CHRISTIAN
CONFESSIONS

CHRISTIAN CONFESSIONS

A HISTORICAL INTRODUCTION

Ted A. Campbell

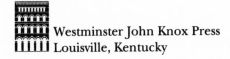
Westminster John Knox Press
Louisville, Kentucky

© 1996 Ted A. Campbell

Scripture quotations, unless otherwise noted, are from the New Revised Standard Version of the Bible, copyright © 1989 by the Division of Chris-tian Education of the National Council of the Churches of Christ in the U.S.A., and are used by permission.

Book design by Jennifer K. Cox
Cover design by Fearless Designs

First edition

Published by Westminster John Knox Press
Louisville, Kentucky

This book is printed on acid-free paper that meets the American National Standards Institute Z39.48 standard. ∞

PRINTED IN THE UNITED STATES OF AMERICA

96 97 98 99 00 01 02 03 04 05 — 10 9 8 7 6 5 4 3 2 1

Library of Congress Cataloging-in-Publication Data

Campbell, Ted.
    Christian confessions : a historical introduction / Ted A. Campbell. — 1st ed.
        p.   cm.
    Includes bibliographical references and index.
    ISBN 0-664-25650-3 (alk. paper)
    1. Christian sects.   2. Theology, Doctrinal—Comparative studies.
    3. Creeds—Comparative studies.   I. Title.
    BR157.C36   1996
    230'.09—dc20
                                     95-46675

To my parents
Gene Allen Campbell and Lucretia Cammack Campbell

Contents

Tables

Preface

In recent years I have become convinced of the need for a straightforward textbook designed for students and Christian leaders that will set out the historic teachings of Christian traditions in a comparative framework. To my knowledge, no such text is currently available in print. There are a number of particular contexts in which such a text is needed. In particular, I have long sensed the need for something like a "map" of historic Christian teachings as an introduction to theological studies. This is especially critical in a time when theological seminaries have become more regionalized because of the older average age of their students, a situation in which even denominational seminaries attract students who represent a wide variety of Christian traditions. For many of the same reasons, moreover, I sense the need for a means by which a baseline in historic Christian teaching can be given in order to enable critical discussion of contemporary issues in Christian thought or practice (for example, in an integrative course on the understanding and practice of various forms of ministry in the churches).

Moreover, it is my belief that a comparative study of historic Christian teachings should be a resource for Christian leaders more broadly, and not just for professional leaders but for lay Christian leaders as well who wish to be better informed about Christian belief. One of the strongest trends in contemporary church life in the United States has been the tendency for people to move from the tradition in which they were raised to other Christian traditions, selecting church membership more on the basis of services offered than traditional doctrine or teachings. This trend suggests the need for a guide not only for persons who want to understand their new church identities in a broad framework but also for Christian leaders who want to be able to engage in serious conversation with persons from quite diverse traditional backgrounds.

This book grows very much out of my experience. I went up to Oxford University at Michelmas term 1977 with the intention of learning about my Methodist roots. This was not very bright, for I quickly realized that though the university had a college or religious house of studies for almost every major Christian tradition, it had none for Methodists at that time. What I found instead was an ecumenical feast: Old Testament tutorials from Ian Braylee at the Jesuit house, Congregationalist George Caird's lectures on New Testament

theology, New Testament tutorials from John Muddiman at the
Anglo-Catholic St. Stephen's house, Hebrew lessons at Evangelical
Anglican Wycliffe Hall just down the street, Patristics tutorials from
Eastern Orthodox Archimandrite (now Bishop) Kallistos Ware, lec-
tures in systematic theology from Liberal and High Church Anglican
John Macquarrie, and theology tutorials from John Saward, an Anglo-
Catholic on the very edge of conversion to Roman Catholicism. The
fact that my parents became members of a traditionally Pentecostal
denomination while I was away in Britain increased my awareness of
the breadth of Christian traditions.

Returning to the United States, I did pursue my interests in
Methodist history and theology, but my program was guided in part
by Professors Albert C. Outler and John Deschner of Southern
Methodist University. Professors Outler and Deschner had long been
engaged in the Ecumenical movement, and they encouraged me to
study Methodist theology within a broad ecumenical context. Given
the opportunity to teach undergraduates at Southern Methodist University in the fall of 1983, moreover, I decided to offer my first course,
an undergraduate course in "Teachings of the Christian Churches."
Over the last eleven years I have taught this course repeatedly, though
in the rather different context of theological seminaries, using John
Leith's *Creeds of the Churches* to supply the primary texts for students.
In the last three years, moreover, I have become a Methodist partici-
pant in the Faith and Order Working Group of the National Council
of Churches of Christ in the United States. This too has given me op-
portunities to understand Christians from a wide variety of traditions.

To see the long view, the astronomical perspective, seems to be my
curse. How do the parts fit in the whole? What is the shape of the
whole Christian tradition? What are the most consistently problematic points of division on Christian teaching? These are the questions
that have consistently interested me. In an age of ever-increasing spe-
cialization I am convinced that the broad view must be kept constantly in mind, but I find that the call to see the long view in our time
is a particularly heavy burden to bear. I find that it makes me constantly open to the criticism that I have failed to see nuances, failed to
account for more detailed work, failed to account for particularities of
traditions, failed to express *depth* in my passion for *breadth*. Like my
mentor Albert Outler, I must confess to the fear that I am but a dilet-
tante. The pain is most acute when I realize that these criticisms are almost always correct, and I become defensive and resort to the ques-
tionable excuse that an expression of the broader perspective does not
allow for every expression of particularity. But this really can become

an excuse for carelessness and negligence, and, in the particular area of understanding traditional Christian teachings, carelessness and negligence can do immense harm to the cause of visible Christian unity. I offer this work with trepidation, then, but I also offer it in the hope that it will serve the cause of Christian unity.

Although I must take responsibility for the contents of this book, I have benefited from the insights of readers from widely different ecclesial backgrounds. I acknowledge with gratitude the assistance of those who have read drafts of parts of this manuscript and have offered helpful criticism and suggestions. In particular, I want to thank the following readers: Professor Mark Achtemeier, University of Dubuque Theological Seminary; Professor John Ford, CSC, Catholic University of America; Dr. Arthur Freeman, Moravian Theological Seminary; Professor Douglas Foster, Abilene Christian University; Professor Paul L. Gritz, Southwestern Baptist Theological Seminary; Brother Jeffrey Gros, Ecumenical Secretariat of the National Catholic Bishops Conference; Mr. Bert Haloviak, Office of Archives and Statistics, General Conference of Seventh-day Adventists; Professor Mickey Mattox, Concordia College in Illinois; Professor Paul Meyendorff, St. Vladimir's Theological Seminary; Dr. Byron Stuhlman, scholar and author of Anglican and liturgical studies; Professor Geoffrey Wainwright, The Divinity School, Duke University; and Professor John H. Young, Queen's Theological College, Kingston, Ontario.

Many others have read smaller parts of the work; I deeply appreciate their help in every case. I would note, again, that the reader must hold me and not them responsible for the words that follow. I also wish to express thanks to the academic dean and the faculty of Wesley Theological Seminary, who have encouraged and supported me in this project as well as reading drafts.

There are others who have helped in concrete ways. Students in my course on "Teachings of the Christian Churches," offered at Southern Methodist University, Duke Divinity School, and Wesley Theological Seminary, have consistently helped with the framing and explication of doctrinal issues. The Faith and Fellowship Class of the congregation of which I am part, Rockville United Methodist Church, read preliminary drafts of these materials in the spring of 1994, and their reactions helped in the writing of the work. I am particularly grateful to Faculty Secretary Jane Jenkins of Wesley Theological Seminary, who entered the list of denominations that forms Appendix 1 of this work, and to Ms. Lisa McKee, a student assistant who read over the manuscript for consistency.

I offer heart-felt thanks to my immediate family—Dale, Elizabeth, and Lydia. They have often detected the glazed looks at the dinner table that served as an outward and visible sign that their husband and father was away working on the book, even when materially in their presence. I dedicate this book to my parents—my first teachers in Christian doctrine.

Abbreviations and Printed Editions of Confessional Documents

In the "Sources" paragraphs of the text and in notes to the text, I have utilized the following list of abbreviations for primary and secondary texts. Wherever possible, I have cited confessional documents from John Leith's collection of *Creeds of the Churches*. In other cases, I have cited the published edition noted below. All references to Christian scripture are to the New Revised Standard Version (NRSV) unless otherwise noted.

Abstract of Principles   "Abstract of Principles of Southern Baptist Theological Seminary," Louisville, Ky., 1859. In Leith, pp. 339–343.

Anglican Articles of Religion   "Thirty-nine Articles of Religion of the Church of England," adopted during the reign of Elizabeth I, 1563. In Leith, pp. 266–281.

ANF   Alexander Roberts, James Donaldson, and Cleveland Coxe, eds. *The Ante-Nicene Fathers*, 10 vols. Buffalo: Christian Literature Publishing, Co., 1885–1887.

Assemblies of God Statement of Fundamental Truths   Sixteen paragraphs expressing Assemblies of God teaching, as revised in 1969. In Melton, pp. 357–360.

Baptism, Eucharist and Ministry   Also referred to informally as "BEM." Report of the Faith and Order Commission of the World Council of Churches (Faith and Order Paper no. 111). Geneva: World Council of Churches, 1982.

Baptist Faith and Message   "Report of the Committee on Baptist Faith and Message," adopted by the Southern Baptist Convention, 1925. In Leith, pp. 343–352.

Basis of Union of The United Church of Canada   Doctrinal statement adopted at the formation of The United Church of Canada in 1925 and included in the Church's *Manual* since then. The text used here is cited as it appears in the UCC *Manual* 1993 (q.v.), pp. 11–16.

BEM   See *Baptism, Eucharist and Ministry*.

Book of Common Prayer (1559)   John E. Booty, ed. *The Book of Common Prayer, 1559: The Elizabethan Prayer Book.* Washington, D.C.: The Folger Shakespeare Library, 1976.

Book of Common Prayer (1662)   W. M. Campion and W. J. Beamont, eds. *The Prayer Book Interleaved with Historical Illustrations and Explanatory Notes Arranged Parallel to the Text,* 10th ed. London, Oxford, and Cambridge: Rivingtons, 1880.

Book of Common Prayer (USA 1979)   *The Book of Common Prayer and Administration of the Sacraments and Other Rites and Ceremonies of the Church, Together with The Psalter or Psalms of David, According to the Use of The Episcopal Church.* New York: Church Hymnal Corporation and The Seabury Press, 1979.

Briggs   Charles Augustus Briggs. *Theological Symbolics.* New York: Charles Scribner's Sons, 1914.

Calvin, *Institutes*   See McNeill.

Catechism of Philaret   A catechism adopted by Russian Orthodox bishops in 1839. In Schaff, 2:445–542.

Catechism of the Catholic Church   Catholic catechism approved by the apostolic constitution *Fidei Depositum* of John Paul II, October 11, 1992. I have cited the uniform paragraph numbers in the work as well as page numbers from the American translation: *Catechism of the Catholic Church.* Washington, D.C.: United States Catholic Conference, 1994.

Chicago-Lambeth Quadrilateral   A statement of four prerequisites for ecumenical union drawn up at first by the House of Bishops of the Protestant Episcopal Church in the USA at Chicago in 1886; subsequently revised and adopted by the Lambeth Conference of Bishops of the Anglican Communion in 1888. In the *Book of Common Prayer (USA 1979)*, pp. 876–878.

Church of God, Cleveland, Tenn., Declaration of Faith   "Declaration of Faith of the Church of God" (and related documents), Cleveland, Tennessee. In Melton, pp. 334–336.

Confession of Faith in a Mennonite Perspective (1995)   *Confession of Faith in a Mennonite Perspective: Draft Recommended to Delegates for Adoption at the General Conference Mennonite Church Triennial Sessions and the Mennonite Church General Assembly, July 25–30, 1995.* This confession was approved by assemblies of both denominations in July 1995 with minor changes in wording.

Denzinger and Hünermann   Henricus Denzinger and Petrus Hünermann, eds. *Enchiridion Symbolorum Definitionum et De-*

clarationum de Rebus Fidei et Morum, 37th ed. Freiburg: Herder, 1991.

Flannery   Austin P. Flannery, ed. *Documents of Vatican II.* Grand Rapids: Wm. B. Eerdmans Publishing Co., 1975.

Fundamental Beliefs of Seventh-day Adventists   An Adventist statement of twenty-seven central beliefs originally developed in 1872 and revised most recently in 1980. In *Seventh-day Adventists Believe . . . A Biblical Exposition of Twenty-seven Fundamental Doctrines*. Washington, D.C.: Ministerial Association, General Conference of Seventh-day Adventists, 1988.

Heppe   Heinrich Heppe. *Reformed Dogmatics: Set Out and Illustrated from the Sources*, trans. G. T. Thomson and ed. Ernst Bizer. London: George Allen and Unwin Ltd., 1950.

Leith   John Leith, ed. *Creeds of the Churches: A Reader in Christian Doctrine from the Bible to the Present*, 3rd ed. Atlanta: John Knox Press, 1982.

Klotsche   E. H. Klotsche. *Christian Symbolics, or, Exposition of the Distinctive Characteristics of the Catholic, Lutheran and Reformed Churches as Well as the Modern Denominations and Sects Represented in This Country*. Burlington, Iowa: Lutheran Literary Board, 1929.

McNeill   John T. McNeill, ed. *Calvin: Institutes of the Christian Religion*, Library of Christian Classics, 2 vols. Philadelphia: Westminster Press, 1960.

Melton   J. Gordon Melton, ed. *Encyclopedia of American Religions: Religious Creeds*. Detroit: Gale Research Inc., 1988.

Mennonite Confession of Faith (1963)   A statement of belief adopted by the Mennonite General Conference in 1963 and also affirmed by the Mennonite Church. This is the document that was revised in 1995 as the "Confession of Faith in a Mennonite Perspective" (see above), but it contains some material not included in the latter. In *Mennonite Confession of Faith: Adopted by the Mennonite General Conference, August 22, 1963*. Scottdale, Penn. and Kitchener, Ontario: Herald Press, 1963.

Methodist Articles of Religion   "Twenty-five Articles of Religion," derived from the "Thirty-nine Articles of Religion of the Church of England" and adopted by the Christmas Conference, Baltimore, 1784. These "Articles of Religion" remain as doctrinal standards in the African Methodist Episcopal (AME) Church, the African Methodist Episcopal Zion (AMEZ) Church, the Christian Methodist Episcopal (CME) Church, and the United Methodist Church (UMC). In Leith, pp. 354–360.

Meyer and Vischer   Harding Meyer and Lukas Vischer, eds. *Growth in Agreement: Reports and Agreed Statements of Ecumenical Conversations on a World Level.* Ramsey, N.J.: Paulist Press, and Geneva: World Council of Churches, 1984.

Moravian *Ground of the Unity*   A Moravian statement of doctrine developed after World War II and revised most recently in 1995. The printed edition to which we refer is the 1982 edition; references to the 1995 revision are based on a photocopy of the statement as revised.

Nazarene Articles of Faith   "Articles of Faith of the Church of the Nazarene." In the *Manual/1989.* Kansas City, Mo.: Nazarene Publishing Company, 1989.

Neuner and Dupuis   J. Neuner and J. Dupuis, eds. *The Christian Faith: Doctrinal Documents of the Catholic Church,* 5th ed. New York: Alba House, 1990.

New Hampshire Confession   "The New Hampshire Confession," adopted by the New Hampshire Baptist Convention, 1833. In Leith, pp. 334–339; Schaff, 3:742–748.

NPNF   Philip Schaff and Henry Wace, eds. *A Select Library of Nicene and Post-Nicene Fathers of the Christian Church.* Two series with fourteen volumes in each series. Buffalo: Christian Literature Publishing Co., 1886 (first series) and 1890 (second series). Reprint edition, Grand Rapids: Wm. B. Eerdmans Publishing Co., 1979.

Origins   Publication of the Documentary Service of CNS, the Catholic News Service. Some English translations of Roman Catholic documents are cited from this periodical.

Pelikan   Jaroslav Pelikan. *The Christian Tradition: A History of the Development of Doctrine,* 5 vols. Chicago: University of Chicago Press, 1971–1989.

Pentecostal Holiness Articles of Faith   Articles of Faith of the International Pentecostal Holiness Church. In Melton, pp. 352–353.

Piepkorn   Arthur Carl Piepkorn. *Profiles in Belief: The Religious Bodies of the United States and Canada,* 4 vols. New York: Harper & Row, 1977.

Schaff   Philip Schaff, ed. *The Creeds of Christendom: With a History and Critical Notes,* 3 vols. Harper & Row, 1931. Reprint edition, Grand Rapids: Baker Book House, 1993.

Schmid   Heinrich Schmid. *The Doctrinal Theology of the Evangelical Lutheran Church*, trans. Charles A. Hay and Henry E. Jacobs, 3rd ed., revised. Minneapolis: Augsburg Publishing House, 1899.

TAC   This denotes my own translations of passages from biblical or historical documents.

UCC *Manual* 1993   The *Manual* of The United Church of Canada. 29th revised edition. Toronto: The United Church Publishing House, 1993.

United Holy Church of America Articles of Faith   "Articles of Faith of the United Holy Church of America." In Melton, pp. 408–409.

Ware   Timothy [Kallistos] Ware. *The Orthodox Church*, 2nd ed., revised. London: Penguin Books, 1993.

Schema of Doctrinal Traditions or Families

1 Eastern Orthodox

Greek Orthodox	ethnic/patriarchal
Russian and other Slavic Orthodox Churches	(not doctrinal)
Antiochian or Syrian Orthodox	traditions

Interlude 1 A: Assyrian Church of the East ("Nestorian")
Interlude 1 B: Oriental Orthodox ("Monophysite") Churches

Coptic (Egyptian and Ethiopian)	ethnic/patriarchal
Syrian	(not doctrinal)
Armenian Apostolic	traditions

Interlude 1 C: The Mar Thoma Church
Interlude 1 D: Russian Old Ritualists

2 Roman Catholic

Interlude 2 A: Old Catholics and Other Separated Catholic Churches

3 Reformation and Union Churches

Lutheran Churches
Anglican Churches
Reformed Churches
  Presbyterian
  Congregationalist
Union Churches
  Union Churches (Lutheran/Reformed)
  United/Uniting Churches

4 Evangelical and Free Churches

Anabaptist Churches
Baptist Churches
Friends (Quakers)
The Moravian Church
Methodist Churches
Restorationist Churches
Dispensationalist Churches
Adventist Churches
Holiness Churches
Pentecostal Churches

Divisions of Major Christian Traditions

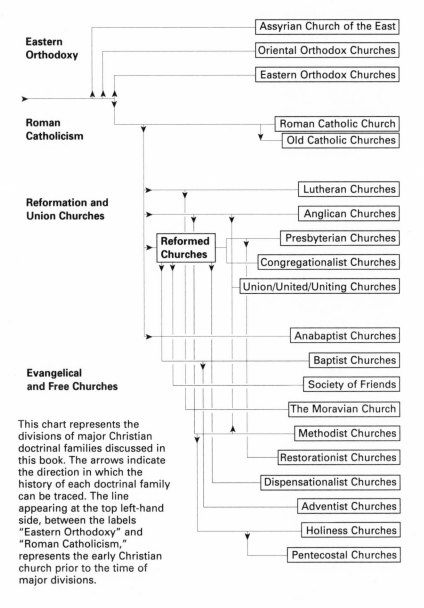

This chart represents the divisions of major Christian doctrinal families discussed in this book. The arrows indicate the direction in which the history of each doctrinal family can be traced. The line appearing at the top left-hand side, between the labels "Eastern Orthodoxy" and "Roman Catholicism," represents the early Christian church prior to the time of major divisions.

Introduction

And, in a town where everyone was either Lutheran or Catholic, we were neither one. We were Sanctified Brethren, a sect so tiny that nobody but us and God knew about it, so when kids asked what I was, I just said Protestant. It was too much to explain, like having six toes. You would rather keep your shoes on.[1]

This is a book that tries to take the shoes off and explain the toes. We can certainly explain who the Catholics and Lutherans are, and there are enough clues lying around to say something about the Sanctified Brethren themselves.[2] This book intends to explain what major families of Christian churches have historically taught and how their teachings inform the identities of their traditions.

Throughout the two thousand years of its history, the Christian community has evolved in a variety of cultural forms and formal divisions. Eastern (originally Greek-speaking) and Western (Latin-speaking) Christians grew apart from each other, and from A.D. 1054 no longer shared communion with each other. The Protestant Reformation in the 1500s brought about a series of divisions within the Western church, and it set in motion a tendency toward fission that continues unabated to this day. But the broad religious toleration allowed since the Enlightenment, and then the movement for visible Christian unity (the Ecumenical movement) in the last hundred years, have brought Christians of im-

1. Garrison Keillor, *Lake Wobegone Days* (New York: Viking Penguin, 1985), p. 101.
2. Although the "Sanctified Brethren" are Garrison Keillor's fictive creation (see the reference above), they bear enough resemblances to other Evangelical groups—especially "Exclusive" Darbyite Brethren churches—that we can make some intelligent surmises about them. See 4.0.7.

1

mensely varied traditions face-to-face with one another—Lutherans and Catholics and Sanctified Brethren and . . . well, it is a very long list now (see Appendix 1), and not just in Minnesota, but in Singapore and Peru and Kenya as well. Although the Ecumenical movement has worked to define common grounds for belief and work between Christians, many question today whether anything distinctively Christian would remain once the layers of division are stripped away (see 5.3).

We should be clear from the start that traditional Christian identities rest not only on their teachings or doctrines but on the multitude of historical quirks and accidents (and providences?) that have made the Orthodox, Anglican, Pentecostal familes, as well as others, what they are. But teachings are important, and it is especially important to know how different churches identify *their* teachings. Without considering how churches describe themselves, we are likely to reduce Christians to stereotypes or popular misconceptions at the level of children, calling names at one another.

"Catholics stink."

"You stink so bad you think everybody does. You stink so bad, you make flowers stink."

"The Pope is dumb, he can't even speak English."

"You're so dumb you're going to hell and you don't even know it."

"Am not."

"Am too."[3]

So this book takes very seriously what Christian churches say about themselves, and that means taking seriously what Christians agree to teach.

0.1 Doctrine: What Christians Agree to Teach

"What Christians agree to teach" is what we shall call *doctrine*. Doctrine is not quite the same thing as "theology": theology may be done by individuals and represents their reflection on a religious tradition. But Christian doctrine, as we shall investigate it in this book, reflects the beliefs of *groups* of Christians (typically churches or denominations), and reflects *consensus* or agreement about what they should teach together.[4]

---

3. Keillor, *Lake*, p. 120.
4. Cf. Jaroslav Pelikan, *The Christian Tradition: A History of the Development of Doctrine*, 5 vols. (Chicago: University of Chicago Press, 1971–1989), 1:1, where doctrine is defined as "What the church of Jesus Christ believes, teaches, and confesses on the basis of the word of God." Pelikan stresses the corporate nature of doctrine in pp. 1–4, and suggests the difference and interrelatedness between doctrine and

How do we know what Christians have agreed to teach? This is not as simple as it might appear. Most churches have doctrinal statements, such as the Augsburg Confession for Lutherans, or decrees of Ecumenical Councils for Eastern Orthodox Christians. But the issue of what churches agree to teach is not always as simple as that. Anglicans, for instance, have "Thirty-nine Articles of Religion," but many Anglicans—with firm allegiance to their tradition—have serious questions about some of the Articles. Some Anglican priests have cassocks with thirty-nine buttons, and always leave specific buttons unfastened! So in the case of Anglicans (including Episcopalians in the United States and in Scotland) we must consider not only their Articles of Religion, but also the *Book of Common Prayer*, which has informed Anglican doctrine perhaps as much or (for some Anglicans) more than the Articles. In other churches, hymns will be used as an important indication of what Christians have agreed to teach. Sometimes it is important to consider contemporary resolutions or doctrinal statements to the extent that they reflect a broad consensus about what Christian groups have agreed to teach.

The use of contemporary doctrinal statements is admittedly limited in this book, however, because a book of this scope cannot deal with particular denominations. Arthur Carl Piepkorn's *Profiles in Belief*, for example, is a massive, four-volume study of the teachings of particular denominations in the United States and Canada alone.[5] But because there are literally hundreds of denominations in North America, Piepkorn's work had to give extremely limited space to most denominations. In this book we have elected to describe larger "families" of Christian traditions, such as Lutheran or Pentecostal families of churches, within which there has been a historical consensus about what to teach. When we ask what the Lutheran *family* of churches has agreed to teach, then, what appears most prominent is the Augsburg Confession, Luther's *Small Catechism*, and perhaps other Lutheran confessional documents in the *Book of Concord*. A doctrinal statement or resolution adopted by a particular Lutheran denomination will have to be given less weight in this book than those historic

---

"theology" in his assertion that "it is usually difficult, and sometimes impossible, to draw the line of demarcation between the teachings of the church and the theories of its teachers" (p. 3), where "the theories of [the church's] teachers" represents what I have called "theology."

5. Sidney Mead's *Handbook of American Denominations* offers a more convenient guide to larger North American Christian groups, and J. Gordon Melton's *Encyclopedia of American Religions* offers an even more expansive consideration of North American religious groups.

documents received by Lutherans across denominational boundaries. Appendix 1 gives a list (though incomplete) of denominations, indicating where, in the denominational families represented in this book, a particular denomination should fit. But readers should be aware of the fact that particular denominations may have doctrinal statements, clarifications, or resolutions in addition to the historic documents that define the identity of the broader family of churches of which they are part.

In considering Christian doctrine as that which Christians have agreed to teach, then, this book places considerable emphasis on the historic creeds, confessions, and catechisms by which corporate groups of Christians have defined commonly held beliefs. We have not attempted in this book to describe emerging new theological trends; rather, we have tried here to understand the traditional doctrines that remain in place as corporately agreed-upon teachings of the churches, however they may be challenged by contemporary thought.

For some churches, traditional doctrinal statements have been questioned, not so much because of the inroads of contemporary criticism, but more prominently because of a historic Evangelical predilection to mistrust nonscriptural doctrinal statements. In fact, for some traditions (for instance, the noninstrumental Churches of Christ in the United States) the one thing agreed on is that there should be *no* doctrinal statements. In this case, we obviously cannot study doctrinal statements as such, and we shall have to describe their consensus on what to teach on the basis of such things as their history, their hymnody, and their agreed practices.

The traditional word for the study of doctrine expressed in historic creeds is *symbolics*, from the Greek word *symbolon*, the word that is used to denote a "creed." Moreover, a work such as this one that compares the doctrines of different Christian traditions was traditionally called a study of *comparative symbolics*.[6] But there has been very little interest in comparative symbolics in the last seventy-five years.[7] Why

---

6. On the definition of symbolics and comparative symbolics, see Charles Augustus Briggs, *Theological Symbolics* (New York: Charles Scribner's Sons, 1914), pp. 3–33; and E. H. Klotsche, *Christian Symbolics, or, Exposition of the Distinctive Characteristics of the Catholic, Lutheran and Reformed Churches as Well as the Modern Denominations and Sects Represented in This Country* (Burlington, Iowa: Lutheran Literary Board, 1929), pp. 13–20.
7. Documented works on comparative symbolics in English in this century can be described rather quickly. We have cited above the works of Briggs (*Theological Symbolics*, 1914) and Klotsche (*Christian Symbolics*, 1929). We should also include Theodore Edward William Engelder's *Popular Symbolics* (St. Louis, Mo.: Concordia Publishing House, 1934). These were practically the only works available

should this be? The reason is probably that this period corresponds to the rise and flourishing of the Ecumenical movement, which stresses what Christians hold in common, rather than the distinctives of each tradition. The Ecumenical movement, in fact, had utilized the method of comparative symbolics early in the twentieth century through the 1950s, when it was recognized that comparative symbolics alone could not bring about a new basis for ecumenical unity. But the Ecumenical movement has entered a new situation in which, I am convinced, traditional doctrinal distinctives have again become important. It is to this new ecumenical context that we turn in the next section of this chapter.

0.2   The New Ecumenical Context

The Ecumenical movement today faces a critical juncture in its history, and in some respects the movement has been radically challenged in recent decades. In this book we presuppose an ecumenical context for the understanding of Christian teachings. That is to say, we presuppose the attempt on the part of Christians of varied traditions to understand each other, to work with one another, and to strive toward the goal of the visible unity of our visibly divided churches. But the new context of ecumenism makes the understanding of particular doctrinal teachings extremely important now, and so in what follows we must explain how the changing nature of the Ecumenical movement bears on the need for better understandings of the teachings of the churches.

The new ecumenical context in which the teachings of the Christian churches will be explained here answers in many ways to a broad cultural movement that some describe as "Postmodernism." Post-

---

until the publication of Arthur Carl Piepkorn's *Profiles in Belief* (published posthumously in 1977). Piepkorn's work is highly denomination-specific (i.e., it gives accounts of specific denominational organizations) and is specifically limited to the churches of the United States and Canada. The great advantage of Piepkorn's work is its attention to detail in dealing with specific North American churches. Along with these we might consider Jaroslav Pelikan's five-volume study of *The Christian Tradition: A History of the Development of Doctrine* (cited above), which does not follow denominational lines but gives the reader a chronological history of the development of Christian doctrine. A notable coincidence is that all of these—Briggs, Klotsche, Engelder, Piepkorn, and Pelikan—were or are all Lutherans! But this probably speaks (favorably) of the high importance attached to doctrinal formulation among traditional Lutherans. We may also note and distinguish the enterprise of "dogmatics" or "symbolic theology," that is, theological reflection on the inherited doctrines of a Christian tradition, such as Karl Barth's *Church Dogmatics* or Part Two of John Macquarrie's *Principles of Christian Theology*.

modernism reacts against "Modernism," and we shall argue that the Ecumenical movement, since the last part of the nineteenth century and through the early 1970s, has been a distinctly Christian expression of Modernism. The advent of Postmodernism (or perhaps, Postmodernisms) has important implications for the understanding of Christian doctrinal traditions today.

In the first place, let us clarify some terms by drawing a distinction between modernity and Modernism. *Modernity*, as we use the term here, represents the whole complex of social and cultural conditions that began to develop in the 1600s and 1700s, involving industrial economies (as opposed to older agricultural or mercantile economies), urbanization, stress on democratic and participatory forms of government (as opposed to monarchy), the search for broader religious toleration (as opposed to civil establishments of religion), and views of human knowledge grounded in reason or in reflection on our experience (as opposed to tradition). Although modernity may have originated in Europe and North America, it has become a fact of worldwide culture and society since the 1800s. We take *Modernism* here to denote a more specific cultural movement that flourished from the 1880s through the 1960s, the movement that stressed the attempt to find a truly global, international culture as opposed to the divisive national, ethnic, and religious traditions that had prevailed in the past.

Modernism, then, is the cultural movement that attempted to overcome the particularities of traditions. Modern architecture, for example, rejected traditional architectural styles (such as classical or Gothic) and developed a new style, free of the encumbrances of tradition. The so-called International Style of architecture describes the rectangular concrete-and-glass-and-steel monoliths that until recently dominated the skylines of great cities. The architects who designed these buildings tried very hard to avoid the particularities of traditions, including architectural traditions (like the classical or Gothic styles), national traditions (the new buildings were "International"), and the particularities of specific places (no matter where they were located, from Houston to Singapore, they all have essentially the same form). Modernism in art and literature also reflected the passion to avoid traditional patterns and to develop newer and more purely artistic styles. In the area of political life, Modernism stressed the overcoming of traditional ethnic and cultural divisions and the attempt to build a new society free of the national and ethnic divisions of the past: the Union of Soviet Socialist Republics was perhaps the masterpiece of political Modernism.

The Ecumenical movement in Christianity flourished at the same time as the flourishing of Modernism, and one can easily perceive the parallels between them. Just as Modernism reacted against the particularities of architectural and artistic traditions, so the Ecumenical movement reacted against the visible divisions of churches. Just as the "International Style" was an expression of Modernism in architecture, so the progenitors of the Ecumenical movement understood "ecumenical" as representing "the whole world" (the *oikoumene*), or at least, the whole Christian world. For the Ecumenical movement, unity in Christ was more important than traditional divisions. The expression of distinctive traditional identity was typically seen as a hindrance to the mission of the church in the modern world.

Now, to be fair, it must be said that ecumenical Christian leaders did not foresee a complete loss of traditional identities: many held out an ecumenical vision of the "sharing of gifts," in which each tradition would bring to the whole Church its own particular gifts, grounded in its own identity and history. Some ecumenical leaders, in fact, insist that the Ecumenical movement never intended the formation of a "Greatest Common Denominator" church in which all distinctions would cease. The effect of the Ecumenical movement was not to deny traditional denominational identities but simply to deemphasize traditional differences, emphasizing instead the common ties that bind all Christian believers together.

By the end of the 1960s, ecumenical trends had exerted a deep impact not only at global and national levels but at the local church level as well. Denominational distinctions by this time were seen much less rigidly than in the past, and many Christians (particularly in the United States) began to see traditional differences as being relatively unimportant.[8] Perhaps a more positive way of stating this would be to say, with Joan Brown Campbell, that "the typical church member lives ecumenically—and without apology."[9] The Ecumenical movement, then, was a Christian expression of Modernism, but not just among intellectuals and church leaders; it was a movement that has deeply affected the ways in which Christians relate to one another today. There are some signs, though, of a reaction in the direction of traditional distinctiveness in recent years.

8. Jean Caffey Lyles, "The Fading of Denominational Distinctiveness," *Progressions: A Lilly Endowment Occasional Report* 2:1 (January 1990): 16–18. Lyles calls on the work of Robert Wuthnow and Wade Clark Roof in substantiating the claim that traditional identities had been fading for some time.
9. Joan Brown Campbell, "The State of the Ecumenical Movement" in *Yearbook of American and Canadian Churches*, ed. Kenneth B. Bedell (Nashville: Abingdon Press, 1993), p. 2.

Whether it is appropriate or not to speak of "Postmodernism" (it does seem like a contradiction within itself), there are clear signs that the flourishing of Modernism, or at least of older forms of Modernism, has drawn to an end. It can be questioned whether older forms of ecumenism have come to an end as well. Sometime in the 1970s, Modern architecture gave way to a Postmodern style that incorporated elements of older architectural traditions in surprising ways (for example, the broken pediment forming the top of the AT&T building in New York), and utilizing more traditional building materials such as wood and textured stone. Architecture again reflected broader cultural trends, for since the 1970s the particularities of tradition, ethnicity, and nationality have appeared in striking contrast to Modernism's attempts to overcome them. Alex Haley's *Roots*, for example, stressed the particularities of African-American experience, rejecting the notion that African Americans should be dissolved into the melting pot of North American society and culture. The rise of political conservatism in the West in the 1980s was one example of this trend toward the particular (especially the expression of particular national identities), though political conservatism was not the only way in which the move to the particular could be expressed. The collapse of the Soviet Union was perhaps the most striking illustration of the political move to the particular in the 1980s: for so many millions of people, it seemed more important that they were Estonians (or Russians, or Ukrainians, etc.) than that they were part of a modern political entity such as the Soviet Union. Consistently, the late 1970s and 1980s witnessed the rejection of modern unities in favor of traditional, ethnic, and national particularities. When we speak of Postmodernism, then, we denote this general mood of reaction against Modern art, architecture, politics, and culture more broadly, and at the same time, the attempts since the 1970s to express ethnic, regional, national and (as we shall see) religious particularities.[10]

If the Ecumenical movement, then, was a Christian expression of Modernism, where might we find signs of a corresponding Christian expression of Postmodernism? Most obviously, the rise of religious conservatisms and fundamentalisms from the 1970s could be seen as an instance of the antimodernist turn to the particular, though they could as easily be read as "Premodern" rather than "postmodern."

---

10. The account of Postmodernism given here is based in part on that of Steven Connor, *Postmodernist Culture: An Introduction to Theories of the Contemporary* (Oxford: Basil Blackwell, Publisher, 1989), pp. 31–131, and most particularly on his description of Postmodernism in architecture, pp. 66–80.

The prominence of Evangelical Fundamentalism in the United States from the late 1970s was paralleled by the rise of Islamic and even Hindu Fundamentalisms at the same time in other parts of the world. In the same period, Christians in non-Western contexts insisted on the integrity of their cultural traditions and cultural expressions of Christian faith. Ethnic identities within Western cultures stressed their particular experience of Christian faith, such as the experience of African-American Christians in the United States. These expressions of particularity were not necessarily tied to religious fundamentalisms.

Moreover, there were some new assertions of Christian traditional identity from the middle of the 1970s, and these came neither from Fundamentalists nor from persons in third-world contexts, but from Christians who had long identified themselves and their denominations with Liberal Protestantism and with the Ecumenical movement. One simple fact stands out: in the late 1970s and early 1980s, church support for the Ecumenical movement (at least in the United States and Canada) dropped off severely. This could be explained in different ways: perhaps, ecumenical leaders suggested, it was not that the churches had rejected ecumenism; rather, this withdrawal of funding should be seen as a reflection of inflation and other economic trends that had effects on the churches.[11] Although it is true that economic forces have influenced the churches, the priority placed on denominational programs as opposed to ecumenical programs in the last two decades should not go unnoticed. Perhaps, if nothing else, this trend indicates that the Ecumenical movement, as a linked set of institutions, fails to captivate the imagination and affection of church leaders as it once did.

A more telling indication of a growing sense of traditional identity in the last two decades comes typically from younger scholars and pastors who had grown up in so-called mainline traditions and who have lamented the loss of traditional identities. Their call to rediscover denominational tradition has challenged both conservatives (who defend the present status quo of the older denominations) and old-style liberals (who find it difficult to distinguish between new traditionalism and plain old conservatism). The attempt to rediscover and restate the identities of Presbyterianism, Lutheranism, Methodism, and Anglicanism

---

11. In discussing "The State of the Ecumenical Movement" in 1990, this withdrawal of funding was one of the primary trends noted by Joan Brown Campbell, General Secretary of the National Council of Churches of Christ in the U.S.A. Campbell's explanation was that this reflected the effects of inflation and other economic factors, not a problem with the ecumenical movement itself (in the work cited above, pp. 1–2).

(just to name four examples) indicates that the Postmodern concern for the recovery of tradition (in the context of a modern culture that had rejected it) is more than simply a reaction to fiscal crises in the churches, and as this generation of scholars and pastors comes into positions of religious leadership, their concern for traditional identity will be seen more and more clearly, and at every level of the church's life.[12] It is an ironic situation that we face now: on the one hand, *denominational* loyalty seems to have faded to a low ebb; on the other hand, *tradition* consciousness seems to have attained a new peak.

But this situation does not mean that the Ecumenical movement is a relic of the past. It is often said that "Postmodernism is a form of Modernism," and following this insight we may understand that the new (Postmodern) stress on traditional identity presupposes a strong ecumenical (Modern) commitment. In its best expressions in the past, the Ecumenical movement has challenged the churches to be faithful to their particular traditions.[13] A generation of Methodist leaders, to cite the example closest to my experience, began to rediscover John Wesley and their Methodist tradition when challenged by ecumenical contacts with other churches.[14] Ecumenical dialogue led to a revitalization of a particular Christian identity in this case. The engagement of various Evangelical and Free churches in the Ecumenical movement has led to a growing consciousness of their identities as Christian traditions, so that today we may speak of a "Pentecostal tradition," a "Baptist tradition," or a "Dispensationalist tradition," terms that were not at all current thirty years ago.

It may well be that since the publication of *Baptism, Eucharist and Ministry* (or *BEM*, 1982) and subsequent ecumenical discussions on "Confessing the Apostolic Faith Today," the churches are at a point where the Ecumenical movement itself requires a more serious examination of traditional teachings. Edward Cardinal Cassidy, visiting the offices of the National Council of Churches of Christ in the USA, recently remarked that Catholics and other Christians have now come to the point where we are seriously able to discuss the issues that have divided our churches in the past. This situation itself calls for careful, ecumenical discussion of doctrinal traditions. In Cardinal Cassidy's

12. For a further discussion of this renewed sense of traditional identity, with specific reference to Methodist tradition, see my article "Is It Just Nostalgia? The Renewal of Wesleyan Studies," *Christian Century* 107:13 (18 April 1990), 396–398.
13. Robert T. Handy, "Denominationalism and Ecumenism: Opposition or Symbiosis?" *Criterion* 23:1 (Winter 1984), 2–6.
14. Here I have in mind Colin Williams, Albert C. Outler, and Frank Baker. Williams explained in the introduction to his study of *John Wesley's Theology Today* (Nashville: Abingdon Press, 1960) that ecumenical contacts had led him to his research on Wesley's theology (pp. 5–7).

words, "we must dig deep into our theological and doctrinal roots. In the present situation, that makes the going more difficult—but no less important."[15]

This book, then, attempts to understand traditional Christian teachings in such a way that it may contribute to ecumenical understanding. This calls, as we have noted above, for careful attention to how the churches themselves describe and hand on their own teachings, and for careful comparisons between these traditional teachings. It also calls for a consideration of common Christian roots, including common roots in New Testament Christianity.

0.3   Christian Consensus in the New Testament

All the Christian traditions described in this book understand themselves as descendants of the Christian community founded by Christ and the apostles. Each Christian tradition has its own way of accounting for the continuity between the apostolic Church and their own churches. But what evidence is there in the New Testament for a consensus about Christian teachings, as we have described above? The diversity within New Testament literature is widely acknowledged, and in fact the recognition of the diversity of the New Testament literature and the communities represented in it has been a consistent contribution of biblical scholarship in the last two centuries. In a sense, one could argue, the New Testament as a whole represents a consensus about central Christian teachings. But the fact is that the list of books that form the New Testament, the canon of New Testament scriptures, was not widely agreed upon until the middle of the second century, and even then it was not the complete list we have now but the core list of gospels and epistles. A definitive list matching the one we now have was not given until the middle of the fourth century.[16] Is there any evidence within the New Testament, then, for an early consensus about central Christian teachings, from which the historic churches derive their central teachings? In what follows we consider some evidence for such an early consensus, though, as we shall see, it does not resolve many of the key issues that have divided churches since the New Testament age.[17]

15. Cited by Joan Brown Campbell, "State of the Ecumenical Movement," p. 3.
16. Werner Georg Kümmel, *Introduction to the New Testament*, trans. Howard Clark Kee (London: SCM Press, 1975), part two, pp. 475–499.
17. The crucial issues dividing the earliest Christian communities tended to be practical rather than theological ones, for example, the issue of whether Gentile (male) believers were obliged to be circumcised. For a survey of issues regarding unity and diversity in the New Testament, see Craig C. Hill, *Hellenists and Hebrews: Reappraising Division within the Earliest Church* (Minneapolis: Fortress Press, 1992), and especially the conclusion, pp. 193–197.

The earliest evidence for Christian agreement or consensus on central teachings comes in two passages of Paul's first letter to the Corinthians. The letters of Paul, including 1 Corinthians, were actually written before the Gospels—they are the earliest Christian literature. Within 1 Corinthians, written in the middle of the first century, there are two passages in which Paul reports the words by which he had "received" and "handed on" the Christian message.[18] We have placed the expressions "received" and "handed on" in quotation marks, because in the language of the New Testament, they are technical terms for the common, ancient practice of reciting a form of words "received" by one generation and "handed on" to the next.

In 1 Corinthians 11:23–25, Paul wrote:

> For I received from the Lord what I also handed on to you, that the Lord Jesus on the night when he was betrayed took a loaf of bread, and when he had given thanks, he broke it and said, "This is my body that is for you. Do this in remembrance of me." In the same way he took the cup also, after supper, saying, "This cup is the new covenant in my blood. Do this, as often as you drink it, in remembrance of me."

Apparently, when Paul used the expression "from the Lord," he meant that the message came from Christ through the agency of those who had told the narrative to him (parallels in the Synoptic Gospels are significant on this point). Similarly, in 1 Corinthians 15:3–4 Paul uses this same technical language about "receiving" and "handing on" to tell the basic story or narrative of Christ's death and resurrection:

> For I handed on to you as of first importance what I in turn had received: that Christ died for our sins in accordance with the scriptures, and that he was buried, and that he was raised on the third day in accordance with the scriptures. . . .

At this point (in 1 Corinthians 15) Paul went on to recount numerous witnesses to the resurrection of Christ, probably supplementing the words he had received, but at verse 11 he noted, "Whether then it was I or they, so we proclaim and so you have come to believe." Paul was not giving an original story in these two passages; rather, he re-

---

18. Although C. H. Dodd's *The Apostolic Preaching and Its Developments* (1956) laid out a basic thesis about the *kerygma* of the primitive community, a more mature treatment reflecting subsequent developments in scholarship is offered in Hans Conzelmann, pt. 1 of "The Kerygma of the Primitive Community and the Hellenistic Community," *An Outline of the Theology of the New Testament* (London: SCM Press, 1969, based on the German edition of 1968), pp. 27–93.

peated the words by which the Christian message had been "handed on" to him. If 1 Corinthians was written in the middle of the first century, then these passages contain a form of words by which Christians told the simple, primitive narrative of their faith in the earliest decades after Christ's crucifixion and resurrection.

It might be objected that what is contained in these two passages is not so much doctrine as narrative, an account of what Christ had done. But the narrative indicates what the earliest Christians seem to have agreed on at this point, and it carries theological presuppositions, for example, that Christ's death was "for our sins."[19] Before particular Christian teachings were challenged, and before the churches began the laborious process of responding to challenges to its teachings, Christian communities simply proclaimed "Jesus Christ, and him crucified" (1 Cor. 2:2b) in much the same terms that Paul gives in these passages. It should come as little surprise, however, that the earliest Christian creeds (used typically at baptisms) should echo again these words: that Christ was "crucified . . . on the third day he was resurrected . . ." and so on. The basis of ancient Christian unity lay in the simple proclamation of Christ's death and resurrection.[20]

Even if there is some evidence of Christian consensus or at least common presuppositions in the time of the New Testament, we must not imagine that Christianity was ever undivided. True, the Acts of the Apostles portrays the Christian community in the period immediately after Pentecost as a remarkably unified one:

> All who were believed were together and had all things in common; they would sell their possessions and goods and distribute the proceeds to all, as any had need. Day by day, as they spent much time together in the temple, they broke bread at home and ate their food with glad and generous hearts, praising God and having the goodwill of all the people. And day by day the Lord added to their number those who were being saved.
>
> (Acts 2:44–47)

But soon after this, "the Hellenists complained against the Hebrews" in the Christian community "because their widows were being neglected in the daily distribution of food" (Acts 6:1). A solution was arrived at, but divisions continued in the early Christian communities.[21]

19. Conzelmann, "Kerygma," pp. 64–71.
20. We should note at this point, for Catholics and Protestants alike, that the creed traditionally called the "Apostles' Creed" does not date from apostolic times. It is very similar to early Christian baptismal creeds, but did not appear in its current form until the eighth century A.D.
21. Hill, *Hellenists and Hebrews*, examines these controversies in detail.

By the time Paul wrote 1 Corinthians, he faced a Christian congregation severely divided into factions:

> For it has been reported to me by Chloe's people that there are quarrels among you, my brothers and sisters. What I mean is that each of you says, "I belong to Paul," or "I belong to Apollos," or "I belong to Cephas," or "I belong to Christ." Has Christ been divided?
>
> (1 Cor. 1:11–13a)

It is not obvious that these particular divisions were doctrinal—they may have been simply political divisions in the Corinthian congregation. But the epistles of the New Testament give abundant evidence of doctrinal divisions among the earliest Christians. In the first letter to the Corinthians, Paul had to deal with misunderstandings about the nature of Christ's resurrection (1 Corinthians 15), and this was in fact the point at which he recited the story about Christ that he had received. In other letters Paul had to deal with false teachers of various descriptions (often their teachings were not described), and the later New Testament epistles (1 and 2 Timothy and Titus, for example) consistently urge their readers to hold fast to the teachings that they had received and not be turned aside by false prophets and false teachers. It is clear from these letters that divisions—doctrinal and otherwise—existed from the very earliest days of the Christian communities.

0.4   The Format of This Book

From this point, we may proceed historically to consider the development of particular Christian traditions and their teachings. The first four chapters of this book explain a major Christian tradition or a broad family of traditions: the traditions of Eastern Orthodox churches (chapter 1), the Roman Catholic Church (chapter 2), Reformation and "Union" Churches (chapter 3), and Evangelical and Free Churches (chapter 4). In the case of Eastern Orthodox and Roman Catholics, these divisions between traditions are fairly clear and they describe discrete Christian "communions"; that is, churches that do not ordinarily admit members of other churches to their celebration of the Lord's Supper (or, what is called the Eucharist). In the case of the various Protestant churches, the distinctions are not so clear, and we have had to make some fine (and perhaps controversial) judgments in making these distinctions. It should be kept in mind that many of these distinctions, especially in chapters 3 and 4, are rather analytical; that is, they are devised as teaching tools, and in reality many Protestant churches share traits across these boundaries. For our part, we shall try to be fair in describing the various Protestant traditions to note problems of categorization.

One problem that this format will present for Protestant readers is that the progression of these four chapters may well be from the least to the most familiar. But historically, it makes sense to consider Orthodoxy and Catholicism before taking up Protestantism, since Protestantism developed from the Catholic tradition in the 1500s.

Each of these four chapters are divided into short sections and begin with a historical introduction (identified with the section number .0 in each chapter). In these introductions, we have tried to give a narrative, that is, to tell a story, explaining how the traditions became separate. We also describe the historical factors that have shaped their identities (for example, long contact with and often captivity by Muslims, in the case of Orthodox Christians) and some of the diversity that exists within Christian traditions.

After the historical introduction in each of these four chapters, the teachings of the churches are described in four general categories. The first category is teachings about *religious authority* (identified with section number .1 in each chapter), that is, how do churches understand the authority of the Bible, of church traditions, of bishops and perhaps the Pope, and of human reason and experience? A second category describes beliefs about *God and Christ* (identified with section number .2 in each chapter), including the doctrine of the Trinity and even teachings about Mary, the mother of Jesus, since teachings about Mary have almost always been an expression of beliefs about Christ. A third category describes teachings about *human nature and salvation* (identified with section number .3 in each chapter). How do the churches describe the fallen state of humankind? How do we get out of this fallen condition? How are grace and faith and good works related in this process? What is the ultimate end or goal of the Christian life? The final category concerns the issues of *church, ministry, and sacraments* (identified with section number .4 in each chapter), and asks how the various churches understand the church itself, its ministry, and the most important religious acts in which the church engages. Each section is further divided into subsections that consider particular points of doctrine.

In each of these four chapters, attention must be given to diversity of doctrine and to the expression of doctrine in historic creeds. Diversity is especially important in dealing with the various Protestant traditions. For instance, Anglicans have always laid a particular stress on the teachings of the early Christian church. This sometimes stands in contrast to Reformed (or Evangelical) understandings of religious authority, although for most Anglicans it does not challenge their commitment to the Bible as the primary source of religious authority. In every case, we shall attempt to document our discussions of Christian teachings with reference to specific agreed-upon doctrinal statements, or at least to the hymns, prayers, and worship practices of a particular Christian tradition.

In each of the substantive sections (sections identified as .1 through .4 in chapters 1–4) we have given short summary statements for every subsection on major points of doctrinal agreement, followed by paragraphs explaining in more detail these points. We have used a system of numbering for these summary statements: following the section numbers (for example, section 3.2) there will be further periods and numbers or letters identifying particular statements. In general, *a period followed by a number indicates a subpoint;* for example, statements 3.4.4.1 and 3.4.4.2 are subpoints under statement 3.4.4 (and all these come in section 3.4). *A period followed by a letter,* however, *indicates a point of doctrinal contrast,* so that statements 3.4.4.2.a and 3.4.4.2.b present alternative points of view under point 3.4.4.2). The use of points of contrast is particularly important in dealing with the diversities of Reformation and Union churches in chapter 3 and with the massive diversities of Evangelical and Free churches in chapter 4. The enumeration of summary statements allows us to follow cross-references, which appear parenthetically through the text.

All these together will prepare for chapter 5, which is shorter than the other four chapters. In this chapter we shall (1) give an account of ecumenical attempts to forge Christian consensus in doctrine (5.1); (2) state as broadly as possible where points of unity exist between churches and where critically divisive issues still separate the churches (5.2); (3) ask what core of distinctly Christian teachings exists across the boundaries of Christian traditions (5.3); and (4) ask about communities at the boundaries or periphery of historic Christian teaching (5.4). This chapter is followed by a short conclusion to the work.

Although the book is laid out according to four major families of Christian traditions, there are at least two other ways in which the book can be used: (1) Appendix 2 gives sequences of subsections appropriate to particular families of Anglican and Protestant tradition (for examples, sequences for Adventists and Lutherans). Readers who wish to consider a particular doctrinal tradition may elect to follow one of the sequences. By using the list of denominations in Appendix 1, the reader can link the name of a particular denomination to its broader tradition family; and (2) It is also possible to read the book "laterally," that is, by reading the historical introductions sequentially, then reading each of the sections on religious authority, and so forth. "A Doctrinal Comparative Schema," which is given in Appendix 3, and the points of comparative reference noted in the text allow for this kind of reading. Courses organized by topics rather than Christian traditions may elect to read the book in this fashion, and the hypertext version of the book will allow readers to navigate easily on either axis (that is, either by traditions or by major themes).

The study of comparative doctrine is not an easy subject. Much that follows will not be quite as interesting as a Christian rock concert or even as stimulating as a good sermon well delivered. A good deal of what follows involves vocabulary study, because different Christian traditions have developed their own "languages," their own distinctive terms and uses of terms, by which they explain and communicate their traditional teachings. Orthodox speak of "mysteries," of the "Divine Liturgy" and the "Theotokos." Catholics speak of "purgatory" and "papal infallibility" and the "Blessed Virgin." Reformed folk consider the relative values of "infralapsarianism" and "supralapsarianism," and Evangelicals may speak in a kind of insider's code about being "saved" and "sanctified" or "baptized with the Holy Spirit." We have not hesitated in what follows to use these traditional "languages"; in fact, to understand a tradition with any depth it is necessary to learn the terms it employs.

1

Teachings of the Ancient Councils and Contemporary Eastern Orthodoxy

1.0 Historical Background to the Ancient Councils and Contemporary Eastern Orthodoxy

There are churches where even today the New Testament is read aloud—and understood—in the language in which it was written. There are other churches that conduct public worship today in a language little different from the Aramaic spoken by Jesus himself. There are congregations today that trace their origins to the very presence, in their own cities, of Jesus' apostles.

The churches to which we refer here are conventionally described as "Eastern Orthodox" churches, and they include Greek, Slavic, Antiochian or Syrian Orthodox, and a number of other Orthodox churches. At least 187 million Christians today, about a tenth of all members of Christian churches, are part of Eastern Orthodox Churches.[22] Although Orthodox Christians were severely restricted during the period of the Soviet Union in this century, their religious traditions are currently undergoing renewal in many ways.

Why should we consider Eastern Orthodox churches before the Roman Catholic Church? Both Catholics and Eastern Orthodox consider their churches to maintain an unbroken succession reaching back to the ancient churches founded by the apostles. The Eastern Orthodox Churches of today developed from Christianity in the Eastern, Greek-speaking Mediterranean in antiquity, where there existed a long unity

22. David B. Barrett, "Annual Statistical Table on Global Mission: 1994," in *International Bulletin of Missionary Research* 18:1 (January 1994), 25. Hereafter cited as "Barrett (1994)."

of Greek or "Hellenistic" civilization from the fourth century B.C. through the fifteenth century A.D., and extending even into the present time.[23] ("Hellenistic" denotes the culture not only of Greece but also of the large area of the Mediterranean and the Near East where there was a strong influence of Greek culture after the conquests of Alexander the Great.) I have found it convenient to begin with the consideration of Eastern Orthodoxy for reasons that are fairly practical. Eastern Christianity emerged in the geographical areas where Christianity itself first emerged; it preserved the language of the New Testament (common or *koinē*, Greek) as its medium of communication, and it held a special regard for the seven Ecumenical Councils in the period A.D. 325–787, councils that expressed the unity of most Christians in the first millennium after Christ.[24] When we take up Roman Catholic teachings in chapter 2, we will have to go back to the beginning and consider the distinctive development of Western Christianity.

1.0.1   The Primitive Church (before A.D. 325)

The Orthodox Churches today believe themselves to be the inheritors of the ancient Christian faith expressed in the New Testament and taught consistently through the centuries in an unbroken tradition up until the present time. They share with Roman Catholics a common history up through the eleventh century A.D. when Eastern and Western Christianity formally divided, and they share with almost all Christians the inheritance of the first three Christian centuries, the period that is often described as the "primitive" church. This generally denotes the period up until A.D. 313, when the emperor Constantine formally allowed toleration of Christianity in the Roman Empire, or perhaps to A.D. 325 when the same emperor called together the (First) Council of Nicaea.

In these earliest centuries Christians were persecuted off and on by Roman authorities, who would frequently insist that citizens should offer incense to the *genius* (or spirit) of the emperor as a sign of respect and patriotism. Jews had traditionally refused this civic devotion, and in fact were granted a formal dispensation from the Roman law, in return for which they agreed to pray for the emperor. Although some Christians early on claimed Jewish identity as grounds for their re-

23. The origins of this long unity of Hellenistic civilization are described in F. E. Peters, *The Harvest of Hellenism* (New York: Simon & Schuster, 1970).
24. There is also precedent in scholarship: both Klotsche and Piepkorn begin with Orthodoxy: Klotsche, pp. 29–56; Piepkorn, 1:31–116.

fusal to participate, Christians in general were conscious of their separate identity from Judaism and were frequently put to death by civil authorities when their "disrespect" was made known. The first centuries, then, were the centuries of persecution and martyrdom in the Christian churches' experience.

Even in these early centuries, the Christian churches in the Mediterranean world faced some doctrinal issues that forced them to develop consensus on important teachings. From the early second century there were Christian groups who thought of Jesus primarily as a revealer of secret wisdom. Very typically, these groups would maintain that the creator of the material world was a lower deity, that the Hebrew Scriptures (the Old Testament to later Christians) were the creation of a false god, and that Jesus himself did not truly suffer and die, but only appeared to do so. These beliefs are sometimes considered together under the title of Gnosticism, though the name (from *gnosis*, secret or esoteric "knowledge") does not fit all of them. Gnostic teaching forced such Christians as Irenaeus, bishop of Lyons in Southern France in the late second century, to catalog the teachings of the "heretics" and to explain the church's teachings in response to them.

Around A.D. 200 another set of teachings emerged that again forced the churches to think together about their understanding of God and Christ. These teachings maintained that God the Father became Christ the Son, and that "the Father suffered" in the Son. Sometimes called Modalism (or Sabellianism or Patripassianism; see table 2), these teachings forced such Christians as the African Tertullian of Carthage to clarify the churches' belief that though Christ is worshiped as God, there must be some difference between Father, Son, and Holy Spirit.

Other Christians in the early centuries were concerned to relate Christianity, originally Semitic, to its new context in the Hellenistic culture of the ancient Mediterranean. In the middle of the second century Justin Martyr of Rome wrote an *Apology* for the Christian faith addressed to sophisticated Hellenistic peoples. In the early third century A.D. the African Christians Origen and Clement, both lay teachers (through most of their careers) in Alexandria, developed highly sophisticated expressions of the Christian faith utilizing the terminology and concepts of ancient Greek philosophy and incorporating many religious ideas of the ancient Hellenistic world, such as Origen's claim that all rational souls (the souls of angels, humans, and even demons) existed with God before they fell and came into material bodies.

All these developments in Christian teachings prior to A.D. 325

forced Christians to think very seriously about the issue of authority in Christian teachings. As early as A.D. 190, a consensus was developing in the churches later regarded as orthodox (at this point, this includes Eastern and Western churches) that there were four consistent tests of Christian truth. The first was the test of *continuity with Hebrew scripture* (what Christians would later call the Old Testament), which the various Gnostic groups had denied. A second test was *continuity with apostolic writings*, what we would call the New Testament, though there remained some dispute over exactly which writings should be read as scripture in Christian congregations. A third test was *continuity with an accepted "rule of faith,"* similar to what we might call a "creed." In forms given by the writers Irenaeus and Hippolytus (both around A.D. 200), these early "rules of faith" were used for candidates professing the faith at their baptisms and had developed from the simple form of words about Jesus given in 1 Corinthians 15:3–5 and other places in the New Testament. A fourth and final test of Christian truth emerging by the end of the second century was *continuity with apostolic bishops*, that is, an unbroken succession of bishops in churches founded by one of the original apostles of Jesus. Irenaeus thought that the succession of bishops in such churches (he named Rome in particular) was a guarantee of the faithfulness of their teachings.[25]

1.0.2   The Period of Ecumenical Councils (A.D. 325–787)

In A.D. 313 the Roman Emperor Constantine issued a series of acts formally allowing the toleration of Christianity within the empire. He eventually allocated funds for building Christian churches and tried to intervene in church affairs, especially when he feared that divisions in the Christian churches (now influential in the empire) might threaten the unity of the state. For the first time, Christians could worship publicly and Christianity could become "comfortable" in the Roman world.

It was at about the time of the Emperor Constantine, just at the moment when Christianity attained a degree of respectability in the Roman Empire, that some Christians began to withdraw from cities and live their lives, either by themselves alone or in communities, away from the world so they could focus on the spiritual struggle. Beginning with Anthony of Egypt around A.D. 320, Christians in increasing numbers gave themselves over to the "monastic" life, attempting to follow Christ by practicing "celibacy" (singleness) and living an entirely devoted life. Monasticism spread rapidly from Egypt to Pales-

---

25. Pelikan, *The Christian Tradition,* 1:108–120.

tine and Syria, and from these places around the Mediterranean world, and by the end of the fourth century A.D. Christian monasticism had spread to the cities as well as the isolated areas where the movement had flourished earlier. The monks would play a leading role in the church in the centuries to follow, and in Eastern Christianity their communities would be centers for education and spiritual life, from which bishops and other leaders were drawn.

One of the clearest signs of the Emperor Constantine's interest in Christian affairs was his calling together a council of Christian bishops, which met at the town of Nicaea in Asia Minor in A.D. 325. The Council of Nicaea—we should call this one more technically the First Council of Nicaea—initiated a long period of councils, all called together by imperial authority and represented by bishops from East and West. Seven of these councils are regarded by Eastern Orthodox and Roman Catholic Christians alike as having special significance for the ancient Christian consensus regarding the faith. These seven councils are referred to as Ecumenical Councils (from the word *oikoumene*). For Eastern Orthodox Christians, the Ecumenical Councils are particularly definitive: Orthodox Christians today look forward to the time when a new Ecumenical Council will resolve contemporary issues dividing the churches, though they believe that a council will not be truly "ecumenical" until Christians from the whole world are represented at it. Because the Ecumenical Councils were so foundational for Eastern Christianity, we shall deal with their teachings below (especially in section 1.2), but at this point it is important to have a sense of when and why the Ecumenical Councils were called. See table 1 for a list of the seven Ecumenical Councils.

Each of the seven Ecumenical Councils dealt with doctrinal issues facing Christians in their day. It is often difficult for contemporary Christians to understand the vehemence and urgency with which the ancient Christians viewed these issues. Bear in mind that almost all of them had to do, one way or another, with the doctrine of Christ's in-

Table 1. Seven Ecumenical Councils

Date	Council	Teachings Condemned
325	I Nicaea	Arianism
381	I Constantinople	Arianism
431	Ephesus	Nestorianism
451	Chalcedon	Monophysitism
553	II Constantinople	(Moderate Nestorianism)
680	III Constantinople	(Moderate Monophysitism)
787	II Nicaea	Iconoclasm

carnation, that is, Christ's becoming human. I shall argue (see 5.3) that this teaching is at the heart of Christian faith. The ancient Christians involved in these conflicts understood themselves to be dealing not with peripheral issues but with issues central to Christian life and belief.

The First Council of Nicaea (325) was the first Ecumenical Council, and it was called to deal with the issue of Arianism. Arianism was an influential system of beliefs, popular with the imperial court through most of the fourth century A.D., which claimed that though Christ is divine, Christ is not fully God in the same way that God the Father is fully and eternally God. Christ, the Arians maintained, was a creation (or "creature") of God and did not exist from eternity as the Father had existed. The Council of Nicaea developed a creed, the original Nicene Creed, which held against the Arians that Christ is "God from God, light from light, true God from true God, of one substance [or being] with the Father, begotten and not created." The council condemned in harsh language the Arian teaching that Christ was a creation of the Father (see table 2).

Although the First Council of Nicaea ruled against the Arians, Constantine himself came to sympathize with the Arians, and his successors officially adopted Arian doctrine. Through the fourth century A.D. the teachings of the council of 325, and especially its claim that Christ was "of the same substance with the Father," were strenuously debated. Through the efforts of Athanasius of Alexandria (an African bishop and theologian) and a group of Asian theologians from the region of Cappadocia, the consensus in the churches came back around to affirming the original Nicene Creed, with the section on the Holy Spirit expanded to make it clear that the Holy Spirit was also equally God as were the Father and the Son. This reaffirmation of Nicaea came at the First Council of Constantinople, which is now reckoned as the second Ecumenical Council and which met in the new imperial city of Constantinople (modern Istanbul) in A.D. 381. The creed used in churches today and popularly called the "Nicene Creed" is actually

Table 2. Issues in Trinitarian Teachings Leading Up to the First Council of Nicaea (A.D. 325)

Modalism	Nicene Doctrine	Arianism
Stressed unity of Father and Son	Attempted to balance unity and difference between Father and Son	Stressed difference between between Father and Son
Son *is* the Father	Son is "of the same substance" as the Father	Son is of "different substance" than the Father

the creed of this council. For this reason, it is sometimes referred to, rather technically, as the Niceno-Constantinopolitan Creed. When we refer to the "Nicene Creed" from this point, readers should understand that it is this creed (of 381) to which we refer.

The next four Ecumenical Councils all dealt with specific issues concerning the relation of human and divine in Christ. Although almost all took it as a given that Christ was fully divine (as the earlier Councils had taught) and at the same time a real human being, the relationship between the human and divine became a subject of intense controversy. One important option was to maintain that Christ involved two completely different natures, indeed two completely different persons, one human and one divine. This teaching, stressing the difference between the human and divine and the completeness of each of the two persons, is called Nestorianism (see table 3). Nestorianism was rejected at the third Ecumenical Council, the Council of Ephesus (A.D. 431).

At the opposite extreme from Nestorianism was the option of stressing the unity of human and divine in Christ, to the point of claiming that Christ had one nature, and was one Person, divine and human, with Christ's humanity virtually subsumed by his divinity. This option is referred to as Monophysitism, and it prevailed especially in ancient Alexandria. Monophysitism (along with Nestorianism) was condemned at the fourth Ecumenical Council, the Council of Chalcedon in A.D. 451. In contrast to both Nestorianism and Monophysitism, the Council of Chalcedon maintained that Christ involves two complete natures (human and divine) in one Person of Christ (see table 3). The positions ruled out by the councils of Ephesus and Chalcedon resulted in the exclusion of Christians whose traditions persist until today. These are the "Assyrian Church of the East" (see Interlude 1 A) and the "Oriental Orthodox" Churches (see Interlude 1 B).

Although the Nestorians remained a fairly small group on the

Table 3. Issues about Christ Leading Up to the Council of Chalcedon (A.D. 451)

Nestorianism	Chalcedon	Monophysitism
2 Persons	1 Person	1 Person
2 natures	2 natures	1 nature
Stressed integrity or distinctness of divine and human in Christ	Attempted to balance distinctness of divine and human in Christ	Stressed unity of divine and human in Christ

eastern fringes of the empire, the Monophysite churches condemned by the Council of Chalcedon represented a powerful segment of the empire. The next two Ecumenical Councils, both of which met in Constantinople, resulted from attempts to compromise with the Monophysite churches. These were the Second and Third Councils of Constantinople, which met in A.D. 553 and 680, and which are reckoned respectively as the Fifth and Sixth Ecumenical Councils. Eventually, all attempts at compromise failed and Monophysite churches (now referred to as "Oriental Orthodox" churches) remained separate in Egypt, Ethiopia, Syria, Persia, Armenia, and other places (see Interlude 1 B).

The seventh and last Ecumenical Council (at least, the last of the Ecumenical Councils of the undivided ancient church) met back in the location of the first Ecumenical Council. This was the Second Council of Nicaea (A.D. 787), and it was called to deal with the issue of Iconoclasm, that is, opposition to the use of religious images. The custom of paying reverence to religious images, especially images of Christ and the saints, had become particularly prominent in Eastern Christianity. One faction, perhaps influenced by this time by the Muslims' utter rejection of all images of living things, regarded religious icons or images as idols, and proceeded to break images—image-breaking is literally what is meant by "Iconoclasm." Particularly controversial was the issue of whether Christ could be represented by an image: all the older christological issues about the relationship of human and divine in Christ were raised again by the question of how human and divine could be represented iconographically. The Second Council of Nicaea condemned Iconoclasm, and in doing so it approved of the use of icons in a carefully defined way. The council taught that "worship" (*latreia*) is due to God alone, and images cannot be worshiped. But "veneration" or "respect" (*proskunesis,* literally, "bowing the knee") can be paid to human beings whom we revere (such as parents or grandparents), especially to saints and to images that represent the saints to us. It might be noted that though the teachings of the Second Council of Nicaea were eventually approved in the Christian West, it took a whole century before the West agreed, and there was considerable opposition to the use of images in the Western Church.

1.0.3 The Formal Division of Eastern and Western Christianity

The Western reaction to the Second Council of Nicaea points to important differences between the Christian East and West, differences that had been growing for centuries and that led to the formal division of Eastern and Western Churches in A.D. 1054. These differences were grounded in the cultural differences between the Greek-speaking eastern Mediterranean and the Latin-speaking western Mediterranean. The Emperor Constantine, the same one who had allowed toleration of Christianity and called together the First Council of Nicaea, had formalized these cultural distinctions by establishing a separate imperial capital, Constantinople (also called Byzantium), and by dividing the empire into eastern and western administrative units.

Throughout the centuries from Constantine's time up to A.D. 1000, the differences between the Greek-speaking Christian East and the Latin-speaking Christian West had grown more and more pronounced. Some seem trivial in retrospect. Eastern Christians, for instance, had insisted on using leavened bread in the Eucharist, whereas Western Christians had customarily utilized unleavened bread. Other differences lay in the forms of worship used in the East and West. The Western Church often used the "Apostles' Creed," which was virtually unknown in the Christian East. Still other differences lay in nuances and emphases of traditional religious teachings. Eastern Christians had tended to stress the distinctness of the three Persons of the Trinity, where Western Christians consistently emphasized the oneness or unity of God, though all were agreed on the creeds and formulas arrived at by the seven Ecumenical Councils. Moreover, there were political factors. By A.D. 1000 the West had undergone an important rebirth of political power under Charlemagne and his successors in the Holy Roman Empire, while at the same time the Eastern Roman Empire—by this point we should call it the Byzantine Empire—was sorely pressed by the Muslims.

It was against this background of cultural and religious differences, and political struggle, that the Eastern and Western Churches formally divided from each other. The overt issue over which they divided was a question of how the creed—the "Nicene" Creed—was to be said. The creed adopted by the First Council of Constantinople asserted that the Holy Spirit "proceeds from the Father." In Latin-speaking Western Churches, however, it had become customary to say that the Spirit "proceeds from the Father and the Son." The words "and the Son" (in Latin, *filioque*) were approved by the Western Church because the bishop of Rome—the pope—had approved them. Eastern Christians were concerned about this addition to the creed, not only because of the notion of the Spirit "proceeding" from the Son as well as the Father, but more importantly because, as they saw it, no single bishop had the authority to alter or change what an Ecumenical Council of bishops had agreed on.

Underlying the outward issue of the *filioque* clause, then, was the larger issue of authority in the church. This was probably the most important difference that had developed between Eastern and Western Christians since ancient times. Although Eastern Christians were willing to accord the popes—bishops of Rome—the "first place of honor" among the bishops of the church, they were not willing to grant them jurisdiction over other bishops, and they would certainly not grant them authority over Ecumenical Councils. The development of the papacy (the office of popes or bishops of Rome) will be dealt with in section 2.0, but here it must be noted that differing views of the authority of bishops, and especially of the bishops of Rome, lay beneath the outward events that separated Eastern and Western Christians in the Middle Ages.

In the summer of A.D. 1054 then, delegates from Pope Leo IX attempted to reach an agreement with the bishop (now with the title "patriarch") of Constantinople, Michael Cerularius, on the various beliefs and practices separating Eastern and Western churches. Cerularius refused to compromise, and the Western delegates then laid a document on the altar of the great Church of Holy Wisdom (Hagia Sophia) in Constantinople, a document indicating that from the perspective of the Western Church, the Eastern Patriarch and the church authorities of Constantinople were *excommunicate,* that is, outside of the communion of Christian faith, and *anathema,* that is, "cursed." Cerularius returned the favor the next day by announcing the excommunication and anathematization of the Western delegates. This condition existed until the middle of the 1960s, it may be noted at this point, when Pope Paul VI and the patriarch of Constantinople agreed to remove the mutual anathemas; but Eastern and Western Christians still do not share full communion with one another.

1.0.4   The Rise of Slavic Christianity

Even before the formal division of Eastern and Western Christianity, Eastern Christians in communion with Constantinople had begun the process of Christianizing the Slavic peoples of Central and Eastern Europe, to the north of the Byzantine Empire. In the 800s A.D., the evangelists Cyril and Methodius began preaching among the Slavic peoples, and Cyril himself developed an alphabet (still called the "Cyrillic" alphabet, used for modern Russian) to represent Slavic tongues. Christianity was accepted in Bulgaria in A.D. 864–865, and though Western missionaries were also at work there, the nation decided by A.D. 870 to accept the practices of Eastern Christians. At about the same time, Serbia became Christian, but wavered many centuries between Eastern and Western customs before finally siding with the East.

The first Christian missionaries came to Russia in the ninth century A.D. The Russian prince Vladimir was baptized in 988, and when the division came between Eastern and Western Christianity in 1054, Russian Christianity followed Constantinople and the East. Eastern Christianity had already been established in Georgia, and eventually it expanded into Rumania, Ukraine, and some areas of Poland.

1.0.5   Orthodoxy and the Struggle with Islam

The Islamic religion originated in Arabia in the seventh century A.D., and by the middle of that century Muslim armies had conquered Palestine, Syria, Egypt, and many other lands where Eastern Christianity had flourished. The official policy of Islam toward Jews and Christians, whom they called "peoples of the Book," was one of toleration, though "proselytization," making converts to Christianity, was forbidden under penalty of death. In fact, many Muslim states attached severe taxes and other penalties to adherents of non-Muslim faiths. Most seriously, Muslim armies continued the attempt to take the Christian stronghold of Constantinople. Although they did not accomplish this goal until 1453 A.D., the entire period from the 600s through the 1400s was marked by deep insecurity on the part of Eastern Christians in the face of the Islamic threat.

It should be recalled that the last two of the seven Ecumenical Councils took place after the Islamic threat had emerged, and both the attempt to compromise with Monophysite Christians and the attempt to deal with the issue of Christian veneration of images may be understood as motivated by the threat of Islam to the Byzantine Empire. Eastern Christians were also tempted during this period to make compromises with the Christian West in exchange for pledges of military support; in fact, some of the Western-led Crusades against Islam were directly aimed at supporting Constantinople, but the Western Christian forces of the Fourth Crusade sacked Constantinople and set up a temporary Latin kingdom there in 1204. This event served to strain relations between Eastern and Western churches, and is remembered as one of the numerous tragedies in the history of Eastern Christianity.

On two occasions, Eastern bishops actually gave in to the demands of the Western Church that the expression "and the Son" should be said in the creed. At councils held in Lyons (1273) and Florence (1439), Eastern delegates agreed to the *filioque* and so technically effected reunions of Western and Eastern Churches. But although Catholics would regard both of these councils as fully Ecumenical, in neither case did the majority of Eastern bishops accept the results once they were reported in the East. In a few areas, though, the reunion was accepted, and this is why in some places there are "Eastern-Rite Catholic" churches. Perhaps the best known of these is the Catholic Church in Ukraine, which maintains communion with Rome (and says "and the Son" in the creed) but worships according to ancient Eastern patterns. In Lebanon and other areas there were Christians who accepted this reunion (or later reunions) and so became Eastern-Rite Catholics.

1.0.6   Early Modern Orthodoxy

The fall of Constantinople to the Ottoman Turks in 1453 marked a huge defeat for Eastern Christianity. The great Church of Holy Wisdom became an Islamic mosque. Christians were forced to pay severe taxes to the state, and of course they were forbidden from making new converts. Patriarchs often became lackeys of the Turkish state, and more than a hundred of them were murdered, kidnapped, or otherwise forcibly removed from office by rivals. It was a dismal age for Greek Christianity (up until the Greek War of Independence in the 1820s), described by Steven Runciman as the period of "the great church in captivity."[26]

But while Greek Christianity's influence dwindled, Russian Christianity grew in importance, corresponding to the rise of Russia on the global political stage in the late fifteenth century. With the patriarch of Constantinople unable to oversee the vast areas that looked to him as a symbolic head of the church, the position of bishop of Moscow was raised to the level of patriarch in 1589, and from that time the Orthodox began to think of Moscow as a "third Rome" (after Rome itself and Constantinople). It might be noted at this point that Orthodox patriarchates were eventually established in Rumania, Bulgaria, Georgia, and Serbia as well as Russia.

During this period Eastern Christianity was forced to rely on Western Christian institutions, especially for the education of church leaders. Some Orthodox leaders refer to this period as the "Western Captivity" of the Eastern churches. It was during this period that Eastern Christianity also had to deal with the Protestant Reformation. The Reformation was not well understood in the East, and it would be as accurate to say that Eastern Christianity was not well understood by the Protestant Reformers. There were some abortive attempts to form al-

---

26. Steven Runciman, *The Great Church in Captivity: A Study of the Patriarchate of Constantinople from the Eve of the Turkish Conquest to the Greek War of Independence* (Cambridge, U.K.: Cambridge University Press, 1968).

liances of Eastern Christians and Protestants against Catholics, and some Eastern Christian (Greek and Russian) priests were educated in the West. One patriarch of Constantinople in the 1620s and 1630s turned out (it was discovered after his election) to have Calvinist leanings, and the Confession of Faith he composed was rejected and replaced with a truly Orthodox confession, authored by the patriarch of Constantinople, Dositheus. The Confession of Dositheus (1672) is an important indication of Eastern Orthodoxy's reaction to both Catholicism and Protestantism in the early modern period, and we shall refer to it at some points in what follows.

1.0.7 The Soviet Eclipse of Orthodoxy

Just as the rise of Islam and the eventual overthrow of Constantinople had provided setbacks for Greek Christianity, the emergence of the Soviet state in 1917–1918 offered an enormous setback to Russian Christianity and eventually to Slavic Christianity more broadly. The Soviet state embraced atheism, and its official attitude toward religion resembled in some ways the policies of Islamic states toward Christians and Jews: religious worship was technically tolerated, but proselytization and evangelization of all forms were forbidden. The Soviets did not tax religious believers more than other citizens, but active members of Christian churches were not allowed to be members of the Communist Party and so could not advance in the Soviet political system. Orthodox Churches in the Soviet state were no longer given the subsidies on which they had come to rely in centuries past. Moreover, although the official policy of the Soviet state was to tolerate religious worship, for most of the seventy years of the Soviet Union, the state maintained a de facto policy of destroying the churches. Bishops and priests who resisted the state were identified as "counterrevolutionaries," and thousands of Russian Orthodox leaders were imprisoned. It has been estimated that more than twelve thousand priests alone were either executed or died through poor treatment under the Soviet regime. By the middle of the twentieth century there was a notable shortage of priests, seminaries and monasteries were closed, and church attendance waned significantly, with elderly women forming the bulk of the faithful remnant in Russia.

Since the 1820s, however, when Greece became independent of the Ottoman Empire, Greek Christianity had emerged from its period of captivity and by the beginning of the twentieth century was in a position to play an influential role in the Christian world, especially in the Ecumenical movement. In 1920 the patriarch of Constantinople issued an encyclical letter (an open letter for readers throughout the world) addressed to "all the churches of Christ" appealing for "closer intercourse and mutual cooperation" between Christians. Greek Orthodox Christians followed this appeal by engaging in conversations with Protestants and Catholics alike. In 1961, other Orthodox churches, including Russian Orthodox, began sending delegates to the World Council of Churches. In 1963, as we have noted above, the patriarch of Constantinople and the pope removed the anathemas that their churches had placed on each other's delegates in A.D. 1054, and this action, along with Catholic statements in the Second Vatican Council, opened the way for improved Catholic-Orthodox dialogue.

1.0.8   Orthodoxy since the Fall of the Soviet Union

Since the dissolution of the Soviet Union in the early 1990s, Orthodoxy has undergone a notable revival, though it is too early to estimate the extent to which this will influence the formerly atheist states. Many seminaries have reopened, and participation in Orthodox rites has increased. At the same time, the relaxation of laws forbidding evangelization has opened the former Soviet states to new missionary efforts, especially by Evangelical Protestant groups. Eastern Orthodox leaders have signaled intense concern about Protestant encroachments, and they feel that these Protestant endeavors threaten ecumenical dialogue in failing to recognize the integrity of Orthodox Christianity in its own settings. Unfortunately, most of the Protestant groups engaged in this new missionary activity are not themselves engaged in ecumenical dialogue with the Orthodox.

In a different area, Orthodox participants in the Ecumenical movement have expressed increasing concern over the last decade about their perception that the movement is so dominated by Liberal Protestantism that their voice is not effectively heard. Such contemporary issues as the ordination of women are seen as enormous obstacles to Orthodox participation in the movement.

Finally, in closing this historical sketch, we might note that Orthodoxy has undergone a kind of revival in the West in recent years. In the middle of the 1980s an "Evangelical Orthodox Church" was formed in North America, largely from formerly Evangelical members of the "baby boom" generation who combined folk songs strummed on the guitar with the use of incense and icons and Byzantine liturgy. These were received into Orthodox communion by the Antiochian Orthodox Diocese of America, and (in a very controversial move) their priests were recognized en masse as being validly ordained. Although they are a relatively small group, they stand for a larger revival of interest in Eastern Christianity in recent years. Another sign would be the consistent attempts on the part of Anglicans, Methodists, and others in the same period to find their own connections to the ancient Eastern churches.

1.1   Orthodox Teachings on Religious Authority

The outline of Eastern Orthodox teachings that follows relies on a number of historic documents, many of which are available in English translation in John Leith's *Creeds of the Churches*. (These documents have been specifically cited in the sources paragraphs.) This account relies heavily on the statements of the seven Ecumenical Councils, which Orthodox churches hold in particularly high regard, and on the Confession of Dositheus (1672) and the Russian Catechism of Philaret (1839). The latter documents cannot always be utilized, because at some points they illustrate a tendency of Orthodox teachers in their periods to utilize characteristically Western terminology (such as "transubstantiation" or "purgatory"), which have not been subsequently held as binding on Orthodox expressions of the faith. I have also relied consistently on Bishop Kallistos Ware's *The Orthodox Church*, which is the most standard treatise on Orthodoxy in the English language and a book that readers are encouraged to study for greater detail and depth.

1.1.1   *What Eastern Orthodox churches teach about the source of religious authority:* Eastern Orthodox churches agree in teaching that the source of all religious authority is the unbroken and unfailing holy tradition of the church as a whole, through which God speaks to humankind.

Sources: Confession of Dositheus, decree 12 (in Leith, p. 496; Schaff 2:417). Catechism of Philaret 16–23 (in Schaff, 2:448–449). Ware, *Orthodox Church*, 2nd ed., revised (London: Penguin Books, 1993), pp. 195–199. Klotsche, 2:2 (pp. 34–35).

Comparative Cross-References: Roman Catholic, 2.1.1; Reformation and Union, 3.1.1; Evangelical and Free, 4.1.1a–d; Ecumenical, 5.2.1.

To the outside observer, especially to a Protestant, almost everything about Eastern Orthodoxy represents continuity with ancient tradition. Liturgies in ancient languages (Greek, Syriac, Old Slavonic), chanting in modes and melodies quite alien to the Western ear, incense, lamps and candles, Byzantine-style icons, perhaps even the absence of pews—all these convey a remarkable sense of continuity with antiquity. To understand Eastern Christian views of authority in the church, it is important to keep in mind this sense of continuity of tradition, for it underlies the Eastern Christian understanding of authority: even the authority of the Bible is understood by the Orthodox as an expression of an unbroken tradition in which God has continually spoken to humankind and through which God has continued to work within the church. The Orthodox recognize a particular inheritance as holy tradition, the ongoing, creative work of God in the church, the basis of all church authority.

The seventh Ecumenical Council—the last regarded as ecumenical by the Eastern Churches—met at Nicaea in A.D. 787 and looked back over the long tradition that had already gone before. In dealing with the issue raised by the use of religious images (or icons) in churches, the council referred to "all the ecclesiastical traditions handed down to us" and "the divinely inspired authority of our Holy Fathers and the traditions of the Catholic Church (for, as we all know, the Holy Spirit indwells her)."[27] "Catholic Church" here refers to the "whole" or "complete" church throughout the whole world (kath' holos means "through the whole"), and in fact this statement was written before the formal division of Eastern and Western (Roman Catholic) churches. The council took as a fact acknowledged by everyone that the Holy Spirit dwells within the Church and continues to inspire it. Similarly, responding at least partially to Protestant claims, the Confession of Dositheus (1672) states that the Holy Spirit "doth not immediately [that is, without mediators], but through the holy Fathers and Leaders of the Catholic Church, illuminate the Church."[28]

This Orthodox stress on the presence of the Holy Spirit in the tradition of the church illuminates their insistence that "tradition" does not mean the static repetition of that which has been done in the past for the sake of the past. It should heighten our sensitivity to their concern that tradition is a living and creative reality in the contemporary Church.[29] We have stated above that Eastern Orthodox agree in teaching that holy tradition is not only unbroken, but also unfailing. Perhaps a sharper way to state this would be to say that holy tradition (including the Scriptures) is "infallible," but the meaning is the same: God does not fail or err, and God has inspired the Scriptures and the ancient councils in which the church's consensus was laid out. Holy tradition, then, can be described by the Orthodox as "infallible" or "inerrant,"[30] though Orthodox teachers are equally consistent in maintaining that holy tradition can never be reduced to any particular texts. Rather, it exists dynamically within the ongoing life of the church.

27. In Leith, p. 55.
28. Confession of Dositheus, decree 12 (in Leith, p. 496; Schaff, 2:417).
29. Timothy [Kallistos] Ware, The Orthodox Church, 2nd ed., revised (London: Penguin Books, 1993), pp. 195–199.
30. Ibid., pp. 210, 243–244.

The Orthodox sense of holy tradition differs rather sharply from Protestant understandings of biblical authority, in which a clean break is seen between the Bible and later traditions. Later traditions are typically seen by Protestants as corrupt, and the Bible is seen as standing over against the church, correcting and reforming it. The Orthodox sense of tradition is closer to that held by Roman Catholics, who also emphasize an unbroken tradition as the grounds of authority. Both Catholics and Orthodox see the unbroken succession of bishops from the time of the apostles to our own time as a primary symbol of the continuity of tradition in the church. But as we shall see, Catholics understand the bishops of Rome (popes) to be the central representatives of this tradition, and although Eastern Christians might be convinced to revere the bishop of Rome as having the highest place of "honor" in the church, they are not willing for a single bishop, or even a succession of bishops in one place, to have authority over the tradition in which the consensus of the church has been expressed.

This sense of tradition is one factor that often makes the understanding of Roman Catholicism as well as Eastern Orthodoxy a difficult task for Protestants. Protestants tend to utilize the language of the Bible and the language of the modern world with little or no intervening traditional or technical language. In the cases of Orthodoxy and Catholicism, there is a huge inheritance not only of traditions about worship and devotion, but also of technical language inherited from tradition about Christian doctrine, that is, technical language describing consensus about Christian teaching. There is no escaping this, no easy way to translate these technical terms, without avoiding issues and truths that Catholics and Orthodox take to be foundational. So in what follows we will often utilize the technical language of Orthodox (and in chapter 2, "Teachings of Roman Catholicism," Catholic) tradition, with technical terms denoted by quotation marks. These should serve to remind Western readers, especially Protestant readers, that the quoted terms are often not to be understood in their usual senses, but will have to be explained in the text.

The Orthodox sense of tradition also presents a critical issue in contemporary ecumenical dialogue. The discussion of issues like the ordination of women inevitably leads back to discussions of the grounds of religious authority. For Protestants, new readings of the New Testament text and reliance on reason and experience may open up possibilities not easily accepted by Orthodox leaders. This is crucial in the case of Orthodoxy, precisely because the Orthodox have been fully involved in the Ecumenical movement, most visibly in their participation in the World Council of Churches since 1961. In recent years, Orthodox leaders involved in contemporary ecumenical dialogue have expressed frustration over their perception that their own sense of the authority of tradition has little voice or respect in the Ecumenical movement.[31]

1.1.2 *What Eastern Orthodox churches teach about the relationship between scripture and church tradition:* Eastern Orthodox churches agree in teaching that the Scriptures and later tradition, especially the Ecumenical Councils, complement each other.

Sources: Confession of Dositheus, Decree 2 and Questions 1–3 (in Leith, pp. 486–487, 506–508; Schaff, 2:402–403, 433–435). Catechism of Philaret, 25–61 (in Schaff, 2:450–455). Ware, *Orthodox Church,* pp. 199–202. Klotsche, 2:2 (pp. 34–35).

Comparative Cross-References: Roman Catholic, 2.1.1; Reformation and Union, 3.1.1, 3.1.2.a–c; Evangelical and Free, 4.1.1.a–c; Ecumenical, 5.2.1.

This claim follows naturally from the earlier explanation of the Orthodox understanding of tradition, but it goes a step further in stating that the Bible and later traditions are understood by the Orthodox as mutually supporting each other. The Confession of Dositheus reflects the Orthodox understanding that tradition gave the Scriptures to the church, not the other way around. The Scriptures require tradition, moreover, to explain their hidden meanings. At some points in their histories, especially due to fear of private interpretation of scripture advocated by Protestants, Orthodox churches have discouraged vernacular (modern language) translations of the Scriptures, though present-day Orthodox churches encourage laity to study vernacular translations, and the vernacular is now read in worship.[32]

Orthodox Christians use the entire Bible as it is found in Greek. For the New Testament, the Bible used by Orthodox is the same as that of other Christian groups. For the Old Testament, however, the Orthodox use the ancient translation called the Septuagint (from *septuaginta,* "seventy," for the seventy translators believed to have produced it). Orthodox generally hold that the Septuagint was itself divinely inspired. At some points the Septuagint differs from the Hebrew text of the Old Testament, and it also includes ten books not present in the Hebrew Bible. These latter books are referred to by the Orthodox as Deuterocanonical books or the *Apocrypha,* and although some Ortho-

31. "Reflections of Orthodox Participants" in the Seventh Assembly of the World Council of Churches (Canberra, 1991), pars. 7–8, in *Signs of the Spirit: Official Report, Seventh Assembly* ed. Michael Kinnamon (Geneva: WCC Publications, 1991), p. 281.
32. Confession of Dositheus, qu. 2 (in Leith, p. 507; Schaff, 2:402–403).

dox councils (in the 1600s) declared them to be of equal authority with the rest of the Bible, there is not a widespread consensus on this today.[33] What non-Orthodox might want to recognize, though, is that at certain points the biblical texts used by Orthodox may differ from those received in other traditions.

After the Scriptures, the seven Ecumenical Councils of the ancient church (see 1.0.2, above) hold a particular authority for Orthodox Christians. The Ecumenical Councils, above all, are the authorized interpreter of the Scriptures for the Orthodox.[34] They are understood to form the core of tradition, "holy tradition," and speak in a uniquely unfailing (or "infallible") way because they represent the consensus of bishops from the whole church. But in stating they represent such a consensus, it must not be supposed that this "consensus" existed at the time of the councils themselves. In fact, the long perspective, the consensus gained through centuries, gives the Ecumenical Councils their unique authority. For this reason also the Orthodox reject some councils at which Eastern and Western bishops were present, but which were not accepted subsequently in Orthodox churches. An example would be the Council of Florence, which in A.D. 1439 technically effected a reunion of Eastern and Western Churches. Once the Eastern delegates returned home and announced the results of the council, they were largely rejected (except by some bishops and their churches, who became "Eastern-Rite Catholics," see 1.0.5, above). The Ecumenical Councils must represent a consensus across the world and across the centuries. But for the Orthodox, it is quite possible that there could be again an Ecumenical Council, and some contemporary ecumenical advocates have proposed that the churches should work toward just such a council.

Roman Catholics, like the Orthodox, see the Scriptures and later traditions as mutually interpreting each other, although again the succession of bishops of Rome will be seen as establishing the central unity of the church's teachings for Catholics. Protestants have traditionally rejected the notion of mutual interpretation between the Bible and tradition. For Martin Luther himself, a recognition of the fallibility of Ecumenical Councils was a key step in his movement toward the work of the Reformation. Although Protestants may utilize creeds

33. Confession of Dositheus, qu. 3, declares these books to be canonical along with the rest of Christian scripture (and chides St. Cyril for calling them "apocrypha"; in Leith, pp. 507–508); but cf. Ware, *Orthodox Church*, p. 200, on contemporary Orthodox views of the Deuterocanonical books.
34. Confession of Dositheus, decree 2 (in Leith, pp. 486–488) and decree 12 (in Leith, p. 496).

from the ancient councils (most notably, the "Nicene" Creed), they tend to use these only so far as they find them compatible with the teachings of the Bible (see 3.1.1, 4.1.1.a–b).

1.1.3 *What Eastern Orthodox churches teach about the authority of Christian tradition after the Ecumenical Councils:* Eastern Orthodox churches agree in teaching that there are other traditions, less authoritative than the Ecumenical Councils, which nevertheless guide the life of the church.

Sources: Catechism of Philaret, 24 (in Schaff, 2:449–450). Ware, *Orthodox Church,* pp. 202–207. Klotsche, 2:1 (pp. 31–33).

Comparative Cross-References: Roman Catholic, 2.1.5; Reformation and Union, 3.1.2.a–c; Evangelical and Free, 4.1.3.a–b; Ecumenical, 5.2.1.

Having noted the Eastern Orthodox reverence for tradition, it is important now to note that all traditions are *not* equal in the eyes of Orthodox Christians. Some traditions, especially those representing the broadest consensus of faith (that is, the Ecumenical Councils) are understood as "holy tradition." Some traditions even beyond the ancient councils are almost universally received by Orthodox churches, and there is in fact no clear dividing line between "holy tradition" and lesser traditions. Examples of traditions received broadly by Orthodox churches would be the use of later councils and their decrees, the use of specific liturgies, consistent reference to certain ancient and medieval theologians and spiritual writers (the "fathers" of the church), and even the consistent use of certain icons in the churches. The liturgy is particularly important: the patterns of worship utilized in Orthodox churches are very ancient and are understood as sources of the church's spiritual and moral teachings.

Still other traditions used by Orthodox Christians may be national or local. In addition to the languages used in worship, a number of rites and customs differ between Greek, Russian, Syrian or "Antiochian," and other Orthodox communions. Orthodox churches are often tied closely to national and ethnic identities, so Greek or Russian churches in the West will often be centers of cultural life for the Greek or Russian communities as a whole.

1.2   Orthodox Teachings on God and Christ

Before we proceed to consider the technical vocabulary that Orthodox Christians use to describe God, perhaps we should note that many Orthodox spiritual writers insist that because God is an unspeakable mystery, human beings are not really capable of saying anything, positively, about God. At best, they insist, we can only say what God is *not:* everything we know is limited or finite, so we might say that God is "infinite" (or, "unlimited"). But in saying this, we have not said so much what God really *is,* as what God *is not.* But despite our human limitations, it is possible to say some things positively about God, because God has been revealed to us. Remember that, for Orthodox Christians, God has been revealed not only in Christ and in the Christian scriptures but also in the continuing tradition of the church. This is one of the points, as we have suggested above (see 1.1.1), where there is considerable technical language derived from tradition describing consensus in faith (so beware of quoted terms in the following account).

1.2.1 *What Eastern Orthodox churches teach about the nature of God as the Holy Trinity:* Eastern Orthodox churches agree in teaching that God is three "Persons" in one "substance," that the three Persons differ in their "modes of origin" (the Father is unbegotten, the Son is begotten, and the Spirit proceeds), and that the three Persons "interpenetrate" each other in all acts of God.

Sources: Nicene and Constantinopolitan Creeds (in Leith, pp. 30–31; Denzinger and Hünermann, items 125–126 and 150, pp. 62–64, 83–85; Schaff, 2:57–61; *NPNF* 2:14:3–7). Confession of Dositheus, decree 1 (in Leith, p. 486; Schaff, 2:401–402). Catechism of Philaret, 76–96, 238–251 (in Schaff, 2:458–462, 481–483). Ware, *Orthodox Church*, pp. 208–218. Klotsche, 2:3 (pp. 35–37).

Comparative Cross-References: Roman Catholic, 2.2.1; Reformation and Union, 3.2.1; Evangelical and Free, 4.2.1.a–b; Ecumenical, 5.2.2.1.

The Orthodox Churches (in this case, along with Roman Catholics and most Protestant churches) accept the teachings of the first two Ecumenical Councils, the First Council of Nicaea (A.D. 325) and the First Council of Constantinople (A.D. 381), as establishing parameters for belief about God. The creed adopted at Nicaea in 325 was subsequently expanded in 381, and this is the creed said in most churches today as the "Nicene" (or "Niceno-Constantinopolitan") Creed. Orthodox say the creed as it was given by the council:

> We believe in one God, Father all-powerful, maker of heaven and earth, of all things seen and unseen.
>
> And in one Lord Jesus Christ, the only-begotten Son of God, begotten from the Father before all ages, light from light, true God from true God, begotten not created, of the same substance as the Father, through whom everything came into being, who for us human beings and for our salvation came down from heaven, and was incarnate [or, took flesh] by the Holy Spirit and the Virgin Mary and became human, was crucified on our behalf

under Pontius Pilate, and suffered and was buried, and rose on the third day according to the scriptures, and ascended into heaven, and sits at the right hand of the Father, and is coming again with glory to judge the living and the dead, of whose kingdom there will be no end.

And in the Holy Spirit, the Lord and life-giver, who proceeds from the Father, who is together worshiped and glorified with the Father and the Son, who spoke through the prophets, and in one holy, catholic, and apostolic church. We confess one baptism for the forgiveness of sins. We look forward to the resurrection of the dead and the life of the coming age. Amen.[35]

You will recall (see 1.0.2) that this creed was directed against the Arians, who taught that Christ is a lesser divine being than God the Father. Christ, the Arians maintained, is a "creature" or "creation" of God. The Council of Nicaea responded by insisting that Christ is "of the same substance with the Father," that is, that Christ is equally, eternally God and not a creation of God. The same truth was underscored by the creed's insistence that Christ is "true God from true God," that Christ is "begotten not created"—since things that are begotten are the same beings as their parents are and things that are created or made are not what their creators or makers are.

Although the original creed of 325 simply ended with "And in the Holy Spirit," the creed as adopted in 381 expanded the section on the Holy Spirit to make it clear that the Spirit too is equally God with the Father and the Son. The Spirit is "together worshiped and glorified with the Father and the Son." Note that in the section on the Holy Spirit, the creed states that the Spirit "proceeds from the Father," not "from the Father and the Son," the customary wording in Western churches—Protestant and Catholic. This is a point (perhaps the most critical point) at which Orthodox insist that the creed should be used in the form in which the council adopted it, not as later amended. With its language about the Son being "begotten" and the Spirit "proceeding," the creed laid the foundation for the Orthodox understanding that the Persons of the Trinity differ in their "modes of origin," that is, the Father is unbegotten, the Son is begotten by the Father, and the Holy Spirit proceeds from the Father.

---

35. TAC; based on Greek text as given in Denzinger and Hünermann, item 150, pp. 83–85; cf. Leith, p. 33; Schaff, 2:57–58. We might note that the text of the Niceno-Constantinopolitan creed is not actually found among the documents from the First Council of Constantinople, but was given in the preface to the "Definition of Faith" of the Council of Chalcedon (451), where it is attributed to the Council of 381 at Constantinople. Despite this technicality in the derivation of the text, however, there seems to be little dispute that this was the text as given by the First Council of Constantinople.

The first councils of Nicaea and Constantinople laid the foundation for Orthodox understanding of God as Trinity, that is, "three in one," though the term "Trinity" is not actually used in the creed. The church's technical language about three "Persons" in one divine "substance" in the Trinity was developed to find consensus on issues that seriously divided Christians in the third and fourth centuries, and this technical language cannot be understood apart from the actual crises that provoked the churches to develop this language in the first place. By affirming that God is three Persons, the church ruled out the Modalist teaching that the Father and the Son (and perhaps the Holy Spirit) are all simply the same with no differences whatsoever between them. On the other hand, by affirming that Father, Son, and Holy Spirit are one in substance, the church ruled out the Arian teaching that the Son is a lesser being than the Father. By the time of the Council of Constantinople in 381, the church also affirmed that the Holy Spirit is equally God with the Father and the Son.

We should note in closing this subsection on the Trinity, that this doctrine, however clothed in technical theological language, lies at the heart of Eastern Orthodox belief and piety. Underneath the debates about divine substance and modes of origin, ancient Christians believed that they were clarifying the most important truth and the most uncompromisable practice known to humankind, namely, their belief that Jesus Christ is God and their practice of worshiping Christ as God. Arianism had to be ruled out, as they saw it, because the Arian view of Christ as a lesser being would imply worshiping a creature rather than the creator.

The Orthodox (and Catholic) insistence on affirming the Trinitarian faith as handed down by the early Christian councils has had a noticeable effect on contemporary ecumenical dialogue. When the Faith and Order Commission of the World Council of Churches neared the completion of its landmark study of *Baptism, Eucharist and Ministry* in the early 1980s, it began to focus its dialogues around the theme of "Confessing the Apostolic Faith Today." In these discussions the Nicene Creed has become a central point of discussion, because it is affirmed not only by Orthodox and Catholics but by the majority of Protestant churches as well. The agreed statement of the Santiago Faith and Order meeting of 1993 stressed the importance of the Nicene

36. "On the Way to Fuller Koinonia: The Message of the World Conference," par. 6; in *On the Way to Fuller Koinonia: Official Report of the Fifth World Conference on Faith and Order*, ed. Thomas F. Best and Günther Gassman (Faith and Order Paper no. 166; Geneva: World Council of Churches Publications, 1994), p. 226.

faith in developing ecumenical discussion.[36] Trinitarian doctrine does provide some potential problems for ecumenical dialogue with Orthodox churches, though. Orthodox participants in the Ecumenical movement have stated their concern in recent years that the World Council of Churches has been so dominated by Liberal Protestantism that it has compromised its original commitment to historic Trinitarian faith.[37]

1.2.2   What Eastern Orthodox churches teach about the two natures of Christ: Eastern Orthodox churches agree in teaching that Christ is one "Person" in two "natures" (divine and human), and that there are two "operations" (or "energies") and two wills in Christ, corresponding to the divine and human natures.

Sources: Definition of Faith of the Council of Chalcedon (in Leith, pp. 35–36; Denzinger and Hünermann, items 301–302, pp. 142–143; Schaff, 2:62–65; *NPNF*, 2:14:262–265). Anathemas of the Second Council of Constantinople, 1–11 (in Leith, pp. 46–50; Denzinger and Hünermann, items 421–436, pp. 194–201; *NPNF*, 2:14:312–314). Definition concerning the Two Wills and Energies in Christ of the Third Council of Constantinople (in Leith, pp. 51–53; Denzinger and Hünermann, items 556–558, pp. 257–259; Schaff, 2:72–73; *NPNF*, 2:14:344–346). Confession of Dositheus, decrees 7–8 (in Leith, pp. 490–491; Schaff, 2:408–409). Catechism of Philaret, 150–154, 178–183, 192–237 (in Schaff, 2:468–481). Ware, *Orthodox Church,* pp. 225–229. Klotsche, 2:6 (pp. 42–43).

Comparative Cross-References: Roman Catholic, 2.2.3; Reformation and Union, 3.2.2; Evangelical and Free, 4.2.2; Ecumenical, 5.2.2.2.

The ancient understanding of the Trinity was developed in the fourth century A.D. and formalized at the Councils of 325 and 381. The next four Ecumenical Councils all dealt with the issue of the relationship between the divine and the human in Christ. As the reader will see from the thesis given above, this is another point where tradition has given considerable technical language to describe the ancient consensus in which contemporary Orthodoxy is grounded.

Again, as with the controversies over the Trinity, the controversies over the human and divine in Christ emerged in response to specific teachings that caused immense concern in the churches, in this case beginning in the early fifth century A.D. All sides in these conflicts seem to have agreed on two basic facts: first, that only God can save human beings; and second, that only by Christ's complete participation in human nature could humans be saved. It was, then, necessary for all parties to speak in some way of Christ's divinity (Christ's identity as God) and of Christ's humanity. But given these points of agreement, how could the church agree on teaching about the human and divine in Christ?

Two conflicting positions emerged in the early fifth century A.D.

37. "Reflections of Orthodox Participants," in Kinnamon, par. 3, p. 280.

On one end were the teachings of Nestorianism, which stressed the distinction between the human and the divine in Christ to such a degree that they could speak of "two Persons" of Christ, perhaps even "two Christs" (one human and the other divine). Nestorianism seemed to threaten the unity of divine and human in Christ. On the other end from Nestorianism were the teachings of Monophysitism, which stressed the unity of the human and divine in Christ to such a degree that they asserted not only a single Person in Christ but also a single "nature" in Christ (a combined divine/human nature; "monophysite" comes from the terms *monos*, "one," and *physis*, "nature").[38] Monophysitism seemed to threaten the distinctiveness of divine and human in Christ.

The third Ecumenical Council met at Ephesus in A.D. 431 and condemned Nestorian teachings. From that time until today, Nestorian churches have existed as separate communions in the East (see Interlude 1 A). The fourth Ecumenical Council met at Chalcedon in A.D. 451 and issued a statement condemning both Nestorian and Monophysite teachings. The churches that at that time affirmed Monophysite teachings remain separate until the present, though they prefer not to be called Monophysite now (see Interlude 1 B). The Councils of 431 and 451 thus marked the first formal Christian divisions that resulted in separate churches still in existence today.

The large majority of remaining churches, from which both Eastern Orthodoxy and Roman Catholicism are derived, affirmed the "Definition of Faith" developed at the Council of Chalcedon. Whereas Nestorians had insisted on two natures and two persons in Christ, and Monophysites had insisted in one nature and one Person in Christ, the Chalcedonian definition asserted that Christ is *one Person in two natures,* one entirely human nature and one entirely divine nature.[39]

It is sometimes difficult for Western Christians to understand how these differences over technical terminology could lead to serious rifts

38. I should perhaps add a defensive note at this point about my representation of these conflicts. It was sometimes said that one party (the "Antiochene" party of which Nestorianism was the most exaggerated instance) stressed the humanity of Christ, and the other party (the "Alexandrian" party of which Monophysitism was the most extreme example) stressed the divinity of Christ. There are some elements of truth in this: Antiochene theologians did stress the humanity of Christ (but also the integrity of Christ's divine nature as a separate "Person") and one exaggerated version of Alexandrian teaching—that of Apollinaris of Laodicea—denied the human soul of Christ. But I believe that it is more instructive to see the conflict not so much "divinity versus humanity" as competition between accounts of how divinity and humanity coexisted in Christ. This is, I think, fairer to all sides in the fifth-century controversy.
39. Chalcedonian Definition of Faith (in Leith, pp. 35–36).

in the church. Admittedly, church politics played a role: there were serious political issues involved in the struggles between the "sees" (centers headed by leading bishops) of Constantinople, Alexandria, and Rome. One might argue moreover that the technical language adopted about the "natures" and the "Person" of Christ adopted at Chalcedon do not themselves really tell much about who Christ is (within himself); rather, they mark an agreement about how the church would use language in referring to Christ. For most Christians, the Chalcedonian formula of "one Person in two natures" sufficed; for Nestorians and Monophysites (each for their own reasons) the Chalcedonian formula was unacceptable, and so the divisions remained. But even so, the conflicts over the natures and Person of Christ cannot be reduced to merely political or merely verbal struggles; Christians of all sides in these conflicts understood that what was at stake was ultimate: what was at stake was the church's understanding of Christ's work in bringing about human salvation.

Although the Nestorian churches did not pose a serious threat to the remaining Orthodox Christians, the Monophysite churches represented a fairly significant minority of churches in Syria, Palestine, and Egypt. There were ongoing attempts to find a compromise between Orthodox and Monophysites, especially after the Muslim invasions of the areas of Monophysite strength in the seventh century A.D. The fifth Ecumenical Council (the Second Council of Constantinople) met in A.D. 553 and condemned some ancient theologians whose works were seen as leaning in the direction of Nestorianism.[40] Although it was hoped that this might please Monophysites and so draw them to accept the Chalcedonian formula, it did not in the end bring about the desired reunion.

Another attempt to bring about a reunion with the Monophysite churches suggested that the Orthodox should hold to the "one Person, two natures" formula but add to it a further expression, such as the claim that there is but "one operation" or "one will" in Christ. Although these offered some hope for a period in the seventh century A.D., they too did not succeed. The sixth Ecumenical Council (the Third Council of Constantinople) met in A.D. 681, after the Muslim invasions of the Near East, and condemned Monothelitism (the teaching that there is one will [thelema] in Christ) and also condemned Monenergism (the teaching that there is one "energy" or "operation" [energeia] in Christ). In condemning Monothelitism and Monenergism, the sixth Ecumenical Council defined for Orthodox (and Roman

40. Anathemas of the Second Council of Constantinople, 4–5 (in Leith, pp. 47–48).

Catholics) that there are two "operations" and two wills in Christ, each of these corresponding to Christ's human and divine natures.[41]

The insights of Nicaea and Chalcedon are remembered by Orthodox in the manner in which the hand is held to make the sign of the cross. The tip of the thumb of the right hand is joined to the tips of the two fingers adjacent to the thumb. The remaining two fingers rest against the palm of the hand. (In Orthodox custom, the sign of the cross is made from right to left, unlike Catholics who move left to right.) Orthodox spiritual teachers take this hand position as a reminder of the central Orthodox teachings on the Trinity and on Christ: the three fingertips together represent the three Persons of the Trinity (defined at Nicaea), and the two remaining fingers represent the two natures in the one Person of Christ (defined at Chalcedon).

We should underscore that in developing a technical traditional language to describe unity in the faith, the Orthodox have never insisted that simple believers have to know this language in order to be saved. Faith is a matter not so much of knowledge as of trust (see 1.3.5, below). Generations of Orthodox believers have gone to church, gone through the sacraments that mark the passages of life, and have simply believed in Christ and trusted the traditions handed on to them. But if we intend to understand Orthodox consensus in the faith (and that is the point here), then it is important to delve somewhat into the technical language, as better educated Orthodox believers would do. That is why we have tried to describe this language here.

1.2.3 *What Eastern Orthodox churches teach about Mary, the mother of Jesus:* Eastern Orthodox churches agree in teaching that the Blessed Virgin Mary is the "Mother of God" as the Mother of the whole Christ, and that she is a virgin eternally. Moreover, Orthodox Christians teach that the Blessed Virgin Mary was assumed bodily into heaven after her death.

Sources: Anathema of Cyril of Alexandria approved at the Council of Ephesus, 1 (in Denzinger and Hünermann, item 252, p. 126; *NPNF*, 2:14:206). Definition of Faith of the Council of Chalcedon (in Leith, pp. 35–36; Denzinger and Hünermann, items 301–302, pp. 142–143; Schaff, 2:62–65; *NPNF*, 2:14:264). Confession of Dositheus, decree 8 and question 4 (in Leith, pp. 491, 508; Schaff, 2:408–409, 435–443). Catechism of Philaret, 185–191 (in Schaff, 2:471–472). Ware, *Orthodox Church*, pp. 257–261. Klotsche, 2:4 (p. 38) and 2:5 (p. 42).

Comparative Cross-References: Roman Catholic, 2.2.4; Reformation and Union, 3.2.3; Evangelical and Free, 4.2.4.

Remember the Nestorians who insisted on the clear separation between the divine and human in Christ? Nestorius started the whole

---

41. Statement of Faith of the Third Council of Constantinople (in Leith, pp. 51–53).

controversy when he preached a sermon against the custom of calling
Mary *Theotokos*, "God-bearer" or "Mother of God." God cannot have
a mother, Nestorius reasoned, for this would confuse humanity and
deity together. Other Christians reacted sharply against Nestorius's
attack, defending the title *theotokos* by reasoning that Mary is the
mother of the whole Christ, human and divine, and is as much
"Mother of God" as mother of the human nature of Christ. In condemning Nestorius, the Ecumenical Councils of Ephesus (A.D. 431)
and Chalcedon (A.D. 451) affirmed the use of the term *theotokos* applied to Mary.[42]

Eastern Orthodox Christians not only apply the title *theotokos* to the
Virgin Mary but also "venerate" her as a saint and pray for (in this
context "pray for" simply means "ask for") her intercession. The seventh and last Ecumenical Council (the Second Council of Nicaea) met
in A.D. 787 to consider the issue of the churches' use of religious images or "icons." In considering this issue the council made a careful
distinction between "worship," which is due God alone, and "veneration" or respect (*proskunesis*), which may be paid to the saints, angels,
and religious images that represent them. Orthodox confessions will
sometimes state that Mary is to be paid a degree of veneration higher
than that of other saints [*huperdouleia*].[43] Although we can say correctly that Orthodox and Catholic Christians respect or "venerate" the
Virgin Mary in a special place among the saints, it is quite incorrect to
say that they "worship" her, and Protestants need to cleanse this misunderstanding from their collective memories. "Veneration" is often
understood on the analogy of the respect that one would pay to parents or leaders. Intercessory prayers directed to Mary (and other
saints) are understood not as replacing prayer to God but as asking for
the prayers of a Christian friend.

Long before the controversies of the fifth century A.D. it had become customary for Christians to reverence Mary's virginity. Even in
the second century A.D. Christian books suggested that Mary remained a virgin even after the birth of Jesus. If Protestants ask about
the New Testament references to Jesus' brothers and sisters (Matt.
12:46; 13:55–56; Mark 3:31; Luke 8:19–20) and references to James as
"the Lord's brother" (Gal. 1:19), Catholics and Orthodox respond that
the terms in Greek can denote cousins, and that Joseph might have
had other children by a previous wife. The doctrine that Mary re-

42. Chalcedonian Definition of Faith (in Leith, p. 36).
43. Decree of the Second Council of Nicaea (in Leith, pp. 55–56); cf. Confession of
Dositheus, decree 8 and question 4 (in Leith, pp. 491 and 508).

mained a virgin through Jesus' conception and birth and beyond seems not to have been disputed in the ancient church; Ecumenical Councils consistently use the expression "ever virgin" to refer to Mary.[44]

Moreover, although it is not defined in Ecumenical Councils, Orthodox Christians generally teach that Mary was assumed bodily into heaven after her death; this is celebrated in Orthodox life as the *dormition* (literally, "sleeping") of the Blessed Virgin.[45] We might note that although Catholics formally teach that Mary herself was conceived "immaculately"; that is, without the stain of original sin, the doctrine of the "immaculate conception" of Mary has not been widely accepted by Orthodox Christians. Moreover, although Catholics teach that Mary was assumed bodily into heaven, they maintain that this may have happened before her natural death. With these exceptions however, Orthodox and Catholics generally agree in their veneration of the "Blessed Virgin Mary," particularly in their use of the expression "Mother of God" to refer to her and in their affirmations of her perpetual virginity and her bodily assumption into heaven. Protestants have historically rejected these doctrines, although Lutherans and Anglicans affirm the term *theotokos,* and some Anglicans (those who favor a more Catholic expression of the Anglican tradition) have been receptive to the other Marian doctrines (see 3.2.3 and 4.2.4).

1.3   Orthodox Teachings on Human Nature and Salvation

We now turn to consider how Orthodox churches account for the human condition and the possibility of our deliverance (salvation) from this situation. Whereas the basic Orthodox teachings about God and Christ were laid down in the Ecumenical Councils, Orthodox teachings about human nature and salvation developed more from devotional and especially from monastic writings. These teachings, in the broadest understanding, tended not to be much disputed in Orthodox circles and so did not become the subject of larger councils.[46] Such later Orthodox documents as the Confession of Dositheus,

---

44. For example, in the anathemas of the Second Council of Constantinople VI (in Leith, p. 48). The doctrine of perpetual virginity is defined more formally in the Confession of Dositheus, decree 7 (in Leith, p. 490).

45. Ware, *Orthodox Church,* pp. 260–261.

46. There was an extended controversy in Eastern Christian circles over the propriety of certain monastic practices of prayer, and whether Christians can experience the "uncreated light" of God, but these controversies were not addressed by Ecumenical Councils.

written in the 1600s, deal more explicitly with issues of human nature and salvation, so that in this section we must rely more on ancient devotional works and later councils than on the ancient councils.

1.3.1 *What Eastern Orthodox churches teach about human nature:* Eastern Orthodox churches agree in teaching that human beings were created in the "image" of God, with reason and freedom, and in the "likeness" of God, with holiness and immortality.

Sources: Confession of Dositheus, decree 14 (in Leith, pp. 497–498). Ware, *Orthodox Church,* pp. 218–222. Klotsche, 2:5 (pp. 41–42).

Comparative Cross-References: Roman Catholic, 2.3.1; Reformation and Union, 3.3.1; Evangelical and Free, 4.3.1; Ecumenical, 5.2.3.

Orthodox churches teach that human beings were created in the "image and likeness of God." Orthodox spiritual writers and theologians frequently use these terms to distinguish that which we have lost as a result of the human fall into sin (the likeness of God) from that which humans retain after the fall (the image of God). The original state of human beings, according to Orthodox teachings, was characterized by reason, holiness, immortality, and freedom (or power, or ability) to do what God requires. Reason and freedom constitute the image of God that still remains in human beings after the fall; holiness and immortality constitute the likeness of God that has been lost as a result of the fall. Note that each of these four terms (holiness, immortality, reason, and freedom) is understood to be an attribute of God and together describe "godliness," and godliness is not only the original condition of human beings but also the goal toward which human beings should now strive.

1.3.2 *What Eastern Orthodox churches teach about the fall of humankind:* Eastern Orthodox churches agree in teaching that human beings suffered disease, corruption, and death as a result of the disobedience of the first human beings.

Sources: Confession of Dositheus, decrees 3, 6 (in Leith, pp. 487–490). Ware, *Orthodox Church,* pp. 222–225. Klotsche, 2:5 (pp. 41–42).

Comparative Cross-References: Roman Catholic, 2.3.1; Reformation and Union, 3.3.1; Evangelical and Free, 4.3.1; Ecumenical, 5.2.3.

According to Orthodox teachings, human beings lost their original immortality and holiness. In losing holiness they fell into sin; in losing immortality they became susceptible to disease, corruption and death. Immortality and holiness, then, describe the "likeness" of God lost in the fall, and for Orthodox Christians the religious life is a quest to recover this lost likeness. We should note, though, that Orthodox do not teach that human beings inherit the guilt of Adam's sin (as Western churches, both Protestant and Catholic, are inclined to teach); rather, Orthodox stress that it was the results of the sin of our first human parents, namely, the human inheritance of disease and death, that passed on to human beings. All human beings are responsible for their own sins.[47] And in spite of our loss of the "likeness" of God, Orthodox maintain that we retain certain aspects of God.

1.3.3 *What Eastern Orthodox churches teach about the gifts of reason and freedom remaining after the fall:* Eastern Orthodox churches agree in teaching that human beings retain both reason after the fall and a degree of grace that gives freedom to avoid sin and to believe in Christ.

Sources: Confession of Dositheus, decree 14 (in Leith, pp. 497–498). Ware, *Orthodox Church,* pp. 221–222. Klotsche, 2:5 (pp. 41–42).

Comparative Cross-References: Roman Catholic, 2.3.2; Reformation and Union, 3.3.2; Evangelical and Free, 4.3.1; Ecumenical, 5.2.3.

Though human beings have lost the "likeness" of God in the fall, they nevertheless retain the "image" of God, however distorted. This divine image includes reason and a degree of freedom to avoid sin. The term "reason" in the Greek used by Eastern theologians is *logos,* the same term translated "Word" at the beginning of John's Gospel: "In the beginning was the Word [*logos*], and the Word was with God, and the Word was God" (John 1:1). Human beings, along with angels and devils are understood to be "reasonable" or "rational" (*logikos*) beings, and it is "reason" in this sense that distinguishes human beings from animals. "Reason" is a central concept for Eastern Christian theologians. Sometimes Plato and other pre-Christian philosophers will appear among the images of saints in Eastern churches. How could this be? Because, they respond, God has shared "reason" with human beings, and some who lived even before Christ expressed the "reason" that is part of the nature of God. The Word was, after all "the true light, which enlightens every human being" (John 1:9a; author's translation).

Not only do human beings participate in "reason" after the fall but they also share a degree of "freedom," in the sense of freedom to avoid sin. This is why Orthodox churches state that all human beings are responsible for their own sin and cannot attribute their sin to their first parent (Adam). On this point, Eastern churches differ from Western

47. Confession of Dositheus, decree 6 (in Leith, pp. 489–490); cf. Ware, *Orthodox Church,* pp. 218–221.

church traditions (Catholic and Protestant) that have insisted that all later human beings have inherited the guilt of Adam's sin and that in their natural state human beings have no power or freedom to resist sin. Does this mean, then, that Orthodox churches teach that human beings can resist sin by themselves? (This would be the heresy identified in Western churches as Pelagianism.) No, Orthodox churches would say, because the "image" of God remaining in human beings is in itself a kind of grace, a power or ability given by God and not from ourselves. In other words, our freedom to avoid sin is not entirely our own, it is a gift of God, although it is given to every human being and is present with us from birth.

We might note, in regard to the contemporary ecumenical dialogue, that although Eastern Christian views of human nature and the human predicament differ from a long line of Western Christian thinking on these issues (what we shall call the "Augustinian" strain of Western Christian thought, see 2.3.1 and 3.3.1), there are some important "exceptions" within Western Christian tradition. As we shall see, some Catholics (like the Jesuits in the 1590s) would argue that God gives a kind of grace to all human beings that enables them to turn to Christ (see 2.3.3), and Protestants identified as "Arminian" (including Methodists and most of their descendants in Holiness and Pentecostal churches) have argued similarly (see 3.3.3.b and 4.3.2.b). In this particular respect they bear more similarities to Eastern Christian traditions than to "Augustinian" Western traditions.

1.3.4 *What Eastern Orthodox churches teach concerning the goal of human existence:* Eastern Orthodox churches agree in teaching that the goal of human existence is "divinization," the recovery of the original human "likeness" to God.

Sources: Ware, *Orthodox Church*, pp. 231–238.

Comparative Cross-References: Evangelical and Free, 4.3.6.b; Ecumenical, 5.2.3.

According to Athanasius of Alexandria, Christ "became human in order that we might become divine."[48] This idea—that human beings aspire to "divinity"—is perhaps the most central and distinctive idea of Eastern Christianity. The specific term for this process is *theosis*, which I have translated "divinization." It comes from the term for

---

48. Athanasius, "On the Incarnation of the Word," 54; my translation; text in *Enchiridion Patristicum: Loci Sanctissimorum Patrum, Doctorum, Scriptorum Ecclesiasticorum,* ed. M. J. Rouët de Journel, 24th ed. (Barcelona: Herder, 1969), item 752, p. 261.

God, *theos*, and could even be translated "deification." What was the purpose of Christ's incarnation, his becoming human? According to Athanasius and a long-held consensus of Eastern Christian thought, it was so that we might become like God, divine. In the words of a Liberal Protestant hymn,

> Our spirits are thine.
> Remold them, make us, like thee, divine.[49]

Christ became incarnate so that we might be restored to those aspects of God, the "likeness" of God, that we lost in the fall, namely, holiness and immortality.

The word "divinization" implies a process in which human beings grow more and more godlike. As we shall see in the next subsection (1.3.5), this process centers on "mysteries" given by God to the church through which grace is shared. Eastern Christians are likely to visualize this process in the lives of Christian saints, perhaps especially those monks (men and women) who have renounced the world, decided to live entirely for God, and whose lives consistently take on the characteristics of God. This "ascetic" process is seen by Eastern Christians preeminently in the life of Jesus himself, so that Christian monks are seen as literally following Christ in a life of celibacy devoted to meditation and prayer, constantly growing in the process of divinization.

As the Christian grows in holiness, so she or he grows in "immortality," living less and less for the things of this world and more and more for the world that is to come. Eastern Christians tend to see the culmination of religious life as a state or condition in which one has almost completely divorced oneself from worldly obstructions, such as food and drink and even sleep. In this state the religious person's life is spent almost constantly in prayer and meditation, so that death marks an almost natural transition from this life to that life of eternity for which he or she was already living.

This process is not reserved for monks, even if they provide a paradigm of the religious life. Ordinary folk also participate in this process. Orthodox Christians will say short, customary prayers over the most common acts of life, such as lighting candles in the evening when darkness comes. They are taught to recite the name of Jesus or simple prayers privately and constantly to themselves. Perhaps the best known of these simple prayers is the so-called Jesus Prayer, in which

49. Earl Marlatt, "Are Ye Able," 1926, in *The United Methodist Hymnal: Book of United Methodist Worship* (Nashville: United Methodist Publishing House, 1989), no. 530.

many Eastern spiritual traditions have been grounded. The prayer is
"Lord Jesus Christ, Son of God, have mercy on me, a sinner."[50] The
point of constant recitation is that repetition leads the soul to focus consistently on Christ, and by doing so the believer grows constantly closer
to God. In this way the most ordinary Christians can participate in the
process of "divinization," the heart of Eastern Christian spirituality.[51]

1.3.5 *What Eastern Orthodox churches teach about the role of
"mysteries" in the Christian life:* Eastern Orthodox churches agree in
teaching that through certain "mysteries," which have outward form
and inward spiritual power, God gives grace to human beings.

Sources: Ware, *Orthodox Church*, pp. 274–277. Klotsche, 2:8 (p. 45).
Comparative Cross-References: Roman Catholic, 2.3.6.

Not only do human beings receive the grace of the divine "image" remaining in them, with the "reason" and "freedom" it conveys, but
through the "mysteries" of the church they are able to receive grace
throughout their lives. These "mysteries" are rites or acts that are understood as privileged moments of communication with God, in which
grace is given to human beings. They include Baptism, the Eucharist, and
other acts of the church such as anointings, ordination, marriage, and
penance. We shall discuss the meaning of "mysteries" for the Orthodox
below (see 1.4.4, along with specific discussions of baptism, 1.4.5, and the
Eucharist, 1.4.6), but at this point we should take note of the importance
of the "mysteries" in the pursuit of divinization. The "mysteries" are the
normal process or means by which the Orthodox pursue the religious life.
There is no pursuit of divinization outside of the church, since the church
and its rites were intended by God to be the normal means by which
God's power is shared with human beings (see also section 1.4, below).

1.3.6 *What Eastern Orthodox churches teach about the process of
growth in the Christian life:* Eastern Orthodox churches agree in
teaching that divine grace cooperates with human free will in the
pursuit of "divinization," leads human beings to such a faith as
produces good works, and brings human beings finally to the
recovery of the divine "likeness."

Sources: Confession of Dositheus, decrees 3, 9, 13–14 (in Leith, pp. 487–489, 491,
496–498). Ware, *Orthodox Church*, pp. 231–238. Klotsche, 2:9 (pp. 51–53).
Comparative Cross-References: Roman Catholic, 2.3.4; Reformation and Union, 3.3.5;
Evangelical and Free, 4.3.5; Ecumenical, 5.2.3.

50. Ware, *Orthodox Church*, p. 65. As Ware notes, the text given here is the more
modern form; in older usage the expression "a sinner" was omitted.
51. For a more extensive introduction to Eastern Christian spirituality, cf. Kallistos Ware, *The Orthodox Way* (1979; reprint, Crestwood, N.Y.: St. Vladimir's Seminary Press, 1990).

The grace given in human nature and given even more abundantly through Christ, the church, and the church's "mysteries" cooperates with the free will that is itself part of the divine "image" in humankind. Orthodox theologians sometimes utilize the term "synergy" (*sunergeia*, "cooperation") to describe this working-together of the divine and the human in the process of salvation.[52] Again, Eastern patterns diverge from typically Western teachings at this point, since Western teachings tend to stress the divine work in salvation.

As Orthodox churches state the matter, our salvation is by faith, but it is not by faith alone: salvation comes by such a faith that produces good works. Here they may quote James 2:17, "So faith by itself, if it has no works, is dead." Faith, as Orthodox churches understand it, involves head and heart and hands. Nevertheless, Orthodox teachings clarify that good works themselves are the result not of human goodness but of the goodness of God, since it is God's grace that works within us to produce them. In the words of the Confession of Dositheus, "But for the regenerated to do spiritual good . . . it is necessary that he be guided and [empowered] by grace . . . so that he is not able of himself to do any work worthy of a Christian life."[53]

The final goal of salvation is the recovery of the divine "likeness." This goal is the completion of the process of "divinization," and it is frequently described by Orthodox spiritual writers as "perfection." Their term "perfection" (*teleiosis*) comes from the word for "goal" or "end" (*telos*), and it carries the sense of the final goal toward which the religious life is directed. In "perfection," the lost holiness and immortality that characterize God are rejoined to the freedom and "reason" that remains within us, and the human being is brought to a state even higher than that of our first parents.[54]

1.3.7 *What Eastern Orthodox churches teach concerning life after death:* Eastern Orthodox churches agree in teaching that believers will share joy in Christ after death, and those who reject Christ will suffer eternal punishment. They agree in teaching, further, that there

52. Confession of Dositheus, decree 3 (in Leith, pp. 487–489).
53. Confession of Dositheus, decrees 9 (on the necessity of faith; in Leith, p. 491), 13 (the need for a faith that produces works; in Leith, pp. 496–497), and 14 (the continuing need for grace; in Leith, pp. 497–498). The quoted portion is from Leith's version, p. 498, but I have rendered "prevented" as "empowered," since this translation used "prevent" in the obsolete sense of "coming before" an event to empower it or make it happen.
54. Confession of Dositheus, decree 14, states this goal: "But in the regenerated, what is wrought by grace, and with grace, maketh the doer perfect, and rendereth him worthy of salvation" (in Leith, p. 497), although the Confession does not go on to detail the recovery of the divine likeness; cf. Ware, *Orthodox Church*, pp. 231–238.

is an intermediate state between death and the final judgment in which believers who have not attained the "likeness" of God may continue to be perfected.

Sources: Confession of Dositheus, decree 18 (in Leith, pp. 505–506). Ware, *Orthodox Church*, pp. 261–263. Klotsche, 2:10 (pp. 53–54).

Comparative Cross-References: Roman Catholic, 2.3.7; Reformation and Union, 3.3.7; Evangelical and Free, 4.3.7.

Traditional Orthodox teaching maintains that those who have believed in Christ will share fellowship with Christ through eternity and those who reject Christ will face punishment. According to the Confession of Dositheus, persons go immediately to joy in Christ or to the torments of punishment, even though the joy of believers will not be complete until after the final judgment.

This point does not need much elaboration, but it should be noted that the Orthodox belief in the need for "perfection" raises a critical problem: what of those believers who have died in sincere faith, but who have not come to the goal of recovering the lost "likeness" of God? Orthodox churches respond that there is a state beyond death where believers continue to be perfected and led to full divinization. Though some Orthodox teachers have described this intermediate state as "purgatory," others prefer to distinguish it from the Roman Catholic understanding of purgatory, insisting that it is not necessarily a place of punishment but rather a place of growth. Protestant readers might note that for Orthodox and Catholics, this notion of an intermediate state (or purgatory) does not at all imply that unbelievers can somehow be saved; it is understood as a place of purification or growth, or both, only for those who have believed in Christ.[55] Although Orthodox teachers maintain that belief in such a state is necessary, there is little speculation as to what it might be like.

1.4   Orthodox Teachings on Church, Ministry, and Sacraments

1.4.1 *What Eastern Orthodox churches teach about the nature of the church:* Eastern Orthodox churches agree in teaching that the church is the spiritual and material body of those who believe in Christ.

Sources: Confession of Dositheus, decrees 10–11 (in Leith, pp. 491–492 and 495–496). Ware, *Orthodox Church*, pp. 239–248. Klotsche, 2:7 (pp. 43–45).

---

55. The Confession of Dositheus (decree 18; in Leith, pp. 505–506) does reflect a Western-style notion of purgatory, but Ware (*Orthodox Church*, pp. 254–255) indicates that there is now a wide variety of Orthodox belief on this issue.

Comparative Cross-References: Roman Catholic, 2.4.1; Reformation and Union, 3.4.1; Evangelical and Free, 4.4.1; Ecumenical, 5.2.4.1.

Readers will have gathered already that for the Orthodox the church is not simply a human institution. The church is not just a building, and it is even more than "the people." The church bears the "character" (*charakter* in Greek means "imprint") of Christ, and it is a kind of "incarnation," or perhaps it might be more appropriate to say that the church extends the incarnation of God in Christ. It is itself a sacrament or "mystery," an outward, material form in space and time that nevertheless bears inwardly the presence of God through its history. Contemporary Orthodox theologians have stressed that the church is constituted, above all, by its celebration of the Eucharist, and in this sense too it is a mystery in which Christ is present in our world.[56] The church is really "the body of Christ" (Rom. 12:5; 1 Corinthians 12) presently existing in our world, both spiritually and materially. The church contains all those who believe in Christ, even in spite of their sins and failings, and the Spirit continues to be present in the church just as the Spirit was present on the day of Pentecost. Because of the Spirit's continuous presence, Orthodox regard the church as "unfailing" or "infallible," and as noted above, the church's "unfailing" character is expressed through its long tradition (see 1.1.1, above).[57]

"So do Orthodox Christians think they're the only Christians?" In fact, some Orthodox do believe this. Because they believe that the church is necessary to salvation, and the Orthodox churches form the only true church, it would seem to follow that those outside of Orthodox churches cannot be saved. But other Orthodox reason differently on this matter. While holding to their belief that Orthodox churches form the church in the truest sense, they argue that there can be less-than-complete ways of participating in the church. Orthodox participation in the Ecumenical movement has never implied that they should relinquish their belief that Orthodoxy is the truest church, but on the other hand their participation and their address "To All the Churches of Christ" (1920) seem to imply recognition of the Christian character of other churches.[58] Also, because the Orthodox accept baptisms performed in other churches, this implies a recognition of the Christian character (or at least intent) of other churches.

56. John D. Zizioulas, *Being as Communion: Studies in Personhood and the Church* (Crestwood, N.Y.: St. Vladimir's Seminary Press, 1985), pp. 20–23, 143–169.
57. Confession of Dositheus, decrees 10–11 (in Leith, pp. 491–492 and 495–496); cf. Ware, *Orthodox Church*, pp. 239–248.
58. Ware, *Orthodox Church*, pp. 307–311.

1.4.2 *What Eastern Orthodox churches teach concerning the hierarchical nature of the church, and the office of bishop:* Eastern Orthodox churches agree in teaching that the church is "hierarchical" in that it is governed by bishops, but is not "monarchical," except in the sense that Christ is its head.

Sources: Canons of the First Council of Constantinople, 3 (in *ANF*, 14:178). Confession of Dositheus 10 (in Leith, pp. 491–495). Ware, *Orthodox Church,* pp. 248–254. Klotsche, 2:7 (p. 44).

Comparative Cross-References: Roman Catholic, 2.4.3; Reformation and Union, 3.4.2.a–d; Evangelical and Free, 4.4.2.a–c.

Orthodox churches hold bishops in high regard and see bishops as outward signs of the church's unity. The Confession of Dositheus quotes a fifth-century teacher who said, "The dignity of the bishop is so necessary in the Church, that without him, neither Church nor Christian could either be or be spoken of."[59] Moreover, some bishops are given higher honor in the churches, such as the bishops of ancient "sees" (the most ancient city-churches), who are referred to as "patriarchs." There are, as we have noted above, some more recent "patriarchates," especially in Slavic countries, where bishops have been elevated to the honor of "patriarchs." The church's structure, especially its use of deacons, priests, and bishops, is understood as a form of sacred leadership: a "hierarchy" (from *hieros*, "sacred," and *arche*, "rule" or "leadership").

Although the Orthodox churches understand that the church is necessarily "hierarchical," they reject the idea that it should be "monarchical," that is, governed by a single bishop. On this point Orthodox differ most clearly from Roman Catholics, since Catholics regard the bishops of Rome (or "popes") as having authority over other bishops. The Orthodox bishop (with the title "ecumenical patriarch") of Constantinople may speak on behalf of Orthodox churches, but he does so only when representing the consensus of their bishops in consultation with one another. Most Orthodox today would be willing to grant the bishops of Rome the "primacy of honor" in the church, especially since that title was granted to them by the First Council of Constantinople,[60] but they will not grant the bishops of Rome jurisdiction over other bishops. Only Christ is the head of the church in this sense. This was a principal issue underlying the division of Eastern and Western churches in 1054, since the Western churches claimed the authority of the bishops of Rome in adding the expression "and the Son" to the Nicene Creed.

59. Confession of Dositheus, decree 10 (in Leith, p. 492).
60. First Council of Constantinople, canon 3 (*ANF*, 14:178).

We can note at this point that although Orthodox priests cannot marry, married persons *can* become Orthodox priests, that is, one might be married *before* one is ordained priest. Married priests are the norm in many Orthodox countries, where they may even retain secular occupations, functioning simply as a local expert who happens to know how to perform the liturgy. It is a long-standing custom in Orthodox churches, however, that bishops are always drawn from the ranks of priests who belong to religious orders, so that Orthodox bishops are always celibate. Orthodox churches do not ordain women, and they see the ordination of women as one of the obstacles to ecumenical dialogue.[61] In modern Greece and other Orthodox contexts there are sometimes lay preachers, typically middle-class persons educated at universities and having taken some religion courses, who will preach, because it is not the norm for local priests to preach.

1.4.3 *What Eastern Orthodox churches teach concerning the use of religious images or icons in worship:* Eastern Orthodox churches agree in teaching that the church rightly "venerates," but does not "worship," material images of Christ, of the Blessed Virgin Mary, and of the saints and angels. They agree, further, in teaching that these material images convey the reality of spiritual things.

Sources: Definition concerning Sacred Images of the Second Council of Nicaea (in Leith, pp. 55–56; in Denzinger and Hünermann, items 600–603, pp. 276–277). Confession of Dositheus, question 4 (in Leith, pp. 508–516). Ware, *Orthodox Church,* pp. 206–207, 271–272. Klotsche, 2:4 (pp. 38–39).

We have noted above (see 1.0.2 and 1.2.3) that the Second Council of Nicaea (A.D. 787) made a careful distinction between the "worship" that is due God alone and the "veneration" that should be paid to the saints (including the Virgin Mary) and to religious images (or "icons") of Christ, the saints, and the angels. Religious images are understood in Eastern churches as being like the "mysteries" in that they combine material form with spiritual reality (see 1.4.5, below).[62] These images fill the walls and ceilings of Orthodox churches, and they are believed to convey the spiritual presence of those they represent. When they are combined with incense, candles, lamps, and the recitation of liturgy, they convey the sense that Orthodox worship is a kind of interface between earth and heaven.

61. "Reflections of Orthodox Participants," in Kinnamon, par. 6, p. 281.
62. Decree of the Second Council of Nicaea (in Leith, pp. 55–56); cf. Confession of Dositheus, question 4 (in Leith, pp. 509–510); cf. Ware, *Orthodox Church,* pp. 277–278.

1.4.4 *What Eastern Orthodox churches teach concerning the "mysteries" of the church:* Eastern Orthodox churches agree in teaching that the "mysteries" are privileged moments of communication with the divine that combine material forms with spiritual reality.

Sources: Confession of Dositheus, decree 15 (in Leith, pp. 498–500). Ware, *Orthodox Church,* pp. 281–283, 285–286, 295–303. Klotsche, 2:8 (pp. 45–51).

Comparative Cross-References: Roman Catholic, 2.4.5, 2.4.5.2, 2.4.5.4–7; Reformation and Union, 3.4.3; Evangelical and Free, 4.4.3.a–c.

According to Eastern Christian thought, God is a mystery, and "a God who is comprehensible is not God."[63] But "mystery" may hold for Eastern Christians a more specific and technical meaning, namely, an event that has both an outward form and an inward spiritual power, what the Western church would call a "sacrament." In the words of the Confession of Dositheus, "the Mysteries consist of something natural, and of something supernatural; for they are not bare signs of the promises of God."[64] Even this may reflect the Western influence on Dositheus, however; contemporary Orthodox teachers prefer to speak of the mysteries as those moments or events in which human beings share communion with God. Christ himself was a "mystery" in this sense, combining the outward form of a human being with the inward and mysterious presence of God, and the church is also a "mystery," combining external form with the inward presence of God. But there are other acts that can be counted as "mysteries," which also share the character of acts in which human beings share communion with the divine. Preeminent among these, in the eyes of Orthodox churches, are Baptism and the Eucharist (or the "Divine Liturgy," as Orthodox are apt to say). Since the 1600s, Orthodox churches have generally agreed that in addition to Baptism and the Eucharist, five other acts count as "mysteries"; these are chrismation, ordination, marriage, penance, and the anointing of the sick.[65] Baptism and the Eucharist will be discussed below. We should note at this point that chrismation is the anointing following baptism in which the Holy Spirit is invoked on the person baptized. Chrismation answers to "confirmation" in Western (Catholic and Protestant) churches, but the Orthodox do not require this mystery to be administered by a bishop, and they do not separate it from

63. Ware, *Orthodox Way,* p. 13.
64. Confession of Dositheus, decree 15 (in Leith, p. 499).
65. In fact, the Confession of Dositheus lists these five along with Baptism and the Eucharist as seven specific mysteries (decree 15; in Leith, pp. 498–499), and Ware states that a consensus did not exist through Orthodox history as to the enumeration of the mysteries until the seventeenth century; Ware, *Orthodox Church,* p. 275.

Baptism as Western Christians do when infants are baptized and then confirmed at a later date. Ordination is the act in which by the laying on of hands a man is ordained as a deacon, priest, or bishop. Marriage is the mystery in which a man and woman are united together to create a family. Penance is the mystery by which a woman or man who has sinned is reconciled to the church, following confession to a priest. Anointing of the sick is the mystery in which persons in any grave illness are prayed for and anointed with oil.

1.4.5 *What Eastern Orthodox churches teach about baptism:* Eastern Orthodox churches agree in teaching that by baptism human beings are incorporated into the church and are given new birth in Christ.

Sources: Confession of Dositheus, decrees 15–16 (in Leith, pp. 498, 500–502). Ware, *Orthodox Church*, pp. 277–278. Klotsche, 2:8:1 (p. 45).

Comparative Cross-References: Roman Catholic, 2.4.5.1; Reformation and Union, 3.4.3.1; Evangelical and Free, 4.4.4.a–b; Ecumenical, 5.2.4.2.

Among the "mysteries" of the church, Baptism and the Eucharist hold special importance for most Christians, including those of Eastern Orthodox churches. With almost all Christian churches, Orthodox churches teach that baptism is the means instituted by Christ himself by which human beings are incorporated into the church. With Roman Catholics and most Reformation churches, they agree that baptism confers new birth in Christ (the technical term for this is "regeneration") and that through baptism, Christ gives forgiveness of all sins committed up until that time. In this latter respect, Orthodox (and Catholics and many in the Reformation churches) differ from most Evangelical Protestants, who have traditionally insisted that the new birth in Christ occurs in a distinctive religious experience—a "conversion" experience. With almost all churches, Eastern Orthodox churches teach that baptism is a one-time event, not to be repeated.[66]

Orthodox churches baptize by immersion, three times "in the name of the Father and the Son and the Holy Spirit." The baptismal service is accompanied by an anointing, which the Orthodox call "chrismation," in which it is believed that the gift of the Holy Spirit is given. Baptism and chrismation are followed immediately by the Eucharist. This process is the same for adults who are baptized and for infants, who likewise are immersed, chrismated, and given the Eucharist all in the same service. This differs clearly from the Western (Catholic

---

66. Confession of Dositheus, decree 16 (in Leith, pp. 500–502), although the Confession of Dositheus focuses primarily on the forgiveness of sin in baptism and not on incorporation into the church; cf. Ware, *Orthodox Church*, pp. 277–278.

and Protestant) practice of confirmation, which is dissociated from Baptism and put off until later.

1.4.6 *What Eastern Orthodox churches teach about the Eucharist:* Eastern Orthodox churches agree in teaching that in the Eucharist the bread and wine become in reality the body and blood of Christ, and as such are worthy of "worship" as well as "veneration."

Sources: Confession of Dositheus, decrees 15, 17 (in Leith, pp. 499, 502–505). Ware, *Orthodox Church,* pp. 279–288. Klotsche, 2:8:3 (pp. 46–48).

Comparative Cross-References: Roman Catholic, 2.4.5.3; Reformation and Union, 3.4.3.2.a–c; Evangelical and Free, 4.4.5.a–b; Ecumenical, 5.2.4.3.

The meal that Christ instituted is given various names by Christian traditions. We have used the common ecumenical term "Eucharist" (from *eucharistia,* "thanksgiving"), but Catholics may refer to its celebration as the "Mass," Protestant groups may call it the "Lord's Supper" or "Holy Communion," and Orthodox churches generally refer to it as the "Divine Liturgy." The Divine Liturgy is the center of the life of Orthodox churches.

Like Roman Catholics, Lutherans, and many other Christians of the Reformation traditions, Eastern Orthodox churches insist on the true presence of Christ himself in the Eucharist. Although some Orthodox statements have utilized the more typically Catholic term "transubstantiation" (see 2.4.5.3, below) to explain how Christ is present in the Eucharist, other Orthodox statements simply state the belief that in the meal Christ instituted, bread and wine become in reality the body and blood of Christ, and the whole liturgy links believers to the sacrifice of Christ. Because the bread and wine have truly become Christ, Christ is offered true worship in them, not only the "veneration" that is due human saints.[67] The following hymn, based on the Greek "Liturgy of St. James" from the fourth century A.D., reflects the worship of Christ's real, bodily presence in the Eucharist:

Let all mortal flesh keep silence,
And with fear and trembling stand;
Ponder nothing earthly-minded,
For with blessing in his hand,
Christ our God to earth descendeth,
Our full homage to demand.[68]

67. Confession of Dositheus, decree 17 (in Leith, pp. 502–505); cf. Ware, *Orthodox Church,* pp. 283–287, who explains that even when the term "transubstantiation" is used by Orthodox, it is not understood in its distinctively Catholic sense.
68. Hymn from the "Liturgy of St. James," in *The United Methodist Hymnal,* trans. Gerard Moultrie, no. 626.

Orthodox churches do not share the Eucharist with other churches. They understand the Eucharist to be a sign of full "communion" not only with God but with one another. As such, they cannot share the Eucharist with those with whom communion has been in fact broken. As Orthodox representatives to the Canberra Assembly (1991) of the World Council of Churches (WCC) expressed it,

> The Orthodox are sorry that their position with regard to eucharistic communion has not been understood by many members of the WCC, who regard the Orthodox as unjustifiably insisting upon *abstinence from eucharistic communion*. The Orthodox once more invite their brothers and sisters in the WCC to understand that it is a matter of *unity in faith and fundamental Orthodox ecclesiology*, and not a question of a triumphalistic stance.
>
> For the Orthodox, the eucharist is the supreme expression of unity and not a means towards unity.[69]

Although non-Orthodox cannot share the Eucharist with Orthodox Christians, there is a part of the service that they can share. At the end of the Orthodox liturgy, the priest will share with the congregation the remaining bread that has been blessed but that was not used (consecrated) in the Eucharist. This "after-gift" (*antidoron*) is a historical remnant of the ancient love-feast that accompanied the Eucharist, and non-Orthodox persons will often be invited to share in it.[70]

The Orthodox liturgy incorporates words and music, lights, smells, images, vestments, priest and deacons, and actions and responses of the Orthodox faithful such as making the sign of the cross. In very traditional Orthodox services there are no pews or seats (except around the walls), the people do not necessarily read specific parts of the service, and a Western observer can gain the impression of a combination of charismatic freedom with liturgical form. The liturgy conveys in a powerful way the continuing reality of the Orthodox connection to Christ and to the Spirit's presence in the long history of the church.

---

69. "Reflections of Orthodox Participants," in Kinnamon, par. 6, p. 281; italics as in original.
70. Ware, *Orthodox Church*, p. 288.

Interlude 1 A
The Assyrian Church of the East ("Nestorian")

There remain today some churches that are descendants of those supporters of Nestorius who insisted on the separation of integral divine and human
"Persons" in Christ. Although Nestorian churches once spread from Syria to
China to India, they were limited to Persia, Turkey and Syria early in this cen-
tury. Severely persecuted, many Nestorians converted to Catholicism and are
now referred to as "Chaldean" Catholics. Many if not most of the remaining
Nestorians fled to the West. The surviving Nestorians refer to themselves as
the "Assyrian Church of the East," and their patriarch now resides in San
Francisco. In the mid-1980s, it was estimated that there were some 180,000
Nestorians throughout the world.[71]

Interlude 1 B
Oriental Orthodox ("Monophysite") Churches

The Oriental Orthodox churches are those that were traditionally described in
Western literature as "Monophysite" because they rejected the Chalcedonian formula of "one Person in two natures" and insisted on the formula "one
nature" (Greek *mia phusis*) "of the Word of God incarnate." These churches
hold considerable strength in Syria, Iran, Iraq, Turkey, Armenia, Egypt, and
Ethiopia and with a small community in India. Today they prefer to be called
"Oriental Orthodox" rather than "Monophysite." They have engaged in serious ecumenical dialogue with Eastern Orthodox churches and have very
nearly concluded agreements that will allow intercommunion and mutual
recognition of ordinations between their churches and the Eastern Orthodox.
The five principal groups of Oriental Orthodox Churches are (1) Coptic (Egypt),
(2) Syrian, (3) Armenian, (4) Ethiopian (which became independent of Coptic
hierarchy in 1950), and (5) the Malankara "Syrian" Church of India. ("Syrian"
here refers to the use of Syriac language in the liturgy.) These groups share
communion with one another and so are separated only ethnically, not theologically.

Interlude 1 C
The Mar Thoma Church

The first Jesuit missionaries to India, in the 1590s, were quite surprised to
find Christians on the Malabar coast (southwestern India). The historical origin of these "Thomas Christians" (from the belief that their communities
were founded by the Apostle Thomas) remain obscure: some scholars hy-
pothesize that they were originally Nestorian, though by the 1500s they sub-

71. Barrett, ed., "Global Table 27" in *World Christian Encyclopedia: A Comparative
Study of Churches and Religions in the Modern World, AD* 1900–200 (Nairobi: Oxford
University Press, 1982), p. 793.

mitted to the Monophysite (Oriental Orthodox) patriarchs of Persia. After centuries of Catholic and Protestant evangelization, the Mar Thoma churches were seriously divided, with some churches becoming Anglican or Roman Catholic, and some remaining within the communion of the Oriental Orthodox (the Malankara Syrian Church referred to in Interlude 1 B).[72] The church that bears the name Mar Thoma Church is a descendant of the Thomas Christians who accepted some Western practices and theology but remained independent. Their status as an ancient Eastern church reformed by contact with Western traditions marks them as an important "bridge" community between the Christian East and Protestantism. It is estimated that the membership of the Mar Thoma Church today is approximately two million.

Interlude 1 D
Russian Old Ritualists

A schism occurred within the Russian Orthodox Church when the patriarch of Moscow, Nikon, reformed the liturgy in 1654 to bring it into accordance with Byzantine customs. The reforms he advocated seem very slight in retrospect, but many Russian Christians regarded Nikon as a traitor to their national traditions. Although Nikon himself was deposed, his reforms were sanctioned by the Russian Church. Many who objected to them became separate and came to be known as "Old Believers" or "Old Ritualists." A concern of Russian church historians is that the Old Ritualists have sometimes been interpreted in the West as a Russian analog to the Protestant Reformation. This is far from the case: their own liturgy differs only slightly from that of the Russian Orthodox, and they did not at all object to traditional Orthodox theology. If anything, they understood themselves as upholding the older traditions. There were a number of spiritualist sects that emerged in Russia in the 1700s and 1800s, but not all of these had direct connections with the Old Ritualists.

72. Stephen Neill, *A History of Christian Missions,* The Pelican History of the Church (Harmondsworth, Middlesex: Penguin Books, 1964), pp. 142–148, 269–272.

2

Teachings of Roman Catholicism

2.0 Historical Background to Roman Catholicism

The Roman Catholic Church is by far the largest Christian body in the world; in fact, most members of Christian churches are Roman Catholics. By 1993 it was estimated that the total number of Catholics had reached one billion. This is clearly a majority of the 1.9 billion members of Christian churches worldwide, and it represents almost one-fifth of the total population of our planet (estimated in 1994 to be 5.6 billion people). Moreover, the number of Roman Catholics has increased very rapidly in recent decades, almost doubling in the twenty-four years between 1970 (688 million Catholics) and 1994 (more than 1 billion).[73]

When Protestants consider the immense size of the Roman Catholic Church, they are sometimes tempted to fall back on stereotypes of Catholicism inherited from the Middle Ages, especially the stereotypical view that most Catholics are Christian in name only but have not seriously and personally embraced Christian faith. Although this may be true in some places (and it is obviously also true of many Protestants), Catholics have developed remarkably successful programs for forming persons in Christian faith. Perhaps the most obvious example of this process would be the "Rite of Christian Initiation for Adults" (RCIA), which is not only a ritual but an extensive, year-long program in Christian formation for adults coming to baptism.

Since the early 1960s, Roman Catholicism has undergone a process of modernizing and updating its teachings and practices. Part of this

73. Barrett (1994), p. 25, lines 1, 11, and 34. The previous year's report (1993) indicated one billion Catholics for the first time.

process has been the opening of ecumenical contacts with other Christian bodies. Catholics now participate in the Faith and Order Commission of the World Council of Churches, the commission whose particular task is to examine issues of doctrine and life that have traditionally divided Christians. Moreover, Catholics have instituted "bilateral" dialogues with a number of other Christian traditions, including Orthodox, Anglican, Lutheran, Reformed, Methodist, Baptist, and Pentecostal. Through these dialogues, Protestants have come to know Catholic life and teachings somewhat better. This and the next four sections will examine Catholic history and Catholic doctrine before returning to questions about the contemporary ecumenical relationships of Roman Catholicism in chapter 5.

Just as Eastern Christianity developed in the Greek-speaking eastern end of the Mediterranean in antiquity, Western Christianity developed in Latin-speaking areas of Africa and Europe in ancient times, roughly the western half of the Mediterranean, an area including Italy, southern Gaul (France), Spain, and the northern coast of Africa all the way from Gibraltar to the borders of Egypt. Western Christianity grew in parallel with Eastern Christianity, but a number of factors made the Western Christian experience differ from that of the Eastern churches.

2.0.1   The Founding of Roman Christianity

Christianity came to the capital of the Roman Empire very early on, certainly by the middle of the first century A.D. and probably within a decade of Christ's crucifixion and resurrection. Paul's letter to the Romans addressed a church he had not yet visited, but the Acts of the Apostles concludes with Paul in Rome "proclaiming the kingdom of God and teaching about the Lord Jesus Christ with all boldness and without hindrance" (Acts 28:31). A cryptic reference to "your sister church in Babylon" (or simply "she who is in Babylon") in 1 Peter may be a veiled reference to Peter's presence in Rome (1 Pet. 5:13). But although the New Testament speaks explicitly only of Paul's presence in Rome, early Christian tradition consistently represents the apostle Peter as also traveling to Rome, founding the church there, and being crucified there. An early bishop, Irenaeus of Lyon, writing in southern Gaul in the 180s A.D., gave a complete list of bishops of Rome, beginning with Peter himself and continuing up until his own time.

The early centuries were ones of persecution for Latin-speaking as well as Greek-speaking Christians. In Latin-speaking areas, controversies grew up especially from the time of the Decian persecution, the first empire-wide persecution of Christians that occurred in the mid-third century A.D. These controversies focused on the issue of sacraments administered by "lapsed" bishops, that is, bishops who had given in to the Romans and had offered incense to the emperor's *genius* (spirit), or perhaps handed over Bibles or other church paraphernalia to the Romans. Many Western Christians, "Novatianists" in Rome itself and later "Donatists" in Africa, took the stringent view that sacraments administered by such bishops could have no validity. For example, they would rebaptize persons who had been baptized by lapsed bishops. Although Western Christians eventually rejected these views, it might be noted that a strain of rigorism existed within the earliest Western Christian communities.

In the third and early fourth century A.D. there seems also to have been a tendency on the part of Western Christians to emphasize the oneness or unity of God in discussing the Trinity. Although "Modalism," the teaching that considers the Father and the Son (and perhaps the Holy Spirit) as different "modes" of the one Godhead, may have originated in the East, its best known advocates were all Western (such as Tertullian's adversary Praxeas and the teacher Sabellius). Even at the time of the First Council of Nicaea, many stressed the unity of God, and at least one prominent teacher supported by Western church leaders (Marcellus of Ancyra) understood the creed's expression "of one substance with the Father" to mean that Christ and the Father were identical except for the temporary work of Christ in creation and redemption.

The Christian community at Rome clearly exerted broad influence in the ancient church. Irenaeus, himself bishop of Lyons, looked to the bishops of Rome as guardians of true Christian doctrine against the heretics. For him, the living tradition of a Christian community founded by an apostle was even more important than written scriptures, and Rome was for him the primary example of such an apostolically founded community, with the bishops of Rome representing in themselves the continuity of faith from the apostles. By the time of the First Council of Constantinople (A.D. 381) the bishops of the church concurred, as stated explicitly by the council, that the bishop of Rome should have the "first place of honor" (or "primacy of honor") among all the bishops of the church. By this time, Christianity was officially tolerated in the empire by the actions of the Emperor Constantine.

2.0.2 Roman Christianity and the Fall of Old Rome

But within a few decades after the First Council of Nicaea, the empire was attacked by Germanic peoples invading from the north. By the early fifth century A.D., Rome and most of Italy was in the hands of the invaders, and in 476 the last Roman emperor in the West was deposed. Although many of the invading Germanic peoples had already embraced Christianity, many were Arian, and many others were not Christian at all.

Observing the fall of Rome from the far side of the Mediterranean was the African Bishop Augustine of Hippo. In his book *The City of God*, he reflected on the passing of the earthly Rome and the permanence of the heavenly city. Augustine bequeathed to Western Christianity in the Middle Ages not only an account of how God's justice could be reconciled with the awesome events of the fall of Rome but also a theological inheritance that would characterize Western thought for centuries to come. Augustine stressed the utter fallenness of humanity and the inability of humans to do any good without God's help. Augustine read Romans 9—11 and applied Paul's words about the calling of Israel to the salvation of individual men and women. Our salvation, he reasoned on this basis, is entirely God's work, God chooses or "predestines" those whom God will save. Aware of typically Eastern Christian thought through monks whom he had encountered, Augustine rejected their theology as relying too much on human effort. His writings indicate the clear beginnings of divisions between Western and Eastern Christians in ways of thinking about human nature and salvation.

After the fall of "Old Rome" (Constantinople considered itself to be the "New Rome"), through centuries of chaos brought about by the invasions of the empire and the establishment of Germanic principalities in Western Europe and Africa, the Christian church became more and more the cultural center of the Latin-speaking world. At some points, in fact, the bishop of Rome was left as the only civil authority in the city of Rome, and the church began to acquire extensive properties and civil authority. One result was that the power of Roman bishops increased during this period.

Monasticism, which had originated in the Christian East, found a distinctly Western expression in the monasteries founded by Benedict of Nursia in the sixth century A.D. Benedict's practically crafted *Rule* for the monastery at Monte Cassino eventually became the pattern by which all Western monasteries were governed. Perhaps the longest resistant to the Benedictine pattern were the ancient monasteries that had been founded in the Celtic regions of the British Isles, but by the eighth century A.D., Benedictine and Roman practices had prevailed over the Celtic churches as well. For centuries after this time, all Western monks were Benedictine.

Two centuries after the fall of Old Rome, another tragedy fell to Western Christianity. This was the loss of Latin-speaking Africa to Muslims in A.D. 640–650 and the loss of most of Spain to the Muslims in early 700s. By A.D. 720, Latin-speaking Christianity was at its lowest ebb, consisting geographically of Italy, France, the British Isles, and some regions of western Europe adjacent to France. After A.D. 720, Muslim armies from Spain were pressing into France, threatening the very existence of Western Christianity.

2.0.3   Roman Christianity and the Carolingian Empire

At this time, in the eighth century A.D., the balance of power between Western Europe and the Eastern Roman (Byzantine) Empire began to shift. Frankish armies turned back the Muslims in southern France and initiated the long process of the *reconquista*, the "reconquest," of Spain, a process that would carry on through the 1400s. The Frankish generals and their descendants established a powerful kingdom, the precursor of modern France, and on December 25, A.D. 800, their King Charles I (Charles the Great, or Charlemagne) was crowned and proclaimed "Augustus" by the pope. "Augustus" was a title of ancient Roman emperors, so for the first time since A.D. 476 there was an emperor in the West. The narrative of Western Europe in the later Middle Ages was dominated politically by the "Holy Roman Empire." With the Byzantine Empire threatened constantly by Islam through this period, the West emerged in the following centuries as the dominant Christian power.

The emergence of the Holy Roman Empire brought about a renewal of Latin culture, the "Carolingian Renaissance," and closely tied to this was a renewal of Western church life. New schools were established (often based at monasteries or cathedrals), church offices were regularized, and new provisions were made for Christian initiation and formation. At this time Western Christians began to separate "confirmation" (which earlier had been a baptismal anointing) from Baptism itself and to reserve it for older children (see 2.4.5.2).

Also during the Carolingian period, Western Christians began to recite the Nicene Creed as part of the Mass (a Western term for the celebration of the Eucharist), and bishops of Rome began insisting that the expression "and the Son" should be said in the clause on the Holy Spirit. At about the same time the "Apostles' Creed" was used in the form in which we now know it. As we have seen in chapter 1, the expression "and the Son" in the Nicene Creed was one issue over which Eastern and Western churches would eventually split, although it would take two hundred years for the disagreement to issue in the final break between the churches.

The controversy over this issue indicates that by the Carolingian period the bishops of Rome had expanded their authority over the other bishops of the church that they had exercised in the West for many centuries (in addition to the "primacy of honor" granted to them at the First Council of Constantinople). Through the centuries, moreover, other terms had been applied to the bishops of Rome. They were called "popes" (originally from the Greek term *pappas*, for "father") and "pontiffs" (in Latin, *pontifex*, the title of a high Roman religious official); these words lie behind the terms "papacy" and "pontificate," which describe the office of the bishops of Rome. By the Carolingian period they represented the unity of the Western church, and in a broad sense, the unity of Western European culture.

2.0.4   Roman Christendom in the Late Middle Ages

In the late Middle Ages, the very power of the Roman church brought about some critical problems, problems frankly acknowledged by Catholics today. During the late Middle Ages Western Christians engaged in one of the most misguided enterprises in Christian experience, namely the attempt to defeat Islam militarily, and specifically to reclaim the holy places in Palestine from the Muslims. The Crusaders (from Spanish *cruzado*, "crossed," that is, those who bore the cross on their armor) had some initial successes in the early 1100s, but in the end they were unable to hold territories gained through conquest. Also in the late Middle Ages, Western Christians instituted Inquisitions to seek out heretics, Jews, and Muslims in Western countries and to punish them, sometimes by civil penalties, sometimes by torture, sometimes by death.

Moreover, there were intense internal struggles in Western Europe over the papacy itself; at some points there were two successions of rival claimants to the papacy, and during one period in the 1300s there were three rival claimants. The very wealth of the church, even of well-established monastic houses, could lead to corruptions, such as the buying and selling of church offices. In many places, secular princes "owned" the right to appoint priests to parishes (local churches and their immediate area) and even bishops to dioceses (the larger area over which a bishop presides). In many places there was little concern for the education or spiritual formation of laity.

A series of Catholic reform movements addressed some of these issues in the life of the church in the late Middle Ages. Reforms began with religious orders: Benedictine reformers tried to enforce the rule of their order, and eventually new monastic orders were formed, which challenged the moral laxity of the older Benedictine houses. In the early 1200s, Francis of Assisi led a startling renewal movement that insisted on absolute poverty and a life of itinerant preaching. At about the same time a Spaniard named Dominic organized a movement of men and women who also lived by begging and felt particularly called to ministries of teaching and preaching. The Franciscans and Dominicans would devote enormous energies to these tasks in the centuries to come.

The reforms not only affected people in religious orders, but also influenced the life of medieval Catholicism as a whole. The monk Hildebrand, who became Pope Gregory VII in the late eleventh century, embarked on a broad program of reforms, including attempts to outlaw lay appointments of church officials and the buying and selling of church offices. In the 1300s and 1400s, in response to the disputed claimants to the papacy, a movement arose that sought to reform the church by means of councils of bishops. Advocates of this movement, called Conciliarism, would sometimes argue, as Eastern Christians had done, that a council held authority over popes. It was also in this period (with Ottoman Turks threatening the imminent destruction of Constantinople) that Eastern delegates to the Council of Florence relented and agreed to use the Western form of the Nicene Creed. But remember that their compromise was not broadly accepted in the East. Councils in the 1400s did resolve the disputed claims to the papacy, but although councils would be used many times in the future to bring about Catholic reforms, the Latin-speaking church did not in the end accept the Conciliar teaching that popes were subject to councils of bishops.

Finally we should note late medieval reforms in the Western church that were concerned with spirituality, that is, with the practices of prayer and devotion, and in general the living of the Christian life. A movement called "Modern Devotion" flourished in the 1300s and 1400s, and it called Christians to devoted following of Christ. The movement was responsible for the popularity of crucifixes in Catholic churches (rare before this time), and is perhaps best illustrated in Thomas à Kempis's devotional classic, *The Imitation of Christ*. Advocates of Modern Devotion stressed the importance of priests in hearing confessions, and they helped make universal in the Western church an elaborate literature designed to aid priests in prescribing appropriate "penances" (signs of sincere repentance) for those whom they shepherded.

2.0.5   The Catholic Reformation

When the Augustinian monk and Professor Martin Luther called for church reforms early in the sixteenth century, he was understood at first as one more in a long train of Catholic reformers. Luther's movement and other movements springing up in Western Europe in his time would eventually bring about a break with medieval Catholicism, namely, the Protestant Reformation. But we should note at this point that Catholics themselves underwent a process of significant reforms in the 1500s. Historians conventionally called these reforms the "Counter-Reformation," but that seems to suggest that only the Protestants were trying to reform the church and Catholics were trying to stop the reforms. It is fairer to speak of these reforms, within the structure of the Catholic church, as a "Catholic Reformation."

Like almost all Catholic reform movements, the Catholic Reformation began with the establishment of new religious orders and renewal in the life of the old orders. In Spain the Carmelite order was renewed by the mystical teachings of Teresa of Avila, and her pupil, John of the Cross. In the middle of the 1500s a new order emerged around a Spanish student at the University of Paris, Ignatius Loyola, and some of his companions. Calling themselves the "Society of Jesus," the Jesuits took traditional vows of poverty, chastity, and obedience, and a special vow to go wherever the pope should order them to go for the salvation of souls. Not only did the Jesuits provide the church with an army of teachers and preachers in the work of reform in centuries to come, but they developed techniques (such as the "retreats" pioneered by Ignatius himself) by which laity could be led to deeper spiritual lives. Further, the Jesuits' unique relationship to the papacy allowed them a great degree of independence from local bishops, so much that many local bishops would later find them a threat.

The primary instrument of the Catholic Reformation, beyond the religious orders, was the Council of Trent, which met between 1545 and 1563 and issued reforms in both Catholic theology and Catholic practice. Protestants have traditionally thought of the Council of Trent as directed primarily toward the suppression of the Reformation, but more recent historical studies have suggested some important parallels between the work of the Protestant Reformers and the reforms of the Council of Trent. Most notably, the council was concerned with the intelligibility of the Christian faith, that is, with teaching the faith to laity in order to form them as Christians. The Council of Trent reversed the medieval pattern according to which parish priests were not trained to preach (and not expected to preach), and insisted on thorough education to aid priests in the work of preaching and teaching the faith. The council revised Catholic liturgies, authorized a revision of the Latin Bible used in Catholic churches, and spent a great deal of effort clarifying Catholic doctrine, partly in response to Protestant claims. In the exposition of Catholic doctrine below, we shall refer to the Council of Trent at a number of points.

Also in the 1500s, the century of the Catholic Reformation, Catholicism began to expand far beyond the confines of Western Europe. Catholics had already established small mission stations on the western coast of Africa in the late 1400s following Portuguese explorations. Franciscans, Dominicans, and other orders accompanied Spanish *conquistadores* to the New World, establishing Christian enclosures with schools, churches, and hospitals. From the late 1500s the Jesuits became involved in the missionary effort, with Ignatius of Loyola's companion Francis Xavier traveling to India, Southeast Asia, and Japan. By the late 1500s, Jesuit missionaries were active in China. A great deal of the numerical strength of Roman Catholicism today results from the missionary efforts that were begun in this period.

2.0.6   Early Modern Catholicism

The four hundred years between the end of the Council of Trent (1563) and the beginning of the Second Vatican Council (1962) can be described as the age of Tridentine Catholicism, since Catholicism in this period was largely guided by the reforms of Trent. ("Tridentine" is the adjective denoting "Trent.") In this period Catholicism faced the challenges of "modernity," as we have tried consistently to utilize that term, but through most of this long period Catholicism proved stoutly resistant to modern tendencies. Catholic liturgy remained fixed in the form Trent had given it, with the Mass said in Latin (with a few approved exceptions, for example, in "Eastern-Rite" Catholic churches). Catholic systematic and moral theology became largely an enterprise of cataloging and commenting on the precepts from Trent, in the light of the philosophy and theology of Thomas Aquinas.

In the 1800s, Catholic leaders became particularly concerned with modern culture; in fact, they were among the first to give it the name "Modernism." Consistently through this period Catholic teachers expressed the view that Catholicism was the only true expression of the Christian faith, and that Protestants and Orthodox alike stood outside the faith. Perhaps the most important sign of Catholicism's reaction against modernity in this period was its adoption at the First Vatican Council (1869–1870) of a formal definition (for the first time) of the "infallible" (unfailing) teaching authority of the popes in matters of faith and morals. Many progressive Catholics opposed this definition, and in fact some Catholics became independent due to their opposition to it (see Interlude 2 A). But the definition of papal infallibility was seen by traditionalists as upholding the church's authority against the destructive and iconoclastic tendencies of modernity.

A notable revival of Catholic spirituality and church growth occured in the 1800s throughout Western Europe and in the later years of the 1800s in North America, where immigration from historically Catholic countries expanded the Catholic population considerably. This revival occurred in spite of growing "anticlerical" sentiment in Europe, that is, public opinion strongly prejudiced against the church, priesthood, and traditional church institutions. New religious orders sprang up, many of them oriented toward ministry to the poor in the growing cities of Europe and North America. The conversion of Anglican leader John Henry Newman to Catholicism at mid-century signaled a growing sense of respectability on the part of Catholics in the traditionally Protestant English-speaking world. Newman's eloquent defense of Catholic faith rejected the prevailing Liberalism of his era, and yet in some ways it also reflected a moderate form of modern thought: Newman saw Catholicism's sense of doctrinal "development" as a version of historical progress, and "progress" was a key concept in European thought throughout the 1800s.

The later years of the 1800s and the first half of the 1900s, in general, found Roman Catholicism staunchly defending its traditions and teachings against the encroachments of Liberalism and Modernism. A notable Catholic movement, often described as "Catholic Modernism," offered a breathtakingly modern understanding of Catholic faith in its adoption of contemporary philosophy, but it was consistently rejected as heretical by Catholic leaders. Perhaps more influential for the future development of Catholic thought was the rise of "Neo-Thomism" in the period between World War I and World War II, a more moderate attempt to express Thomistic philosophy (the philosophy of Thomas Aquinas) in light of modern philosophical and scientific challenges. Despite these developments, however, the institutions of Catholicism and Catholic leadership remained firmly committed to older traditions and firmly opposed to compromises with Modernism through the 1950s.

2.0.7 Catholicism since the Second Vatican Council

Vatican II, held between 1962 and 1965 under the leadership of Pope John XXIII (who died in 1963) and then Pope Paul VI, marked Catholicism's rapid and in many ways unexpected embrace of the modern world. Aware of moderate Catholic advocates of *aggiorna-*

mento, "updating" the church's teachings and practices, John XXIII ascribed his decision to call the council to divine inspiration. Like the Council of Trent before it, Vatican II dealt with reforms in almost every aspect of the church's life and teachings. Masses in vernacular languages and utilizing local and native customs were not only approved but encouraged, education for teaching and preaching was again encouraged, and proposals were adopted for a much more active role by bishops in governing the church in consultation with the papacy. This last shift in administrative structure reflected important changes in Catholic understandings of the nature of the church, also expressed at the council.

The council affected Catholic life at every level. Theological reflection was opened up to allow "experimental" theological inquiries. Catholics have become fully involved in the critical study of the Bible. New programs for the education and formation of laity (such as RCIA, mentioned at the beginning of this chapter) have been developed, and a new catechism has been published. The Mass and other rites have been thoroughly revised. Catholic leaders in developing countries were at the forefront of the development of liberation theologies, and although the Vatican has expressed concern over more radical expressions of liberation theology, Catholics' identification with the poor and oppressed has provided an inspiring witness to other Christian churches in the period since the mid-1960s.

One of the most important changes in Catholic life, with regard to the interests of this study, was Catholicism's embrace of the Ecumenical movement in two documents issued by the council, one concerning relationships with Eastern Orthodox churches, and the other with ecumenism more broadly. It was a dramatic moment during Vatican II when Pope Paul VI met the ecumenical patriarch of Constantinople to remove the anathemas their churches had placed on each other's representatives nine hundred years before. Protestant as well as Orthodox observers had been invited to the council, and one of the council's last acts, in December 1965, was a service of prayer for Christian unity. Since the council, the Vatican has established secretariats to promote Christian unity. Catholics have been engaged in the Faith and Order Commission of the World Council of Churches, and they have engaged in bilateral dialogues with most larger Christian traditions. This work has been carried on most recently by Pope John Paul II, whose decree *Ut Unum Sint* ("That they may be one . . .") of May 30, 1995, offers repentance on behalf of Catholics for their role in Christian strife and divisions in the past, and it opens up new possibilities for visible unity between Catholics and other Christian communions.[74]

Vatican II also encouraged the revision and updating of Catholic programs for teaching the Christian faith. After a lengthy process of reflection, discussion, and consultation, Pope John Paul II gave formal approval to a new Catholic catechism (a manual to teach the essentials of Christian faith) on October 11, 1992, the thirtieth anniversary of the opening of the council. This catechism, published in English in the summer of 1994 as *The Catechism of the Catholic Church*, gives insight into contemporary Catholic consensus on Christian faith, and has been utilized throughout chapter 2 of this book.

2.1   Catholic Teachings on Religious Authority

The sketch of contemporary Roman Catholic teachings that follows is grounded in a number of historic documents. As with chapter 1, English versions of many of these documents are available in John Leith's *Creeds of the Churches*. I have utilized the documents of the ancient Christian councils, which Catholics affirm along with Eastern Orthodox Christians and many Protestants. I have also had access to the statements of later Catholic councils, such as the Fourth Lateran Council (1215), the Council of Trent, and the First and Second Vatican Councils. In addition to these, I have referred to decrees or letters of the popes that Catholics have accepted as reflecting a consensus about their faith and practices. The most recent documents utilized are the *Catechism of the Catholic Church* (1992) and the papal encyclical on ecumenical relations, *Ut Unum Sint* (1995).

2.1.1   *What the Roman Catholic Church teaches about the authority of the Bible:* The Roman Catholic Church teaches that the Christian scriptures, interpreted by the traditions of the church, are the authoritative source of the church's teachings and practice.

Sources: Council of Trent, "Decree concerning the Canonical Scriptures" and "Decree concerning the Edition and Use of the Sacred Books" (in Leith, pp. 401–405; Neuner and Dupuis, pp. 76–79) and the Creed of the Council of Trent (in Leith, p. 440). Vatican II, "Dogmatic Constitution on Divine Revelation" (in Flannery, pp. 750–765; Neuner and Dupuis, pp. 92–96). *Catechism of the Catholic Church*, 50–141 (in American translation, pp. 19–38).

Comparative Cross-References: Eastern Orthodox, 1.1.1–2; Reformation and Union, 3.1.1, 3.1.2.a–c; Evangelical and Free, 4.1.1.a–b; Ecumenical, 5.2.1.

74. Papal encyclical of Pope John Paul II: *Ut Unum Sint*, 30 May 1995 (English translation published in *Origins: CNS Documentary Service* 25:4 [June 8, 1995]: 49–72).

On this broad point, belief in the authority of scripture interpreted by church traditions, Catholic and Eastern Orthodox are largely in agreement (see 1.1.1 and 1.1.2). It was customary to say, even among some Catholic theologians until recently, that Catholicism maintained the "equal authority" of the Bible and tradition, and some statements of the Council of Trent do suggest an equality of authority between them. But the Council of Trent was particularly concerned to respond to Protestant teachings that the Scriptures *alone* were authoritative for the church, and the decrees of Trent at other points suggest a priority of scripture (rightly interpreted) over later traditions. Moreover, more recent Catholic statements have preferred to speak, as in the summary above, of the authority of the Bible interpreted by subsequent and authorized church traditions. The various documents of Vatican II illustrate this high regard for scripture in practice by their constant reference to the Bible, as well as in a separate statement on divine revelation, laying out contemporary Catholic views of scripture.[75] The *Catechism of the Catholic Church* (1992) places scripture first in its discussion of religious authority, and it refers to "the living tradition of the whole Church" as one of three criteria by which Christians can be sure that they are reading the Scriptures in accordance with the Spirit who inspired the Scriptures.[76] Like Orthodox Christians, Catholics believe that the Holy Spirit has never ceased to speak through the history of the church, and Christians can trust the continuing voice of the Holy Spirit, through the church's tradition, to interpret the Scriptures rightly.

In addition to the sixty-six biblical books accepted by Protestants, Catholics (as well as Orthodox, see 1.1.2) also utilize the Apocrypha, that is, the ten books that appeared in the Greek and subsequently Latin Bibles but not in Hebrew manuscripts. Just as the Eastern Orthodox use the Septuagint along with the Greek New Testament as their received version of scripture, so Catholics utilize the Latin Vulgate version, originally translated by Jerome in the fourth century, as their received scripture. But it should be noted that following the Council of Trent and Vatican II, Catholics have extensively revised the Vulgate text to bring it into harmony with the original Hebrew, Aramaic, and Greek texts. Their use of the Vulgate does not mean that they refuse to use the texts in their original languages, and in fact the

---

75. Council of Trent, "Decree concerning the Canonical Scriptures" and "Decree concerning the Edition and Use of the Sacred Books" (in Leith, pp. 401–405) and the Creed of the Council of Trent (in Leith, p. 440). Vatican II, "Dogmatic Constitution on Divine Revelation" (in Flannery, pp. 750–765).
76. *Catechism of the Catholic Church*, 113 (in American translation, pp. 32–33).

vernacular biblical texts used in Catholic liturgy are based on the original languages and are typically produced ecumenically (as is the case
with English translations now in use in Catholic liturgy).

Moreover, Catholics do provide vernacular translations of scripture for the study and devotional use of the laity. One Protestant mis-
conception about Catholicism is the notion that Catholics forbid
laypersons from reading the Scriptures. Catholics like to point out that
there were authorized, Catholic versions of the Bible in German long
before Luther produced his translation. Although it is true that at
some points Catholics discouraged the use of vernacular translations
(as did the Orthodox), for fear that scriptures would be read apart
from the tradition that interprets them, Catholics now expend considerable energies in making biblical texts available and in sponsoring programs of biblical study for the laity.

2.1.2 *What the Roman Catholic Church teaches about the interpretation of the Bible:* The Roman Catholic Church teaches that the
locus of traditional interpretations of the Scriptures lies with the
church's hierarchical order, and especially with its bishops.

Sources: Vatican II, "Dogmatic Constitution on the Church," 3 (in Leith, pp. 469–480;
in Flannery, pp. 369–387). *Catechism of the Catholic Church* 888–890 (in American
translation, p. 235).

Comparative Cross-References: Eastern Orthodox, 1.1.3; Ecumenical, 5.2.1.

Prior to Vatican II, this thesis about the centrality of the church's
bishops in interpreting scripture might have been omitted, jumping
from the centrality of scripture and tradition to papal authority (see
2.1.4). But Vatican II clarified that the teaching authority of the papacy
lies within, not outside of, the "college" of bishops ("college" here
simply denotes a "gathering together"), that is, the bishops of the
church acting together. The "Dogmatic Constitution on the Church"
of Vatican II states that

> by divine institution bishops have succeeded to the place of the
> apostles as shepherds of the Church, and he who hears them, hears
> Christ, while he who rejects them, rejects Christ (cf. Luke 10:16).[77]

In fact, the council went on to provide for regular consultation between
the Vatican and Catholic bishops throughout the world, a level of consultation that had not been previously exercised. This new process of col-
legial consultation is only beginning at the present time, and is the subject of much discussion among contemporary Roman Catholic leaders.

77. Vatican II, "Dogmatic Constitution on the Church," 3:20 (in Leith, p. 472).

2.1.3 What the Roman Catholic Church teaches about the authority of the bishop of Rome within the "college" of bishops: The Roman Catholic Church teaches that within the "college" of bishops, the bishop of Rome is conceived as standing at the head, on the analogy of the relationship between the apostle Peter and the "college" of apostles.

Sources: First Council of Constantinople, canon 3 (in *ANF*, 14:178). Vatican II, "Dogmatic Constitution on the Church," 3:20 (in Leith, pp. 471–472; in Flannery, pp. 371–372). *Catechism of the Catholic Church*, 880–885 (in American translation, pp. 233–234). Papal encyclical of Pope John Paul II: *Ut Unum Sint*, par. 95 (*Origins* 25:4, pp. 69–70).

Catholic doctrinal statements consistently state that the bishop of Rome, the pope, stands in the same relation to other bishops as Peter stood in relation to the apostles.[78] Jesus said, "And I tell you, you are Peter, and on this rock I will build my church, and the gates of Hades will not prevail against it" (Matt. 16:18). Catholics have long understood this to mean that Jesus placed Peter in a position of authority among the other apostles. Just as the authority of the apostles passed from them to the bishops of the church, so Peter's role as "prince of the apostles" passed from him to his successors as bishops of Rome.

The notion of the bishops of Rome as successors of Peter relies on the tradition, stated plainly in the late second century A.D. by Bishop Irenaeus of Lyons, that Peter was the original founder of the church at Rome, and that he was succeeded by an unbroken line of bishops in that office. Irenaeus himself gave a list of all the bishops of Rome, from Peter up until his own time. The First Council of Constantinople (A.D. 381) assigned to the bishops of Rome the "primacy of honor" among the bishops of the church.[79] Moreover, the doctrinal leadership of the bishops of Rome was often acknowledged in the ancient church (for example, when Pope Leo submitted a resolution that was accepted at the Council of Chalcedon in 451), although bishops of Rome seldom interfered in the internal affairs of other churches in antiquity. In any case, Catholics take these indications of ancient reverence and respect as indicating that the "primacy" (first place) of Rome and the Roman bishops' teaching authority was acknowledged even by other ancient churches. Throughout the early Middle Ages, the authority of the bishops of Rome increased, so that by the Carolingian period (see 2.0.3) Catholics understood the pope's "primacy" as involving "supremacy" or jurisdiction over all bishops in the church. This claim on

78. Creed of the Council of Trent (in Leith, p. 441); Vatican I, "First Dogmatic Constitution on the Church of Christ," introduction and chapters 1–3 (in Leith, pp. 448–454); Vatican II, "Dogmatic Constitution on the Church," 3:18–19 (in Leith, pp. 470–471).
79. First Council of Constantinople, canon 3 (in *ANF*, 14:178).

the part of the papacy has remained as one of the most crucial issues dividing Catholics from other Christians, although the papal encyclical *Ut Unum Sint* of May 1995 hints at the possibility that Catholics may be willing to reconceive the "primacy" of the Pope in ways that could open up unity with Eastern Christians.[80]

2.1.4   *What the Roman Catholic Church teaches about the infallible teaching authority of the bishops of Rome:* The Roman Catholic Church teaches that bishops of Rome teach "infallibly" due to divine protection when they speak on a specific doctrinal issue in their capacity as supreme teacher in the church.

Sources: Vatican I, "First Dogmatic Constitution on the Church of Christ," chapter 4 (in Leith, pp. 454–457). Vatican II, "Dogmatic Constitution on the Church," 3:25 (in Leith, pp. 477–480; in Flannery, 379–381). *Catechism of the Catholic Church* 891–892 (in American translation, pp. 235–236).

In addition to the question of papal supremacy, the issue of the infallible teaching authority of the bishop of Rome is a closely related, controversial point in Catholic doctrine, affecting Catholic relationships with both Eastern Christian churches and Protestants. It must be understood in the light of what has been said above, namely, that Catholics understand the tradition of the church, especially represented by its bishops, to be the authorized interpreter of scripture, and that the bishop of Rome stands at the head of the "college" of bishops. The doctrine of the infallible teaching authority of the pope was first stated as formal dogma at Vatican I (1870). These are the terms in which the council stated the doctrine:

> We teach and define that it is a dogma divinely revealed: that the Roman Pontiff, when he speaks *ex cathedrā*, that is, when in discharge of the office of Pastor and Doctor of all Christians, by virtue of his supreme Apostolic authority he defines a doctrine regarding faith or morals to be held by the Universal Church, by the divine assistance promised to him in blessed Peter, is possessed of that infallibility with which the divine Redeemer willed that His Church should be endowed for defining doctrine regarding faith or morals: and that therefore such definitions of the Roman Pontiff are irreformable of themselves, and not from the consent of the church.[81]

Some specific points about this definition ought to be noted. First, infallibility is not ascribed to the pope as a human being; rather, it is

---

80. Papal encyclical of Pope John Paul II: *Ut Unum Sint*, par. 95 (*Origins* 25:4, pp. 69–70).
81. Vatican I, "First Dogmatic Constitution on the Church of Christ," chap. 4 (in Leith, pp. 454–457; quotation is on pp. 456–457).

ascribed to the presence of the Holy Spirit in the continuing life of the church, and the Holy Spirit speaks through the pope as a designated channel. Catholic teaching would agree with the assertion that only God is, in the end, infallible. A question remaining would be, "Where is the place where we find God's infallible teaching authority?" For conservative Protestants, the only form in which divine infallibility remains in the world is in the text of the Bible itself. For Eastern Orthodox Christians, as we have seen, this divine infallibility resides in the continuing tradition of the church as a whole, expressed principally in Ecumenical Councils of bishops. Catholics understand the bishops of Rome as standing at the center of this continuing tradition, and therefore some of the pronouncements of the bishops of Rome can be regarded as reflecting divine infallibility.

A second point follows from the previous sentence: only *some* statements of the popes are understood as conveying this infallible authority. In the first place, according to the definition, the bishop of Rome must speak *ex cathedrā*. This literally means "from the chair" or "throne," and it means that statements may be considered as representing an exercise of infallibility only when the pope issues them "in discharge of the office of Pastor and Doctor of all Christians." In the second place, again according to the definition, the pope must be speaking on "a doctrine regarding faith or morals" for a statement to be considered infallible. In fact, the number of statements issued under these criteria is rather small. Some Catholics would say that only two papal statements qualify as "infallible" statements by strict definition: the definitions of the doctrines of Mary's "immaculate conception" and her bodily "assumption" into heaven (see 2.2.4).

A third point on the doctrine of papal infallibility is that although it was approved by a large majority of the bishops at Vatican I, it was opposed by an influential minority of Catholics and interpreted in different ways by other Catholics, and it is possible to read the "Dogmatic Constitution on the Church" of Vatican II as qualifying the doctrine of papal infallibility by placing it within the context of the teaching authority of the "college" of bishops. One point that Newman and others contested was the last phrase of the definition, which says that infallible declarations are "irreformable of themselves, and not from the consent of the church." Although it would appear that this statement itself could not be seriously qualified in any way (if it is itself "irreformable"), nevertheless, it may be understood as meaning simply that a papal decision cannot be appealed; it might nevertheless be subject to continuing clarification and interpretation.

This is, I think, an important point to note in our attempt to understand the teachings of Roman Catholicism in the light of modern tendencies in general and the Ecumenical movement in particular. One of the consistent tendencies of modernity is its stress on representative and participatory forms of governance, as contrasted with monarchical forms of governance. The doctrine of papal infallibility as defined at Vatican I seemed to contradict modernist notions of participatory governance (and democratic, relativistic theories of truth) as clearly as could possibly be done. But Vatican II does qualify (or at least clarify) the understanding of the pope's authority in the church in a direction that contemporary Catholics see as being both more biblical and more theologically accurate, namely, in its understanding that the pope always teaches as a representative of the "college" of bishops.

2.1.5 *What the Roman Catholic Church teaches about the authority of Ecumenical Councils:* The Roman Catholic Church teaches that Ecumenical Councils derive their authority from their having included the participation or approval of bishops of Rome.

Sources: Vatican I, "First Dogmatic Constitution on the Church of Christ," chap. 3 (in Leith, pp. 452–453). Vatican II, "Dogmatic Constitution on the Church," 3:20–21, 25 (in Leith, pp. 472–473, 478–479). *Catechism of the Catholic Church*, 884 (in American translation, p. 234).

Comparative Cross-References: Eastern Orthodox, 1.1.2–3; Reformation and Union, 3.1.2.a–c; Evangelical and Free, 4.1.2.a–c, 4.1.3.a–b; Ecumenical, 5.2.1.

From what has been said above it should be apparent that Catholicism has a different emphasis than Eastern Orthodoxy, which has historically maintained that councils, especially those acknowledged as Ecumenical Councils, stand over all individual bishops of the church (including the bishops of Rome). A similar principle was proposed in the Conciliar movement in Western Christianity in the 1300s and 1400s, and in fact it was invoked as a way of resolving the problem of the divided papacy in the 1400s. But the Catholic stress on the unique role of the bishops of Rome within the "college" of bishops implies that the authority of Ecumenical Councils includes their approval by the whole church, which must include the bishop of Rome, at least in the form of subsequent "reception" by the bishop of Rome. Vatican I asserted that the Roman pontiff has authority over all bishops, so that councils of bishops cannot have a higher authority than that of the bishops of Rome. Vatican II explained in explicit terms that Ecumenical Councils derive their authority from the participation or approval of the bishops of Rome: "A council is never ecumenical unless it is confirmed or at least accepted as such by the successor of Peter."[82]

With this definition of the authority of an Ecumenical Council, we should observe that Catholics acknowledge fourteen councils as having the status of Ecumenical Councils in addition to the seven acknowledged by Eastern and Western churches alike, giving a total of twenty-one Ecumenical Councils acknowledged by Rome. Vatican II was the most recent Ecumenical Council in the Roman reckoning. After Vatican II, Pope Paul VI began to speak of the later fourteen councils as "Latin Councils" or "General Synods of the West," terminology that might be found more conciliatory in dialogue with Eastern Orthodox Christians.

2.2   Catholic Teachings on God and Christ

Catholic teachings concerning God and Christ will be found largely compatible with the Orthodox teachings discussed in section 1.2. There are a few nuances in Western emphases concerning God and Christ, and only a couple of points at which Western divergences from Eastern patterns have become church-dividing issues, most notably, the question of the "double procession" of the Holy Spirit (see 2.2.2).

2.2.1   What the Roman Catholic Church teaches about the nature of God as the Holy Trinity: The Roman Catholic Church teaches that God is three "Persons" in one "substance," and that the three persons differ in their "modes of origin" (the Father is "unbegotten," the Son is "begotten," and the Spirit "proceeds").

Sources: Nicene and Constantinopolitan Creeds (in Leith, pp. 30–31; in Denzinger and Hünermann, items 125–126 and 150, pp. 62–64, 83–85). Fourth Lateran Council, canon 1 (in Leith, p. 57). Council of Trent, "Decree concerning the Symbol of Faith" (in Leith, p. 401). Catechism of the Catholic Church, 198–325 (in American translation, pp. 54–84).

Comparative Cross-References: Eastern Orthodox, 1.2.1; Reformation and Union, 3.2.1; Evangelical and Free, 4.2.1.a–b; Ecumenical, 5.2.2.1.

On this basic doctrine of Trinitarian theology there is wide agreement between Catholic, Orthodox, and most Protestant churches (see 5.1). The Nicene Creed is utilized in Catholic masses (but see 2.2.2, below), and the Trinitarian doctrine has been affirmed, according to its

82. Vatican I, "First Dogmatic Constitution on the Church of Christ," chap. 3 (in Leith, pp. 452–453); Vatican II, "Dogmatic Constitution on the Church," 3:20–21, 25 (in Leith, pp. 472–473, 478–479; quotation is on p. 475); cf. Catechism of the Catholic Church, 884 (in American translation, p. 234).

formulation in the First Councils of Nicaea and Constantinople, consistently through Catholic history. It was stated at the beginning of the first canon of the Fourth Lateran Council (1215) in this manner:

> We firmly believe and openly confess that there is only one true God, eternal, beyond measure and unchangeable, incomprehensible, omnipotent and ineffable, the Father, the Son, and the Holy Spirit: Three persons but a single essence, substance, or nature that is wholly one; the Father proceeding from none, the Son proceeding from the Father alone, and the Holy Spirit from both in like manner; without beginning and having no end forever: the Father begetting, the Son being begotten, and the Holy Spirit proceeding; having the same substance, the same equality, the same omnipotence, and the same eternity. . . .[83]

Similarly, the Council of Trent's "Decree concerning the Symbol of Faith" begins by reciting the Nicene Creed.[84]

If there is general agreement between Eastern and Western churches in the use of Nicene language to describe the doctrine of the Trinity, it might be argued that there are some nuances, some differences in emphasis, between East and West on this issue. The Western church, at least in antiquity, tended to emphasize the unity or oneness of God, as contrasted with the Eastern church's tendency to emphasize the threeness or the distinctions between the three persons. Many early Western creeds begin with the words, "We believe in one God. . . ." Modalism, the heresy that identified the Father and the Son as "modes" of the one God and failed to recognize a distinction between them, was most typically held in the West in the period before the Council of Nicaea. When pressed for metaphors for the Trinity, Western thinkers tended to find metaphors within a single human personality, such as Augustine's use of the metaphor of a single person with memory, will, and intellect. These metaphors tend to be strong on unity and relatively weak in expressing diversity within the godhead. Eastern Christians, by contrast, were far more often tempted by the Arian heresy, which stressed the difference between Father and Son. When pressed to find metaphors for the Trinity, even the most orthodox of Eastern thinkers, such as the Cappadocian writers of the fourth century A.D., turned to the image of three men united by a common humanity. This metaphor seems strong on diversity and correspondingly weak on unity. But East and West agreed in ruling out the

---

83. Fourth Lateran Council, canon 1 (in Leith, p. 57).
84. Council of Trent, "Decree concerning the Symbol of Faith" (in Leith, p. 401).

extremes of Modalism and Arianism, and both found unity in the wording of the creed, despite differences in emphasis between them.

2.2.2 What the Roman Catholic Church teaches about the double procession of the Holy Spirit: The Roman Catholic Church teaches that the Holy Spirit "proceeds from the Father and the Son."

Sources: Nicene (Constantinopolitan) Creed, Western form (as given in Denzinger and Hünermann, item 150, pp. 83–85). *Catechism of the Catholic Church*, 246–248 (in American translation, pp. 65–66).

Comparative Cross-References: Eastern Orthodox, 1.2.1; Reformation and Union, 3.2.1; Evangelical and Free, 4.2.1.a; Ecumenical, 5.2.2.1.

Of course, on this one point Eastern and Western Christians did *not* agree in the wording of the creed. Eastern Christians say, "from the Father"; Western Christians since the ninth century A.D. (the period of the Carolingian renaissance) have said, "from the Father and the Son." The excerpt from the Fourth Lateran Council quoted above and the creed of the Council of Trent and other Catholic doctrinal statements will show this insistence on the Spirit's proceeding "from the Father and the Son." The Catholic doctrine is referred to as the doctrine of the "double procession" of the Holy Spirit, as contrasted with the Eastern church's affirmation of a "single procession" (from the Father only).

What is at stake in this controversy? We have argued above that lying behind it was the issue of authority, that is, whether bishops of Rome had the authority to change or add to the wording of a creed given by an Ecumenical Council. But there were significant differences over the doctrine itself, and these focused on the question of how the equality of the three Persons of the Trinity is best expressed. East and West have always agreed on the equality of the Persons, but Western theologians argued that adding the words "and the Son" was a more appropriate expression of the equality of the Persons. Without these words, they argued, God the Father would appear to be the only source of the godhead, and so could be seen as having priority over the Son and the Holy Spirit. Eastern theologians reasoned differently. The expression "from the Father" (without "and the Son") expressed better the equality of Persons, as they saw it, since it would be unbalanced to have the Son originating from the Father only and the Spirit originating from the Father and the Son. If it seems remarkable that a difference over such an issue as this could lead to nine hundred years of division between Eastern and Western churches, remember that there were many issues lying beneath the surface of the division, with the issue of the authority of the bishops of Rome (who authorized the expression "and the Son") chief among the underlying issues. In recent ecumenical discussions, moreover, Catholics and Orthodox have come to realize that the two positions they have taken on the expression "and the Son" may express complementary truths. This may mark an important breakthrough, suggesting that the contested wording of the creed is no longer the church-dividing issue it once was.[85]

It is important to note, with respect to ecumenical relationships, that Anglican and Protestant churches that use the Nicene Creed use it in the Western form, that is, with the expression "and the Son." This may seem surprising, given the fact that the expression was authorized by the teaching office of the papacy, which Protestants rejected. The fact is, however, that Eastern Christianity and its reasons for rejecting this expression were not well understood in the 1500s, and it is likely that early Protestants believed that "and the Son" was part of the original wording of the creed. The Episcopal Church in the United States has voted in principal to remove the expression "and the Son" from the creed as it appears in their prayer books, although this decision is contingent on approval by the broader Anglican communion (see 5.2.2.1). The World Council of Churches Faith and Order Commission and the Faith and Order Working Group of the National Council of Churches of Christ in the United States are in process of addressing this issue.

2.2.3 What the Roman Catholic Church teaches about the two natures in Christ: The Roman Catholic Church teaches that in the one Person of Christ were united two complete "natures," one divine and the other human.

Sources: Definition of Faith of the Council of Chalcedon (in Leith, pp. 35–36; in Denzinger and Hünermann, items 301–302, pp. 142–143). Anathemas of the Second Council of Constantinople 1–11 (in Leith, pp. 46–50; in Denzinger and Hünermann, items 421–436, pp. 194–201). Definition concerning the Two Wills and Energies in Christ of the Third Council of Constantinople (in Leith, pp. 51–53; in Denzinger and Hünermann, items 556–558, pp. 257–259). Fourth Lateran Council, canon 1 (in Leith, p. 57). *Catechism of the Catholic Church,* 422–682 (in American translation, pp. 106–178).

Comparative Cross-References: Eastern Orthodox, 1.2.2; Reformation and Union, 3.2.2; Evangelical and Free, 4.2.2; Ecumenical, 5.2.2.2.

On this point Catholics agree with Orthodox and most Protestants in affirming the formula of the Council of Chalcedon, that Christ is "one Person in two natures." Just as the Fourth Lateran Council reaffirmed Trinitarian doctrine after the break with the East, so it affirmed the doctrine of Christ:

> And finally the only-begotten Son of God, Jesus Christ, made flesh by the Trinity in all its persons together, conceived of Mary,

---

85. *Catechism of the Catholic Church,* 248 (in American translation, pp. 65–66).

ever Virgin, with the cooperation of the Holy Spirit, made true man, composed of a rational soul and human flesh, one person in two natures, showed the way to life with greater clarity.[86]

The same language of one Person in two natures was affirmed consistently by later Catholic doctrinal statements. It is expressed in the words of the familiar Christmas carol "O Come, All Ye Faithful,"

> True God of true God, Light from Light Eternal,
> Lo, he shuns not the Virgin's womb;
> Son of the Father, begotten, not created;
> O come, let us adore him, . . .
> Christ the Lord.[87]

With this recognition of general agreement between Catholics and other Christians on Chalcedonian formula of "one Person in two natures," we may pause to look a bit more deeply at the ways in which Catholics express devotion to Christ. The Mass itself is understood as a way of paying devotion to Christ (see 2.4.5.3), and Catholic devotion to the mother of Jesus must be seen, ultimately, as a way of devotion to Jesus himself (see 2.2.4). The "Modern Devotion" movement of the fourteenth and fifteenth centuries focused on the following or "imitation" of Christ, and the crucifix, present everywhere in Catholic culture, became popular at this time. Medieval Catholics often meditated on the wounds of Christ—the marks of the thorns in his brow, the wound in his side where he was pierced by a Roman soldier, and the nailmarks in his hands and feet. From the 1600s it became very popular among Catholics to pay devotion to the "Sacred Heart" of Jesus. This does not indicate a morbid devotion to Jesus' anatomy: Catholics understand the Sacred Heart of Jesus as symbolizing God's love for all humanity, Christ's own human love, and the love that is born in Christians as they follow the example of Christ.[88] Devotion to the Sacred Heart of Jesus is a personal and emotional and popular way of paying reverence to Christ himself, and the symbolism of the Sacred Heart is almost as widespread in Catholic culture as the symbol of the crucifix.

2.2.4 *What the Roman Catholic Church teaches about Mary, the mother of Jesus:* The Roman Catholic Church teaches that the Blessed Virgin Mary is the "Mother of God" (as Mother of the whole Person of Christ) and affirms her "perpetual virginity," her bodily "assumption" into heaven, and her "immaculate conception."

86. Fourth Lateran Council, canon 1 (in Leith, p. 57).
87. Latin hymn by John F. Wade, in *The United Methodist Hymnal*, trans. Frederick Oakeley, no. 234.
88. Ted A. Campbell, *The Religion of the Heart* (Columbia, S.C.: University of South Carolina Press, 1991), pp. 36–40.

88   Christian Confessions

Sources: Anathema of Cyril of Alexandria approved at the Council of Ephesus 1 (in Denzinger and Hünermann, item 252, p. 126). Definition of Faith of the Council of Chalcedon (in Leith, pp. 35–36; in Denzinger and Hünermann, items 301–302, pp. 142–143). Apostolic Constitution *Munificentissimus Deus* (in Denzinger and Hünermann, items 3900–3904, pp. 1100–1101; in Leith, p. 458). Papal bull. *Ineffabilis Deus* (in Denzinger and Hünermann, items 2800–2804, pp. 774–776; in Leith, pp. 442–446). *Catechism of the Catholic Church*, 487–511, 963–975 (in American translation, pp. 122–128, 251–254).

Comparative Cross-References: Eastern Orthodox, 1.2.3; Reformation and Union, 3.2.3; Evangelical and Free, 4.2.4.

Catholics often make the point, especially in conversations with Protestants, that when they speak of Mary, they are speaking of Jesus Christ. This does not mean that the two are simply the same, but it means that teachings about Mary are inevitably related to teachings about Christ. Following the Ecumenical Councils of Ephesus and Chalcedon, Catholics understand Mary to be the Mother of God, as the mother of the whole Christ, both divine and human.[89] Following the teachings of the Second Council of Nicaea, Catholics are forbidden to "worship" Mary, since she is not God, but they are encouraged to "venerate" Mary, and images of her, with the highest degree of veneration that can be paid to a human saint.[90] There are three doctrines by which Catholics make their belief about Mary more explicit.

The first of these is the doctrine of the perpetual virginity of Mary. Completely consistent with Eastern Christian teachings at this point (see 1.2.3), Catholics insist that Mary remained a virgin through the conception and birth of Jesus, and beyond. This means, again like Eastern churches, that they take scriptural references to Jesus' brothers and sisters to refer to stepbrothers and stepsisters, or possibly cousins. Virginity has been highly prized by Christians since ancient times, and the Catholic insistence on the perpetual virginity of Mary reflects their sense of her exalted state, "blessed . . . among women" (Luke 1:42).

The second specific doctrine about Mary affirmed by Catholics is the doctrine of her bodily assumption into heaven. This teaching maintains that at the end of her life, Mary was received into heaven by God as a foretaste of the resurrection of all Christians. Like the doctrine of perpetual virginity, the doctrine of Mary's assumption into heaven is also affirmed by Eastern Christians and relies on early Christian traditions outside of the New Testament. Taught consistently through the Middle Ages, the doctrine was not formally de-

89. Council of Ephesus, anathemas of Cyril of Alexandria approved by the Council, no. 1 (in Denzinger and Hünermann, item 252, p. 126); Definition of Faith of the Council of Chalcedon (in Denzinger and Hünermann, item 301, p. 142; in Leith, p. 36).
90. Decree of the Second Council of Nicaea (in Leith, pp. 55–56).

fined by the Catholic Church until 1950.[91] The definition of this doctrine is considered to be one of the few exercises of the infallible teaching authority of the papacy. We may note that this teaching is very close to that of Eastern churches, although Eastern Christians consistently maintain that Mary was assumed bodily into heaven after her natural death, whereas the Western church leaves open the question of whether the assumption was before or after Mary's death.

The third specific doctrine about Mary taught by Catholics is taught formally by Catholics alone, and that is the doctrine of the immaculate conception of Mary. According to this doctrine, Mary herself was conceived (by her mother and father) "without stain of original sin." In other words, sin is passed to all human beings at the time of conception (see 2.3.1), but in the case of Mary's conception this condition was miraculously avoided. (Note that this does not refer to the conception of Jesus, which was also "immaculate" in that it was free from original sin; this doctrine refers only to the conception of Mary.) The doctrine thus safeguards the sinlessness of Jesus, who according to Catholic teaching was the only child of Mary (and of course not the child of Joseph). Although the doctrine of the immaculate conception of Mary had been taught since the Middle Ages, it was not formally defined as doctrine by Catholics until 1854.[92]

In popular Catholic piety, devotion to the Blessed Virgin Mary occupies a central role, and in some Catholic cultures this devotion will have very specific and sometimes local overtones. Mexican Catholics, for instance, pay devotion to Our Lady of Guadalupe, commemorating an appearance of Mary to a Native American peasant near Mexico City in 1531. Devotion to Mary is most often expressed by use of the "Hail Mary" (in Latin, Ave Maria), an address to Mary that utilizes the words of the angel to Mary in Luke 1:28 and adds a prayer for the Christian:

> Hail Mary, full of grace,
>   The Lord is with thee.
> Blessed art thou among women,
>   And blessed is the fruit of thy womb, Jesus.
> Holy Mary, Mother of God,
>   Pray for us sinners,
>   Now and at the hour of our death.[93]

---

91. Apostolic Constitution *Munificentissimus Deus* (in Denzinger and Hünermann, items 3900–3904, pp. 1100–1101; in Leith, p. 458).
92. Papal bull., *Ineffabilis Deus* (in Denzinger and Hünermann, items 2800–2804, pp. 774–776; in Leith, pp. 442–446).
93. *Catechism of the Catholic Church*, 2676–2677 (in American translation, pp. 643–644).

2.3   Catholic Teachings on Human Nature and Salvation

Catholic leaders often feel that their views on human nature and salvation have been seriously misunderstood by Protestants, because Protestants have often told their own story or narrative as a story of Luther's rejection of the "works righteousness" of Catholicism. In response to this, Catholics often point out to Protestants that Luther reacted against a rather odd version of medieval Catholicism (as it seemed in later perspective), and that Luther's protest in many ways presupposed the rightness or appropriateness of the Catholic sacramental and especially penitential system. Moreover, these older stereotypes have often failed to realize the large common ground between Protestants and Catholics (in contrast to Eastern Orthodox) on the issue of original sin, to which we turn first.

2.3.1 *What the Roman Catholic Church teaches about human nature and original sin:* The Roman Catholic Church teaches that as a result of the sin of the first human beings, "original sin," both the guilt of sin and the punishment for sin (death), have been passed on to all human beings.

Sources: Council of Orange, canon 1 (in Leith, p. 38). Council of Trent, "Decree concerning Original Sin," 1–4 (in Leith, pp. 405–407). *Catechism of the Catholic Church,* 385–421 (in American translation, pp. 97–105).

Comparative Cross-References: Eastern Orthodox, 1.3.1; Reformation and Union, 3.3.1; Evangelical and Free, 4.3.1; Ecumenical, 5.2.3.

The doctrine of original sin is a typically Western Christian way of accounting for the fallen state of humankind. The doctrine was formulated by Augustine of Hippo in the late fourth and early fifth centuries A.D., and it has been maintained consistently by Catholics and the groups to which we shall refer as Reformation churches. It is important to understand, in the background, that Augustine and later Western theologians formulated this teaching against Pelagianism, the belief that human beings, by their own power, can do what God requires and so be saved. There is some serious doubt whether the teacher Pelagius ever believed such an idea, but in Western Christian thought, the term "Pelagianism" denotes this idea of self-salvation. Closely related is another set of teachings that Augustine and Western leaders also sought to refute, and that is the idea that human beings cooperate with God in the working out of salvation. This view has been traditionally called Semipelagianism in Western Christian circles, but readers of this book may recognize that it is very similar to ways in which Eastern Christians had taught about the "synergy" or cooperation of human nature and divine grace (see 1.3.3 and 1.3.6).

With an ardent concern to assert the role of God (as opposed to human beings) in the process of salvation, Augustine stressed that human beings are by themselves incapable of any good, and that all good comes from God alone. According to Augustine and Western Christian traditions following him, both the consequences of sin (death) and the guilt of sin have been passed on hereditarily from our first human parents to every human being after them. In the words of a synod of French bishops meeting in A.D. 529:

> If anyone asserts that Adam's sin affected him alone and not his descendants also, or at least if he declares that it is only the death of the body which is the punishment for sin, and not also that sin, which is the death of the soul, passed through one man to the whole human race, he does injustice to God and contradicts the Apostle, who says, "By one man sin entered into this world, and by sin death: so death passed upon all men because all have sinned" (Rom. 5:12).[94]

As we have seen above (in 2.2.4), Catholics allow only the exceptions of Mary and Jesus in the inheritance of sin.

The Catholic understanding of original sin does stand in contrast to Eastern tradition, which maintains that only the punishment for sin, but not its guilt, was passed on to subsequent human beings. Despite the contrast on this issue, though, this has not been seen as one of the primary or formal issues dividing Orthodox and Catholics.

2.3.2 *What the Roman Catholic Church teaches about the results of original sin:* The Roman Catholic Church teaches that one of the results of original sin is that free will has been so seriously impaired that it is impossible for human beings to return to God by their own power.

Sources: Council of Orange, canon 8 (in Leith, p. 40). Council of Trent, "Decree concerning Justification," chap. 1 (in Leith, p. 408). *Catechism of the Catholic Church,* 402–406 (in American translation, pp. 101–103).

Comparative Cross-References: Eastern Orthodox, 1.3.3; Reformation and Union, 3.3.2; Evangelical and Free, 4.3.1; Ecumenical, 5.2.3.

The Catholic understanding of the human predicament rejects the notion (associated with Pelagianism) that human beings have a free will that enables them to do what God requires. Again, this struck Augustine as leaning too heavily on human initiative rather than divine grace. Augustine and later Western teachers did not deny that human

---

94. Council of Orange, canon 1 (in Leith, p. 38); cf. Council of Trent, "Decree concerning Original Sin," 1–4 (in Leith, pp. 405–407).

beings have free will, but they maintained that as a result of sin, our wills have been so weakened that they are unable to do good without the aid of God's grace. The consistent way in which Catholic doctrinal statements speak of the human will after the fall is to say that it has become "weakened" or "corrupted." The Synod (or Council) of Orange (A.D. 529) maintained that human will has been "weakened through the sin of the first man," and the Council of Trent speaks of free will as "weakened as it was in its powers and downward bent" after the fall.[95] As Catholics understand this teaching, it is not to lessen the beauty of God's creation of humankind, but rather to emphasize our constant need for God's grace.

On this point about the weakness of human will that results from the fall, Catholics stand in close agreement with Lutheran and Reformed traditions, and at least the formal doctrine of Anglicans. Catholics differ from Eastern Orthodox churches on this issue, which teach that the "image" of God remaining in human beings after the fall includes a true free will.

One further aspect of Catholic teaching on sin is the distinction maintained in traditional Catholic moral teaching between mortal and venial sins. The distinction of mortal and venial sins is grounded in 1 John 5:16–17, which speaks of a sin that is "mortal" or "unto death" (KJV) and indicates that not all sins are so serious. This distinction is also grounded in the practice of the early church to exclude from communion those persons who had committed sins so blatant as to offend the community. Mortal sins (from the Latin word for "death") are those that lead to spiritual death, so that if a person dies having committed a mortal sin (and not having been reconciled to the church by the sacrament of penance), that individual will not share communion with Christ and the saints in heaven. Venial sins are those acts that warrant divine punishment, so that if a person dies having committed venial sins (and not having been reconciled to the church by the sacrament of penance), the individual may eventually be with Christ and the saints in heaven, but their sins will still require punishment (according to traditional Catholic teaching, in purgatory; see 2.3.7).

2.3.3 What the Roman Catholic Church teaches about the human need for grace in salvation: The Roman Catholic Church teaches that it is only by God's grace, in virtue of Christ's sacrifice, conveyed by

---

95. Council of Orange, canon 8 (in Leith, p. 40); Council of Trent, "Decree concerning Justification," chap. 1 (in Leith, p. 408).

the Holy Spirit, that human beings can be restored to fellowship with God.

Sources: Canons of the Council of Orange (in Leith, pp. 38–45). Council of Trent, "Decree concerning Justification," chap. 12 (in Leith, p. 416). Paul V, "A Formula for Ending Disputes *De Auxiliis*" (in Denzinger and Hünermann, item 1997, p. 611). *Catechism of the Catholic Church,* 1996–2005 (in American translation, pp. 483–486).

Comparative Cross-References: Eastern Orthodox, 1.3.3; Reformation and Union, 3.3.2; Evangelical and Free, 4.3.1; Ecumenical, 5.2.3.

For Augustine and many later Catholics, a necessary corollary of their understanding of the human predicament is that God alone chooses, or predestines, who will be saved, because salvation must be the work of God alone, not of human beings, corrupted as they are by the fall. Although some Catholic councils taught this doctrine, the Council of Trent was at least ambiguous on the issue. Shortly after the council, Dominicans defended the Augustinian teaching, including its assertion of predestination, against the Jesuits, who insisted that Christ had died for all human beings and therefore salvation must be available to all. The Catholic Church refused to resolve this controversy except to say that Dominicans and Jesuits should refrain from attacking each other.[96]

Despite the church's refusal to resolve this particular controversy, it should be clear from what has been said above that Roman Catholicism consistently teaches that human beings can be saved only by God's grace. This needs to be emphasized, though, because another Protestant misunderstanding about Catholicism is that it somehow teaches "works righteousness," that is, it somehow claims that salvation is based on human works. This may be related to the narrative about Martin Luther's discovery of the meaning of justification by faith, but Catholics point out that Luther was in touch with a rather aberrant form of late-medieval Catholic teaching that was not adopted by Catholics subsequently, and that the main stream of Catholic tradition has consistently stressed that human beings cannot possibly save themselves and must be saved by God's grace.[97] Some ecumenical historians have gone so far as to argue that if Martin Luther had known Catholic works more representative of the position that Catholics would eventually choose, works like Thomas Aquinas's commentaries on Paul's letters, Luther might not have felt such

96. Canons of the Council of Orange (in Leith, pp. 38–45); Council of Trent, "Decree concerning Justification," chap. 12 (in Leith, p. 416); Paul V, "A Formula for Ending Disputes *De Auxiliis*" (in Denzinger and Hünermann, item 1997, p. 611).
97. Council of Orange, canon 25 (in Leith, p. 43); Council of Trent, "Decree concerning Justification," chap. 2 (in Leith, pp. 408–409).

a degree of alienation from Catholicism.[98] As we shall see below
(2.3.5), Catholics do insist that good works are part of the Christian life
and in a sense necessary to salvation, and they will even speak of our
good works "meriting" salvation, but these doctrines are carefully defined so as to make it very clear that we can do no good works, and
we can "merit" nothing, apart from God's grace.

2.3.4 *What the Roman Catholic Church teaches about the process of
the Christian life:* The Roman Catholic Church teaches that salvation
occurs in individual persons in a process in which (1) the human will
is prepared by grace, (2) the human will then freely assents in faith to
the gospel, and (3) the individual submits to baptism, whereby the
person is justified and forgiven of all past sins.

Sources: Council of Orange, canons 5 and 14 and conclusion (in Leith, pp. 39, 41, 43).
Council of Trent, "Decree concerning Justification," chap. 4–8 (in Leith, pp. 409–413).
Catechism of the Catholic Church, 1987–1995, 2001 (in American translation, pp.
481–483, 484–485).

Comparative Cross-References: Reformation and Union, 3.3.4; Evangelical and Free,
4.3.3, 4.3.4.a–b.

How does a man or woman come to faith in Christ? Catholic teaching usually points to three identifiable moments in the process of coming to faith, although these three moments do not necessarily occur in
a particular order. The first is that the human will (weakened by sin)
is prepared by God's grace. This grace, "coming before" our belief in
Christ, is often described as "preparatory" or "prevenient" grace
("prevenient" simply means "coming before"). Preparatory grace
does not guarantee that persons will believe in Christ, but it empow-
ers their will so that what they could not accomplish on their own can
be accomplished by God's help.[99] For Catholics who have believed in
predestination, this preparatory grace is given only to those who are
elect, and it is the means of their election. For those (like the Jesuits in
the 1590s) who argue that Christ died for all humankind, it is stressed
that this preparatory grace is given to all human beings. The second
moment in the process of coming to faith is faith itself, that is, when a
woman or man freely assents to the gospel and believes.[100]

98. Harry McSorley, "Thomas Aquinas, John Pupper von Goch, and Martin
Luther: An Essay in Ecumenical Theology" in *Our Common History as Christians:
Essays in Honor of Albert C. Outler*, ed. John Deschner, Leroy T. Howe, and Klaus
Penzel (New York: Oxford University Press, 1975), pp. 97–129.
99. Council of Orange, canons 5 and 14 and conclusion (in Leith, pp. 39, 41, 43); Council of Trent, "Decree concerning Justification," chaps. 4–6 (in Leith, pp. 409–411).
100. Council of Orange, conclusion (in Leith, p. 43), Council of Trent, "Decree concerning Justification," chap. 8 (in Leith, p. 413).

The third moment—remember that these do not have to occur in this order—is baptism. We shall discuss baptism in more detail below (see 2.4.5.1), but at this point we should note that Catholic doctrine describes baptism as the "instrumental cause" of justification, that is, it is the instrument that God uses to bring about our forgiveness.[101] But if baptism actually brings about forgiveness, what then is the relationship between faith and baptism? Catholics generally have taught that baptism will bring about forgiveness of sins *if a person does not lack faith in Christ*. Since infants do not have faith (or lack it) in this sense, Catholics consider that the faith of the church supplies the infant's lack of conscious faith, and so baptism effects forgiveness of (the guilt of original) sin for infants, and this forgiveness is effective unless the individual rejects faith. For adults, faith is a condition of the forgiveness brought about in baptism, so that a baptism without faith in a mature person would not bring about forgiveness. Note that in the case of an infant baptism, baptism would come before the two steps of preparation and explicit faith.

2.3.5 *What the Roman Catholic Church teaches about the role of merit in human salvation:* The Roman Catholic Church teaches that God's grace continues to lead the baptized person to good works, by which she or he "merits" eternal life.

Sources: Council of Orange, conclusion (in Leith, pp. 44–45). Council of Trent, "Decree concerning Justification," chaps. 10–11, 16 (in Leith, pp. 414–416, 418–420). *Catechism of the Catholic Church*, 2006–2011 (in American translation, pp. 486–487).

Comparative Cross-References: Eastern Orthodox, 1.3.6; Reformation and Union, 3.3.5; Evangelical and Free, 4.3.5; Ecumenical, 5.2.3.

Grace does not stop at the moment when a person believes and is baptized. Grace leads the believer to do good works. Catholic doctrine speaks of our good works "meriting" salvation, but we have placed the term "merit" in quotation marks here to indicate that it is used in a very specialized sense. Protestants have objected historically to the notion that human beings can "merit" anything. Clearly, Protestants understand "merit" to mean something that we earn on our own. But Catholics distinguish between "merit" that is something we earn and the "merit" that is actually given to us by someone else. Only in this latter sense do Catholics speak of good works as "meriting" salvation. Even in good works we do not work alone; our wills work together with God so that even "merit" is not from our work, it is the result of God working within us.[102]

101. Council of Trent, "Decree concerning Justification," chap. 7 (in Leith, p. 412).
102. Council of Orange, conclusion (in Leith, pp. 44–45); Council of Trent, "Decree concerning Justification," chaps. 10–11, 16 (in Leith, pp. 414–416, 418–420).

2.3.6 *What the Roman Catholic Church teaches about the role of sacraments in the Christian life:* The Roman Catholic Church teaches that believers are empowered in the Christian life by the grace given through the Mass (Eucharist). The Roman Catholic Church agrees, further, in teaching that if a believer sins after baptism, she or he can be restored to grace by confession and the sacrament of penance.

Sources: Council of Trent, "Decree concerning Justification," chaps. 7, 14 (in Leith, pp. 411–412, 417–418). *Catechism of the Catholic Church,* 1391–1398, 1468–1470 (in American translation, pp. 351–353, 369).

Comparative Cross-References: Eastern Orthodox, 1.3.5.

We shall discuss all the sacraments, and specifically the Mass (Eucharist) and the sacrament of penance below (see 2.4.5.3 and 2.4.5.4). At this point we should call attention to the link between this section on human nature and salvation and the following section on church, ministry, and sacraments. There is no solitary Christian life in the Catholic understanding. The church exists as a means by which God's grace is constantly available in the world (see 2.4.1), and the sacraments (see 2.4.5) offer specific means of grace stretching through a person's life from beginning to end. In the living of the Christian life, two sacraments stand out as particularly important because they are repeatable. The first is the Mass (a traditional Catholic term for the celebration of the Eucharist), in which Christ's presence offers grace to the recipient (see 2.4.5.3). The other is the sacrament of penance, in which a believer confesses his or her sins to a priest and the priest pronounces "absolution" (an announcement of God's forgiveness) when he is convinced that the individual has sincerely repented (see 2.4.5.4).

2.3.7 *What the Roman Catholic Church teaches about life beyond death:* The Roman Catholic Church teaches that those who finally reject Christ will be eternally punished, but Christian believers share eternity with Christ, and may be purified between death and the final judgment in purgatory.

Sources: Creed of the Council of Trent (in Leith, p. 441). *Catechism of the Catholic Church,* 1030–1032 (in American translation, pp. 268–269).

Comparative Cross-References: Eastern Orthodox, 1.3.7; Reformation and Union, 3.3.7; Evangelical and Free, 4.3.7.

Historic Catholic doctrine maintains that those who finally reject Christ will be eternally punished and that those who believe in Christ will be saved to share eternity with Christ and all the saints. There is not a tight definition as to what constitutes rejection of Christ (this is reserved for God's judgment): Catholic teaching (expressed in Vatican II) recognizes Christian faith in "separated" churches. Some Catholic teachers maintain that persons who have lived according to the grace given them, not knowing of Christ but also not rejecting Christ, may be saved by Christ's grace.

Just as Orthodox Christians teach about an intermediate state between death and the final judgment, so Catholics teach the existence of "purgatory." Such a concept as purgatory seems to be necessary to explain how it could be that a person who has truly believed in Christ but has committed some lesser sin(s) could be made pure before the final judgment. Consider the story of the rich man and Lazarus in Luke 16:19–31. A rich man dies and is tormented, while a poor man goes to "Abraham's bosom." But can this passage describe the state of persons after the final judgment? Not likely, say Catholics, because the rich man asks if he can go warn his five brothers about the fate awaiting them—his brothers were still alive, and so the story can not refer to the time after the final judgment. Catholics take this story to indicate that there must a state or "place" where believers go after death, and in which their lesser (venial) sins are purified.

In traditional Catholic thought, purgatory was associated with a cleansing, purifying flame in which remaining venial sins were atoned for. It was believed that prayers of believers on earth aided souls in purgatory, and perhaps even that good works done by believers could help souls in purgatory.[103] Contemporary Catholic theologians, however, are not as inclined to see purgatory as a place of torment and would see it more as a place where the soul's love for God is made pure.

2.4   Catholic Teachings on Church, Ministry, and Sacraments

2.4.1   *What the Roman Catholic Church teaches about the nature of the church:* The Roman Catholic Church teaches that the church is the spiritual and visible body of faithful Christians, which, as Christ's own body, combines divine and human natures.

Sources: Vatican II, "Dogmatic Constitution on the Church," 1–2 (in Leith, pp. 459–469; in Flannery, pp. 350–369). *Catechism of the Catholic Church,* 748–870 (in American translation, pp. 197–230).

Comparative Cross-References: Eastern Orthodox, 1.4.1; Reformation and Union, 3.4.1; Evangelical and Free, 4.4.1; Ecumenical, 5.2.4.1.

"Now you are the body of Christ . . . ," Paul wrote to the Corinthians (1 Cor. 12:27a). Just as Christ bore in his visible body the divinity

103. Creed of the Council of Trent (in Leith, p. 441).

that was his from eternity, so the church, as Catholics understand it, bears in its visible body the presence of Christ. The church is a kind of sacrament: an "outward and visible sign of an inward and spiritual grace." Vatican II described the church as "a kind of sacrament of intimate union with God . . . ."[104] This does not mean that the church is the body of Christ in the same sense as the earthly body of Jesus, nor in the same sense as the eucharistic elements become the body and blood of Christ. But as Catholics understand it, the church's identity as the body of Christ is more than a mere figure; it denotes that in some mysterious way Christ's presence abides in the church. Catholics stress the importance of the church as a "visible structure," not to be considered separate from the spiritual community of the church.[105]

So we may ask of Catholics as we did of Eastern Orthodox churches, Is the Roman Catholic Church the only true church? "Catholic," after all, means "universal." And again, the response is not unanimous. The Council of Trent appears to have taken a strict view of the subject. After reciting key elements of Catholic faith, the person affirming the Creed of the Council of Trent was to say: "I shall most constantly hold and profess this true Catholic faith, outside which no one can be saved and which I now freely profess and truly hold."[106] Up until the time of Vatican II, Catholic doctrine seemed to maintain that Catholicism was, simply, the one true, universal church. Appealing to the fact that Catholics recognize baptisms performed by other churches does not really help, since Catholics (unlike Orthodox at this point) hold that even non-Christians can perform valid baptisms in cases of emergency.

The "Dogmatic Constitution on the Church" issued by Vatican II approaches this question in a very different way. Rather than giving a hard and fast line separating true believers from all others, the council depicted a series of concentric circles, with the Catholic faithful in the innermost circle, those baptized but outside of Catholic communion in the next circle, and unbaptized persons in the outermost circle.[107] Insofar as religious toleration is a key element in modernity, Vatican II would appear to be far more modern in its approach to this question.

One might ask if it is possible to reconcile these two different views

104. Vatican II, "Dogmatic Constitution on the Church," 1:1 (in Leith, p. 459).
105. Ibid., 1:8 (in Leith, p. 460).
106. Creed of the Council of Trent (in Leith, p. 441).
107. Vatican II, "Dogmatic Constitution on the Church," 2:14–16 (in Leith, pp. 465–468).

of who constitutes the church. Perhaps the discrepancy can be accounted for by stretching somewhat the definition of "this true Catholic faith," which appears in the Creed of the Council of Trent. Although the expression appears most straightforwardly to refer to those who affirm the specific Roman Catholic doctrines professed earlier in the creed (including such items as the church's teaching authority and transubstantiation), a more tolerant reading of the document (and similar Catholic statements) might take "Catholic faith" as denoting the true Christian faith in which all baptized persons participate, at least to some degree.

2.4.2 *What the Roman Catholic Church teaches about the necessity of the church for human salvation:* The Roman Catholic Church teaches that the church, as the earthly mediator of divine grace, is necessary to salvation.

Sources: Fourth Lateran Council, canon 1 (in Leith, p. 58). Creed of the Council of Trent (in Leith, p. 441). Vatican II, "Dogmatic Constitution on the Church," 2:14 (in Leith, pp. 465–466; in Flannery, pp. 365–366). *Catechism of the Catholic Church*, 846–848 (in American translation, pp. 224–225).

Comparative Cross-References: Eastern Orthodox, 1.4.1.

Because the church is the body of Christ, it is never dispensable. Christians constantly need the grace that only the church supplies. The church, then, is necessary to salvation, but given what has been said above, it is not necessary to take this as implying that "the Roman Catholic Church" is necessary for the salvation of every person. "There is one universal church of believers," declared the Fourth Lateran Council, "outside which there is no salvation at all for any."[108] Vatican II states this principle in similar terms, but then restates it in negative terms: "Whosoever, therefore, knowing that the Catholic Church was made necessary by God through Jesus Christ, would refuse to enter her or to remain in her could not be saved."[109] Again, if I am reading it correctly, this allows a greater degree of toleration, for its condemnation applies only to persons who know that the church was instituted by God and who still reject it.

2.4.3 *What the Roman Catholic Church teaches about the hierarchical nature of the church:* The Roman Catholic Church teaches

---

108. Fourth Lateran Council, canon 1 (in Leith, p. 58); cf. the Creed of the Council of Trent (cited above), which states the same (in Leith, p. 441).
109. Vatican II, "Dogmatic Constitution on the Church," 2:14 (in Leith, pp. 465); cf. *Catechism of the Catholic Church*, 847 (in American translation, p. 224).

that the church is ordered by the hierarchical example of the
apostles, with the successors of Peter at its head.

Sources: Vatican I, "First Dogmatic Constitution on the Church of Christ," introduction
and chaps. 1–3 (in Leith, pp. 448–454). Vatican II, "Dogmatic Constitution on the
Church," chap. 3 (in Leith, pp. 469–480; in Flannery, pp. 369–387).

Comparative Cross-References: Eastern Orthodox, 1.4.2; Reformation and Union,
3.4.2.a–d; Evangelical and Free, 4.4.2.a–c.

However much Vatican II may have leaned in the direction of participatory governance in its stress on the role of the "college" of bishops, the bishops themselves stand within the "hierarchy" (sacred leadership) of the church, and this hierarchical structuring of the church, including the position of the bishop of Rome at the head of the hierarchy, is understood by Catholics as essential to the very being of the church. The hierarchical structure of the church centered on the bishop of Rome was explained at great length in Vatican I and reaffirmed in Vatican II.[110] As we have seen above (2.1.2), the hierarchical ordering of the church is the place where the Scriptures are rightly interpreted, according to Catholic understandings of religious authority, and the leadership of the bishops of Rome within the "college" of bishops is the grounds for claims of the papal exercise of infallibility (see 2.1.3 and 2.1.4).

2.4.4 *What the Roman Catholic Church teaches about orders of
ministry:* The Roman Catholic Church teaches that within this
hierarchy are bishops, priests, and deacons, as well as men and
women in religious orders, "permanent deacons," and laity, all of
whom have appropriate ministerial functions to carry on.

Sources: Vatican II, "Dogmatic Constitution on the Church," chaps. 3–4, 6 (in Leith, pp.
469–484; in Flannery, pp. 369–396, 402–407). *Catechism of the Catholic Church,*
871–945 (in American translation, pp. 231–246).

Comparative Cross-References: Eastern Orthodox, 1.4.2; Reformation and Union,
3.4.2.a–d; Evangelical and Free, 4.4.2.a–c; Ecumenical, 5.2.4.1.

To the outsider, the Catholic hierarchy seems an impenetrable maze of church titles and offices. Vatican II includes all Christians in the one category of "the people of God." But to aid in understanding the variety of Catholic offices, it is perhaps best to start out by clarifying the relationships between three basic groups: laity, clergy, and "religious." Laity and clergy are technically exclusive categories (that

---

110. Vatican I, "First Dogmatic Constitution on the Church of Christ," introduction and chaps. 1–3 (in Leith, pp. 448–454); Vatican II, "Dogmatic Constitution on the Church," chap. 3 (in Leith, pp. 469–480).

is, one cannot be both lay and clergy), so that if a man is ordained, then he is part of the clergy, and all other persons (nonordained) are part of the laity. "Religious," however, is a category that overlaps laity and clergy and denotes all persons who are members of religious orders. Typically this means taking specific vows (usually vows of poverty, chastity, and obedience), but some "religious" are ordained and others are not. Monks and nuns are "religious." Although women are not ordained to the Catholic clergy, they are admitted to religious orders.

With these basic distinctions between laity, clergy, and "religious" in mind, we now turn to the clergy. Within the ranks of the clergy there are three basic orders, and all other clerical titles are variations on these orders[111]: (1) The first major order is that of the *deacons* (from *diakonein*, "to serve"), originally those who assisted in the Eucharist, but the term was later applied to a wide variety of assistants in the church and also was used for those ordained as a preliminary step to become *priests*; (2) The second major order among the clergy is that of priests (from *presbuteros*, "elder"), a term that originally designated the elders of a particular congregation. Although only bishops celebrated Eucharist in the early church, priests have been the principal celebrants (or "presidents," that is, presiders) at Mass since the fourth century; and (3) The third major order is that of *bishops* (from *episkopos*, literally an "overseer"), which as early as the first decade of the second century A.D. designated the principal leader of the Christian congregation in a city.

With this distinction of three orders of clergy in mind, we may now note some further variations. Although most deacons are preparing for the priesthood, there are now *permanent deacons* who are committed to nonpriestly ministries in Catholic churches and agencies. The title *monsignor* usually designates one of the leading priests of a diocese, although in some countries it is also a title of respect for a bishop or archbishop. An *archbishop* ("ruling bishop") is the bishop of a large area (an archdiocese) under whom other bishops usually serve.

Historically, within each of the three orders of the clergy there were high-ranking members of their orders called *cardinals* (from the word for "hinge," so by extension, an important or "hinge" person). The office of "cardinal deacon" has fallen out of use, and it has become

---

111. There is strong evidence that in the Middle Ages, the three orders of ministry were reckoned to be those of subdeacons, deacons, and priests, with bishops considered priests with full powers and other priests considered to have limited powers. In the twentieth century, and especially with the teachings of Vatican II, the three orders have been clarified as those of deacons, priests, and bishops, following the ancient pattern enunciated by Ignatius of Antioch early in the second century.

customary since the 1960s that whenever a priest is made a cardinal, he is also consecrated as a bishop, so that at this time all cardinals are bishops or archbishops. Only a small percentage of Catholic bishops are cardinals. The cardinals are called together from time to time to serve as a council of advisers to the pope. When a pope dies, it is the "college of cardinals" that gathers together to elect a new pope.

Vatican II described the hierarchy of the church in such a way that all Catholics—including laity—are understood as having ministries appropriate to their vocations (vocation means "calling"). Bishops have responsibility for teaching, church administration, evangelization, and conferring the sacraments of confirmation and holy orders. Priests have responsibility for carrying on the life of the church in parishes, especially by administering the sacraments of the Mass, Baptism, penance, marriage, and the anointing of the sick. Deacons have a ministry of service, either as a temporary position in preparation for the priesthood or as a permanent office of service. Laypersons have their own responsibilities: according to Vatican II, they can be called "priests" in their own way. Their calling is to sanctify the secular world. Also, in cases of emergency, laypersons can administer the sacrament of Baptism.[112]

2.4.5 *What the Roman Catholic Church teaches about the nature of sacraments:* The Roman Catholic Church teaches that the sacraments are outward signs of invisible grace, instituted by Christ himself.

Sources: Council of Florence (in Leith, p. 61). Council of Trent, "Decree concerning the Sacraments," canons 5–7 (in Leith, p. 426). *Catechism of the Catholic Church,* 1113–1134 (in American translation, p. 289–293).

Comparative Cross-References: Eastern Orthodox, 1.4.4; Reformation and Union, 3.4.3; Evangelical and Free, 4.4.3.a–c; Ecumenical, 5.2.4.1.

The sacraments are central to the life of Roman Catholic Christians: in fact, Catholic life is punctuated by sacraments marking transition points in life (Baptism, confirmation, marriage or holy orders, anointing of the sick) and lived out in the interim by sacraments sustaining believers (the Eucharist and penance). Catholic sacraments correspond to what Eastern Orthodox prefer to call "mysteries," and the Council of Florence (fifteenth century) defined seven sacraments, which correspond to the seven "mysteries" celebrated by Orthodox Christians. This same council clarified that three elements are necessary for all the sacraments: first, a form of words; second, material things that are the "matter" of the sacrament (for example, water in baptism); and third, the in-

112. Vatican II, "Dogmatic Constitution on the Church," chap. 3 (in Leith, pp. 469–480).

tention to do what the church does in celebrating the sacrament.[113] The last point simply means that if a baptism (for example) is performed in a play, even if there is an appropriate form of words and the "matter" of water present, the act would still not qualify as a sacrament because the participants (actors, in this case) did not intend to do what the church does in baptism. Catholic teaching insists that all the sacraments were instituted by Christ. In the case of some sacraments Jesus gave a specific command that an action should be carried on by the disciples (this applies to Baptism and the Eucharist). In other cases the institution of the sacrament is derived from the church's following of Jesus' own acts (such as his ministry of healing, in the case of the anointing of the sick) or from Jesus' consistent teaching (such as his call to conversion or renewal in the case of penance).

Catholicism consistently teaches that the sacraments not only symbolize God's grace but actually convey grace.[114] But this raises a larger issue with the Catholic doctrine of sacraments, namely, the issue of what constitutes a valid sacrament. Can anything keep the sacraments from conveying grace? In ancient times Catholics rejected the notion that the validity of the sacrament depends on the uprightness or virtue of the minister performing it. The sacrament is the church's work on behalf of God, Catholics reason, and even if the person performing the sacrament is unworthy, the sacrament may nevertheless be worthy because of God's work in it. But there are conditions that can be "impediments" or hindrances to the grace offered in the sacraments. One such impediment would be the lack of intention to do what the church intends, as the previous paragraph notes. Another impediment is lack of faith (or rejection of Christian faith) in those receiving the sacraments. What this means is that although the sacraments are effective in conveying grace to infants and others who are incapable of mature faith, they will not be effective for those persons who are capable of faith and do not believe. So the Mass would not convey grace to a person who does not believe in Christ, even if all the other conditions for the sacrament (such as the intention on the part of the priest to do what the church does) were met.[115]

113. Council of Florence (in Leith, p. 61).
114. Council of Trent, "Decree concerning the Sacraments," canons 5–7 (in Leith, p. 426).
115. The Council of Florence stated that the sacraments "confer [grace] on those who receive them worthily" (in Leith, p. 60). Although this might imply that sacraments require (positively) some degree of faith or righteousness to be effective (which would be impossible for infants, for instance), the Council of Trent states this in terms that are more consistent with more recent Catholic tradition, i.e., the sacraments "confer that grace on those who place no obstacles in its way" ("Decree concerning the Sacraments," canon 6; in Leith, p. 426).

2.4.5.1 *What the Roman Catholic Church teaches about the sacrament of Baptism:* The Roman Catholic Church teaches that baptism effects "regeneration," or new birth in Christ, accompanied by the forgiveness of sins.

Sources: Fourth Lateran Council, canon 1 (in Leith, p. 58). Council of Florence (in Leith, p. 61). Council of Trent, "Decree concerning the Sacraments," canons concerning baptism (in Leith, pp. 427–429). *Catechism of the Catholic Church,* 1213–1284 (in American translation, pp. 312–325).

Comparative Cross-References: Eastern Orthodox, 1.4.5; Reformation and Union, 3.4.3.1; Evangelical and Free, 4.4.4.a–b; Ecumenical, 5.2.4.2.

The New Testament proclaims that God "saved us, not because of any works of righteousness that we had done, but according to his mercy, through the water of rebirth and renewal by the Holy Spirit" (Titus 3:5). Catholics understand baptism as the way appointed by Christ himself by which human beings enter the church and participate in the reign of God. Catholics, like Orthodox and many Protestants, associate baptism with the "new birth" in Christ and believe that baptism conveys forgiveness of all sins committed up to that point. For infants, this would mean forgiveness for the guilt inherited by original sin (see 2.3.1). For more mature candidates, it means forgiveness for the guilt of original sin and all sins committed up to that time.[116] Catholic baptisms are usually performed by parish priests, but Catholics have always held that in cases of emergency any person (laypersons, even non-Christians) can perform a valid baptism if they intend to do what the church does in baptism.

Although infant baptisms are statistically the norm for Catholics, recent reforms in Catholic practice present adult baptism in a way in which, at least theologically, infant baptism is seen as an exception. Part of these reforms has been the attempt to integrate mature believers into the faith with a more rigorous program of education and spiritual formation. The "Rite of Christian Initiation for Adults" (RCIA) admits candidates to baptism, confirmation, and Eucharist at the end of a yearlong process of training.

It follows from what has been said above that although baptism is performed only once, it remains a cornerstone event in Catholic life. When Catholics enter a church building, they typically place their fingers in a container of water and make a sign of the cross to remind themselves of their baptism. It reminds them that through Christ's

---

116. Fourth Lateran Council, canon 1 (in Leith, p. 58); Council of Florence (in Leith, p. 61); Council of Trent, "Decree concerning the Sacraments," canons concerning baptism (in Leith, pp. 427–429).

grace they have been forgiven, born again, and made part of the fellowship of the church.

2.4.5.2 *What the Roman Catholic Church teaches about the sacrament of confirmation:* The Roman Catholic Church teaches that confirmation confers the gift of the Holy Spirit.

Sources: Council of Florence (in Leith, p. 61). *Catechism of the Catholic Church,* 1285–1321 (in American translation, pp. 325–333).

Comparative Cross-References: Eastern Orthodox, 1.4.4; Reformation and Union, 3.4.3.

Confirmation is the Catholic equivalent of the Eastern Christian rite of chrismation. But whereas chrismation is an anointing accompanying Baptism, confirmation is usually separated from Baptism. This change between Eastern and Western Christian practices occurred (as many did) in the Carolingian period (eighth and ninth centuries A.D.), and it originally came about because churches in the Frankish kingdoms allowed priests to baptize but only allowed bishops to perform the anointing. Because it might take some time before the bishop was able to come for chrismation, the anointing was separated. Through a long process, the anointing was removed further and further from the time of baptism and became associated with the bishop's "confirming" the faith of candidates, hence the title "confirmation." From the time of the Catholic Reformation, Catholics have insisted on a period of training in the faith ("catechesis") as part of the process of preparation for confirmation.

Catholics understand the rite of confirmation on the basis of Acts 8:14–17:

> Now when the apostles at Jerusalem heard that Samaria had accepted the word of God, they sent Peter and John to them. The two went down and prayed for them that they might receive the Holy Spirit (for as yet the Spirit had not come upon any of them; they had only been baptized in the name of the Lord Jesus). Then Peter and John laid their hands on them, and they received the Holy Spirit.

The bishop administering confirmation prays for the coming of the Holy Spirit, as Peter and John did in this case. It has become customary among Catholics for children to receive First Communion when they are in primary school and to postpone confirmation until they are older than this, often in their early teen years. Confirmation is preceded by a process of catechesis.

It might be noted that although the Catholic pattern of baptism followed by catechesis and confirmation differs from Eastern Christian practice, the Catholic pattern prevailed in the Reformation, so that Lutheran, Anglican, and Reformed churches also practice catechesis and confirmation subsequent to baptism, and many Protestant churches do not admit children to communion until they have been confirmed. Evangelical Protestant churches, by contrast, have tended to stress a conversion experience rather than confirmation, although some Methodist churches have experimented with confirmation in this century. Of course, in the case of an adult convert to Catholicism, baptism and confirmation (and First Communion) come together, as in the Eastern pattern.

2.4.5.3 *What the Roman Catholic Church teaches about the sacrament of the Eucharist:* The Roman Catholic Church teaches that in the Eucharist there is a change or "transubstantiation" of bread and wine into the body and blood of Christ, and that the Eucharist repeats in an "unbloody" manner the sacrifice that Christ made on the cross.

Sources: Fourth Lateran Council, canon 1 (in Leith, p. 58). Council of Trent, "Decree concerning the Most Holy Sacrament of the Eucharist" (in Leith, pp. 429–437). Council of Trent, "Doctrine concerning the Sacrifice of the Mass," chaps. 1–2 (in Leith, pp. 437–439). *Catechism of the Catholic Church,* 1322–1419 (in American translation, pp. 334–356).

Comparative Cross-References: Eastern Orthodox, 1.4.6; Reformation and Union, 3.4.3.2.a–c; Evangelical and Free, 4.4.5.a–b; Ecumenical, 5.2.4.3.

The traditional Catholic term for the celebration of the Eucharist is "Mass," which comes from a Latin expression that was said at the very end of the eucharistic celebration, *Ite, missa est,* literally, "Go, it is the dismissal." This expression is now translated in the Catholic liturgy, "Go, the Mass is ended." The point here is that although the term "Mass" may strike Protestants and Orthodox as unusual, what is meant by it is the celebration of the Eucharist, the supper instituted by Christ himself.

Catholics believe, as Orthodox and many Protestants do, that Christ is truly present, and not just in a symbolic or merely spiritual way, when the Eucharist is celebrated. Since the Middle Ages, Catholics have held to a specific explanation of how Christ is present in the Eucharist, and this explanation centers around the term "transubstantiation." The notion of transubstantiation presupposes a distinction between the substance of a thing, what it is in itself, and its accidents or "appearances," how it appears externally. The doctrine of transubstantiation maintains that the substance of bread and wine are transformed in the Eucharist into the substance of the body and blood of Christ, although the "accidents" or appearances of bread and wine remain.[117]

Insofar as it expresses the literal, bodily presence of Christ in the Eucharist, this doctrine seems closely compatible with Orthodox understanding of the Eucharist, and Orthodox have sometimes utilized the expression "transubstantiation," although they feel that Orthodox faith does not require a specific explanation of Christ's presence in the Eucharist as the Latin church holds. The doctrine of transubstantiation has not been seen, historically, as one of the primary issues dividing Eastern Orthodox and Roman Catholics. The doctrine of transubstantiation also emphasizes, with many Reformation churches' understandings of the Eucharist, the reality of Christ's presence, although Protestants will usually say that bread and wine remain through the Eucharist, and Christ's body and blood are added to (or "under" or "with") them (see 3.4.3.2.a–b). A test of the doctrine of transubstantiation, then, is to ask whether bread and wine exist after the Eucharist is consecrated: the doctrine of transubstantiation maintains that they do not exist in "substance" because their substance has been replaced by the substance of Christ's body and blood. We might note, further, that in *The Catechism of the Catholic Church* (1992), transubstantiation is mentioned but overshadowed by a larger discussion of Christ's presence in the Eucharist.[118]

In addition to teaching the doctrine of transubstantiation, Catholics have taught consistently the doctrine that in the Eucharist, Christ's sacrifice on the cross is represented in an "unbloody" manner. This teaching relies on a fairly elaborate understanding of sacrifice inherited from the ancient world. According to this ancient understanding, sacrifice consists of an offering to God, the change or transformation of this offering (typically by burning), and a partaking (eating or drinking) of part of the offering. The notion of the "sacrifice of the Mass" (or "eucharistic sacrifice") is grounded in the belief that Christ's whole life and death was his offering to God, that his resurrection marked the transformation by which God the Father accepted his offering, and that the eucharistic meal represents the church's partaking of Christ's body that was offered up on our behalf. Because Catholics believe firmly in the reality of Christ's bodily presence in the Eucharist (see the preceding paragraphs), they teach that the Mass

117. Fourth Lateran Council, canon 1 (in Leith, p. 58); Council of Trent, "Decree concerning the Most Holy Sacrament of the Eucharist," chap. 4 (in Leith, p. 432).
118. *Catechism of the Catholic Church*, 1376 (quoting the Council of Trent; in American translation, p. 347).

represents the sacrifice. This sacrifice is one with Christ's offering on Calvary and indeed with God's eternal self-emptying, but it is a very specific re-presentation of Christ's sacrifice, so much so that it is appropriate to say that Christ is "re-sacrificed" in the eucharistic celebration.[119]

Having noted the meaning of transubstantiation and eucharistic sacrifice, we are now in a position to explain why Catholics see the Mass as a truly awesome event, an event that happens not only on earth but also in heaven. Catholics sometimes have the impression that when Protestants go to church, they just "talk about" religion. Catholics don't just talk about it, as they see it, they do it. When a Catholic approaches the altar during Mass, she believes she is approaching the very porch of heaven; she is coming face-to-face with none other than Jesus Christ.

2.4.5.4 *What the Roman Catholic Church teaches about the sacrament of penance and reconciliation:* The Roman Catholic Church teaches that the sacrament of penance and reconciliation offers forgiveness for particular sins committed after baptism.

Sources: Fourth Lateran Council, canon 1 (in Leith, p. 58). Council of Florence (in Leith, p. 61). *Catechism of the Catholic Church,* 1422–1498 (in American translation, pp. 357–374).

Comparative Cross-References: Eastern Orthodox, 1.4.4; Reformation and Union, 3.4.3.

"Therefore confess your sins to one another, and pray for one another, so that you may be healed" (James 5:16). In the early centuries of the Christian church, a believer could be excluded from the Eucharist if she committed a serious sin, that is, a sin that might bring public embarrassment on the congregation. In order to be restored, the sinner was required to make an open and public confession before the congregation. By the early Middle Ages the practice had evolved in the Western church that confessions could be made privately to a priest, and it is customary now for Catholics to make their confession in privacy and with the promise of the priest's confidentiality.

The Catholic's confession of sins is part of the sacrament of penance. The other part is the priest's proclamation or announcement of God's forgiveness and the restoration of the penitent man or woman to communion with the church—their reconciliation to the church. After the resurrection, Jesus said, "Receive the Holy Spirit. If you forgive

---

119. Council of Trent, "Doctrine concerning the Sacrifice of the Mass," chaps. 1–2 (in Leith, pp. 437–439).

the sins of any, they are forgiven them; if you retain the sins of any, they are retained" (John 20:22c–23). Catholics understand this passage to mean that the church, represented by the priest, has the authority to pronounce God's forgiveness in the cases of particular sins. Grounded in these understandings, the sacrament of penance, for Catholics, is a way in which a believer can confess and receive Christ's forgiveness through the church. Like other sacraments, the grace offered in penance can be impeded, or blocked, by some obstacles. One of these, in the Catholic understanding, is a lack of sincerity on the part of penitents, that is, those seeking forgiveness. The priest hearing a Catholic's confession and giving absolution must be convinced that the penitent is sincere. In addition, the priest will often assign a penance, which is a particular work to be performed. If the person's sin is that they have stolen something, for example, they must promise to return what they have stolen (or its equivalent). If their sin is that they have said something false, they may be asked to retract what they have said, at least to the parties involved. But in cases where no retribution can be made, the penitent may be asked simply to recite a set of prayers (the Lord's Prayer, or perhaps the "Hail Mary").[120]

In the way Catholics understand this sacrament, the priest's absolution (his pronouncement of forgiveness) is granted not on the basis of the person's actually doing these good works or penances but on the basis of God's offer of reconciling grace and the person's intention, the sincerity of their repentance. That is, if a person has stolen something and confesses this, the priest may pronounce absolution when he is convinced that the person is truly sorry and has resolved to return what was stolen. In this sense the Catholics insist the penitential system is not a form of "works righteousness": it is grounded in Christ's work and is (as they see it) a way of applying Christ's work in a specific instance. They point out that Martin Luther himself did not really oppose the notion of penance, but rather opposed abuses of the sacrament. In fact, some Lutheran churches retained penance after the Reformation (see 3.4.3).

2.4.5.5 *What the Roman Catholic Church teaches about the sacrament of the anointing of the sick:* The Roman Catholic Church teaches that the anointing of the sick represents the church's prayers for healing in serious illness.

Sources: Council of Florence (in Leith, p. 61). Paul VI, "Apostolic Constitution on the Sacrament of the Anointing of the Sick" (in *Acta Apostolicae Sedis* 65:1 [January 30,

120. Fourth Lateran Council, canon 1 (in Leith, p. 58); Council of Florence (in Leith, p. 61).

1973]: 5–9). *Catechism of the Catholic Church,* 1499–1532 (in American translation, pp. 375–382).

Comparative Cross-References: Eastern Orthodox, 1.4.4; Reformation and Union, 3.4.3.

"Are any among you sick? They should call for the elders of the church and have them pray over them, anointing them with oil in the name of the Lord" (James 5:14). The sacrament of the "anointing of the sick" does what this passage in James prescribes. The word for elders (*presbuteroi*) is the word from which "priest" is derived, so Catholic priests act as the elders of the church in anointing those who are seriously ill and praying for their healing.

Up until 1973 this sacrament was usually called "last rites" (informally) or "extreme unction" (formally; "extreme" means "last," and "unction" means "anointing"). The sacrament was usually administered only when it was believed that a person was very near death, and the sacrament was associated not only with prayers for healing but as a preparation for death and the life of the world to come.[121] In 1973, as part of the ongoing reforms in Catholic liturgical life started by Vatican II, the sacrament was redefined as "anointing of the sick," and it is now performed more frequently, in fact, in any case of serious illness.[122] In this revised version, the Catholic rite has become much more similar to the Orthodox practice (and understanding) of the anointing of the sick. Many Protestant churches also have begun to experiment in the last thirty years with rituals of prayer and anointing for sick persons.

2.4.5.6 *What the Roman Catholic Church teaches about the sacrament of marriage:* The Roman Catholic Church teaches that in the sacrament of marriage, men and women are joined together to form a family in ministry to the world.

Sources: Council of Florence (in Leith, p. 61). Vatican II, "Dogmatic Constitution on the Church," 4 (in Leith, pp. 481–484; in Flannery, pp. 388–396). *Catechism of the Catholic Church,* 1601–1666 (in American translation, pp. 400–415).

Comparative Cross-References: Eastern Orthodox, 1.4.4; Reformation and Union, 3.4.3.

In the earliest centuries, Christian churches did not perform marriages; marriage was a civil ceremony and the churches (East and

121. The Council of Florence uses the term "extreme unction" (in Leith, p. 61) and associates the sacrament with physical as well as spiritual healing.
122. Paul VI, "Apostolic Constitution on the Sacrament of the Anointing of the Sick," *Acta Apostolicae Sedis* 65, no. 1 (January 30, 1973): 5–9.

West) recognized the validity of civil ceremonies. By the early Middle Ages, the church had begun to witness marriages, taking over much of the Roman civil practices of marriage except that Christians insisted on the "indissolubility" of marriage, that is, Christians did not allow for divorce, whereas Roman law had allowed it. By the ninth century A.D. some theologians considered marriage to be a sacrament, and the Council of Florence (fifteenth century A.D.) listed marriage as one of the seven sacraments.[123] Catholic teachings hold that the priest does not actually perform the sacrament of marriage; the couple who are married are themselves the ministers of the sacrament, to which the priest is an authorized witness. This contrasts with the Orthodox position, in which the priest is the minister of the sacrament and second marriages are possible, although these differences have not been seen historically as church-dividing issues between Catholics and Orthodox.

Catholic views of marriage are closely tied to Catholic understandings of the ministries of men and women in common or ordinary life, that is, life outside of ordination or religious orders. Although medieval and early modern Catholic teaching often spoke of marriage as a "lower" way of serving God than celibacy and religious orders, Vatican II and subsequent Catholic teachings have described marriage and family life as a unique vocation through which God works to sanctify the secular world, and they even speak of the "priesthood" of laypersons:

> Though they differ from one another in essence and not only degree, the common priesthood of the faithful and ministerial or hierarchical priesthood are nonetheless inter-related. Each of them in its own special way is a participation in the one priesthood of Christ.[124]

Though it would be mistaken to take this as an indication of the equality of lay and clerical ministries, it marks an important step toward a broader appreciation of Catholic understandings of ministry.

A central part of the vocation of the family, in Catholic teaching, is the procreation of children. Although it is beyond the scope of this book to deal with the social and moral teachings of the churches, we can note here that Catholic opposition to abortion and artificial birth control is grounded in the Catholic understanding of the sacredness of human life along with its understanding of marriage as a sacrament

123. Council of Florence (in Leith, p. 61).
124. Vatican II, "Dogmatic Constitution on the Church," 2:10 (in Leith, pp. 462–463).

and the importance of the bearing of children in the vocation of the Christian family.

2.4.5.7 *What the Roman Catholic Church teaches about the sacrament of holy orders:* The Roman Catholic Church teaches that in the sacrament of holy orders men are given grace for the particular ministries of deacons, priests, and bishops.

Sources: Council of Florence (in Leith, p. 61). *Catechism of the Catholic Church,* 1536–1600 (in American translation, pp. 383–399).

Comparative Cross-References: Eastern Orthodox, 1.4.4; Reformation and Union, 3.4.3.

In our consideration of the hierarchical nature of the church (see 2.4.3 and 2.4.4) we have distinguished clergy as those who are ordained as deacons, priests, and bishops, and we have noted that there are many further distinctions made by Catholics within these three basic forms of ordained ministry. Catholics consider ordination to be a sacrament and believe that it conveys divine grace for these ministries.[125] As mentioned above, women are not admitted to ordination, and traditionally only celibate men were admitted in the Latin Church. There has been some movement on this last point, however. With the reestablishment of the office of permanent deacons, it has become permissible for married men to be ordained to this office. Moreover, Catholics have recently allowed some Anglican priests (and some of them married) to become Catholic priests, and so there are a very small number of married Catholic priests, though celibacy is still by far the norm in the Latin Church. (Married priests are also allowed in Eastern-Rite Catholic churches.)

In the case of ordination, as well as baptism and confirmation, Catholics teach that the sacrament conveys an "indelible" (unerasable) character, and that for this reason these sacraments cannot be repeated, that is, once one is baptized, one may need to be restored to the church's communion (through the sacrament of penance), but one cannot be rebaptized, or reconfirmed, or reordained.[126]

---

125. Ordination is stated clearly as a sacrament by the Council of Florence (in Leith, p. 61).
126. Ibid.

Interlude 2 A
Old Catholics and Other Separated Catholic Churches

There are a few "Catholic" bodies in the world that have formally separated from Roman Catholicism. The "Old Catholics" include a few Catholic Churches in Belgium and the Netherlands that separated in the early 1700s over their support of "Jansenism," a movement that stressed a strongly Augustinian theology and maintained that the grace offered in the sacraments was conditioned upon the interior affections of recipients. In the late 1800s, after Vatican I and its definition of papal primacy and infallibility, a number of more progressive Catholic priests and laypersons became separate. In 1889 they entered into communion with the Jansenist churches, affirming the seven Ecumenical Councils but not papal supremacy over the church. In 1925 the Old Catholics recognized the validity of Anglican ordinations, and from 1932 they have been in full communion with Anglicans throughout the world.

If the Old Catholics represent the "left" of the Catholic world, there have emerged since the 1970s some separated Catholic churches on the "right." After the reforms of Vatican II, many traditional Catholics felt that the Catholic Church had abandoned traditional Catholicism, especially the Catholicism defined at the Council of Trent. Many priests and some bishops continued to celebrate Mass according to the Tridentine liturgy (and in Latin). In June of 1990 Swiss Archbishop Marcel Lefevre performed illicit (according to Catholic church law) ordinations of bishops who subscribed to strictly Tridentine views of the church and its sacraments. In the act of performing these episcopal ordinations he "excommunicated himself" (in the eyes of Roman Catholics), and so the churches allied around his call for a revival of Tridentine Catholicism became separate.

We should note that at some points in Catholic history there have been schisms occasioned more by culture and ethnicity than by particular theological beliefs or liturgical practices. Polish Catholics in the United States formed a separate Polish Catholic Church early in the twentieth century. In the late 1980s a number of African-American Catholics in Washington, D.C. became separate over their insistence on a distinctly African-American expression of Catholicism.

3

Teachings of Reformation
and Union Churches

3.0   Historical Background to Reformation
and Union Churches

Chapter 3 of this book considers the teachings of three traditions
that originated in the established churches of newly emerging nation
states of Western Europe in the 1500s. These are the Lutheran, Reformed, and Anglican traditions. As a result of the Reformation movement, the unity of the Christian church in Western Europe was frag-
mented. In the aftermath, the dominant churches in the nations of
Western Europe took on the character of national churches (whether
Protestant or Catholic), with the governing authorities of each nation
determining which tradition would be "established" as the religion of
the nation. While the constitutional ties of particular churches to national governments have been attenuated or severed since that time,
the traditions considered in chapter 3 nevertheless originated in "established" churches, and their character as European state-supported
churches during the Reformation distinguishes them from the Anabaptists of that era and from later "Evangelical" and "Free" Protestant churches (churches that have historically stressed a personal experience of conversion and a voluntary church). We might note that
the distinction between "Established" and "Free" churches looms
large in the sensitivities of European Christians, but not so much in
the understandings of Christians in the United States and wherever
there has been little experience of establishments of Christianity. Both
the criteria of (1) a personal experience of conversion (distinguishing
"Evangelical" Christian communities from "Classical" Protestant
churches) and (2) the stress on a voluntary church (distinguishing

"Free" churches from "Established" churches) figure in the distinctions between the communities considered in chapters 3 and 4 of this book.

In addition to considering the historic Reformation churches, chapter 3 also considers the teachings of churches that have come into existence by the union of two or more of these three Reformation traditions in particular countries. Although the "Union" churches do not share the established character of the older Reformation churches, they grew from the union of Reformation traditions (and in some cases other traditions). In some cases they were established European churches; an example of this would be the Union Church of Prussia, which combined Lutheran and Reformed traditions. In more recent cases Union or United churches have been associated with particular political states or regions even if not "established" by political states. Examples of these would be The United Church of Canada, the Church of South India, the Church of North India, and the Uniting Church of Australia. It is estimated that combined membership of Reformation and Union churches today amounts to around 250 million persons.[127]

We should note at the beginning some different terms that may be used to describe churches in the Reformation traditions. Most Lutheran churches are identified by the name "Lutheran" in English, though in German and other languages the term "Evangelical" (*evangelisch*) or its equivalents may be utilized. "Evangelical" in this sense basically denotes "Protestant" as opposed to "Roman Catholic," but the term is significantly different from the "Evangelical" Protestant churches described in chapter 4. "Reformed" churches include Presbyterian and Congregationalist churches as well as those that bear the name "Reformed." "Anglican" churches include churches identified in Scotland and in the United States as "Episcopal."

These church traditions are represented today by a number of particular denominations and by international organizations that relate their many denominations together. The Lutheran World Federation and the World Alliance of Reformed Churches are representative bodies that attempt to promote common interests and sometimes speak ecumenically on behalf of their member denominations. The Lambeth Conference of Bishops is somewhat different, being an assembly of Anglican bishops from the whole world, but the Lambeth Conference

---

127. See table 4 below and the footnote accompanying it. Total membership in these bodies for 1985 was estimated at 231 million; given the significant growth that Christian churches have experienced since that time, it seems to me that 250 million is a workable rough estimate of the memberships of these three traditions and "Union" churches.

has established a continuing body, the Anglican Consultative Council, that functions along with the bishops to define common interests on behalf of global Anglicanism. Anglicans also refer to the churches that recognize communion with one another as the "Anglican Communion," of which both the Lambeth Conference and the Anglican Consultative Council are deliberative and advisory bodies. These organizations and their current estimated memberships, along with membership figures for Union churches, are shown in table 4.

The identification of three traditions as "Reformation Churches" has been made for analytical purposes in this book. In reality, it is impossible to make a definitive distinction between "Reformation" and "Free Church" or "Evangelical" Protestant groups because there are so many points of overlap between them. We have distinguished "Reformation" churches as embracing the three traditions that (1) have historically stressed the grace of new birth in Christ given in the sacrament of Baptism (as contrasted with churches that have stressed a personal experience of conversion) and that also (2) grew from state-supported churches in the 1500s (in contrast to "Free," that is, non-established and voluntary churches). But readers should be aware of some consistently problematic points with the identification of "Reformation" churches as a coherent group.

One admittedly problematic point has to do with the identity of Anglican churches as "Reformation" churches. We have preferred to use the term "Reformation" rather than "Protestant" in chapter 3

Table 4. Global Organizations Representing Reformation and Union Churches, and their Estimated Memberships in 1985*

Tradition	Organization	Estimated Membership (million)
Lutheran	Lutheran World Federation	75
Reformed	World Alliance of Reformed Churches	40
Anglican	Anglican Communion (Lambeth Conference of Bishops/Anglican Consultative Council)	50
Union	(Including ecumenical United or "Uniting" churches)	66
TOTAL		231

*Note: Membership statistics for 1985 as given in Barrett, ed., *World Christian Encyclopedia*, pp. 792–794. The figure for Anglicans is for member churches of the Anglican Consultative Council. The figure for the Lutheran World Federation includes full members (39 million) and permanent observers (36 million). Each of these traditions would have grown in the period since 1985. A further problem is that some United churches participate in tradition-specific federations (for example, The United Church of Canada participates in the World Alliance of Reformed Churches); it is not clear how much this overlap would affect the total figures in this table.

partly because many Anglicans react strongly against the title "Protestant." The largest Anglican body in the United States has recently undergone a process of definition over its traditional name, the "Protestant Episcopal Church," and now allows the use of the name "The Episcopal Church" without the controversial adjective "Protestant." Those Episcopalians who identify strongly with the Catholic inheritance of Anglicanism (sometimes identified as "Anglo-Catholics") object to being identified as "Protestants" at all. Anglicanism, as they see it, is an expression of catholic (not necessarily Roman Catholic) faith. The Prayer Book, the maintenance of an unbroken succession of bishops from the time of the apostles, traditional stress on the reality of Christ's presence in eucharistic celebration: all these suggest to them that Anglicanism should be distinguished from other churches that emerged at the time of the Reformation.

While acknowledging this consistent problem with Anglican identity, we have included them with Reformation churches for a number of reasons. First, the Church of England did emerge during the time of the Reformation in parallel with the rise of Continental Protestant churches. Through the end of the 1500s there could be little question of Anglicanism's identification as a Protestant body, and after 1600, Anglicans, even "high churchmen," identified themselves as "Protestant" in the simple sense of being "non-Roman Catholic." There remains, moreover, a considerable nucleus of Anglicans who still understand themselves to be "Protestant." Second, with respect to the particular topic of this book, formal church doctrine, the Thirty-nine Articles of Religion and the Homilies of the Church of England strike an unquestionably Protestant tone, however much Anglo-Catholics may argue that they are capable of Catholic interpretation. There are indeed a number of points about Anglicanism that distinguish it from Lutheran and Reformed traditions, and many of these will be noted in the text following. Perhaps one of the most distinctive points is Anglicanism's latitude in doctrinal issues, which has itself enabled expressions of Anglicanism that are quite Catholic, on the one hand, and other expressions of Anglicanism that are unquestionably Evangelical, on the other.

There are other contestable points about the grouping made in chapters 3 and 4 of *Christian Confessions*. Anabaptist churches originated in the 1500s, at the same time as other Reformation traditions, although they were never state-supported and have always insisted on a solely voluntary church. We have found it more congruous to consider them among Free Churches in chapter 4. Methodist and Moravian Churches bear considerable similarities to Presbyterian and

Anglican and Lutheran churches, and many Methodists and Moravians would prefer to be considered in the company of these Reformation traditions instead of in chapter 4. But Methodist and Moravian Churches have historically stressed a personal moment of conversion (sometimes also holding to the grace of regeneration, or new birth, given in baptism), they have always functioned as Free churches and have followed the Free-church model of a voluntary religious communion. For these reasons we shall consider them as representing more ecclesial and sacramental expressions of the Evangelical and Free churches considered in chapter 4.

3.0.1 Forerunners of the Reformation

We turn then to consider the historical origins of Reformation and Union churches, and we must begin by noting some of their medieval precursors. The churches of the Reformation came into existence in the 1500s, but there were medieval movements that foreshadowed some of their characteristic emphases. In the account of Catholic history in chapter 2 (see 2.0), we noted a number of reform movements in the Middle Ages, such as new monastic orders, reforms brought about by papal authority, and reforms brought about by councils of bishops. In addition to these were movements that questioned the very basis of medieval Catholicism. In the 1100s, a religious movement emerged in southern France and northern Italy led by Peter Waldo. He and his followers, the "Waldensians," preached itinerantly, translated the Scriptures into vernacular languages, and called for deep reforms in the church's life. Excommunicated and persecuted for centuries, the Waldensians persisted through the time of the Reformation and are united today with Methodists in Italy.

The movement associated with John Wycliffe (ca. 1330–1384) in England also stressed vernacular translation of the Scriptures and itinerant preaching against the corruptions of the church. Wycliffe, an Oxford philosopher, questioned a whole range of medieval religious institutions, including the celibacy of the clergy, the monastic life itself, the authority of the popes, and the doctrine of transubstantiation. Wycliffe argued that the Bible should be the sole criterion of religious authority and that the only true church is the "invisible" church of God's elect. Wycliffe's followers, known as "Lollards," persisted in England up until the time of the Reformation when they joined ranks with leaders supporting Protestantism.

Wycliffe's teachings were transmitted to Bohemia and his books were read by a popular professor and preacher in Prague, John Huss (ca. 1372–1415). Huss shared Wycliffe's sentiments about the authority of scripture and gained support from students and fellow faculty at the University of Prague. He was excommunicated for his beliefs in 1411. Offered safe passage to the Council of Basle in 1415, he was apprehended and burned at the stake. The same council also ordered that Wycliffe's body should be exhumed and burned. Although some of Huss's followers remained in communion with Catholics, who at first gave permission for some of the suggested reforms, some Hussites became independent after the reforms were withdrawn, and they would eventually form the basis of the Bohemian Brethren. These, after centuries of persecution and exile, became the "Ancient Unity" of Moravian Brethren (see 4.0.4).

3.0.2   The Lutheran Reformation

The movements associated with Peter Waldo, John Wycliffe, and John Huss remained rather small and none won lasting support from political states, although Wycliffe and Huss had argued that civil governments ought to be able to reform the church. By the time of Martin Luther the political situation in Europe had changed significantly, so that a number of states and imperial cities in the northern, German-speaking regions of the Holy Roman Empire were actively seeking greater freedom from the combination of Roman supremacy in the Catholic Church and the closely allied political power of the Hapsburg family of Spain and Austria.

Martin Luther (1483–1546) was a leader of the Augustinian order, vicar over eleven monasteries and professor of Holy Scripture at Wittenberg University. Sometime between 1512 and 1515[128] Luther became convinced that when the letters of Paul speak of the "righteousness of God" they do not mean the "active" righteousness by which God is just and requires justice of us. Rather, he discovered, this expression denotes the "passive" righteousness by which God justifies sinners (accepts them as forgiven) on the basis of faith only, not on the basis of any human works or human merit or human righteousness. This discovery about God's role in salvation seems to have led Luther to a chain of questions about accepted teachings: about the church's role as the mediator of salvation, about the necessity of priests as mediators between God and human beings, and about current abuses of

---

128. The precise date is disputed, especially because of a discrepancy in Luther's own accounts: the preface to his *Latin Writings* seems to place this event after his issuing the "Ninety-five Theses" in 1517, but other accounts place his change of mind about the nature of "the righteousness of God" earlier than the Ninety-five Theses; I have followed the latter version.

the practice of confession and the sacrament of penance. To protest the abuse of penance, he issued in 1517 a series of ninety-five Latin propositions or "theses" disputing rather fine points about the practice of penance. His arguments provoked debates, at first within his order, and many became convinced by his arguments.

From 1519 to 1520, Luther's views became more strident and more publicly known at the same time. In public disputations he questioned the teaching authority of popes and of Ecumenical Councils. He issued public works encouraging secular princes to undertake the work of reforming the church in their regions, and he attacked the doctrines of transubstantiation and of the sacrifice of the Mass. Excommunicated in 1521, he was threatened with the fate of John Huss, and he was forced into hiding for a period. In the later 1520s, though, more and more political leaders, states, and imperial cities took up Luther's views. Churches in these states began to allow the marriage of priests, to encourage monks to leave monasteries, and to abolish fast-days, private confession, and private masses.

By 1526 Luther's movement had attracted the attention of the Holy Roman Empire, and an imperial council held in that year (in the emperor's absence) decreed that each state or imperial city should decide on its own form of religious life. But the Emperor Charles V, himself supporting moderate religious reforms, would not accept this degree of liberty within the empire, and he called a second council in 1529 that he attended personally. This council decreed against the Reformers and insisted on fidelity to Catholic faith. Those leaders who "protested" this council were referred to as *Protestantes,* the immediate root of the term "Protestant." The imperial council met again in the city of Augsburg the next summer, where the Protestants, led by Philipp Melanchthon, submitted a confession of faith that would eventually serve as the most universally accepted of Lutheran doctrinal statements, the Augsburg Confession (1530).

Martin Luther's remaining years were spent in the work of reformation in the German states. He himself offered further doctrinal statements (the Schmalkaldic Articles) and catechisms for teaching the faith. But significant doctrinal disputes divided the churches identified with Luther, and these disputes persisted beyond his death in 1546. After three decades of struggles over the role of the moral law in the life of Christians (see 3.3.5), over the doctrine of predestination (see 3.3.3.b), over the nature of Christ's atoning work, and over Christ's presence in the Eucharist (see 3.4.3.2.a), Lutherans finally agreed on a "Formula of Concord." This was incorporated, along with the Augsburg Confession, Luther's catechisms, and other documents into the *Book of Concord* (1580), which was accepted by most Lutheran churches. It might be noted, however, that not all Lutheran churches have accepted the entire *Book of Concord*. The Augsburg Confession and possibly the "Small Catechism" remain the only universally accepted doctrinal statements in Lutheran churches. The Lutheran confessions and other doctrinal statements included in the *Book of Concord* are listed in table 5.

We should note, further, that Lutheranism spread from the German states and cities of the Holy Roman Empire to Denmark and Sweden within Luther's lifetime. Eventually the movement would result in the establishment of churches throughout Scandinavia and the Baltic, with less influential churches in Silesia, Hungary, and elsewhere in central and eastern Europe.

3.0.3 Zwingli, Calvin, and the Reformed Tradition

The Reformed tradition emerged at almost exactly the same time as Lutheranism, and its first representative, Ulrich Zwingli, may not have known of Luther's work until his own reforming work was underway. Zwingli (1484–1531) had been trained in the traditions of Renaissance Humanism, with its stress on the discovery of ancient Latin and Greek literature and philosophy. This interest, for Zwingli and for Catholic reformers such as Desiderius Erasmus, seems to have led naturally to a rediscovery of ancient Christian literature and to the rediscovery of the New Testament in Greek, first published by Erasmus in 1516. Zwingli had come to preach at the Great Minster in Zurich in 1518 and in the next year launched a series of sermons interpreting New Testament books in serial order, urging reforms based on New Testament teachings. Zwingli encouraged civic leaders to abolish the invocation of saints and monastic houses; urged them to reject the doctrines of purgatory, papal authority, transubstantiation, and the sacrifice of the Mass; attacked the practices of clerical celibacy and

Table 5. Principal Lutheran Confessional Documents
Included in the *Book of Concord*

Confessional Document	Date
Luther's Small Catechism	1529
Luther's Large Catechism	1529
Augsburg Confession	1530
Apology of the Augsburg Confession	1531
Schmalkaldic Articles	1537
Treatise on Power and Primacy of the Pope	1537
The Formula of Concord	1577

fast-days; and eventually prevailed on the city council in Zurich, who adopted his reforms. In his later years he was called on to assist the work of Reformation in other Swiss cities, and attempted to build alliances with other Reformation leaders. On one occasion in 1529, the Colloquy of Marburg, he actually met with Luther and other German Reformation leaders, but although there was substantial agreement between them in some areas, they failed to reach agreement on the question of how Christ is present in the Eucharist. This remained a divisive issue for Protestant churches (see 3.4.3.2.a–c).

Zwingli had been a contemporary of Martin Luther. The next and best known figure in the Reformed tradition, John Calvin (1509–1564), represented a new generation of Protestant reformers, and he took up the work of Reformation in Switzerland a few years after Zwingli's death. Calvin had studied law at Orleans and then he studied theology at the University of Paris; in fact, his time as a student there may have overlapped Ignatius Loyola's years at the same university by a few months. Although his earlier years were given to classical studies, by the early 1530s Calvin felt a calling to aid the work of reform in the churches, inspired by his study of the New Testament. Persecuted by authorities in Paris, Calvin fled at first to Basle in Switzerland, where he hoped to live a quiet life as a scholar. At this time he produced a first edition of his systematic exposition of Christian teaching, the *Institutes of the Christian Religion*, first published in 1536. Later in the same year the reformer of Geneva, William Farel, demanded that Calvin should join his work there. After some initial success in their work of reformation, the city council turned against Farel and Calvin, and in 1538 the two were forced to flee.

Calvin spent the next three years in Strasbourg, where he supported the reform efforts of Martin Bucer. Bucer had been one of Luther's original supporters in the Augustinian order, and he had been one of the most internationally known of the early reformers. With Bucer's counsel, Calvin produced a new edition of the *Institutes of the Christian Religion*. Finally, in 1541, the city council of Geneva welcomed Calvin back to the city, where he spent the remainder of his life.

After a long period of continuing resistance, Calvin's supporters eventually controlled the council, and from about 1555 the city of Geneva under his stern and impassioned leadership became a model for religious and civil reform known throughout Europe. The church was thoroughly reorganized, with a governing consistory composed of lay and clergy leadership. Trials were instituted to prosecute those who offended church law (such as failure to attend worship services).

Educational systems were devised, the University of Geneva was established, hospitals to care for the poor were built, and even sanitation systems were reformed. Geneva attracted Christian leaders from many European states, including exiles from Britain during the reign of Queen Mary (see the next subsection).

The churches that looked to the reforms of Zwingli and especially Calvin as their inspiration have been described traditionally as "Reformed," though sometimes the adjective "Calvinist" is applied to this broad group of churches. Reformed churches were established in many of the cities and cantons of Switzerland, in some areas of France (where they came to be known as "Huguenots"), in Holland, in some of the northern areas of Germany, in some areas of Hungary and Poland, in Scotland (under the leadership of John Knox) and in England. The narrative of the Reformed churches in the British Isles is tied to the story of the English Reformation, whose particular development we shall consider in the next subsection. At this point we should note that "Swiss Reformed," "Dutch Reformed," "Huguenots," and "German Reformed" describe particular national varieties of the Reformed tradition, along with Scots, Irish, and English Presbyterians and Congregationalists.

Although the Reformed tradition does not have an equivalent of the Lutheran *Book of Concord*, there are a number of confessions and catechisms that express a consensus of Reformed belief. Some of the more prominent Reformed doctrinal statements are listed in table 6. Of these the Heidelberg Catechism and the Westminster Confession and Catechisms are the most widely used, though the Westminster documents date from a somewhat later period, the 1640s in Britain.

3.0.4   The English Reformation and the Anglican Tradition

The narrative of the Reformation in the British Isles shows a pattern very different from the narratives of Lutheran and Reformed origins. The Reformation in Britain proceeded by a series of abrupt reversals

Table 6. Principal Reformed Confessional Documents

Confessional Document	Date	Reformed Body Represented
First Helvetic Confession	1536	Swiss Reformed
Scottish Confession	1560	Scottish Presbyterians
Heidelberg Catechism	1562	German Reformed
Second Helvetic Confession	1566	Swiss Reformed
Articles of Synod of Dort	1619	Dutch Reformed (and others)
Westminster Confession	1647	British Presbyterians
Westminster Catechisms	1648	British Presbyterians

in religious policy that were tied closely to the sentiments of the reigning monarchs, a colorful lot indeed: Henry VIII, and then three children by three of his six wives, Edward VI (son of Jane Seymour), Mary Tudor (daughter of Catherine of Aragon), and Elizabeth I (daughter of Anne Boleyn).

Under Henry VIII (r. 1509–1547), the church in England became legally separate from Roman Catholicism, though it retained a moderate but predominantly Catholic theology and liturgy. Frustrated with the pope's refusal to grant an annulment of his marriage to Catherine of Aragon, Henry secured a series of parliamentary acts in the 1530s that successively disentangled English churches from all papal ties and ties to any foreign religious authority and redirected church taxes to the British crown. By the end of his reign the church in his kingdom could be described as "English Catholic" or "nonpapal Catholic" because it was independent but had not adopted much of Protestant doctrine or of typically Protestant liturgical practices.

Under Henry's son Edward VI (r. 1547–1553), the English church became more thoroughly identified with the Reformed tradition. Though Edward himself was too young to take an active role in the religious controversies, his regents favored a more consistent reform of the English church. New prayer books were issued, in English, and a series of Articles of Religion were drawn up reflecting Reformed doctrine.

The premature death of Edward VI led to the reign of Mary Tudor (r. 1553–1558). Mary was the daughter of Henry's first wife, Catherine of Aragon. Closely related to the Hapsburg family and so allied to the Holy Roman Empire and the papacy, Mary's religious policy was to return the entire nation to Roman Catholicism. Many Protestant leaders, including the archbishop of Canterbury, Thomas Cranmer, were publicly executed. Many who favored Reformed doctrine and liturgy fled to the European continent, and some ended up in Calvin's Geneva.

Mary's brief reign was followed by the lengthy rule of her half-sister Elizabeth I (r. 1558–1603), daughter of Henry's second (and Protestant) wife, Anne Boleyn. Elizabeth and her chosen religious leaders rejected the extremes they perceived in Calvinism on the one hand and Roman Catholicism on the other. The compromise reached during her reign was more complex, involving a prayer book that retained more of Catholic liturgical traditions than other Protestant churches had retained, balanced by Thirty-nine Articles of Religion that were more Calvinistic than Elizabeth herself would have preferred. The Church of England established during her reign did indeed hold to a *via media*, a "middle of the road," between historic Catholicism and Reformed faith, but it was a settlement held together in the person of Elizabeth, and even during her lifetime divisions in the church appeared.

Those favoring a national church "purified" according to Reformed patterns came to be known as Puritans. During Elizabeth's reign the Puritans pressed at first for liturgical simplification, then eventually for changes in church government, with bishops being consistent objects of their disapproval. By Elizabeth's death in 1603, the Puritans were prepared to press a long list of reforms, and had hopes that her successor James I would implement them, since he had grown up as a Scottish Presbyterian. But the Puritans' hopes were dashed by James's support for the Anglican party, setting up nine further decades of political, social, cultural, and religious struggles in Britain.

Those who did not share the Puritans' attempts to remake the English church on the model of Geneva are referred to in retrospect as "Anglicans," although the term is confusing because up until 1662 Puritans were technically "Anglican" in the sense that they understood themselves to be part of the established church. The "Anglican" party (now using the term to denote non-Puritans) developed their own literature in the Elizabethan period in the works of such theologians as John Jewel of Salisbury and Richard Hooker, whose *Laws of Ecclesiastical Polity* laid out a basic apology for Anglicanism as preserving the best of Catholic and Reformation traditions.

3.0.5 Reformation Churches in the Early Modern Period

The idea of religious toleration was largely unaccepted at the beginning of the 1600s, and each European state had an "established" (state-supported) form of Christianity. The seventeenth century on the European continent and in the British Isles witnessed the spectacle of Christians going to war against Christians, and in this Christian warfare, differences in church doctrine and church practices were often seen as basic causes. The Thirty Years' War (1618–1648) on the European continent pitted Protestant cities and states in northern Europe against Catholic states in the south. Very little was accomplished by the war, except that some areas of northern Germany officially adopted Reformed faith. Similarly, the English Revolution (1640–1660) pitted Puritans against Anglicans, both struggling to define the form of Christianity that was to be adopted in the national church.

This period of inter-Christian warfare had important cultural side-effects within the Reformation churches. One effect was to encourage the careful definition of church doctrine, to make clear what it was that was contested on the battlefield. Lutheran and Reformed theologians developed a Protestant "scholastic" tradition, carefully defining and defending their churches against other denominations. Although Anglicanism did not develop a body of scholastic theology, Anglican writers of the 1600s explored early Christian texts in Greek and Latin, attempting to show that Anglicanism had faithfully followed the church of the first four or five centuries after Christ.

A second effect of the inter-Christian wars of the 1600s was a serious questioning of knowledge grounded in tradition (and scripture). It was during the first year of the Thirty Years' War that René Descartes began his philosophical quest to find in mathematical logic a surer basis for human knowledge. It was only a decade before him that Francis Bacon had laid plans for a reformation of human learning based on scientific observation rather than tradition. Although at first these challenges to tradition-based knowledge did not have a direct effect on Christian faith, by the 1690s they had led to the rise of Deism, and to widespread questioning of traditional religious belief. This attempt to find better ways of knowing than tradition offered, and to question tradition-based knowledge, is described as the European Enlightenment.

A third effect of the religious warfare of the 1600s was the rise of religious movements in Catholic, Orthodox, Protestant, and even European Jewish circles, all of which had in common a stress on the heart and the affections as the center of religious life. Some English Puritans developed a concern for the centrality of religious experience, and in Lutheran and Reformed churches the movement called Pietism expressed a similar religion of the heart. By the 1700s these movements for heartfelt religious faith, reacting against the dull scholasticism and perceived spiritual "dryness" of older Protestant churches, would usher in the Evangelical Revival in Britain and the first Great Awakening in the British colonies in North America. One of the most important ideas of the Pietistic movements was their deemphasis on traditional doctrinal distinctions in their stress on the religious affections and religious experience.[129]

It is at this point, the development of movements for a religion of the heart within Reformation churches, that we may make an important link to the next chapter. The Evangelical Protestant churches described in chapter 4 developed from the background of Anglican and Reformed Evangelicalism and Lutheran Pietism. But although some

129. The subject of my earlier study of *The Religion of the Heart* (cited above).

churches became separate, there remained significant Evangelical (or Pietist) movements within each Reformation tradition.

3.0.6   Reformation and Union Churches in the Nineteenth Century

In the 1800s Reformation churches continued to have strong Pietist or Evangelical parties, but they were influenced by two new tendencies: the tendency of Protestant Liberalism to express Christian faith in terms and concepts drawn from Enlightenment philosophy and an opposing tendency of new movements for confessional orthodoxy to oppose modern tendencies of Liberalism and to insist on the integrity and truth of their traditions.

In many respects, Protestant Liberalism grew out of the inheritance of Pietism. Friedrich Schleiermacher has been credited as "the signer of the last will and testament of Pietism" and at the same time as "the founder of Protestant Liberalism." Liberalism built on Pietism's stress on religious experience and on Pietism's more tolerant attitude toward other Christian traditions, but Liberalism utilized the Enlightenment's concern for reason and reflection on human experience in ways that challenged Pietism and Evangelicalism. Consistent with their concern for reason and experience in contrast to the supernatural elements they perceived in Christian scripture and tradition, Liberals stressed the humanity of Christ, an optimistic view of the human situation, and a correspondingly optimistic estimate of historical progress, sometimes interpreted as the outworking of the kingdom of God in human society.

An important part of Liberal Protestant reinterpretation of Christian faith was its utilization of modern biblical criticism. Although Christians had asked critical questions about the text of the Bible for centuries, it was during the late 1700s and early 1800s that Christian scholars began to try to probe beyond or behind the texts themselves to ask if biblical books relied on earlier written or oral traditions, or if the words of Jesus in the Gospels might be accounts of early Christian belief but not the actual words of Jesus himself. The application of historical critical study to the Bible challenged traditional Christian understandings of the faith, and although many Christians resisted, Liberal Protestants often found the results of biblical criticism consistent with their efforts to reinterpret the faith.

Another aspect of Protestant Liberalism important for understanding the teachings of the Reformation churches and especially for the development of Union churches was the union of Lutheran and Reformed churches in Prussia in the early decades of the 1800s. Prussian rulers believed that the division of northern German churches into Lutheran and Reformed detracted from the unity of the state, and so they supported (and eventually forced) the union of the churches. Early Liberal theologians such as Schleiermacher tended to support these efforts also. Schleiermacher's *The Christian Faith*, the original Liberal Protestant systematic theological study, was explicitly written to promote the church union in Prussia.

But Liberalism in general and the union of the Prussian churches in particular provoked a strong reaction, the second important trend or tendency in Reformation churches in the 1800s. This was the trend toward confessional orthodoxy on the part of Lutheran and Reformed churches, and toward recapturing a sense of Catholic faith on the part of many Anglican Christians. Some Lutheran and Reformed Christians in Prussia reacted strongly against the forced union of their churches and this led to their engagement in the defense of their traditions. From the 1820s Lutheran churches saw the rise of a New Lutheran party that stressed fidelity to the Lutheran confessions, and in fact some Prussian churches withdrew from the Union Church and became independent "Old Lutheran" churches. (It is perhaps confusing, but "New Lutheranism" and "Old Lutheran" churches reflected the same tendency to stress traditional Lutheran identity.) Advocates of the "New Lutheranism" rejected Pietism on the one hand and Liberalism on the other, stressing the importance of traditional doctrine and traditional Lutheran liturgies.

At about the same time in the United States, a group of German Reformed theologians at their seminary in Mercersburg, Pennsylvania, attempted to recapture the distinct identity of Reformed faith and its deeper roots in Catholic tradition. They rejected revivalism, on the one hand, and the inroads of theological Liberalism, on the other, and parallel to the "New Lutherans," they stressed the faith contained in Reformed creeds and the centrality of liturgical life for the Reformed tradition. Although the Mercersburg theologians were a small minority, they seemed to spark a wider interest in recovering Reformed tradition, felt in Presbyterian and Reformed churches throughout the world.

A similar movement for recapturing traditional identity was felt in Anglican circles in the 1830s in the Oxford movement or Tractarianism. Leaders of the Oxford movement reacted against Evangelicalism, on the one hand (most had grown up as Evangelicals), and rationalism (or Liberalism) on the other. They stressed the continuity of Anglicanism with ancient Christianity, and some attempted to reconnect Anglicanism with its medieval Catholic roots. All stressed the importance of liturgy and traditional Christian doctrine. The Oxford movement led to the development of an influential party within global Anglicanism, a party to which we shall refer as Anglo-Catholicism. Anglo-Catholics, as the name suggests, saw Anglicanism not as an expression of Protestantism but rather as a distinct expression of the ancient Catholic heritage of Christianity. At many points, Anglo-Catholic views and emphases will have to be distinguished among the teachings of the churches described below. The emphases of Anglo-Catholicism were felt not only in academic circles but among many parish clergy as well:

> He would willingly have made the service more ornate than had been usual in the low-church parish of Blackstable, and in his secret soul he yearned for processions and lighted candles. He drew the line at incense. He hated the word protestant. He called himself a Catholic. He was accustomed to say that Papists required an epithet, they were Roman Catholic; but the Church of England was Catholic in the best, the fullest, and the noblest sense of the term.[130]

At the end of the 1800s, then, the Reformation churches found themselves stretched between three identifiable parties or camps. In each case there was a Liberal camp that stressed integration with modern culture. In each case, there was a confessionalist or "High Church" camp that opposed compromise with modernity and stressed continuity with tradition. In addition to these two camps or parties, there remained strong Pietist or Evangelical parties within all the Reformation churches. Perhaps the majority of leaders in the Reformation and Union churches at this time did not think of themselves as belonging to any one of these parties, but they illustrate the range of options generally available to the churches of the Reformation tradition at the turn of the century.

3.0.7   Reformation and Union Churches in the Twentieth Century

Two twentieth-century movements have greatly influenced Reformation and Union churches. These are the Ecumenical movement, which seeks the "visible unity" of churches, and the theological movement known as Neo-Orthodoxy, which attempted to overcome the Liberal-Conservative polarity inherited from the 1800s.

In its earliest years in this century, the Ecumenical movement was

---

130. W. Somerset Maugham, *Of Human Bondage* (New York: The Modern Library, reprint of 1915 edition), p. 31.

dominated by Protestant churches, both Reformation and Evangelical, or Free-Church, Protestants. We have suggested in the introductory chapter that the Ecumenical movement may be understood as a Christian expression of Modernism, and just as Modernism attempted to transcend national and traditional cultures, so the Ecumenical movement sought the visible unity of the churches by transcending traditional denominational divisions. Building on early twentieth-century movements for unity in missionary work, unity in "Life and Work," and unity in "Faith and Order," the World Council of Churches was formally organized in Amsterdam in 1948, and it became the principal instrument of ecumenical work on the part of Reformation and Union churches (see 5.1).

One of the most important results of the Ecumenical movement, for our purposes in this chapter, has been the founding of a number of national "United" or "Uniting" churches. The Reformation traditions, along with Methodists, have been consistently the backbone of these United churches. In 1925 the Methodists, Congregationalists, and the majority of Presbyterians in Canada formed The United Church of Canada. In India, two united churches have been formed: the Church of South India (1947, embracing Anglicans, Congregationalists, Presbyterians, Methodists, and others), and the Church of North India (1970, embracing Anglicans, British Methodists, Congregationalists, Presbyterians, Baptists, Disciples of Christ, and the Church of the Brethren, a Baptist group with roots in Germany). In 1977 a Uniting Church in Australia was formed from Methodists, Congregationalists, and Presbyterians, with the name "Uniting" symbolizing their commitment to expanding visible unity among the churches.

In some cases ecumenical involvement has caused Reformation and Union churches to restate or reformulate their own doctrinal stances. A notable case is the Chicago-Lambeth Quadrilateral developed in the context of ecumenical discussions on the part of Anglican leaders. Originally adopted by the House of Bishops of the Protestant Episcopal Church in the United States at a meeting in Chicago in 1886, the statement of four principles for inter-Christian dialogue and cooperation was adopted in a revised form by the Lambeth Conference of Bishops, representing global Anglicanism, in 1888. The inclusion of the Chicago-Lambeth Quadrilateral in contemporary Anglican prayerbooks alongside the Articles of Religion indicates a growing tendency to see it as reflecting a broad consensus of Anglican belief.

With the Chicago-Lambeth Quadrilateral we are only now able to give a more complete list of documents that reflect historic Anglican doctrinal consensus. Although Anglicanism has never defined itself in confessional terms as Lutheran and Reformed traditions did, there are nevertheless certain documents that describe Anglican consensus in the faith. From the period of Elizabeth I are the Thirty-nine Articles of Religion and the two books of Homilies, whose authority is grounded in the Thirty-nine Articles. From somewhat later is the *Book of Common Prayer* (including its catechism) adopted in 1662, and then from the 1800s the Chicago-Lambeth Quadrilateral. These documents are listed in table 7.

A second important trend that has influenced the Reformation and Union churches in the twentieth century is the theological movement called Neo-Orthodoxy, which reacted against the Liberalism inherited from the nineteenth century and sought a more Christ-centered and biblical faith, though refusing to bow to Fundamentalism or uncritical versions of confessional orthodoxy. Represented by such influential theologians as Karl Barth, Emil Brunner, Dietrich Bonhoeffer, and the brothers Reinhold and H. Richard Niebuhr, Neo-Orthodoxy revived traditional Protestant emphases on the authority of scripture, on the fallenness of humankind, on the omnipotence and transcendence of God, on the importance of the visible structures of the church, and on the church's role as a body that confesses the faith boldly before the world. But while reviving these more traditional emphases of Protestantism, Neo-Orthodoxy took a generally positive attitude toward modern biblical criticism and encouraged direct Christian involvement in the crises of modern political, social, and economic life. Neo-Orthodoxy inspired theologians such as Dietrich Bonhoeffer, who openly opposed Nazism, and it would provide a theological ground for Protestant involvement in the Civil Rights movement in the United States in the 1960s.

At the end of the twentieth century, Reformation and Union traditions are undergoing important changes. Most of their denominations throughout the world are no longer supported by political states, and in many countries where they are (in the United Kingdom, Germany, and elsewhere) citizens who belong to nonestablished churches can

Table 7. Principal Documents Reflecting Anglican Doctrinal Consensus

Document	Dates
Thirty-nine Articles of Religion	1563 and 1571
Two Books of Homilies	1547 and 1571
The Book of Common Prayer	1662
The Chicago-Lambeth Quadrilateral	1886 and 1888

elect to have their "church taxes" diverted to their own denominations. In Europe and North America, most of the Reformation and Union churches have seen consistent decline in membership since the 1960s, and although they continue to gain members elsewhere in the world, their gains even there tend to fall below the rate at which the population is increasing. In the latter part of the twentieth century this may reflect the extent to which Reformation and Union churches have been overshadowed in third-world contexts by Evangelical and especially Pentecostal churches, which we shall consider in chapter 4.

3.1 Teachings of Reformation and Union Churches on Religious Authority

The churches that emerged as a result of the Reformation, as well as modern Free churches, Evangelical churches, and churches that grew from ecumenical mergers, present a number of problems in the comparative study of their agreed-upon teachings, and one problem is that although they agree across denominational lines on some issues, they differ on other issues. For this reason, some of the subsections below will apply to all the Reformation and Union churches (for example, see 3.1.1), but theses whose enumeration ends with a lower-case letter (for example, see 3.1.2.a) will apply to some particular group of these churches. We have tried consistently to use numbers to indicate subheadings, and letters to indicate alternative headings.

The accounts of the doctrines of Reformation and Union churches framed below are based largely on the Protestant confessional documents listed above in tables 5, 6, and 7. As in previous chapters, many of these documents are available in English translation in Leith's *Creeds of the Churches*. Because of the deep influence of theological Liberalism and a more widespread mood of theological pluralism in many of the historic Reformation and Union churches, we have felt more honest to state summaries in chapter 3 in the form "Reformation and Union *traditions* teach . . . "rather than claiming "Reformation and Union *churches* teach . . . ," since some modern Reformation and Union churches have added contemporary doctrinal statements that call into question or seriously qualify historic teachings of their traditions. At one point, moreover, I have ventured a formulation that is grounded more in my own intuition of doctrinal development than in traditional doctrinal statements: I have added a subsection on the role of reason, experience, and modern biblical criticism in contemporary Protestant churches influenced by Liberalism (see 3.1.2.d). It is my judgment, in this case, that this trend has so seriously challenged traditional doctrinal beliefs, and is held by such a seriously large contingent of people in churches, that it needs to be mentioned beside traditional formulations.

3.1.1 *What Reformation and Union traditions teach about the authority of the Bible:* Reformation and Union traditions agree in teaching that the Bible is the final, authoritative source of Christian teachings.

Sources: Augsburg Confession, preface (in Leith, p. 65; Schaff, 3:4), cf. conclusion of the section of initial articles, the preface to the section on disputed matters, and the conclusion to the Confession (in Leith, pp. 78–79, 106; Schaff, 3:26–27, 28, 73). Formula of Concord, Epitome, introduction 1 (in Tappert, p. 464; Schaff, 3:93–94). Second Helvetic Confession, 1 (in Leith, pp. 132–134; Schaff, 3:237–238, 831–833). Westminster Confession 1 (in Leith, pp. 193–196; Schaff, 3:600–606). Anglican Articles of Religion 6–7 (in Leith, pp. 267–269; Schaff, 3:489–492). Anglican Homilies "A Fruitful Exhortation to the Reading and Knowledge of Holy Scripture" and "The Second Part of the Sermon on the Knowledge of Holy Scripture" (in Leith, pp. 231–239). Chicago-Lambeth Quadrilateral, point 1 (in the *Book of Common Prayer* [USA, 1979], p. 877). Basis of Union of The United Church of Canada, preface and Article II (UCC *Manual* 1993, pp. 11 and 12).

Comparative Cross-References: Eastern Orthodox, 1.1.1–2; Roman Catholic, 2.1.1; Evangelical and Free, 4.1.1.a–b; Ecumenical, 5.2.1.

The traditional doctrinal statements of Reformation and Union churches broadly agree in teaching that there can be no authority higher than the authority of scripture. Protestants of all persuasions see the Bible as standing over the churches, reforming their life and teachings. In this respect, Protestant teachings contrast with those of Orthodoxy and Catholicism, where the Bible is seen as part of a long continuity of God's work, complemented by the authority of later church teachings. The reverence for scripture in Reformation traditions is illustrated by the following incident from W. Somerset Maugham's *Of Human Bondage:*

> "I'll put some books under him," said Mary Ann.
>
> She took from the top of the harmonium the large Bible and the prayer-book from which the Vicar was accustomed to read prayers, and put them on Philip's chair.
>
> "Oh, William, he can't sit on the Bible," said Mrs. Carey, in a shocked tone. "Couldn't you get him some books out of the study?"
>
> Mr. Carey considered the question for an instant.
>
> "I don't think it matters this once if you put the prayer-book on the top, Mary Ann," he said. "The Book of Common Prayer is the

composition of men like ourselves. It has no claim to divine authorship."

"I hadn't thought of that, William," said Aunt Louisa.[131]

Although the Lutheran confessions do not have separate articles on the authority of scripture, the Formula of Concord states that the Scriptures are "the only rule and norm, according to which all doctrines and all teachers alike must be appraised and judged."[132] Moreover, the Lutheran confessions presuppose consistently that scripture is the basis for the reform of the church. The Augsburg Confession submitted to the Holy Roman Emperor a body of teachings "setting forth how and in what manner, on the basis of the Holy Scriptures" the Lutherans understood the Christian faith. In practice, the Lutheran Confessions consistently refer to scripture to validate their teachings.[133]

Reformed confessions and catechisms, and the Anglican Articles of Religion and the *Book of Homilies*, include articles and other materials that deal directly with the authority of scripture. The Westminster Confession asserts that God has given the Scriptures to make clear God's will to humankind and that the authority of the Scriptures is grounded in their divine inspiration.[134] The Westminster Confession, following the Anglican Articles at this point, also makes the claim that the Scriptures contain all things necessary to salvation.[135] Thus, however later traditions might clarify the teachings of scripture, they cannot add anything that is essential to human salvation. Only the Scriptures offer the totality of saving knowledge. The first Anglican Homily, "A Fruitful Exhortation to the Reading and Knowledge of Holy Scripture," urges readers to

> search for the well of life in the books of the New and Old Testament, and not run to the stinking puddles of men's traditions, devised by men's imagination, for our justification and salvation.[136]

---

131. W. Somerset Maugham, *Of Human Bondage*, p. 16.
132. Formula of Concord, Epitome, introduction 1 (in Theodore G. Tappert, trans. and ed., *The Book of Concord: The Confessions of the Evangelical Church* [Philadelphia: Fortress Press, 1959], p. 464; Schaff, 3:93–94).
133. Augsburg Confession, preface (in Leith, p. 65), cf. conclusion of the section of initial articles, the preface to the section on disputed matters, and the conclusion to the Confession, all of which appeal to the clarity of scripture in grounding the Lutherans' claims (in Leith, pp. 78–79, 106).
134. Westminster Confession, 1:1, 1:4 (in Leith, pp. 193, 195).
135. Westminster Confession, 1:6 (in Leith, pp. 195–196); Articles of Religion, 6 (in Leith, p. 267).
136. "A Fruitful Exhortation to the Reading and Knowledge of Holy Scripture" (in Leith, p. 232).

The more recent Anglican Chicago-Lambeth Quadrilateral as expressed in 1888 affirms "The Holy Scriptures of the Old and New Testaments, as 'containing all things necessary to salvation,' and as being the ultimate standard of faith."[137]

Although the historic confessions of the Reformation make this consistent claim about the priority of the Bible's authority, there are at least two ways in which adherents of Reformation and Union churches might themselves question this claim. First, many Anglicans prefer to speak, as Orthodox and Catholics do, of the continuity of the Bible and later tradition. On this point they cite Anglicanism's consistent use of early Christian tradition as clarifying and standing in continuity with biblical teachings (see 3.1.2.c). A second and very different objection might come from Liberal Protestants, who would question whether the Bible must be seen as standing over all other authorities. They argue that the Bible reflects primitive views of the universe (such as the six-day creation story in Genesis) and of human culture (such as the subjection of women to men) that have proven unacceptable after further progress in scientific knowledge, historical experience, and critical reflection. For this reason, many Liberal Protestants (but not all!) would reject the notion that the Bible stands over other authorities (see 3.1.2.d on this point).

But granted the general agreement of historic creeds of the Reformation on the final authority of scripture, how do Reformation and Union churches go about the interpretation of scripture? Because the Lutheran confessions do not address this issue directly, it is difficult to answer this question on their behalf, although we can make some reasonable claims based on the general ways in which Lutheran confessions interpret scripture (see 3.1.2.a). In the case of Reformed (see 3.1.2.b) and Anglican (see 3.1.2.c) traditions, we can be somewhat more specific. We have also felt that it is important in this consideration of means of interpreting scripture to consider how Protestant Liberalism has affected the interpretation of scripture (see 3.1.2.d).

3.1.2.a *What Lutheran tradition teaches about the interpretation of the Bible:* Lutheran tradition agrees in regarding the Bible as its own best interpreter. Lutheran tradition generally agrees, further, in the use of Christian traditions in the interpretation of scripture, so far as these interpretations do not contradict scripture and reflect a consensus of Christian teaching or practice.

137. Chicago-Lambeth Quadrilateral, point 1 (in the *Book of Common Prayer* [USA, 1979], p. 877).

Sources: Augsburg Confession, conclusion of the section of initial articles, the preface to the section on disputed matters, and the conclusion to the Confession (in Leith, pp. 78–79, 106; Schaff, 3:26–27, 28, 73). Apology of the Augsburg Confession 4 (in Tappert, p. 108). Formula of Concord, Epitome, 5 (in Schaff, 3:126–130; Tappert, pp. 477–479). Piepkorn, 2:47–49; Schmid, pp. 38–91, par. 6–12.
Comparative Cross-References: Eastern Orthodox, 1.1.2–3; Roman Catholic, 2.1.2–4; Evangelical and Free, 4.1.2.a–c, 4.1.3.a–b.

Lutheran interpreters of their own tradition point out that Luther himself and the Lutheran confessions after him consistently speak of the clarity of the Scriptures, suggesting that scripture itself is the best interpreter of scripture.[138] That is to say, if a passage of scripture is unclear, it should be compared to other passages whose clarity will illuminate the unclear passage. This is largely consistent with the way in which Reformed churches have explicitly formulated their understanding of the interpretation of the Bible (3.1.2.b).

A distinctive Lutheran stress in the interpretation of the Bible is the careful distinction drawn between Law and Gospel (or "Promise"), a distinction made explicitly in the Apology of the Augsburg Confession and the Formula of Concord. The distinction of "Law" and "Gospel" must not be seen as a simple distinction between the Old and New Testaments. By "Law," Lutheran interpreters mean the commandments of God, especially the Ten Commandments, as binding on persons in their quest for salvation, wherever in the Bible this demand for righteousness may be found. By "Gospel" or "Promise," Lutherans mean the grace of God through Christ that saves us in spite of our inability to follow God's Law. One of the Lutherans' principal arguments against their Catholic opponents was that late medieval Catholic theology had subverted the message of the Gospel and had read even the work of Christ in a "legalistic" way, that is, they had read the work of Christ as simply laying more demands of obedience on Christians.

Beyond its concern with the scriptural grounding of Christian teachings, the Augsburg Confession refers repeatedly to "the universal Christian Church" or "what is common to the Christian church."[139] This, along with the prominent presence of the Apostles' Creed, Nicene Creed, and Athanasian Creed at the beginning of the *Book of*

138. Piepkorn, 2:47–49; Heinrich Schmid, *The Doctrinal Theology of the Evangelical Lutheran Church*, trans. Charles A. Hay and Henry E. Jacobs, 3rd. ed., revised (Minneapolis: Augsburg Publishing House, 1899), pp. 68–80, par. 10.
139. Augsburg Confession, conclusion of the section of initial articles, the preface to the section on disputed matters, and the conclusion to the Confession (in Leith, pp. 78–79, 106; Schaff, 3:26–27, 28, 73).

Concord indicates that Lutheran traditions are receptive to the use of tradition subsequent to the Bible, especially as it represents a consensus of Christian teaching, although it does not imply that these subsequent traditions could ever have authority over the Bible. Rather, they are seen as being consistent with the Bible (or put differently, they do not *contradict* biblical teachings) and reflect a consensus of the church.

It should be noted, in connection with this point, that Lutherans value consensus in the church very highly. Not only do the Lutheran confessional documents speak consistently about that which is common to Christians but they also witness to the centrality of corporate consensus in the faith for Lutherans. In ecumenical discussions, Lutherans gently but consistently press other Christians to consider how Christians can work toward a visible consensus in faith. It may be this concern for the importance of consensus and doctrine that explains why almost all English-language books comparing Christian teachings have been written by Lutherans. The very same tendency may explain, paradoxically, the divisiveness of Lutherans outside of Germany into a variety of synods, each distinguished by particular doctrinal concerns.

3.1.2.b   *What Reformed tradition teaches about the interpretation of the Bible:* Reformed tradition agrees in teaching that the Bible itself, because of its intrinsic unity and clarity, is its own best interpreter, that the inward witness of the Holy Spirit confirms the truth of scripture to believers, and that church councils and synods have authority only so far as they reflect biblical truths.

Sources: Second Helvetic Confession 2 (in Leith, pp. 135–136; Schaff, 3:239–240, 833–834). Westminster Confession 1 (in Leith, pp. 193–196; Schaff, 3:600–606).

Comparative Cross-References: Eastern Orthodox, 1.1.2–3; Roman Catholic, 2.1.2–4; Evangelical and Free, 4.1.2.a–c, 4.1.3.a–b.

What the Lutheran creeds imply about the interpretation of scripture, Reformed creeds state explicitly. The Westminster Confession says:

> The infallible rule of interpretation of Scripture is the Scripture itself; and therefore, when there is a question about the true and full sense of any Scripture (which is not manifold, but one), it must be searched and known by other places that speak more clearly.[140]

140. Westminster Confession, 1:9 (in Leith, p. 196; Schaff 3:605); cf. Second Helvetic Confession, 2 (in Leith, p. 135; Schaff, 3:239, 833).

Two things might be noted about this passage that consistently characterize Reformed understandings of the Bible. The first is that it speaks of the unity of the Bible: "which is not manifold, but one." The Bible must be read in the light of its overall message, which in Reformed parlance is sometimes called "the analogy of faith" (Rom. 12:6).[141] The second matter is that this passage presupposes what the Westminster Confession states two paragraphs above, that the Bible's meaning is clear: the things necessary for salvation are "so clearly propounded and opened" that they may be understood by using "the appropriate means,"[142] and for this reason less clear passages of scripture are to be interpreted by clearer passages.

Perhaps a different way of stating this point would be to say that, from the perspective of Reformed churches, later traditions have often obscured rather than clarified the meaning of biblical texts. The Reformation as a whole felt a sense of excitement over the "discovery" of the meaning of biblical texts. There could be no clearer illustration of this than Zwingli's daily practice of reading biblical texts aloud in Hebrew or Greek, then in German, then carefully expounding the meaning of the text and drawing out their implications for the reform of Zurich. The Reformed tradition as a whole has traditionally stressed the importance of clergy being trained in biblical languages in order to understand appropriately the original meaning of biblical texts.

One important sign of the Reformed tradition's regard for scripture was that in their first two centuries, Reformed churches favored the singing of scriptural passages alone, especially the Psalms, in worship. Hymns, as we know them, were not widely used until the time of Isaac Watts in the early 1700s. The Reformed tradition developed in its first two centuries a tradition of "metrical psalmody," that is, paraphrasing psalms in English verse so that they could be more easily sung by the congregation. A classic example is William Kethe's paraphrase of the One Hundredth Psalm (1561):

> All people that on earth do dwell,
>   Sing to the Lord with cheerful voice.
> Him serve with mirth, his praise forth tell;
>   Come ye before him and rejoice![143]

141. TAC; The expression may be confusing, because it is traditionally translated "in proportion to faith" (NRSV) in English versions, but in Greek the term is *analogian tes pisteos*, "analogy of faith."
142. Second Helvetic Confession, 2 (in Leith, p. 135); Westminster Confession, 1:7 (in Leith, p. 196).
143. In *United Methodist Hymnal*, no. 75.

Reformed Christians were not alone in this practice: Anglicans also restricted singing in worship to metrical psalms (and some liturgical chants) until the eighteenth century.

Having said, however, that the Reformed (and in its own ways, Lutheran) tradition has stressed the clarity and ultimate authority of the Bible, we might ask if this means that the Reformed tradition teaches a doctrine of biblical *infallibility* or *inerrancy* (meaning that the Bible does not fail or err in its teachings) as is taught among Fundamentalist churches (see 4.1.1.b). On the one hand, it must be said that the Reformed confessions, especially the Westminster Confession, do indeed speak of the infallibility of the Word of God, and Christian scripture is identified as the "written Word."[144] On the other hand, infallibility was but one of the attributes ascribed to the Scriptures by medieval Catholic theologians as well as the Reformers. The term was not much disputed between Catholics and Protestants at the time of the Reformation, it was not used as the primary test of a doctrine of scripture, and it was not held over against modern scientific claims as is the case with Fundamentalists (see 4.1.1.b). In the Reformers and the Protestant confessions, the assertion of biblical infallibility must be seen as a small part of the large enterprise of reforming the church by returning to the teachings that the Reformers perceived to be clearly and consistently taught in the Bible.[145] We may note that the Basis of Union of The United Church of Canada asserts that the Bible is "the only infallible rule of faith and life."[146] We might faithfully answer the question about "biblical infallibility" in the Reformation age, then, by saying that the Reformation traditions did in fact teach a doctrine of biblical infallibility, but in a different context and with very different accents than later Fundamentalists would.

One point on which the Westminster Confession follows Calvin's *Institutes* is in its claim that the "inward witness of the Holy Spirit"

144. Second Helvetic Confession, 1 (in Leith, pp. 132–133; Schaff, 3:237–238, 831–833); Westminster Confession, 1:2 and 1:5 (in Leith, pp. 193–195; Schaff, 3:601, 602–603).
145. There was an extended debate in the late 1970s and early 1980s over the issue of whether the Protestant Reformers believed in biblical "infallibility" in the sense in which contemporary Fundamentalists believed at that time. Some interpreters of the Reformation stressed the distinction between the "written Word" as having an authority only derivative of the "incarnate Word" (Christ), much as twentieth-century Neo-Orthodox theologians had done. These views are generally rejected in a convincing overview of beliefs about biblical authority in this period, including the issue of biblical infallibility, in Richard A. Muller, *Post-Reformation Reformed Dogmatics: Holy Scripture: The Cognitive Foundation of Theology*, vol. 2 (Grand Rapids: Baker Book House, 1993), pp. 51–86.
146. Basis of Union of The United Church of Canada, Article 2.

confirms the truth of scripture for believers.[147] That is to say, the same Spirit who inspired scripture in the first place works within human beings to convince them of the truth taught by the Scriptures. This "inward witness" does not have to be associated with unusual religious experience, but it can simply mean the growing conviction on the part of a Christian that the Scriptures speak authoritatively to us.

One further point needs to be made about the Reformed tradition's understanding of the authority of scripture, and that has to do with its use of ancient Christian writings and church councils. Reformed confessions insist that all councils are capable of error, and affirm that doctrines defined by church councils are valid only so far as they concur with the teachings of the Scriptures. Similarly, the Reformed confessions "do not despise the interpretations of the holy Greek and Latin fathers" but insist that these interpretations are helpful only so far as they confirm the truths taught by the Scriptures.[148] In fact, the Reformed confessions and such writings as Calvin's *Institutes* do refer consistently to ancient Christian sources (especially Augustine) and generally condemn the heresies condemned by the ancient councils. If there is a difference in nuance at this point between Reformed tradition, on the one hand, and Lutheran and Anglican traditions, on the other hand, it lies in the tendency on the part of Reformed tradition to look for explicit precedents in scripture for what they teach and do. Lutherans and Anglicans, on the other hand, tend to allow the expression of teachings and practices so long as they do not contradict scripture, but they do not insist on positive or explicit scriptural warrants.

3.1.2.c *What Anglican tradition teaches about the interpretation of the Bible:* Anglican tradition allows a wide degree of latitude in the interpretation of scripture, but it has favored the view that the teachings of the early church should be appropriately utilized in the interpretation of scripture.

Sources: Anglican Articles of Religion 8, 20–21, 34 (in Leith, pp. 269, 273–274, 277–278; Schaff, 3:492, 500–501, 508–509). Chicago-Lambeth Quadrilateral, point 2 (in the *Book of Common Prayer* [USA, 1979], p. 877).

Comparative Cross-References: Eastern Orthodox, 1.1.2–3; Roman Catholic, 2.1.2–4; Evangelical and Free, 4.1.2.a–c, 4.1.3.a–b.

147. Second Helvetic Confession, 1 (in Leith, pp. 133–134); Westminster Confession, 1:5 (in Leith, p. 195); cf. Calvin, *Institutes* 1.7 (in McNeill, 1:74–81). The quotation is from the Second Helvetic Confession as given in Schaff, 3:833.
148. Second Helvetic Confession, 2 (in Leith, pp. 135–136); Westminster Confession, 31 (in Leith, pp. 227–228).

The Anglican Articles of Religion reflect at some points the Reformed insistence on the clarity of scripture: Article 20 insists that interpreters may not set one text against another, and this implies that interpreters are to seek the overall meaning of the Scriptures as a whole. Despite the slighting reference to the "stinking puddles" of human traditions in the first Homily of the Church of England (see 3.1.1), Anglicans have traditionally ascribed considerable significance to the writings of the early church as interpreting and clarifying the Scriptures. John Jewel, bishop of Salisbury during the reign of Elizabeth I, explained an Anglican understanding of the value of ancient Christian works in these terms:

> But what shall we say of the fathers, Augustine, Ambrose, Hierome, Cyprian, etc.? What shall we think of them, or what account may we make of them? They be interpreters of the word of God.[149]

Similarly, Richard Hooker and other early Anglican leaders valued the writings of antiquity as interpreting the meaning of scripture.[150]

The Anglican Articles of Religion reflect a cautious appropriation of the riches of ancient Christianity. The caution is evident in Article 21, which criticizes the authority of Ecumenical Councils, noting that they "may err and have erred" and for that reason they cannot promulgate any doctrine as necessary to human salvation except insofar as it agrees with scripture. With this note of caution, however, the Articles do affirm the same three ancient creeds affirmed by the Augsburg Confession (the Apostles', Nicene, and Athanasian Creeds) in an Article (8) immediately following their Articles on scripture. Moreover, the Anglican Articles assert the right of churches to establish rites and ceremonies in keeping with scripture (Article 20) and condemns those who would break such traditions (Article 34). Similarly, the Chicago-Lambeth Quadrilateral as expressed in 1888 insists on "The Apostles' Creed, as the Baptismal Symbol; and the Nicene Creed, as the sufficient statement of Christian faith"[151] in Anglican ecumenical dialogue. In keeping with these statements, Anglicans have historically sanctioned church teachings and practices so long as they do not contradict scripture, and this allows a great degree of latitude in the acceptance of ancient and medieval practices.

149. Cited in Stanley Lawrence Greenslade, *The English Reformers and the Fathers of the Church* (Oxford: Clarendon Press, 1960), pp. 8–9.
150. Cf. Ted A. Campbell, *John Wesley and Christian Antiquity* (Nashville: Kingswood Books, 1991), pp. 11–15.
151. Chicago-Lambeth Quadrilateral, point 2 (in the *Book of Common Prayer* [USA, 1979], p. 877).

Perhaps even more important for Anglicans than the Articles of Religion is the *Book of Common Prayer*, which serves as a model for the careful use of ancient and medieval church traditions. The prayer book (as its proponents and opponents both recognized) consists of a judicious appropriation of substantial parts of the traditional forms for daily worship, the Eucharist, the pastoral offices, and the rites of ordination, edited from a Reformation perspective. The primary source was an English variant of the medieval Roman traditions of worship, known as the Sarum rite, but the prayer book also drew on Continental and even Byzantine (Eastern Christian) sources.

At two points, in the 1600s and again in the 1800s, the Anglican concern for continuity with ancient Christian tradition became particularly prominent. In the 1600s Anglicans maintained that their church was unique among the churches of Europe in retaining the forms and teachings of ancient Christianity. Other Protestant churches had gone to an extreme in stressing scripture alone, and Catholics had fallen into the opposite extreme of reverencing corrupt medieval practices. Anglican episcopacy and liturgy were defended in the 1600s on the basis of ancient precedent. In the 1800s, a new Anglican revival of interest in ancient Christianity was associated with the Oxford or Tractarian movement and its attempt to identify Anglicanism as a branch of the Catholic tradition. Some Tractarians stressed fidelity to ancient Christian precedents; others went beyond this and emphasized faithfulness to a long tradition that included purer spiritual and liturgical traditions of the Middle Ages. Both of these periods of renewal of the Anglican sense of identity with ancient Christianity have given Anglicanism as a whole a unique sense of connectedness to Christian tradition. Because of this, one of the gifts of Anglicanism is that it may serve as a kind of ecumenical link between Protestant churches, on the one hand, and Catholic and Orthodox churches, on the other.

In addition to their use of ancient Christian traditions, many English Reformers, such as Richard Hooker, favored the use of reason in the interpretation of scripture. It was Hooker who laid out for Anglicanism three criteria of religious authority in his assertion that Anglicans test the authenticity of beliefs and practices by scripture, tradition, and reason.[152] Although reason is not given as prominent a place in Anglican doctrinal standards as scripture and tradition, it has held

---

152. Richard Hooker, *Laws of Ecclesiastical Polity*, 3:8, in *The Works of that Learned and Judicious Divine, Mr. Richard Hooker: With an Account of His Life and Death*, 2 vols. (Oxford: Clarendon Press, 1875), 1:299–314.

a conspicuous place in Anglican theological method.[153] This early assertion of the appropriate use of reason, by Hooker and others, opened ways in which Anglicans would later embrace the use of reason as one of the favored tools of the Enlightenment.

3.1.2.d: *How the Enlightenment has affected Reformation and Union churches' attitudes toward the authority of the Bible:* Since the Enlightenment, Reformation and Union churches have increasingly utilized human reason, reflection on common experience, and critical biblical study itself as means of interpreting the Scriptures.

It should be noted from the first that this thesis is not grounded in traditional doctrinal statements, but relies rather on my intuition and experience, which suggest that since the 1700s all the Reformation and Union churches have been challenged by Enlightenment understandings of human knowledge. On the European continent, a version of Enlightenment thought known as rationalism stressed the importance of reason itself as a surer way of knowledge than tradition had given. In the British Isles, a different version of Enlightenment thought known as empiricism suggested that the surest way of knowledge is by reflection on our experience of the world. Both rationalism and empiricism deeply challenged "traditional" knowledge, and that meant above all knowledge grounded in tradition and scripture. Although the earliest advocates of rationalism (René Descartes) and empiricism (Francis Bacon) did not see their discoveries as challenging accepted religious beliefs, by the 1690s Deism had emerged, grounding itself in these outlooks and denying such central traditional beliefs as the divinity of Christ.

The Enlightenment most deeply affected Protestantism in the rise of Protestant Liberalism, from the early 1800s (see 3.0.7). Although most Liberals of the 1800s and even early 1900s reverenced scripture and their church traditions, they utilized reason and reflection on experience in ways that challenged traditional Christian beliefs (an example would be Schleiermacher's questioning whether Modalism might be preferable to traditional Trinitarian doctrine). Moreover, from about the same time, Protestant Liberalism embraced modern biblical criticism as a way of getting at the core or original meaning of biblical texts. Both developments had the effect of changing traditional Protestant attitudes toward the authority of scripture, and would have effects broadly throughout their understanding of the faith.

153. Henry McAdoo, *The Spirit of Anglicanism* (New York: Charles Scribner's Sons, 1965), pp. 240–414.

3.2   Teachings of Reformation and Union Churches on God and Christ

Although doctrines about God and Christ were not as hotly disputed at the time of the Reformation as issues about religious authority, human nature and salvation, and various issues concerning Christian ministry and sacraments, there were nevertheless some disputed areas, for example, about the role of Mary the mother of Jesus. Moreover, it is important in this account of the teachings of Reformation and Union churches to give a brief description of their understandings of God and Christ to indicate the extent to which their teachings are consistent with those of the ancient Christian churches.

3.2.1 *What Reformation and Union traditions teach concerning the doctrine of the Trinity:* Reformation and Union traditions agree in teaching that God is one substance in three eternal Persons, and that the Holy Spirit proceeds from the Father and the Son.

Sources: Augsburg Confession, 1 (in Leith, pp. 67–68; Schaff, 3:7–8). Westminster Confession, 2–5 (in Leith, pp. 197–201; Schaff, 3:606–614). Anglican Articles of Religion 1 and 5 (in Leith, pp. 266–267; Schaff, 3:487–488, 489). Chicago-Lambeth Quadrilateral, point 2 (in the *Book of Common Prayer* [USA 1979], p. 877). Basis of Union of The United Church of Canada, Articles 1 and 8 (UCC *Manual* 1993, pp. 11–12, 13).

Comparative Cross-References: Eastern Orthodox, 1.2.1; Roman Catholic, 2.2.1–2; Evangelical and Free, 4.2.1.a–b; Ecumenical, 5.2.2.1.

The Protestant Reformation did not alter significantly the doctrine of the Trinity, which it had received from ancient Christianity by way of medieval Catholicism. Following the First Councils of Nicaea and Constantinople, Lutheran, Anglican, and Reformed creeds utilize the language of three eternal Persons (Father, Son, and Holy Spirit) sharing in the one "substance" of God. All these traditions utilize the Nicene Creed in worship (that is, the creed of the First Council of Nicaea in 325 as revised at the First Council of Constantinople in 381). The Anglican Articles (Article 8) and the Chicago-Lambeth Quadrilateral (point 2) specifically approve the Nicene Creed, and it stands at the very beginning of the Lutheran *Book of Concord*. In this general affirmation of the faith of Nicaea, then, Reformation and Union churches are in wide agreement with Catholic and Orthodox churches. Anglican Bishop Reginald Heber's hymn expresses this unity in the ancient Trinitarian faith:

> Holy, holy, holy! Lord God Almighty!
> Early in the morning our song shall rise to thee.
> Holy, holy, holy! Merciful and mighty,
> God in three persons, blessed Trinity![154]

154. Hymn by Reginald Heber, in *United Methodist Hymnal*, no. 64.

Moreover, all three Reformation traditions assert that the Holy Spirit "proceeds from the Father and the Son," following the Western, Catholic form of the Nicene Creed.[155] Although this expression has been defended by Protestant theologians, it was not well understood at the time of the Reformation, and in fact many of the Reformers seem to have thought that it reflects the original form of the creed, which it does not. The Anglican Church of Canada has removed the expression "and the Son" in the version of the creed in its *Book of Alternative Services,* and the Episcopal Church in the United States has voted in principle to remove the expression from the creed but will not make this effective until the change is approved by the Lambeth Conference of Bishops and the Anglican Consultative Council.[156] Similarly, the Reformed Church in America has voted to place the expression "and the Son" in brackets in their worship materials.

Having noted this general agreement on Trinitarian doctrine, we might observe some typical emphases in teachings about God on the part of Reformed and Lutheran traditions. The doctrinal statements of the Reformed tradition have an explicit concern for the omnipotence of God, that is, God's power over all things (from *omnis,* "all," and *potens,* "powerful"). Three separate headings of the Westminster Confession deal with God's providential direction of the universe. The confession asserts that God decrees all things that come to pass, although it does allow for "second causes," that is, God may grant a limited degree of choice to creatures (chapter 3). The confession goes on to define God's power as the creator of all things (chapter 4), and then as the governor of all things (chapter 5). In its discussion of God's providential governance of the universe, the confession again allows for secondary causes, so that human sin cannot be attributed to God. But the tenor of these chapters is to depict God as directly involved in the events of the world, and this sense of the constant governance or providence of God is a hallmark of Reformed understandings of God.

Lutherans also emphasize the omnipotence of God, but add to this emphasis a characteristically Lutheran note, namely, to stress the "hiddenness" of God in this world. Luther and the Lutheran tradition after him taught that although we may have a rudimentary awareness

155. The doctrine of the double procession of the Holy Spirit is stated explicitly in the Westminster Confession, 2:3 (in Leith, p. 197) and in the Anglican Articles of Religion, 5 (in Leith, p. 267). Moreover, the form of the Nicene Creed used by all three of the Classical Protestant traditions has the expression "from the Son"; cf. the form of the creed given in the Lutheran *Book of Concord* (in Tappert, p. 19).
156. John C. Bauerschmidt, " 'Filioque' and the Episcopal Church," *Anglican Theological Review* 73, no. 1 (Fall 1991): 7.

of God known from nature, God's saving purpose in Christ is not immediately knowable, not obvious, in this world. Where, then, do we
find the saving God in this world? Lutherans respond that we find
God where we least expect to, in the humiliated form of the human
Christ. Faith (and only faith) enables us to look at the human Christ
and see the almighty God, creator of all that is. For Lutherans, this
teaching on the hiddenness of God in this world is important not only
for theology but also for spirituality. Its implication is that human beings must be constantly on guard, on the one hand, against the temp-
tation to trust our own reason beyond what God has revealed to us,
and on the other hand, we must expect to be surprised by the way in
which the humblest things (like bread and wine) may become the av-
enues through which God is revealed to us.[157]

In concluding this discussion of the doctrine of the Trinity among
Reformation and Union churches, we might note the effect that Liberal Protestantism has had on this teaching. Although most Liberal
Protestants have professed Trinitarian orthodoxy, there has been a
tendency on their part to open up the boundaries of orthodoxy, in
both Arian and Modalist directions. Stressing the humanity of Christ,
many Liberals (such as Albrecht Ritschl) have been drawn toward a
reading of Christ's work that sounds like the Arians' somewhat-less-
than-fully-divine Christ. On the other hand, Liberal Protestantism has
also stressed the unity of God to such a degree that some theologians
have leaned in the direction of seeing Father, Son, and Holy Spirit as
essentially one without distinction. Friedrich Schleiermacher, who is
thought of as the founder of Liberal Protestantism, suggested that
because the Reformers had not seriously dealt with the doctrine of
the Trinity, the issue should remain open in Protestant churches,
and Schleiermacher himself questioned whether Modalism might
not in the end prove more helpful than ancient forms of Trinitarian
orthodoxy.[158]

3.2.2 *What Reformation and Union traditions teach concerning the
two natures of Christ:* Reformation and Union traditions agree in
teaching that Christ took a complete human nature in the incarnation; thus they agree in affirming the doctrine of Christ as one Person in two natures (human and divine).

---

157. David C. Steinmetz, *Luther in Context* (Bloomington, Ind.: Indiana University
Press, 1986), pp. 23–31.
158. Friedrich Schleiermacher, "The Christian Faith," thesis 172, in *The Christian
Faith,* ed. H. R. MacKintosh and J. S. Stewart (Edinburgh: T. and T. Clark, 1928),
pp. 747–751.

Sources: Augsburg Confession, 3 and 17 (in Leith, pp. 68–69, 73; Schaff, 3:9–10, 17–18). Formula of Concord, Epitome 8 (in Schaff, 3:148–159). Westminster Confession, 8 (in Leith, pp. 203–205; Schaff, 3:619–622). Anglican Articles of Religion, 2–4 (in Leith, p. 267; Schaff, 3:488–489). Basis of Union of The United Church of Canada, Article 7 (UCC *Manual* 1993, pp. 12–13).

Comparative Cross-References: Eastern Orthodox, 1.2.2; Roman Catholic, 2.2.3; Evangelical and Free, 4.2.2; Ecumenical, 5.2.2.2.

The Reformation and Union churches all affirm that Christ united a complete human "nature" with a complete divine "nature" in one "Person." In using these terms they affirm the language used by the Council of Chalcedon (A.D. 451) to describe the incarnation, and in the use of this language they are at one with Catholic and Orthodox teachings about Christ (see 1.2.2 and 2.2.3). In addition to the Chalcedonian language, each of these three traditions add language about Christ reminiscent of the Apostles' Creed or the "tradition" passage about Christ in 1 Corinthians 15:1–11. The Anglican Articles of Religion and the Augsburg Confession (Lutheran) both specifically name the Apostles' Creed. In doing this, they affirm language about Christ that echoes the very earliest form in which the Gospel was preached (see 0.3).

Having noted this broad agreement on the doctrine of two natures in the one Person of Christ and on the primitive words conveying the narrative about Christ, we may note an important controversy that separated Lutherans and Reformed Christians in the age of the Reformation. The difference was on the manner in which human and divine are united in Christ—in a sense, the same issue that had divided the church in the controversies that led to the Council of Chalcedon (see 1.0.2 and 1.2.2). In the age of the Reformation, though, this controversy was related to the question of how Christ could be present in the Eucharist. Luther and the Lutheran confessions after him maintained that Christ is bodily present in the Eucharist (see 3.4.3.2.a). Although Calvin and the Reformed Confessions affirmed Christ's presence (or at least the power and grace of Christ's presence) in the Eucharist, they argued that Christ's body itself could not be present on earth since Christ had ascended bodily to heaven (see 3.4.3.2.b–c). Consequently, Lutherans stressed that Christ's divine and human nature so interpenetrate each other that it is proper to speak of Christ's bodily human nature as being present at the Eucharist. The Reformed confessions rejected this point of view, stressing the distinction between the human and the divine in Christ. But although Lutherans accused the Reformed theologians of Nestorianism on this point and Reformed accused Lutherans of "Eutychianism" (what we have called Monophysitism), all parties agreed to the ancient Chalcedonian definition of two natures in the one Person of Christ, both sides denied the charges of heresy, and all agreed to condemn both Nestorianism and Monophysitism. Thus despite the acrimonious differences that are enshrined in both Lutheran and Reformed confessional documents, the question of divine and human is in all likelihood not a church-dividing issue between Lutherans and Reformed today.

3.2.3 *What Reformation and Union traditions teach about Mary, the mother of Jesus:* Although some Reformation and Union traditions affirm that Mary is the "Mother of God" and affirm the perpetual virginity of Mary, others refused to define these doctrines. The Reformation traditions generally agree in their rejection of the doctrines of the immaculate conception and bodily assumption of Mary.

Sources: Schmalkaldic Articles, 1:4 (in Tappert, p. 292, n. 3). Formula of Concord, Epitome 8:7 (in Schaff, 3:150; Tappert, p. 488).

Comparative Cross-References: Eastern Orthodox, 1.2.3; Roman Catholic, 2.2.4; Evangelical and Free, 4.2.4.

The Lutheran Formula of Concord refers to Mary as the "Mother of God," and the most recently approved *Book of Common Prayer* of the Episcopal Church in the United States includes a translation of the Chalcedonian Definition of Faith, which refers to Mary as *Theotokos*, although its translation elects to render this by the less offensive "Mary the Virgin, the God-bearer (Theotokos)."[159] Since Lutheran, Anglican, and Reformed confessions affirm the faith expressed at the Council of Chalcedon and condemn Nestorianism (see the previous subsection), it could be argued that there is widespread agreement between the Reformation traditions on the affirmation that Mary is *Theotokos*, "Mother of God," although Reformed and older Anglican doctrinal statements do not explicitly use this term. Even this might be disputed by those who would argue that the Reformed confessions (and the Anglican Articles) only affirm the doctrine of "one Person in two natures" affirmed at Chalcedon, but not Chalcedon's use of the term "Mother of God" applied to Mary.[160]

159. *Book of Common Prayer* (USA 1979), p. 864.
160. This is the position taken by Calvin himself, who denied "Nestorianism" because it postulated two Persons in Christ, but Calvin would call Mary only "Mother of our Lord," not "Mother of God" or *Theotokos* (Calvin, *Institutes* 2.14.4 [in McNeill, 1:486–487]). On the other hand, Heppe and some of the Reformed dogmaticians he cites allow for the use of *Theotokos* in a very carefully defined sense. See Heinrich Heppe, *Reformed Dogmatics: Set Out and Illustrated from the Sources*, trans. G. T. Thomson (London: George Allen and Unwin, Ltd., 1950), 17:23; pp. 441–444.

The Latin text of the Lutheran Schmalkaldic Articles refers to Mary
as "ever Virgin," a title traditionally denoting belief in her perpetual
virginity, and Luther himself consistently believed in the doctrine of
perpetual virginity.[161] There is evidence that Zwingli, Calvin, and
early Anglican theologians believed in Mary's perpetual virginity, although an explicit affirmation of this belief does not appear in the Reformed Confessions or in early Anglican doctrinal statements.[162] Neither Lutheran nor Anglican nor Reformed confessions affirm the
doctrines of Mary's immaculate conception or her bodily assumption,
seeing these as grounded in later traditions rather than scripture, although it is important to remember that these were not yet formulated
as Catholic dogma at the time of the Reformation.

Anglo-Catholics interpret the silence of the Thirty-nine Articles of
Religion to allow for belief in some or all of the Mariological doctrines
affirmed by Roman Catholics. A reasonable guess is that only a few
Anglo-Catholics would affirm Mary's immaculate conception, some
more than this would affirm her bodily assumption into heaven, and
a fairly large number would affirm her perpetual virginity.

3.3   Teachings of Reformation and Union Churches on Human Nature and Salvation

Issues about human nature and salvation came to be vigorously debated during the century of the Reformation, so much so that the documents of the Catholic Reformation (the Council of Trent) as well as
Protestant documents deal at length with these concerns. Protestants
generally agreed with Catholics on the doctrine of original sin (see
3.3.1), but understood themselves as differing sharply from Catholic
doctrine in their assertion of the priority of grace without merit (see
3.3.3.a–b) and in their assertion of justification by faith alone (see
3.3.4). Union churches have largely followed Reformation doctrine in
their statements about human nature and salvation.

161. Schmalkaldic Articles, 1:4 (in Tappert, p. 292, n. 3).
162. Formative Anglican theologians of the 1500s and 1600s affirmed the perpetual virginity of Mary on the basis of ancient Christian authority; even Methodist
founder (and Anglican) John Wesley affirmed the doctrine of the perpetual virginity of Mary: John Wesley, "A Letter to a Roman Catholic," par. 7, in *The Works
of the Reverend John Wesley, A.M.*, ed. Thomas Jackson, 14 vols. (London: Wesleyan
Conference Office, 1873), 10:81. On Reformed views, including those of Zwingli
and Calvin, see David F. Wright, "Mary," in *Encyclopedia of the Reformed Faith*, ed.
Donald K. McKim (Louisville, Ky.: Westminster/John Knox Press, and Edinburgh: Saint Andrew Press, 1992), pp. 237–238.

3.3.1 What Reformation and Union traditions teach about original sin: Reformation and Union traditions agree in teaching that as a result of the fall of the first human beings, all subsequent human beings are born corrupted by original sin.

Sources: Augsburg Confession, 2, 19 (in Leith, pp. 68, 74; Schaff, 3:8–9, 20). Formula of Concord, Epitome 1 (in Schaff, 3:97–106). Westminster Confession, 6–7 (in Leith, pp. 201–203; Schaff, 3:615–618). Anglican Articles of Religion, 9 (in Leith, pp. 269–270; Schaff, 3:492–493). Basis of Union of The United Church of Canada, Articles 5–6 (UCC *Manual* 1993, p. 12).

Comparative Cross-References: Eastern Orthodox, 1.3.1–2; Roman Catholic, 2.3.1; Evangelical and Free, 4.3.1; Ecumenical, 5.2.3.

Despite sharp differences between Protestant and Catholic traditions in the Reformation age on issues of human salvation, there was and is a substantial ground of agreement between them on the issue of original sin, for both Catholic and Protestant traditions were shaped by the inheritance of thought from the ancient African Bishop Augustine of Hippo, who stressed the utter fallenness of humankind and our constant need for divine grace. Throughout the Middle Ages, leading up to the Reformation, a variety of opinions developed about "Augustinian" views of the human situation, but the doctrine of original sin remained a constant.

The Augsburg Confession (Lutheran), Westminster Confession (Reformed), and the Anglican Articles of Religion express a doctrine of original sin in terms drawn from the Augustinian tradition, asserting that not only the penalty for sin (death) but the actual guilt of sin is passed on to every human being. The original sin that we inherit, according to the Anglican Article, "deserveth God's wrath and damnation."[163] The Augsburg Confession makes the point that God is not the author of sin, so that "secondary causes" are acknowledged, that is, God allows creatures a degree of freedom, and the sin that every person inherits is a result of the sin of their first parent. Protestants have tended historically to speak of sin and salvation in "forensic" (courtroom) terms. Sin is understood as the transgression of God's eternal law, and salvation is forgiveness for our transgression. The sin of Adam and Eve was understood as their transgression of God's injunction to leave the forbidden fruit alone. At this point, though, the Anglican Article of Religion describes original sin as an "infection of nature," sounding here a note of similarity to Eastern Christian understandings of sin and salvation, which have tended to envision sin as an illness leading to death, and salvation as healing from that illness.

163. Anglican Articles of Religion, 9 (in Leith, pp. 269–270).

Having noted the general agreement between Reformation traditions and Catholicism on the issue of original sin, however, we should also be aware that on some points Reformation understandings of original sin differ from Roman Catholic formulations. It is typical of the Reformation theologians and of the Reformation creeds to state that human beings in their present condition are corrupted "completely" or "in all of their faculties": this belief in the complete fallenness of humankind is described traditionally as the doctrine of total depravity. For many Reformers this meant, in particular, that human reason cannot be trusted after the fall of humankind (and so, all the more reason to rely on scripture as God's revelation). Neither Orthodox nor Catholic doctrine questioned so deeply the ability of human reason after the fall. It also implied, for the Reformers, that human freedom is impaired after the fall, which leads to the next point to be considered.

3.3.2 *What Reformation and Union traditions teach about the loss of human free will:* Reformation and Union traditions agree in teaching that although human beings may retain a degree of free will after the fall, they have lost free will to do any good, especially as respects their salvation.

Sources: Augsburg Confession, 18 (in Leith, pp. 73–74; Schaff, 3:18–19). Westminster Confession, 9 (in Leith, pp. 205–206; Schaff, 3:623–624). Anglican Articles of Religion, 10 (in Leith, p. 270; Schaff, 3:493–494). Basis of Union of The United Church of Canada, Article 3 (UCC *Manual* 1993, p. 13).

Comparative Cross-References: Eastern Orthodox, 1.3.3; Roman Catholic, 2.3.2; Evangelical and Free, 4.3.1.

Consistent with the Augustinian tradition, Reformation and Union traditions teach not only that human reason has been corrupted but that human free will also has been so corrupted by the fall of our first parents that we are unable by ourselves to do any good. We may have "free will" in the sense that we can choose between options, but without the grace of God helping us, all our options are evil ones. Only by divine grace can we do any good. When confronted with the question of how "virtuous pagans" could do good, Reformation theologians would either deny that their acts could be good or would claim that their good works arise from a "common grace" given to all human beings. The way in which the Anglican Article states this claim about God's grace being the ground of all good is to say "Original sin standeth not in the following of Adam (as the Pelagians do vainly boast)," because Adam and Eve had a truly free will, that is, free to do good, to do what God required. But because of the fall, we are not like them. The Article continues by asserting that original sin

is the fault and corruption of the Nature of every man that naturally is engendered of the offspring of Adam; whereby man is
very far gone from original righteousness, and is of his own nature inclined to evil. . .[164]

That is to say in our "natural" state ("natural" literally means "from
birth," but it refers more specifically to our condition on our own,
apart from the grace of God), we have no "free will" to do what is
right.

It is important to note Protestant agreement on this issue of "free
will," and we have placed the term in quotation marks to indicate that
the term is used in a very carefully defined sense. As we shall see in
the next subsections, there are some important disagreements between Protestants on the issue of how God's grace is worked out in
human lives, but even those Protestants who have rejected "predestination" have consistently argued that in our "natural state" we have
no true free will. The difference is not really over free will, but rather
over the extent of God's granting (or renewing) free will by grace.

3.3.3.a What Reformed tradition teaches concerning predestination:
Reformed tradition generally agrees in teaching that God freely elects
or predestines some persons to salvation and others to damnation.

Sources: Heidelberg Catechism, 54 (in Schaff, 3:324–325). Canons of the Synod of
Dort (in Schaff, 3:550–597). Westminster Confession, 3:3–8 (in Leith, pp. 198–199;
Schaff, 3:608–611).

Comparative Cross-References: Eastern Orthodox, 1.3.3; Roman Catholic, 2.3.3; Evangelical and Free, 4.3.2.a–b.

The Reformed churches have been historically consistent in affirming the doctrine that only those who are "elected" or "predestined" or
"chosen" eternally by God will be saved. "For those whom he foreknew he also predestined to be conformed to the image of his Son
. . ." (Rom. 8:29a). The height of human arrogance would be to assert
that we are ourselves somehow responsible for our salvation; the
work of salvation, as Reformed Christians understand it, must be entirely the work of God. The doctrine of predestination was understood
in the 1500s to be "a very comfortable doctrine" because it saves us
from reliance on ourselves and makes salvation entirely the work of
God. We might note that Reformed Christians found themselves at
one on this point with those Catholics who taught a consistently Augustinian doctrine of predestination, such as the Dominicans in the

164. Ibid. (in Leith, p. 269).

1580s and 1590s, and the Jansenists of the 1600s, and in fact other Catholics accused both these groups of being "Calvinists." As we shall see, Lutherans and many Anglicans also insisted on a version of the teaching of predestination.

It is true that some Reformed Christians rejected the doctrine of predestination in the earliest decades of the 1600s. Taking the Dutch teacher Jakob Harmensen (in Latin, "*Arminius*") as their mentor, they argued that Christ died, not for a limited number of the elect, but for all humankind. Christ, the Arminians taught, made it possible for all human beings to have, by grace and not their own work, a degree of "free will" that would enable them to turn to God and be saved. But at a council in Dordrecht (or *Dort*), Holland, in 1619, representatives of Reformed churches throughout Europe adopted five points against the Arminians, which are traditionally remembered in English by the acronym "TULIP":

> Total Depravity
> Unconditional Election
> Limited Atonement
> Irresistible Grace, and
> Perseverance of the Saints[165]

A thoroughgoing Reformed Christian, one who accepts each of these points, will sometimes be referred to as a "Five Point Calvinist," a term that is itself disputed because other Reformed Christians maintain that the "Five Points" go far beyond Calvin's own teaching. "Total depravity" denotes the belief that all aspects of human nature are affected by the corruption of sin (see 3.3.1). "Unconditional election" means that God "elects" or chooses those who will be saved, without consideration of human merit or qualifications. "Limited atonement" means that Christ's work was not for all human beings but for the limited number of those who are predestined to salvation. "Irresistible grace" means that God's grace cannot be resisted by human beings. "Perseverance of the saints" means that those who are predestined to eternal life can never fall completely away from God's grace and so will persevere to the end. Although the Council of Dort was widely affirmed by British and European Reformed churches, many persons in the Reformed tradition since its time have questioned whether it faithfully explicated Calvin's own doctrine of predestination or (as some would argue) went far beyond it in hardening the understanding of predestination in the Reformed tradition.

---

165. Canons of the Synod of Dort (in Schaff, 3:550–597). The "TULIP" acrostic is a traditional mnemonic for remembering the essential points of Dort.

Within the bounds of agreement on the doctrine of predestination, there are a number of disputed points. One question is whether God simply chooses those who will be saved out of the total, damned mass of human beings or whether God chooses *both* those who will be saved *and* those who will be damned. The former view is called single predestination, and is usually considered somewhat milder, since according to this view God does not really choose persons for damnation; rather, damnation was chosen for all human beings by Adam and Eve. The latter view is referred to as double predestination, and it is seen as a sterner but perhaps more consistent view, according to which God determines beforehand both those who will be saved and those who will be damned. The Reformed tradition, as contrasted with Lutherans, has consistently affirmed double predestination in its formal doctrinal statements.

A second question over which Reformed churches are divided is whether God made the "decrees" of predestination considering the fall of humankind into sin, or without consideration of the fall. The former view is referred to as *infralapsarianism,* and is it interpreted as being more lenient or milder because God's act of predestination was made in compassionate consideration of humanity's fall into sin. The latter view is referred to as *supralapsarianism,*[166] and it is interpreted as being a sterner (but again, more consistent) view because it holds that God's decrees of who would be saved and who would be damned were made eternally, not only prior to the creation of humankind, but without consideration of the eventual fall of humanity into sin.

A closely related question is where the doctrine of predestination should be placed in understanding the Christian faith. John Calvin himself placed the doctrine of predestination in his consideration of human salvation, and this seems to imply the infralapsarian belief that predestination was God's gracious response to the fallenness of humankind.[167] Later Reformed theologians, the Council of Dort, and the Westminster Confession of Faith placed the doctrine of predestination in their consideration of the nature of God. This seems to imply the harsher supralapsarian belief that predestination was God's act apart from any consideration of human fallenness. It is on this issue, however, that many Reformed Christians question whether Dort and the Westminster Confession went beyond Calvin in their understandings of predestination.

166. "Infralapsarian" technically means "after the fall" and "supralapsarian" means "before the fall," but despite the use of these terms, Reformed teachers are clear that the "before" and "after" cannot be taken in a temporal sense, since time would be irrelevant in God's view.
167. Calvin, *Institutes* 3.21–24 (in McNeill, 2:920–987).

A fourth question is over the issue of "limited atonement." Some Reformed Christians believe that Christ's death paid the penalty for all human sin, even though it is applied only to those who are elect. Because of their questioning of the L in the "TULIP," they are sometimes referred to as "Four Point" or "Four and a Half Point" Calvinists. "Five Point" Calvinists have traditionally asserted that Christ's work was only for the limited number of the elect.

On each of these four questions, as we have seen, there is a somewhat milder view, which attempts to lessen the shock of "the horrible decrees" (as critics called the thoroughly Calvinist doctrine), and a sterner view. Advocates of the sterner positions very often argue that theirs is more consistent because God's foreknowledge and providence makes each distinction irrelevant: God *knows* in saving some that others are damned, God *knew* that humans would eventually fall and knew beforehand that a decision to elect some would have to be made, and God *knows* that only those predestined to eternal life will be saved by the work of Christ.

By contrast with these rather harsh views, there were advocates of the Reformed tradition who preferred not to define the doctrine of predestination so sharply. The mildest expression of predestination in Reformed confessions comes in the Heidelberg Catechism (1563; written long before the Synod of Dort), where the subject is dealt with only obliquely in response to a question concerning the church. The Heidelberg Catechism states that

> out of the whole human race, from the beginning to the end of the world, the Son of God, by his Spirit and Word, gathers, defends, and preserves for himself unto everlasting life, a chosen communion in the unity of the true faith.[168]

Seeking to reconcile Lutherans and Reformed in northern Germany, this statement allowed for the strict interpretation of predestination noted above, but also allowed for milder readings, for example, the view that God's "choosing" of men and women for salvation is based on a foreknowledge of their use of free will. We have noted above the Arminians, who questioned the doctrine of predestination in the first decade of the 1600s. Similarly, the Cumberland Presbyterian churches, which originated in the early 1800s on the frontier of North America, rewrote the Westminster Confession to omit its teaching on predestination. The Presbyterian Church (U.S.A.) has added a contemporary note on the Westminster Confession that insists that belief

---

168. Heidelberg Catechism, question 54 (in Schaff, 3:324–325).

in divine predestination must be "held in harmony with the doctrine of [God's] love for all mankind, his gift of his Son to be the propitiation for the sins of the whole world, and his readiness to bestow his saving grace on all who seek it. . . ."[169]

Although the doctrine of predestination has been a hallmark of the Reformed tradition through its history, we would not have the accent correct if we were to lay the stress on this doctrine itself. Rather, the stress should fall on the conviction that this doctrine upholds, namely, that salvation is entirely God's work, and none of our acts, not even acts of human will, can bring about our salvation.

3.3.3.b *Views of predestination or alternatives to it in other traditions than Reformed:* Lutheran and Anglican traditions allow a wider degree of belief on the question of why some are saved and others are not. Within these traditions, (1) some affirm a doctrine of predestination, (2) some maintain that a preparatory grace gives all the possibility of turning to Christ, and (3) some refuse to answer the question.

Sources: Formula of Concord, Epitome 11 (in Schaff, 3:165–173). Anglican Articles of Religion, 17 (in Leith, p. 272; Schaff, 3:497–499). Basis of Union of The United Church of Canada, Articles 3–4 (UCC *Manual* 1993, p. 12).

Comparative Cross-References: Eastern Orthodox, 1.3.3; Roman Catholic, 2.3.3; Evangelical and Free, 4.3.2.a–b.

The Lutheran and Anglican traditions have not been as consistent as the Reformed tradition in teaching the doctrine of predestination. The Anglican Articles of Religion include an Article (17) affirming the doctrine, and in fact many early Anglicans and Lutherans believed that God elects or predestines those who will be saved. Martin Luther himself, in contention with Desiderius Erasmus, laid out his belief in this characteristically Augustinian doctrine. After long discussion of the doctrine, the Lutheran Formula of Concord came down in favor of "single predestination," that is, the belief that out of the whole, condemned mass of human beings, God has chosen some for salvation, and the damnation of the rest is due to their inheritance of original sin, not to a decision on the part of God.

Many Anglicans, especially after 1600, identified themselves with the "Arminian" teaching discussed above, that is, the teaching that Christ died for all human beings, who are given a free will to believe by a special grace, a "preparatory" or "prevenient" grace. One im-

169. *Book of Confessions of the Presbyterian Church in the United States of America,* Declaratory Statement concerning the Westminster Confession of Faith, 6:192 (New York and Atlanta: Published by the Office of the General Assembly, 1983).

portant version of this teaching held by some Anglicans and Lutherans, though not enshrined in their doctrinal tradition, resembles very closely the position taken by the Jesuits in contention with (predestinarian) Dominicans in the 1590s, and that is the perspective that God predestines those whom God foreknew would make a free choice to believe in Christ. They read Romans 8:29 ("For those whom he foreknew he also predestined to be conformed to the image of his Son . . .") as supporting this view.

Yet others would say that, in the end, this question cannot be answered because of the limitations of human intellect. This was the position (if it can be called that) arrived at by Catholics in the 1590s and early 1600s, when the pope simply declared that Jesuits should not accuse Dominicans of Calvinism, and Dominicans should not accuse Jesuits of Pelagianism. Many individual theologians in Reformation churches have maintained the importance of such an openness on this issue, and for Lutheran churches that do not receive the Formula of Concord as binding doctrine, the issue does remain open. Union churches typically refuse to resolve the issue, since the Union churches embrace constituents from Reformed and other traditions. The United Church of Canada, for instance, declares that God's providential oversight and purpose is not inconsistent with the free will of humankind, but the church does not prescribe either a traditional doctrine of predestination or an Arminian position.[170]

3.3.4 What Reformation and Union traditions teach concerning justification: Reformation and Union traditions agree in teaching that human beings are justified on the basis of faith alone.

Sources: Augsburg Confession, 4 (in Leith, p. 69; Schaff, 3:10–11). Westminster Confession, 11, 14 (in Leith, pp. 207–208, 209; Schaff, 3:626–628, 630–631). Anglican Articles of Religion, 11, 13 (in Leith, p. 270–271; Schaff, 3:494, 495). Basis of Union of The United Church of Canada, Articles 10–11 (UCC *Manual* 1993, p. 13).

Comparative Cross-References: Eastern Orthodox, 1.3.3; Roman Catholic, 2.3.4; Evangelical and Free, 4.3.4.a–b.

The doctrine of justification by faith alone was a central doctrine of the Protestant Reformation, and all the Reformation churches express this doctrine unequivocally in their historic doctrinal statements. "Justification" denotes the act in which God forgives human beings of their sin. This does not, according to Reformation teachers, imply a fiction on the part of God: God knows that we are sinful and continues

---

170. Basis of Union of The United Church of Canada, Articles 3–4 (UCC *Manual* 1993, p. 12).

to know this, but on the basis of Christ's work and on condition of our faith (itself a gift of grace), God freely forgives our sins.

But what does "faith" mean in this sense? The words translated "faith" and "belief" are actually the same words in the Greek of the New Testament (and in Latin and most European languages). Reformation teachers generally understood "faith" to denote trust in Christ, although the Reformation doctrinal statements differ somewhat in describing the object of this trust. The Anglican Articles of Religion (and the Homily on Justification) simply specify Christ as the object of justifying faith. The Augsburg Confession takes justifying faith to denote our belief *that* Christ died on our behalf and *that* our sins are forgiven for his sake. We have emphasized the word "that" in these sentences, because, for Lutherans, the object of justifying faith is a particular claim about *what* Christ has done. The Westminster Confession takes a somewhat different angle, stating that justifying faith denotes our trust in the things revealed in scripture. These statements do not differ significantly, since Christ is at the center of the Lutheran claim about faith, and Reformed Christians take Christ to be that which is revealed, above all, in scripture.

But we should note, especially for readers from Evangelical backgrounds, that the Reformation view of justifying faith did not necessarily involve belief in a particular kind of religious experience, a conversion experience, as Evangelical churches have traditionally insisted on. For the Reformation churches, justifying faith involves a more objective trust in Christ, not the subjective experience prized by Evangelicals. In fact, for most Reformation churches justification is understood as accompanying baptism (see 3.4.3), and Luther himself could speak of a kind of justifying faith given even to infants in baptism. Although Pietistic or Evangelical movements stressing the subjective experience of conversion have arisen in all the Reformation traditions, Reformation churches have sometimes condemned subjective interpretations of justifying faith, seeing a kind of self-justification, a reliance on our own works or actions, implied in them. For the Reformation churches, the stress is typically placed on the object of our faith (Christ) rather than our own experience of faith.

Now to get the accent or stress on the right point, we must pause here long enough to notice that for Lutherans, the doctrine of justification by faith alone looms over and informs the whole structure of Christian doctrine. As we have seen above, the careful distinction of "Law" and "Gospel" used as a tool for interpreting the Bible by Lutherans is grounded in their insistence that the doctrine of salvation by faith only (and grace only) is an invaluable key to understanding the meaning of the Scriptures as a whole (see 3.1.2.a).

3.3.5 *What Reformation and Union traditions teach concerning good works after justification:* Reformation and Union traditions agree in teaching that good works ought to follow as the "fruits" of faith, but they have no power of themselves to merit human salvation.

Sources: Augsburg Confession, 6, 20 (in Leith, pp. 69–70, 74–77; Schaff, 3:11, 20–26). Formula of Concord, Epitome, 4–6 (in Schaff, 3:121–135). Westminster Confession, 16, 19 (in Leith, pp. 210–211, 213–215; Schaff, 3:633–636, 640–643). Anglican Articles of Religion, 12–14 (in Leith, pp. 270–271; Schaff, 3:494–495). Basis of Union of The United Church of Canada, Article 12 (UCC *Manual* 1993, p. 13).

Comparative Cross-References: Eastern Orthodox, 1.3.6; Roman Catholic, 2.3.5; Evangelical and Free, 4.3.5.

The churches of the Reformation and later Union churches teach consistently that Christian faith ought to lead to a life of righteousness and holiness and specifically ought to lead to good works performed in obedience to Christ. The lifelong process of growth in holiness is traditionally termed sanctification (from *sanctus*, "holy"). The doctrinal statements of these churches make it very clear, however, that although good works might be rewarded in heaven, they themselves have no power to effect human salvation; rather, they come as the result or fruit of the faith by which we are justified. Reformation and Union churches carefully avoid talk of our works "meriting" our salvation in any sense, and they contrast clearly with traditional Catholic teaching on this point (see 2.3.5).

Not only did the churches of the Reformation reject medieval Catholic understandings of human merit but they also consistently rejected the notion that human beings can attain "perfection" as a result of the process of sanctification. For the churches of the Reformation, perfection is associated only with justification, since the righteousness that is given to human beings in justification is the righteousness of God in Christ and therefore perfect. The holiness we acquire in sanctification, however, is always limited by our human inabilities and weakness and so cannot be termed "perfection." This contrasts with Orthodox and Catholic understandings of "divinization" or perfection (see 1.3.4 and 2.3.5) and with the teachings of Wesleyan churches on the possibility of "entire sanctification" or "Christian perfection" in this life (see 4.3.6.b). It is appropriate to note at this point that Anglicans are divided on this issue: those who prize their medieval and Catholic heritage are not reluctant to speak of the goal of the Christian life as perfect love for God or, as a prominent Anglican spiritual treatise of the 1600s was titled, *The Life of God in the Soul of Man*.

Now within their broad agreement on the need for good works following justification, Reformed and Lutheran churches have had an important, historic difference in interpreting the role of God's Law for Christians. In this dispute, "Law" denotes not so much the ceremonial law as the moral law contained in the Old Testament and represented in the Ten Commandments. Lutherans argued that although "the Law always accuses" us of remaining in sin, and although Christians will obey Christ and perform good works as a result of faith, Christians are no longer "bound to" or "servants of" the Law; Christ has freed us from the Law, giving us freedom to do what is right, not out of a sense of obligation but out of a sense of gratitude and love. Reformed Christians agree that the Gospel changes our motivation for doing good works and frees us from the rigor of the Law, but they insist that we are never "free" from the moral law of God, because the Law was given by God to serve as a practical guide for a life lived in gratitude to God. Anglicans, we might note, have been divided on this issue, with more puritanical or Evangelical Anglicans leaning in the Reformed direction, and other Anglicans taking the Lutheran view.

Because of this difference in understanding the role of God's Law in Christian living, it may be said that Reformed tradition (and Anglican doctrine) lays more stress on good works than the Lutheran tradition, which has always suspected a lurking reliance on "works righteousness" in claims that Christians are bound to do good works. This difference in interpretation, moreover, has had some important, practical effects on the ethos of Protestant Christians. Reformed churches, for instance, have traditionally observed Sunday as the "Sabbath" and have traditionally insisted on strict observation of the Sabbath as a day of rest, following the Fourth Commandment. Sporting activities, to take a specific example, were traditionally forbidden for Reformed Christians on Sunday. Lutherans and many Anglicans have not been as inclined to "sabbatarianism," regarding the Christian observance of Sunday as "the Lord's day," replacing the Sabbath of "the old Law" with a new Christian celebration.

3.3.6 What Reformed tradition and some others teach concerning the perseverance of the saints: The Reformed tradition agrees in teaching that those who are elect to salvation cannot finally fall from God's saving grace.

Sources: Westminster Confession, 17–18 (in Leith, pp. 206–213; Schaff, 3:636–640).
Comparative Cross-References: Evangelical and Free, 4.3.6.a.

This point reiterates in its logical place the P of the "TULIP" (see 3.3.3.a), that is, the doctrine of the "Perseverance of the Saints." The Reformed tradition has maintained consistently that those whom God has chosen for salvation cannot finally fall away and lose their salvation. This does not mean that everything will be easy for the elect: they may fall along the way, and they will in any case be faced with temptations and trials. But this doctrine maintains that in the end God's grace will restore them to faith and bring them to final salvation. This doctrine is even maintained by the Cumberland Presbyterian churches, who do not hold to the doctrine of predestination that usually accompanies this teaching of the perseverance of the saints.

3.3.7 *What Reformation and Union churches teach about life beyond death:* Reformation and Union churches generally agree in teaching that after the final judgment those who believe in Christ will share eternal fellowship with Christ and one another, and those who reject Christ will suffer eternal punishment. Some teach that believers will share fellowship with Christ, and those who reject Christ will experience torment, in an "intermediate state" between death and the final judgment.

Sources: Augsburg Confession, 17 (in Leith, p. 73). Second Helvetic Confession, chap. 26 (in Leith, pp. 184–185). Westminster Confession, chaps. 32–33 (in Leith, pp. 228–230). Anglican Articles of Religion, 22 (in Leith, p. 274).

Comparative Cross-References: Eastern Orthodox, 1.3.7; Roman Catholic, 2.3.7; Evangelical and Free, 4.3.7.

The traditional doctrinal standards of Reformation and Union churches reflect the view that beyond death and the final judgment, believers will share fellowship with Christ and with one another through eternity, and those who reject faith in Christ will be cut off from Christ and will suffer eternal punishment. In formal doctrine there is very little speculation on what heaven (eternal fellowship with Christ) or hell (eternal punishment) will be like. All Reformation churches (Lutheran, Reformed, and Anglican) reject the notion of purgatory as a place in which the prayers of those on earth may help those who have died. The Westminster Confession makes it clear that human bodies perish at death, believers go to be with Christ in heaven and unbelievers are tormented, then at the final judgment believers are reunited with their "redeemed" bodies and share eternity with Christ. The belief in a particular state between death and the final judgment was sometimes identified as an "intermediate state," and although in the 1500s Protestants distinguished this clearly from Catholic notions of purgatory then popular, clarification of Catholic teaching since that time (see 2.3.7) has suggested that these ideas may not be so far separate. For this reason, Anglo-Catholics will sometimes speak openly of purgatory, arguing that what is condemned in their Article of Religion was only a medieval corruption of Catholic teaching.

3.4   Teachings of Reformation and Union Churches on Church, Ministry, and Sacraments

Some of the most critical issues that divided Catholics and Protestants at the time of the Reformation were the related issues of the nature of the church, its structure and authority, and its sacraments. Medieval reformers such as John Wycliffe and John Huss had questioned the Catholic understanding of the church, arguing that the only true church is the church of God's elect, which is "invisible" or hidden in this world. Both Wycliffe and Huss had rejected the doctrine of transubstantiation, and in these ways they laid the background for the Protestant Reformers' challenges to inherited views of the church, its ministry, and its sacraments. But despite the challenges, there were some important grounds of continuity between medieval Catholicism and the Reformers, even in the ways in which the Reformers understood the church and its sacraments. These grounds of continuity are as important as the issues that divided the churches, especially in the light of contemporary ecumenical efforts at broader Christian understanding and cooperation. If the visible unity of the church is to be renewed, the issues taken up in this section will have to be very carefully understood and discussed.

3.4.1 *How Reformation and Union traditions, generally, define the church.* Reformation and Union traditions agree in teaching that the visible church is the community of believers in which the Word is preached and the sacraments are administered.

Sources: Augsburg Confession, 7 (in Leith, p. 70; Schaff, 3:11–12). Westminster Confession, 25 (in Leith, p. 222; Schaff, 3:657–659). Anglican Articles of Religion, 19 (in Leith, p. 273; Schaff, 3:499–500). Basis of Union of The United Church of Canada, Article 15 (UCC *Manual* 1993, p. 14).

Comparative Cross-References: Eastern Orthodox, 1.4.1; Roman Catholic, 2.4.1; Evangelical and Free, 4.4.1; Ecumenical, 5.2.4.1.

Most doctrinal statements of Reformation and Union churches follow the Augsburg Confession (1530) in defining three necessary components of the church: (1) a community or gathering of believing Christians,[171] where (2) the Word is preached, and (3) the sacraments are administered. If this seems altogether simple, we might note that the second and third points are usually qualified: the church exists where believers gather and "the Gospel is preached in its purity"

171. The Latin text of the Augsburg Confession has "a congregation of saints" (Schaff, 3:11), but "saints" in this case is used in its New Testament sense, that is, as a synonym for Christian believers. The German text has "the assembly of all believers."

(Augsburg Confession) or where "the pure Word of God is preached" (Anglican Articles). Similarly, the church exists where "the holy sacraments are administered according to the Gospel" (Augsburg Confession) or where "the Sacraments be duly ministered according to Christ's ordinance" (Anglican Articles). These qualifications allow for a wide range of discussion about what defines the purity of the church's preaching, and what constitutes a "duly ministered" sacrament, both of which are necessary to the presence of the church.

We may note, further, that this definition applies to the visible church, that is, the church as it appears to the world. Implied in this (and stated most explicitly in Reformed confessions) is the notion that the true church, consisting of those whom God has chosen for salvation, remains hidden or "invisible" in this world. The idea of the Reformers was that the true church has not always appeared "visibly" to the world, and in their way of thinking, the church was especially hidden during the Middle Ages and became more visible with the reforms of the Protestants in the 1500s. The Westminster Confession emphasizes that the church has sometimes been more or less visible in history. In other words, at some points (the early centuries of the church and especially the New Testament age, and the age of the Reformation) the purity of the church has appeared particularly visible to the world, but at other points the true church has been hidden (especially in the Middle Ages). This stress on the "invisibility" of the true church in this world is understood by Reformed Christians as being closely related to their understanding of election (see 3.3.3.a). For Anglicans and Lutherans, the break between the Middle Ages and the Reformation was not perceived so sharply: Anglicans and Lutherans maintained the very church buildings and cathedrals in which their medieval ancestors had worshiped, and they preserved a perceptible continuity with medieval liturgical practices, however purified at the time of the Reformation (on this point, see 3.1.2.a and c).[172]

3.4.1.a *Distinct emphases of the Reformed tradition concerning the doctrine of the church:* The Reformed tradition adds to the definition of the "visible" church the necessity of discipline within the Christian community.

Sources: Heidelberg Catechism, 54, 81–85 (Schaff, 3:324–325, 336–338). Westminster Confession, 25 and especially 30 (in Leith, pp. 222, 227; Schaff, 3:657–659, 667–668).

172. Scottish Presbyterians also retained medieval church buildings, although they had to be altered in most cases to suit the "plainness" of Reformed taste in church architecture.

The Reformed tradition lays considerable stress on the importance of discipline in the Christian community. Consistent with the strictness of early Christians, Reformed churches have traditionally insisted on careful self-examination in approaching the Eucharist and on careful communal discipline in the Eucharist. The Westminster Confession of Faith maintains that discipline (under the heading of "Church Censures") is necessary to regain those who have offended the community, to restrain evil influences on the community, and to keep the church itself pure. In stricter Reformed communities, discipline was administered in a three-step process, in which (1) the offending member was warned or admonished by the church, (2) the offending person was kept from participation in the Lord's Supper (the traditional term for this was "fencing" the supper),[173] and in the most severe cases (3) the offender could be cut off from communion with (or excommunicated from) the church. In practice, local sessions or congregational assemblies (see 3.4.2.b) determined who should be admitted to communion, who should be excluded or fenced from communion until they had repented and confessed, and who should be cut off from communion.

3.4.1.b *A further emphasis of Congregationalist churches concerning the doctrine of the church: the congregational principle.* Congregationalist churches have historically taught that the church exists primarily as a local body or congregation, which may participate in broader expressions of Christian unity.

Sources: The Cambridge Platform, chaps. 2–4 (in Leith, pp. 387–392). Declaration of the Congregational Union of England and Wales, Principles of Church Order and Discipline (Schaff, 3:733–734).

Congregationalist churches belong to the Reformed tradition and share the Reformed emphasis noted above on the need for discipline within the church. Congregationalist churches are further distinguished by their insistence that the local congregation is the primary expression of the church. This does not deny the reality of "the catholic church," but contrasts with other traditions that see the universal or catholic church as the primary meaning of "church" and see local congregations as particular expressions of the universal church. Congregationalists, in contrast, see local congregations united together by local church covenants as the primary expression of the church, and see larger "associations" of Christians as extensions of the ministries

---

173. In fact, Lutheran churches that continued to recognize penance as a sacrament and practiced private confession also "fenced" the table, linking communion to confession.

of particular congregations. As we shall see, the primary locus of church government, for Congregationalists, lies with the local congregation (see 3.4.2.c).

The Congregationalist stress on the priority of the local congregation carries important ecumenical implications. As we have seen above, it makes the explication of "doctrine" (as we have defined it, consensus regarding Christian teachings) more difficult, since local congregations adopt their own expressions of Christian doctrine (see 3.4.2.c). The stress on the priority of the local congregation also makes formal ecumenical relationships more complex, since they must be expressions of Christian "association," and formal ecumenical relationships cannot be entered into on the part of a Congregationalist denomination except as an expression of the association of congregations. The congregational principle has deeply influenced the Evangelical and Free churches (for example, Baptist churches) considered in chapter 4, and we shall have to return to this principle in considering the variety of Evangelical and Free churches.

Having considered basic definitions of the church, we now come to consider the different ways in which Reformation and Union churches are organized and the closely related question of how they have understood ordained ministries. Although the process of democratization of church order in the last two hundred years has opened up positions for lay leadership in most Reformation and Union churches, the basic patterns of church government remain closely related to patterns of ministerial order. These are important, church-dividing issues, not only for doctrinal and theological reasons but also for quite practical reasons, since the visible disunity of the churches in our time is grounded partly in the churches' differing patterns of church government and ministerial order.

There are three basic patterns of church polity or government that have developed among the Reformation and Union churches: the episcopal, presbyterian, and congregational patterns. Moreover, in some Reformation traditions (Lutherans in particular) particular denominations choose between these patterns, and Union churches tend to combine these basic patterns in various ways. Note that we have used lowercase initial letters for "episcopal," "presbyterian," and "congregational" to indicate that these adjectives describe forms of polity. Of course, Presbyterian churches are characterized by presbyterian polity and Congregationalist churches are characterized by congregational polity. Anglican churches, moreover, are consistently characterized by an episcopal polity, and in the United States and Scotland the term "Episcopal" appears in the names of Anglican denominations. We can say of

Lutherans, though, that some Lutheran churches have an episcopal polity, some have a polity resembling that of presbyterianism, and some have a congregational polity, while others have a mixture or hybrid of these various patterns, so that these adjectives used with lowercase initial letters denote the form of polity and not only the Reformation traditions that have been characterized by them.

3.4.2.a *Reformation and Union patterns of church polity and ministerial order: the episcopal pattern.* The episcopal form of ministerial order and church polity, utilized consistently by Anglicans, presupposes a threefold ordering of ministry into deacons, priests, and bishops. It places primary responsibility for church governance in its bishops, who operate within guidelines set by church assemblies. Some Anglicans, moreover, insist on the necessity of an unbroken episcopal succession from the apostles.

Sources: Chicago-Lambeth Quadrilateral, point 4 (in the *Book of Common Prayer* [USA, 1979], pp. 877–878).

Comparative Cross-References: Eastern Orthodox, 1.4.2; Roman Catholic, 2.4.3–4; Evangelical and Free, 4.4.2.a–c.

Of the three Reformation patterns of church government or polity, the one closest to that of medieval catholicism is the episcopal pattern. The term "episcopal" is derived from the word *episkopos*, "bishop." It denotes a form of church polity that is distinguished by the central role played by bishops in the governing of the church. The episcopal polity presupposes a threefold ordering of ministry into deacons (in traditional Anglican practice, this denoted persons preparing for the priesthood), priests (those who function as ministers in local congregations), and bishops (persons who represent the unity and governance of the church and who perform ordination and confirmation). This pattern, as we have seen in our discussions of Orthodoxy and Roman Catholicism, was clearly expressed as early as the second decade of the second century A.D. and is consistent with Orthodox and contemporary Catholic understandings of ministerial order.[174]

---

174. Although at the time of the Reformation, most Anglicans considered bishops to be priests with full powers and simple priests as having limited powers: this is why early Anglican ordinals referred to the "consecration" rather than "ordination" of bishops. (This was also a relic of the medieval Western understanding of the three orders as being those of subdeacons, deacons, and priests.) By the time of the 1662 prayer book, the term "ordination" was allowed in addition to "consecration" for bishops. Since Anglicans (and Roman Catholics) have clearly affirmed the more ancient threefold pattern of deacons, priests, and bishops, this is of primarily historical interest, but it may bear relevance in ecumenical discussions, since Catholics and Anglicans alike have come to affirm doctrinally the threefold pattern of ministry of deacons, priests, and bishops.

Like many other churches, Anglican churches have moved in the last two decades to restore the office of permanent deacon; that is, a diaconate that is a permanent office for specific ministerial functions and not a transitional step toward becoming a priest. In fact, there have been calls in the last two decades to abolish the "transitional diaconate" in order to assert the integrity of the permanent diaconate as a full and equal ministerial order.

At the time of the Reformation, the Church of England inherited the office of bishop from the medieval English church. Many bishops supported the activities of the English Reformers and in fact some of the English Reformers *were* bishops. The two English archbishops of Canterbury and York were also retained, with the archbishop of Canterbury in particular continuing to serve in his historic role as a symbolic representative of English Christianity. In the Anglican tradition, bishops alone hold the authority to ordain ministers and to install ministers in their parishes, and bishops perform confirmations for all Anglicans. In most Anglican churches, moreover, the bishops together form an assembly that cooperates with other assemblies in legislating changes in the church's life.

This last point suggests another dimension of Anglican church government that must be noted in addition to the Anglicans' characteristic use of bishops. The other dimension is the Anglican use of church assemblies, which set the parameters within which bishops can legally act. The Church of England inherited from the English church of the Middle Ages a Convocation, divided originally into a "House of Bishops" and a separate "House of Clergy." At the time of the Reformation, the Convocation was given authority over church matters, and over the last two hundred years Convocation has evolved into a three-part General Synod, with a representative "House of Laity" in addition to the older Houses of Bishops and Clergy. Any important legislation affecting the Church of England must win the consent of all three Houses of the General Synod. Outside of England, Anglicans have developed national or regional assemblies modeled after the General Synod, with varying degrees of participation by bishops, clergy, and laity.

Another area in which Anglicans follow medieval Catholic practice is in their organization of churches into dioceses, presided over by a single bishop. Dioceses are further subdivided into specific parishes, denoting a local congregation (and in England, the geographical area served by a local congregation). Lay representatives to Anglican assemblies are selected by the parish, and in Anglican tradition there exists in each parish a group of designated local leaders called the vestry, which is also empowered to make certain decisions regarding the congregation and its property. As the Anglican pattern of church government has evolved, annual diocesan assemblies have been utilized in many places, which combined with vestries and the larger Synod or assemblies form a three-level pattern of assemblies: vestries at the congregational level, diocesan assemblies for the diocese, and a national assembly or General Synod for a whole Anglican denomination or national church.

We must note one further matter regarding the Anglican episcopal pattern of church polity: many Anglicans regard an unbroken succession of bishops in the church from the time of the apostles as being necessary to the existence of the church. Although this doctrine of apostolic succession was not expressed in the Anglican Articles or Homilies, nor in the works of such formative Elizabethan theologians as Richard Hooker, it became a passionately defended point in the 1600s, especially in contention with the Puritans. Apostolic succession has clearly evolved as a doctrine, that is, an agreed point of Christian teaching, by many Anglicans since the 1600s, especially by Anglo-Catholics. It is an important factor today in Anglican ecumenical dialogue. The Chicago-Lambeth Quadrilateral (1880s) insists that any future ecumenical unity including Anglicans should maintain "The Historic Episcopate, locally adapted in the methods of its administration to the varying needs of the nations and peoples called of God into the unity of His Church."[175] Although this does not state a doctrine of apostolic succession as such, the expression "historic episcopate" in Anglican lore has usually implied the unbroken succession of bishops through the centuries. This is a particularly important statement, since the Chicago-Lambeth Quadrilateral speaks for Anglicans very broadly, not just for those of the Anglo-Catholic cause. One ecumenical implication of this teaching is that Anglicans who insisted on the doctrine of apostolic succession did not (historically) recognize the ministerial orders of churches without apostolic succession. However, many Anglicans today would argue that although the orders of other churches might be recognized, apostolic succession is nevertheless a gift that Anglicans (and Catholics and others) must bring to the whole church in any future ecumenical unity.

3.4.2.b Reformation and Union patterns of church polity and ministerial order: the presbyterian pattern. The presbyterian pattern of church polity presupposes a single order of pastors who function

175. *Book of Common Prayer* (USA, 1979), pp. 877–878.

together with lay elders. The presbyterian polity involves representative church assemblies, including local congregational
"sessions" linked into larger "presbyteries."

Sources: Westminster Confession, 31 (in Leith, pp. 227–228; Schaff, 3:668–670).
Comparative Cross-References: Eastern Orthodox, 1.4.2; Roman Catholic, 2.4.3–4;
Evangelical and Free, 4.4.2.a–c.

A second distinctive pattern of church government or polity among
Reformation and Union churches is the presbyterian pattern, which is an
instance of a more widespread form of church government referred to as
"synodal" polity. The presbyterian polity has been favored historically
not only by churches named as "Presbyterian" but also by most Reformed churches of the European continent. The synodal pattern has also
been incorporated into many modern Union churches. The presbyterian
pattern of ministry and polity presupposes a single order of pastors. In
various presbyterian churches these may be called "presbyters" or
"teaching elders" (*presbuteros* simply means "elder") or they may be
identified by such titles as "ministers of Word and Sacrament." Also typical of the presbyterian pattern is the use of lay elders or "ruling elders,"
who form the local church session (see below) with the pastor(s) of the
congregation. Many congregations also have other offices, such as that of
lay deacons, who are given particular tasks (such as caring for the poor).
In traditional presbyterian polity, the pastors, lay elders, and deacons are
all ordained to their distinctive ministries, and their ordination is considered permanent even when individuals cease to exercise their office.

The presbyterian pattern of church polity as we know it was originally set by French Reformed Christians late in the 1550s. The pattern involves interlinked church assemblies from the local to the national or denominational level. Most consistently, the presbyterian pattern involves
(1) a local representative assembly called the session, consisting of pas-
tor(s) and ruling elders (lay elders) of a congregation, and (2) a regional
assembly called a presbytery, consisting of all the clergy and some
elected elders representing local sessions. In some areas the local session
may be referred to by the name "consistory" or "consistory court," and
in European continental churches the presbytery may be called a "classis." In addition to these basic components, the presbyterian pattern
very often involves (3) an assembly of representatives from the presbyteries typically called a synod, and finally (4) a General Assembly of representatives from a whole Reformed denomination or national church.

3.4.2.c *Reformation and Union patterns of church polity and
ministerial order: the congregational pattern.* The congregational
pattern of church polity presupposes a single order of ordained

ministers who function together with congregational officials. The congregational polity places primary responsibility for church government in congregational assemblies, united by congregational "covenants."

Sources: The Cambridge Platform, chaps. 3–5, 10–11 (in Leith, pp. 388–392, 392–396). Declaration of the Congregational Union of England and Wales, Principles of Church Order and Discipline (Schaff, 3:733–734).

Comparative Cross-References: Eastern Orthodox, 1.4.2; Roman Catholic, 2.4.3–4; Evangelical and Free, 4.4.2.a–c.

A third basic pattern of church government or polity among Reformation and Union churches is the congregational pattern, which builds on the congregational principle that the local congregation is the primary expression of the church (see 3.4.1.b) and insists on the autonomy or independence of local congregations. Like the presbyterian pattern, the congregational pattern presupposes a single order of ordained ministers, terminology for which may vary from place to place. Like the local "session" of the presbyterian pattern, the congregational polity usually involves a representative assembly of the congregation, or perhaps an assembly of the whole congregation. Unlike the presbyterian pattern, though, the congregational pattern vests almost all critical decisions, including the adoption of church doctrine and practices and the ordination of ministers, in the local congregation. In fact, in some early cases, congregational churches ordained ministers for service to their congregation only, and ordination was not understood as being transferable to any other congregation.

In the tradition of Congregationalist churches, each congregation adopts its own congregational covenant, and in many cases its own articles of faith. Persons joining the congregation take upon themselves the congregational covenant as part of their initiation into congregational life. Although the practice of congregations adopting their own doctrinal statements often makes it difficult to describe doctrine on the part of congregational groups, the articles adopted very often reflect standard Reformed confessions, and sometimes simply indicate that the members of the congregation agree to the Westminster Confession or some other Reformed doctrinal statement.

The congregational principle does not prohibit local churches from working together with or "associating" with other congregations. The "Cambridge Platform," a statement of New England Congregationalist principles from the 1640s, explicitly refers to broader assemblies as "presbyteries," but does not grant these assemblies the central governing functions that they hold in churches organized on the presbyterian pattern. Churches with congregational polity typically participate in broader regional or national associations, which operate by the consent of particular congregations wherever it is felt that cooperation is needed.

3.4.2.d *Reformation and Union patterns of church polity and ministerial order: mixed and hybrid polities.* Lutheran churches permit a variety of expressions of ministerial order and church polity. Other Reformation and Union churches combine episcopal, presbyterian, and congregational patterns of church polity and ministerial order.

Sources: Augsburg Confession, 5, 14, 23, 27–28 (in Leith, pp. 69, 72, 80–83, 91–106; Schaff, 3:10–11, 15–16, 58–72).

Comparative Cross-References: Eastern Orthodox, 1.4.2; Roman Catholic, 2.4.3–4; Evangelical and Free, 4.4.2.a–c.

Although the three patterns described above represent the historic options for church polity among Reformation and Union churches, some churches combine elements of these polities, and Lutheran churches have historically allowed for a variety of patterns both of ministerial order and of church organization. It is important to understand the variety of Lutheran polities with respect to their historical development. Remember, in the first place, that Lutheran churches emerged in German-speaking regions of the Holy Roman Empire in the 1500s. At that time there was no single political state answering to modern "Germany" (not until the late 1800s, in fact); rather, there was a variety of small states, free imperial cities, duchies, electorates, and other political units with varying degrees of autonomy within the loose confederation that the empire had become. Lutheranism was adopted by many of these states, but there was no central Lutheran organization and consequently no single pattern of church organization or ministerial orders. Allegiance to the Augsburg Confession and (in varying degrees) to other confessional documents in the *Book of Concord* provided the only consistent basis for Lutheran unity.

Consequently, various Lutheran churches adopted different forms of church polity. In Scandinavian countries and some areas of Germany, the pattern was to have bishops. In almost every Lutheran church there existed synods of clergy, sometimes subdivided into smaller regional or city groups that would be called a ministerium. Lutheran churches without bishops often have overseers referred to as "superintendents," and it is worth noting that the Latin *superintendens* means "overseeing," the same as the Greek *episkopos*, from which "bishop" is derived. Lutheran superintendents carry on some of the functions of bishops, although they do not typically hold the office for life, as bishops do, and we might note further that although the Swedish Lutherans can claim to have maintained episcopal succession, the Scandinavian Lutheran churches with episcopal polity have not maintained a separate ministerial order of deacons. In other Lutheran churches a modified congregational polity has developed: this is the case with the Lutheran Church, Missouri Synod, in the United States.

Among other churches, especially churches derived from ecumenical unions, the tendency is to combine the historic forms of polity together. In fact, congregationalist and presbyterian polities had often been merged in English-speaking countries. In England for a long period after 1689 Dissenting churches were forbidden from having assemblies except at the congregational level, and this reduced Presbyterians to a congregational polity against their will. In New England and the Old Northwest frontier of the United States, congregations were often formed that were congregational in character but sent representatives to larger assemblies that they called "presbyteries." These churches have sometimes been described as "presbygational" for their blurring the boundary between congregational and presbyterian polity.

The Uniting Church in Australia (1977) and The United Church of Canada (1925) have combined elements of presbyterian and congregationalist polity, along with some Methodist terminology for church assemblies. For example, The United Church of Canada has "Annual Conferences" (a traditionally Methodist term) subdivided into smaller presbyteries. The Church of South India (1947) and the Church of North India (1970) are unique and ecumenically important because they have combined the "historic episcopate" with other forms of polity, preserving the uninterrupted apostolic succession of bishops valued by Anglicans (see 3.4.2.a).

The understanding of the sacraments was a church-dividing issue in the time of the Reformation, not only dividing Reformation churches from Catholics but also dividing various Reformation churches from one another. It remains a central issue in contemporary ecumenical discussions. Under the influence of Pietism, Evangelicalism and Liberalism there was a tendency to deemphasize the importance of sacraments for the Reformers and simultaneously to exaggerate the differences between Reformers and Catholics on the issue of sacramental grace. The exaggerations of this point of view were recognized by Anglican advocates of the Oxford movement, by advocates of the New Lutheranism, and by the Mercersburg School of

Reformed theologians (see 3.0.6). Contemporary ecumenical explorations have again pointed to the centrality of the sacraments for the Reformers.

3.4.3 What Reformation and Union traditions teach about the meaning of sacraments: Reformation and Union traditions generally agree in teaching that the sacraments are means of grace as well as signs of Christian intention, and they generally agree further in limiting sacraments to Baptism and the Eucharist.

Sources: Augsburg Confession, 8, 11, 13 (in Leith, pp. 70, 71, 72; Schaff, 3:12–13, 13–14, 15). Luther's Small Catechism, 4–5 (in Leith, pp. 121–123; Schaff, 3:85–92). Second Helvetic Confession, 19 (in Leith, pp. 161–167; Schaff, 3:285–289, 884–889). Heidelberg Catechism, 65–67 (in Schaff, 3:328–329). Westminster Confession, 27 (in Leith, pp. 223–224; Schaff, 3:660–661). Anglican Articles of Religion, 25–26 (in Leith, pp. 274–275; Schaff, 3:502–504). Anglican Catechism (in Schaff, 3:521). Basis of Union of The United Church of Canada, Article 16, par. 1 (UCC *Manual* 1993, p. 14).

Comparative Cross-References: Eastern Orthodox, 1.4.4; Roman Catholic, 2.4.5; Evangelical and Free, 4.4.3.a–c; Ecumenical, 5.2.4.1.

There is an important ground of unity between Reformation and Union churches in their traditional assertions that sacraments are "means" or channels of God's grace as well as signs or symbols of it. The Augsburg Confession states that "sacraments were instituted not only to be signs by which people might be identified outwardly as Christians, but that they are signs and testimonies of God's will toward us for the purpose of awakening and strengthening our faith." The Anglican Article on this point is even stronger: sacraments, according to it, are

> not only badges or tokens of Christian men's profession, but rather they be certain sure witnesses, and effectual signs of grace, and God's good will towards us, by the which he doth work invisibly in us, and doth not only quicken, but also strengthen and confirm our Faith in him.

That is to say, the Lutheran and Anglican confessions generally understand sacraments to involve both (1) a sign or symbol, and (2) an actual grace conferred by God in the rite. This understanding is underscored in the classic definition of a sacrament in the Anglican Catechism: "an outward and visible sign of an inward and spiritual grace given unto us; ordained by Christ himself. . . ."[176] Very often there is

---

176. Anglican Catechism (in Schaff, 3:521). This definition of a sacrament as an "outward sign of an inward grace" is sometimes attributed to Augustine of Hippo, but the locus from Augustine often cited (*City of God,* 10:5; in Migne, *Patrologia Latina,* 41:282) states only that "A visible sacrifice therefore is a *sacramentum* or sacred sign of an invisible sacrifice."

added to these two elements a third, (3) the use of the words by which Christ instituted the particular sacraments.

The doctrinal statements of the Reformed tradition are not quite as clear as the Lutheran and Anglican statements on the issue of an actual grace conferred by the sacraments, but they do insist on the presence of (1) the thing symbolized, (2) its symbol, and (3) the use of the words of institution. Both the Second Helvetic Confession and the Westminster Confession make a clear distinction between the sign or symbol and the matter that is signified or symbolized. Some Reformed Christians stress this distinction between the thing symbolized and the symbol itself, and insist that a sacrament itself is only a sign or symbol proclaiming Christ, that is to say, the "thing symbolized" is the historic work of Christ recorded in the Gospel. But other Reformed Christians believe that through the sacraments Christ conveys grace. They point out that the "thing symbolized" does not refer simply to the work of Christ in the New Testament but to the present work of Christ in the Christian community. On this reading, then, the Reformed tradition concerning the sacraments is not so far from Lutheran or Anglican understandings and is more consistent with Catholic and ecumenical understandings of sacramental grace.

But what specific acts having outward signs and having been instituted by Christ qualify as sacraments? The general tendency of Reformation doctrinal statements is to limit sacraments to the two "Great" or "dominical" sacraments of Baptism and the Eucharist ("dominical" comes from *dominus*, the "Lord," and refers to sacraments instituted by Christ himself). However, two important exceptions to this general rule may be noted. In the first place, many Anglicans affirm the five other sacraments affirmed by Roman Catholics as "lesser sacraments." They point out that their twenty-fifth Article of Religion refers to them as "commonly called sacraments" and notes that they "are not to be counted for Sacraments of the Gospel" but does not strictly forbid the understanding of them as lesser sacraments. The most recently approved *Book of Common Prayer* of the Episcopal Church in the United States includes a revised catechism in which these five acts are accorded the status of "sacramental rites."[177]

A second exception, with important ecumenical implications, is that many early Lutherans, including Martin Luther himself and early Lutheran doctrinal statements, affirmed penance within their consideration of the sacraments. This may come as a surprise to many Protestants, who are accustomed to think that it was Luther's objections

177. *Book of Common Prayer* (USA 1979), pp. 860–861.

to the penitential system that led to the Reformation. But Luther's objection was really to abuses of the penitential system, and he remained committed to the use of penance and even private confession throughout his life. The Small Catechism has a section on "Confession and Absolution" between its sections on Baptism and the Eucharist, and the Augsburg Confession states that "it is taught among us that private absolution should be retained and not allowed to fall into disuse" in a separate article on "Confession." Most Lutheran churches today do not retain penance as a sacrament, but the provision remains present in their doctrinal statements, and some Lutheran worship books have rites for the reconciliation of a penitent person. Perhaps we should observe, further, that in all the Reformation churches, weddings and ordinations *function* as sacraments, although they have not been historically identified as such.

3.4.3.1 *What Reformation and Union traditions teach about baptism:* Reformation and Union traditions agree in teaching that baptism is the means by which persons are accepted into the Christian community and that baptism conveys the gift of new birth in Christ. They agree, further, in practicing infant baptism.

Sources: Augsburg Confession, 9 (in Leith, pp. 70–71; Schaff, 3:13). Luther's Small Catechism, 4 (in Leith, pp. 120–121; Schaff, 3:85–87). Second Helvetic Confession, 20 (in Leith, pp. 167–169; Schaff, 3:289–291, 889–891). Westminster Confession, 28 (in Leith, pp. 224–225; Schaff, 3:661–663). Anglican Articles of Religion, 27 (in Leith, pp. 275–276; Schaff, 3:504–505). Anglican Catechism (in Schaff, 3:521). Basis of Union of The United Church of Canada, Article 16, par. 2 (UCC *Manual* 1993, pp. 14–15). Heppe, ch. 25 (pp. 611–626). Schmid, 4:2:54 (pp. 536–555).

Comparative Cross-References: Eastern Orthodox, 1.4.5; Roman Catholic, 2.4.5.1; Evangelical and Free, 4.4.4.a–b; Ecumenical, 5.2.4.2.

We now turn to consider the teachings of Reformation and Union churches on the sacrament of Baptism. Two points of very broad agreement may be noted here. In the first place, all the Reformation and Union churches agree that baptism is the distinct act, instituted by Christ, by which human beings are incorporated into the community of the church. In the second place, these churches agree in practicing infant baptism. On the first point, Reformation and Union churches stand in agreement with almost all Christian communities. On the second point they stand in agreement with Orthodox and Catholic practice (see 1.4.5 and 2.4.5.1), differing however with Evangelical and Free churches, which practice believer's baptism only (see 4.4.4.b).

Beyond the fact that baptism serves as the sign of incorporation into the Christian community, Reformation and Union doctrinal statements affirm that through baptism men and women are born again in Christ. Luther's Small Catechism asks the question, "What gifts or benefits does Baptism bestow?" The response is then offered: "It effects forgiveness of sins, delivers from death and the devil, and grants eternal salvation to all who believe. . . ." This is also consistent with what the Augsburg Confession says about the grace of new birth or "regeneration" given in baptism. The Anglican Article is not quite as decisive on this point. It claims that baptism is not only a sign of Christian "profession" but also

> a sign of Regeneration or New-Birth, whereby, as by an instrument, they that receive baptism rightly are grafted into the Church; the promises of the forgiveness of sin and of our adoption to be the sons of God by the Holy Ghost, are visibly signed and sealed; Faith is confirmed, and Grace increased by virtue of prayer unto God.

Because this statement utilizes the language of baptism as a "sign" and "seal," characteristic of the Reformed tradition, it has been argued—especially by Evangelical Anglicans—that this Article should be taken as meaning only that baptism is a "sign" of the new birth, but that it does not necessarily bring about the new birth. On the other hand, the expression "as by an instrument" seems to speak of baptism as not only a sign but also a means of the new birth. The service for baptism in the traditional (1662) Anglican prayer book was clear on this point: after the candidate has been baptized with water and signed with the sign of the cross, the minister prays, "Seeing now, dearly beloved brethren, that this Child is regenerate, and grafted into the body of Christ's Church, let us give thanks. . . ."[178] Moreover, the Anglican Catechism teaches that the inward and spiritual grace given in baptism is "A death unto sin and a new birth unto righteousness. . . ."[179]

Reformed doctrinal statements also associate baptism with the new birth in Christ, although the Reformed confessions are qualified in two particular ways. Many Reformed Christians have questioned the idea of "baptismal regeneration" (see below) and in fact Lutheran treatises on Christian doctrine have traditionally represented Reformed confessions as not teaching that baptism conveys the new birth in Christ.[180] Despite this, the Reformed confessions themselves

178. *Book of Common Prayer* (1662), service for the "Publick Baptism of Infants," p. 186.
179. Anglican Catechism (in Schaff, 3:521).
180. Klotsche, pp. 236–237; Schmid, 4:2:55 (pp. 570–571, and see especially the note on p. 571).

do associate baptism with the new birth in Christ, but there are two important qualifications in the Reformed understanding of this sacrament. The first is related to the Reformed teaching concerning election and is the qualification that baptism brings about new birth in Christ only for those who are elect or predestined to eternal salvation. The second is that later Reformed confessions make an important qualification in stating that the moment at which the sign of water is applied to a person may not be the same moment when that person receives the gift of the new birth in Christ.[181] This separation of the moment when the symbol is enacted from the moment when its object (grace) becomes a reality can be contrasted with the postbaptismal prayer of the Anglican prayer book quoted above, a prayer that implies that as soon as the water is applied, the baptized person *is* born again. Although it is taken by some Reformed theologians to mean that regeneration may occur *before* baptism, this qualification would open up among Puritans and later Reformed Christians the issue of whether baptism itself or a *later,* mature experience of repentance and faith was the true moment at which a person was "born again." As we shall see in chapter 4, this distinction would contribute to the "conversionist" ethos of Evangelical churches.

At this point it might be asked how this Reformation belief that the new birth in Christ is brought about through baptism, even for infants, is consistent with the equally consistent Reformation belief that our justification (and new birth) comes by faith alone? How, in particular, could baptism convey forgiveness and new birth for infants, since infants are not capable of mature faith? The response to these questions on the part of Lutherans and Anglicans is not significantly different from that of Orthodox or Catholics. Although lack of faith in mature persons is an impediment to the grace given in the sacrament, it is not an impediment for infants, precisely because they are incapable of mature faith. In other words, baptism will effect the new birth and forgiveness of sin for infants, and these benefits remain in effect unless the person consciously rejects faith in Christ at some later point. For Reformed Christians, the baptism of an infant brings the child into a covenant relationship with God and the church, which will eventuate in the individual's regeneration, if the individual is among the elect, but not necessarily at the moment at which water is applied.

At this point, too, we may note some differences in interpretation by Lutherans, Anglicans, and Reformed Christians who are simply

181. Westminster Confession, 28:6 (in Leith, pp. 224–225); cf. Heppe, 25:10 (pp. 618–619).

uncomfortable with the notion of baptism bringing about justification and the new birth. In the early 1800s, many Anglicans argued that their Article of Religion taught a view of baptism as the "sign" and "seal" of the new birth, but not as actually conveying the new birth. Other Anglican Evangelicals (such as John and Charles Wesley) and Lutheran Pietists (such as Philipp Jakob Spener and August Hermann Francke) argued that although baptism does effect new birth in infants, most adults have "sinned away" the effects of baptism and stand in need of new repentance and conversion.

With the Eucharist we must reckon with a greater diversity of views on the part of Reformation and Union churches. These were church-dividing issues during the century of the Reformation, with Martin Luther and the Reformer of Zurich, Ulrich Zwingli, sharply divided on the question of how Christ is present in the sacrament. Three broad, historic positions may be identified, although they do not fall conveniently along denominational lines. Within these three historic positions, three levels or degrees of understanding Christ's presence may be considered: first, the literal presence of Christ's body and blood (this may be called "bodily" or "corporeal" presence, from *corpus*, "body"); second, the presence of a unique power (or "virtue") given by Christ in the sacrament; and third, the present remembrance of Christ's suffering, death, and resurrection.

3.4.3.2.a   *What Reformation and Union traditions teach about the Eucharist: Lutheran and Anglican belief in Christ's bodily presence in the sacrament.* Lutheran traditions and many Anglicans agree in teaching that Christ is bodily present in the eucharistic elements, although they deny that the substance of bread and wine are transformed into Christ's body and blood.

Sources: Augsburg Confession, 10 and 24 (in Leith, pp. 71, 83–86; Schaff, 3:13, 34–39). Luther's Small Catechism, 5 (or 6; in Schaff, 3:90–92). Formula of Concord, Epitome, 7 (in Schaff, 3:135–146). Schmid, 4:2:55 (pp. 555–582).

Comparative Cross-References: Eastern Orthodox, 1.4.6; Roman Catholic, 2.4.5.3; Evangelical and Free, 4.4.5.a–b; Ecumenical, 5.2.4.3.

The first is the position maintained consistently by Lutherans and professed by many in the Anglican communion, both by Anglo-Catholics and by a substantial number of more moderate Anglicans, although Anglicans prefer to speak of the "real presence" of Christ in the eucharistic elements.[182] The central idea in both cases, which we

182. But "real presence" can also be taken as denoting what we have called "Virtualism" here; on which see 3.4.3.2.b, and see footnote 184 below.

shall consider together, is that Christ is really and bodily present in the eucharistic elements. Christ's presence is real in that it is not merely symbolic. "This is my body," Luther quoted against Zwingli, and he insisted that "is" should be taken literally. The presence of Christ in the supper is bodily, following the same words of institution: it is the very body of Christ who was born of Mary that is present. The presence of Christ is in the eucharistic elements themselves in a special way, not just in the community or the eucharistic celebration as a whole. Although all the Reformation churches rejected the doctrine of transubstantiation (see 2.4.5.3), maintaining that the substance of bread and wine do not cease to exist in the sacrament, some Lutheran scholars identified their position as consubstantiation, meaning that the substance of the body and blood of Christ are present with (con) the substance of bread and wine.[183] We should note that those who maintain this position also believe that a unique power or grace is given by Christ in the sacrament, and that Christ's work is to be remembered in the sacrament; thus, all three of the degrees of Christ's presence mentioned above would hold for this understanding of the Eucharist.

Anglicans who hold to the "real presence" of Christ in the eucharistic elements often refuse to subscribe to any particular explanation of *how* Christ is present: the mode of Christ's presence, they will say, is a mystery and should not be too carefully defined. Although the Anglican Articles of Religion suggest what we shall call a "Virtualist" understanding of the Eucharist (see the next subsection), Anglicans may point to the eucharistic liturgy of the *Book of Common Prayer* as supporting "real presence" in the sense of bodily or corporeal presence.[184] For example, at the point in the traditional liturgy where the

183. Luther himself did not utilize this term and might have felt uncomfortable with it, given his suspicion of such universal concepts as "substance"; cf. Laurence Hull Stookey, *Eucharist: Christ's Feast with the Church* (Nashville: Abingdon Press, 1993), pp. 180–181, n. 3. Schmid also denies that consubstantiation is the Lutheran view, although he takes the term in a very restricted sense (4:2:55, p. 571).
184. The expression "real presence" itself presents considerable difficulties. In the 1500s, it seems to have denoted what Lutherans meant by "bodily" or corporeal presence and in this sense sixteenth-century Anglicans did *not* affirm "real presence." The famous (or infamous) "Black Rubric" of the 1552 prayer book instructed worshipers that although they should kneel to receive the communion, their kneeling should not be construed as implying "any real and essential presence there being of Christ's natural flesh and blood" (given in the *Book of Common Prayer* [1559], the editor's preface, p. vii). By the 1600s (for instance, with the work of Bishop William Nicholson of Gloucester), "real presence" could be claimed by Anglicans but not with the meaning of corporeal presence; rather, with the meaning we have attached to Virtualism (see the next subsection). Consistent with this, a rubric attached to the Eucharistic rite in the 1662 prayer book rules out corporeal

priest offered the bread to the communicant, he was to say, "The body of our Lord Jesus Christ, given for thee," suggesting the identification of the bread with Christ's body, although this is followed by a sentence urging the communicant to take the bread as a way of remembering Christ's work. In any case, this way of understanding Christ's presence in the sacrament is closest to ancient and medieval understandings of Christ's presence in the Eucharist among the positions taken in the Reformation, and some Anglican interpreters in particular see it as being consistent with Orthodox understandings of Christ's presence in the Divine Liturgy and even with a broad understanding of the Catholic tradition (though, again, rejecting the particular terminology of transubstantiation).

3.4.3.2.b *What Reformation and Union traditions teach about the Eucharist: Virtualist or Receptionist views.* Reformed traditions and the Anglican Articles of Religion agree in teaching that the "virtue" or benefit of Christ is truly present in the Eucharist to those who receive with true faith, or present through the power of the Holy Spirit.

Sources: Calvin, *Institutes* 4.17.10–12 (in McNeill, 2:1370–1373). Westminster Confession, 29 (in Leith, pp. 225–227; Schaff, 3:663–667). Heidelberg Catechism, 76–79 (in Schaff, 3:332–335). Anglican Articles of Religion, 28–31 (in Leith, pp. 276–277; Schaff, 3:505–507). Anglican Catechism (in Schaff, 3:521–522). Basis of Union of The United Church of Canada, Article 16, par. 3 (UCC *Manual* 1993, p. 15). Heppe, ch. 26 (pp. 627–656).

Comparative Cross-References: Eastern Orthodox, 1.4.6; Roman Catholic, 2.4.5.3; Evangelical and Free, 4.4.5.a–b; Ecumenical, 5.2.4.3.

Many Protestant Reformers were uncomfortable with the notion that Christ is "bodily" present in the Eucharist. As we shall see in the next subsection, Ulrich Zwingli and others went so far as to reject altogether the notion that Christ is present in any unique way in the Eucharist. But John Calvin, along with more moderate advocates of the Reformed tradition including those who framed the Anglican Articles of Religion, expressed a considerable degree of unity with Luther (against Zwingli), even though they could not affirm Christ's "bodily" presence in the Eucharist. Calvin and the Reformed confessions main-

---

presence and does not use the term "real," as the Black Rubric had done: the 1662 rubric states that the recipients' kneeling should not imply "any Corporal presence of Christ's natural flesh and blood" (*Book of Common Prayer* [1662], p. 182). With the coming of the Oxford movement in the 1800s the expression "real presence" again seemed to imply something more than Virtualism, approximating to an understanding of the bodily or corporeal presence of Christ in the Eucharist (still denying transubstantiation, though), and it was from this time that some Anglican theologians affirmed a eucharistic presence beyond that of the Virtualist position expressed in the Articles of Religion.

tain that although Christ is not bodily present in the Eucharist (because Christ's body has ascended to heaven), the "power" or "benefit" (*virtus*, "power") of Christ is present, just as if Christ's body itself were present.[185] For this reason, this belief has been historically described as Virtualism. We must note, to be fair, that the term "Virtualism" is not in wide circulation in our time, but it is important to take account of the point of view reflected consistently in Calvin's own works and in the historic Reformed confessions, without conflating it with either "bodily" or "corporeal" presence (in the sense defined above) or the Zwinglian view (in the next subsection).[186] The faithful, according to the Westminster Confession, "receive and feed upon Christ crucified, and all benefits of his death." Even where the Reformed confessions speak of the Eucharist as "signifying" Christ's presence, this does not rule out a unique presence or power signified by the outward elements. The Virtualist understanding of Christ's presence in the Eucharist has been linked historically to the idea that the power of Christ's presence is given only to those who receive it with true Christian faith, that is, it is only available to the elect in Christ. For this reason this belief has been historically described as Receptionism.[187]

The Anglican Articles of Religion utilize language similar to that of Reformed confessions in stating that Christ's body is "spiritually" eaten in the Eucharist (Article 28), and that those who receive without faith receive not Christ but damnation (Article 29). Although the Anglican Article's concern with the "spiritual" presence of Christ can be read as Zwinglian (see the next subsection), it has been historically interpreted as being consistent with the Virtualist or Receptionist understanding of the Eucharist characteristic of moderates of the Reformed tradition. Moreover, the catechism of the *Book of Common Prayer* states that the "benefits" given by the sacrament of the Lord's Supper include "The strengthening and refreshing of our souls by the Body and Blood of Christ. . . ."[188] There is, as noted above, an ambiguity (perhaps intended) in the traditional Anglican ritual for the Eu-

185. Calvin, *Institutes* 4.17.10–12 (in McNeill, 2:1370–1373).
186. John T. McNeill used the term "virtualism" to describe Calvin's sacramental views in his edition of Calvin's *Institutes* (p. 1370, n. 27).
187. A distinction is sometimes drawn between Virtualism, as maintaining that the presence of Christ is associated with the Eucharistic *elements* themselves, and Receptionism, which does not associate the presence of Christ with the elements. My judgment is that this distinction is not as critical as the issue of how Christ is present in the Eucharist, and for this reason I have considered Virtualism and Receptionism together.
188. Anglican Catechism (in Schaff, 3:521–522).

charist at the point at which the priest offers the consecrated bread to the people. After offering the communicant "The Body of our Lord Jesus Christ, which was given for thee, preserve thy body and soul unto everlasting life" (this strongly suggests the "bodily" or "real presence" of Christ), the priest quickly admonishes the communicant to "Take and eat this in remembrance that Christ died for thee, and feed on him in thy heart by faith, with thanksgiving" (this suggests a Virtualist or perhaps even a Zwinglian understanding of the sacrament).[189]

3.4.3.2.c What Reformation and Union traditions teach about the Eucharist: Zwinglian views. Some Protestants since the time of the Reformation have taught that the presence of Christ in the eucharistic celebration is purely symbolic.

Sources: Second Helvetic Confession, 21 (in Leith, pp. 169–176; Schaff, 3:291–295, 891–896).

Comparative Cross-References: Eastern Orthodox, 1.4.6; Roman Catholic, 2.4.5.3; Evangelical and Free, 4.4.5.a–b; Ecumenical, 5.2.4.3.

Other advocates of the Reformed tradition, beginning with Ulrich Zwingli, argued that Christ's presence in the Eucharist is only symbolic. When Christ said, "This is my body," Zwingli argued, the word "is" should be taken as having the same force as the word "am," such as when Christ said, "I *am* the vine." That is to say, the expression means that the bread and wine in the Eucharist represent, signify, or symbolize the body and blood of Christ, but it is an error to think that they convey Christ's literal body or even the benefit of Christ's presence in any unique way. We can affirm, this position maintains, that Christ is "present" just as Christ is present whenever two or three are gathered in his name, but in no other sense should we speak of Christ's presence in the Eucharist. The Eucharist is understood primarily as a way of remembering the work of Christ, a memorial of Christ's saving work. The Second Helvetic Confession, composed by Zwingli's successor Heinrich Bullinger in Zurich, insists that Christ is "spiritually" present in the Supper. In this regard it could be interpreted in a Virtualist way (see the previous subsection), but its sharp distinction between the sign (bread and wine) and the thing signified (the body of Christ) can also be interpreted as meaning that the spiritual presence of Christ is the same as when "two or three are gathered" in Christ's name, and so it may denote that Christ's presence is not unique in the eucharistic celebration.

189. *Book of Common Prayer* (1662), p. 172.

4

Teachings of Evangelical and Free Churches

4.0 Historical Background to Evangelical and Free Churches

Protestants are not all created equal, and the churches described in chapter 4 of this book, though sharing the heritage of the Protestant Reformation, have a different character than the established Reformation churches and the Union churches considered in chapter 3. To illustrate the difference, consider the story of an Evangelical who considered becoming a Lutheran:

> Grandpa Cotten was once tempted toward Lutheranism by a preacher who gave a rousing sermon on grace that Grandpa heard as a young man while taking Aunt Esther's dog home who had chased a Model T across town. He sat down on the church steps and listened to the voice boom out the open windows until he made up his mind to go in and unite with the truth, but he took one look from the vestibule and left. "He was dressed up like the pope of Rome," said Grandpa, "and the altar and the paintings and the gold candlesticks—my gosh, it was just a big show. And he was reading the whole darn thing off a page, like an actor."[190]

In the grandfather's heartfelt approval of the pastor's sermon on grace, there lies a recognition of a kindred Protestant spirit. But then there is also a recognition that in some ways the Lutherans seemed closer to "the pope of Rome" than the Evangelical tradition the grandfather knew—a tradition characterized by informality and spontaneity in

---

190. Keillor, *Lake*, pp. 101–102.

worship, grounded in the conviction that religion is a matter of the heart and not a matter of external show.

If representatives of the ten different families of Evangelical and Free churches considered in chapter 4 were placed in a room together, I have a suspicion that they might say a prayer, sing a hymn together (say, "Amazing Grace") and then break into a fight. Many would not recognize one another as Christians at all, certainly not as kindred spirits among the variety of church traditions. But two identifiable traits distinguish the Christian churches whose teachings are described in chapter 4. In the first place, most churches considered in chapter 4 have stressed a personal experience of conversion, a personal choice or decision to follow Christ, as being central to Christian faith, and in this particular respect they can be described as Evangelical churches.[191] We should note, though, that "Evangelical" in this sense differs very significantly from the sense in which Lutheran churches are traditionally described as "Evangelical" (especially in non-English contexts). In the second place, these churches did not originate as state-supported churches, as the established Reformation churches did, and they have historically insisted on an entirely voluntary church. In this respect they can be described as Free churches.

"Evangelical" (conversionist) and "Free" (voluntary) are therefore not quite the same thing, but there exists a kind of logical relationship between them, in that established churches have tended to support mechanisms that automatically incorporate persons in the religious community, specifically, infant baptism in Anglican, Lutheran, and Reformed traditions. "Evangelical" churches, by contrast, have stressed the centrality of personal choice in conversion, not a rote or institutional performance on the part of an established church.

The borders between "Reformation and Union Churches" (chapter 3) and "Evangelical and Free Churches" (chapter 4) are in reality quite ambiguous. On the one hand, many Moravian and Methodist churches bear more resemblances to historic Reformation and Union churches than to historic Evangelical and Free churches. On the other hand, some Reformed bodies (like the Christian Reformed Church in the United States) share much of the culture of Evangelical churches. One must not imagine, then, that there is a clear line of demarcation here; the distinctions are rather analytical and in reality there are many blurred areas of doctrine

---

191. A full definition of "Evangelical" in this sense would include at least (1) an insistence on the primacy of scripture, (2) the need for personal conversion, and (3) the need for evangelization. The second point, however, expresses more the *differentia specifica* by which "Evangelical" in chapter 4 of this book is distinguished from the Reformation traditions considered in chapter 3.

Table 8. Families of Evangelical and Free Churches
and their Estimated Memberships in 1985[192]

Evangelical and Free Churches	World Organization	Estimated Membership (million)
Anabaptist	Mennonite World Conference	1.2
Baptist	Baptist World Alliance	50.3
Friends (Quakers)	—	0.5
Moravian	Unity of the Brethren	0.7
Methodist	World Methodist Council	31.7
Restorationist	World Convention of Churches of Christ	8.7
Dispensationalist	—	2.0
Adventist	—	6.2
Holiness	Christian Holiness Association	10.1
Pentecostal	Pentecostal World Conference	59.0
(Nonaligned)	—	12.8
TOTAL		183.5

and practice between the Protestant churches described in chapters 3 and 4, and we shall have to note many of these in the text that follows.

The various Evangelical and Free churches considered here can be understood as falling into ten broadly recognizable families, some of which are identifiable by international alliances. The estimated memberships of these groups are listed in table 8. These groups will be described in the historical narrative that follows, but they may be briefly identified at this point. *Anabaptist* churches came into existence at the time of the Reformation in the 1520s and 1530s, insisting on believer's baptism only and strict separation from the secular world including its political, military, and legal structures (see 4.0.1). *Baptist* churches emerged from the English Separatist movement in the early 1600s and have traditionally insisted on believers' baptism (see 4.0.3). *Friends*, or "Quakers," originated during the 1640s in England, stressing the centrality of inward or personal religious experience and rejecting outward sacraments (see 4.0.3). *Moravian* Churches emerged from the

192. Membership statistics based on *World Christian Encyclopedia*, Global Table 27, pp. 792–793. To arrive at these figures I have conflated together the "nonwhite indigenous" churches of a particular tradition with Western expressions of the same tradition, so that (for example) nonwhite indigenous Baptists are added to Baptists in originally Western Baptist denominations. In many cases the memberships given for these denominational traditions will differ significantly from the membership statistics for particular confessional conciliar groups (such as the Baptist World Alliance). I have included the Salvation Army in the Holiness category, and I have included German Baptist ("Dunker") groups in the Baptist category. Most noninstrumental Churches of Christ do not participate in the World Convention of Churches of Christ (despite the name, the membership is largely Disciples of Christ). Moreover, the Christian Holiness Association is not a denominational union, but is the largest distinctively Holiness organization in which Holiness denominations participate.

pre-Reformation tradition of John Huss (see 3.0.1), combined with the fervor of Lutheran Pietism in the early 1700s (see 4.0.4). *Methodist* and other *Wesleyan* churches became separate from the Church of England in the context of the Evangelical Revival of the 1700s. We have noted the problem of definition for Methodists in the previous chapter, because although Methodists are "Free" churches, American and British Methodists share many characteristics of Reformation churches (see 4.0.6). *Restorationist* churches, such as the Disciples of Christ and "noninstrumental" Churches of Christ, emerged on the American frontier in the 1820s and 1830s, and they have traditionally stressed the importance of Christian unity based on the New Testament only, not on creeds or other doctrinal statements (see 4.0.7). *Holiness* churches separated from the Methodists (mostly) late in the 1800s and early in the 1900s, and stress a second religious experience (following conversion) described as "entire sanctification" or the "Baptism of the Holy Spirit," in which a woman or man is freed from remaining sin (see 4.0.7). *Dispensationalist* churches originated in the 1800s in Britain and North America, stressing the expectation of the immediate return of Christ and explaining biblical history by way of a series of distinct "dispensations" (see 4.0.7). *Adventist* churches emerged from religious movements in North America in the 1830s and 1840s, stressing the immediate return of Christ and the detailed interpretation of Daniel and the Revelation anticipating Christ's imminent return (see 4.0.7). *Pentecostal* churches came into existence early in this century, largely from the Holiness movement, and they stress a second spiritual experience, also called "baptism of the Holy Spirit," but which they understand to be an in-filling or empowerment by the Holy Spirit, the initial evidence of which is the gift of speaking in unknown tongues (see 4.0.8). In addition to these ten groups, we must reckon with a large number of denominations and even individual congregations that have no formal alliance with any of these groups, and whose strength is consequently very difficult to estimate.

As we shall see (4.0.2), the Evangelical and Free churches grew out of a cultural tradition that reacted against the dogmatism or scholasticism of European state churches (see 3.0.5). In their very origins these churches inherited a suspicion of formal church doctrine, typically claiming that what one believes in one's heart is far more important than what a denomination says on paper. The most radical expression of this sentiment is found in the American Restorationist churches ("Churches of Christ" and "Disciples of Christ"), which have historically rejected all creeds and insist on the New Testament alone as the basis for Christian unity or consensus in the faith. Other

Evangelical and Free churches have formal creeds or doctrinal standards, but these tend to be less important for them than they are (or were) for the established churches of the Reformation. This makes the following account considerably more difficult to construct in comparison to the previous three chapters.

Moreover, the Evangelical and Free churches are grounded in a principle of voluntary foundation of churches that makes them rife for division, and in fact there are simply thousands of Evangelical and Free-church denominations. It is impossible in the scope of such a work as this to consider all of them. In what follows, we have largely taken Baptists and Methodists and Pentecostals, the three largest families of Evangelical and Free churches, as a basis for discussing the teachings of Evangelical and Free churches, and we have noted other families of traditions especially at points of distinctive doctrinal differences, such as the rejection of creeds for Restorationists, the doctrine of a "baptism of the Holy Spirit" as entire sanctification for Holiness groups, and the rejection of "outward" sacraments for Friends or Quakers.

4.0.1   The Reformation and the Roots of the Free-Church Tradition

The Evangelical and Free churches considered in this chapter emerged from the matrix of European culture in the 1600s and 1700s, and in many ways they were connected to the inheritance of the Protestant Reformation of the 1500s. The Reformation stressed the priority of scripture, and this tendency remained in the Evangelical and Free churches. The Reformation also stressed the centrality of justification by faith, and this too characterized Evangelical churches, although later Evangelicals tended to interpret "faith" as involving a personal religious experience, typically a conversion experience.

Although the Reformation churches described in chapter 3 of this book were state supported, Anabaptist churches in Europe set a visible precedent for voluntary, "Free" churches in the 1500s. Unlike other Reformation traditions, Anabaptist groups did not originate in one particular region or under the leadership of a particular individual. Rather, the churches historically described as Anabaptist came into existence in a number of places almost simultaneously, often with little or no knowledge of the other groups. Because they opposed infant baptism, they were accused of "rebaptizing" those who had been baptized as infants, and for this reason they were called Anabaptists, "rebaptizers." They themselves rejected this title, however, because as they saw it the earlier infant baptism did not count as a valid baptism, and so on their understanding they were not "rebaptizing" but rather "baptizing" for the first time. The rejection of infant baptism first occurred in Switzerland in the 1520s and in some German states in the same decade. Representatives of Swiss and German Anabaptist groups met at Schleitheim near Schaffhausen on the Swiss-German border in 1527 and adopted a brief confession dealing with seven particular issues of concern to them. This confession did not pretend to be the creed of a united church. Other Anabaptist groups came into existence in the 1520s and 1530s in Bohemia (the Hutterites, followers of Jacob Hutter) and in Holland.

Within the ranks of those who opposed infant baptism in the early 1500s, there was a vigorous international dispute about whether Christians could take up arms. Some had opted for using military force in the belief that God would grant them swift victory and establish a Kingdom of the Messiah on earth. After a number of failed exploits, however, this option was almost entirely rejected by those who carried on the Anabaptist tradition after the 1540s. From this point the various Anabaptist movements or churches can be accurately described as pacificist and as "Free" churches, since from this point they opposed state support for their churches and insisted that church membership should be entirely voluntary. Among these groups, the most prominent was the movement associated with Menno Simons, a Dutch religious leader whose churches came to be called Mennonites, from his Christian name. The Mennonites represented a better organized form of the Anabaptist movement, and they gained considerable strength in northern German states as well as Holland in the later 1500s. In 1632 Mennonite leaders met at Dordrecht in Holland and adopted the Dordrecht Confession, a statement of Mennonite beliefs to which we shall refer in the next sections. Significant numbers of Mennonites and some of the less numerous Hutterites immigrated to North America, where there are now a number of denominations of their traditions. In 1963 leaders of two of these denominations, the General Conference Mennonite Church and the Mennonite Church, adopted a *Mennonite Confession of Faith*. This confession was significantly revised in 1995 as the *Confession of Faith in a Mennonite Perspective*, and we shall refer to both documents in the text following. We should note, further, that some Hutterite groups participate in the Mennonite World Conference, making it the most inclusive body representing Anabaptist churches today.

4.0.2   The Religion of the Heart

If the Reformation, and especially the Anabaptist tradition, lay in the background of modern Free churches, the background of Evangelical churches lay in a series of movements throughout Europe in the 1600s and 1700s that stressed personal appropriation of religious faith, movements that we refer to as "the religion of the heart." These movements included expressions in each of the established Reformation traditions: Lutheran and Reformed Pietists, Anglican Evangelicals, and "New Light" Presbyterians and Congregationalists in North America. But the stress on heartfelt religion also characterized European Catholics, who in the 1600s turned increasingly to devotion to the Sacred Heart of Jesus, and among whom such movements as Jansenism and Quietism stressed the personal experience of God. A similar movement affected European Jews, with the rise of Hasidism and its stress (at least early on) on heartfelt love for God, for Torah, and for Israel. In Russia in the 1700s movements originated that stressed immediate spiritual experience, movements that were sometimes (incorrectly) described as "Quakers," acknowledging the similarities to Western European movements.[193] With this cultural background, the origins of Evangelical and Free churches may be seen as part of a very broad trend in modern European culture.

4.0.3   The Origin of the Baptist Churches and the Society of Friends

Baptist churches emerged from the Reformed tradition in England. Although they began more as separate or "Free" churches, they also espoused the Evangelical emphases of the "religion of the heart" movements. It may be helpful to recall that those pressing for a more complete reform of the national church in England were called Puritans (see 3.0.4). A more radical group of Reformed Christians opposed the notion of a national church, opting instead for separate, nonestablished congregations. These were referred to as "Separatists," and they were so persecuted in the early 1600s that some of them fled to Holland where broader religious toleration had been allowed. One Separatist congregation in Amsterdam was led by John Smyth, a former priest of the Church of England. He became convinced that infant baptism was not practiced in New Testament times, rebaptized himself, and convinced his congregation that they should practice believers' baptism only. Some of Smyth's followers returned to England in 1612, led by Thomas Helwys, and from that time Baptist congregations began to develop there.

Smyth and Helwys were Arminians in their belief that Christ's death was for all human beings (see 3.3.3.b and 4.3.2.b), and they

---

193. Campbell, *Religion of the Heart.*

preferred a form of synodal polity similar to that of the Presbyterians. Baptists who believed this way came to be known as General Baptists. Distinct from them in church life were the Particular Baptists who emerged in England in the 1630s and 1640s, taught a Calvinistic doctrine of predestination (see 3.3.3.a and 4.3.2.a), and preferred congregational polity. When Baptists came to North America (as early as 1639), the term Regular Baptists was applied to Calvinistic or "Particular" groups, and Arminian or "General" Baptists were sometimes called Free-Will Baptists. By the 1640s Baptists in Britain were regarded as one of the "Three Congregations" of "Dissenters" (those who dissented from the Church of England), along with Presbyterians and Congregationalists. Baptists tended early on to reflect the concerns of those Puritans and Separatists who have been described as "Pietistic" because of their demand for a godly religious life arising from personal religious experience. In fact, a classic Puritan account of religious life was given by the Baptist pastor John Bunyan in *The Pilgrim's Progress* (1678).

Because most Baptist churches are congregational, they have not been bound (at least traditionally) to denominational doctrinal standards. Nevertheless, there is considerable consistency in historic Baptist statements of faith except at one or two points debated among Baptists (such as predestination). In the account of the doctrines of Evangelical and Free churches given below in this chapter, we have relied on three Baptist doctrinal statements to illustrate the teachings of Baptist churches. These are (1) the "New Hampshire Confession" (1833), (2) the "Abstract of Principles" (1859) of the Southern Baptist Theological Seminary in Louisville, Kentucky, and (3) the "Report of the Committee on Baptist Faith and Message" (1925) adopted by the Southern Baptist Convention. All of these, we might note, come from groups with historic roots in Regular Baptist tradition, although as we shall see, the New Hampshire Confession and the statement of Baptist Faith and Message strike a moderate tone (see 4.3.2.a–b).

In the same century, the 1600s, the Society of Friends or Quakers appeared in England. The 1640s were the years of the English Civil War, when armies representing the Crown (and Anglicanism) fought openly against armies representing the Parliament (and Puritanism; see 3.0.5). During this period a remarkable number of religious movements emerged in England, some of them stressing personal visions and revelations. During this time George Fox began his religious quest, turning from Anglicanism to Puritanism and eventually finding consolation in a vivid religious experience in which he was convinced that Christ had spoken directly to him. Fox preached in the open air across England gathering disciples to himself, sometimes from other religious movements. Rejecting "outward" sacraments, Fox stressed that the only true "baptism" is baptism with the Spirit, and the only true "communion" is our inward communion with God. Fox's followers organized the movement he had begun. One of his followers, Robert Barclay, produced a weighty systematic treatise (in Latin as well as English) laying out basic Quaker teachings. At some points below we shall refer to the main points of Barclay's *Apology* to discuss historic Quaker consensus in the faith.

In their earliest years, both Baptists and Quakers were considered to be illegal religious groups in England (along with Presbyterians and Congregationalists) because at that time only Anglican worship was legally allowed or "tolerated." These groups became legal in 1689 when the British Parliament adopted the Act of Toleration, which allowed "Dissenting" (non-Anglican) congregations to worship publicly under certain controlled conditions, one of which was that their chapels had to be publicly registered. The Act of Toleration was an important turning point in the story of Evangelical and Free churches, because it effectively created the modern idea of a religious denomination, that is, a religious group not sanctioned by the political state but legally tolerated by it.

4.0.4 Moravianism

The principle expression of the "religion of the heart" within Lutheran and Reformed churches was Pietism, a movement that reacted against Protestant dogmatism and insisted on heartfelt experiences of repentance and faith (see 3.0.5). The Pietist movement did not in general result in the formation of separate churches, although there were separate Synods of Norwegian Lutheran Pietists, and the Mission Covenant Church of Sweden, founded in the 1800s, developed from Pietistic Lutheran roots. Another exception might be the Moravian Church, but in its case there was a connection back to the pre-Reformation movement of John Huss in Bohemia and his followers, the Bohemian (later Moravian) brethren (see 3.0.1). A remnant of the Moravian brethren had fled to Germany in the 1720s and were given refuge on the country estate of Nicolaus Ludwig, the Count von Zinzendorf.

Zinzendorf had grown up in a strongly Pietistic Lutheran family, and although he had studied to be a lawyer, he showed interest in religious leadership from a very early age. He reorganized the Moravian settlers on his property, established an extraordinarily disciplined communal life for them, and was eventually selected to be a bishop by them (after being ordained as a Lutheran). True to his Pietist roots, Zinzendorf stressed vivid experiences of repentance and conversion. He had a vast ecumenical vision, according to which he hoped that Moravians would serve as a catalyst for unity among European Protestants. In America, he hoped to draw all Protestants together into a federation of churches. The Moravians also became some of the first Protestant missionaries, and they quickly developed congregations in Greenland, the West Indies, and India. In North America, they established colonies in Georgia, Pennsylvania, and North Carolina.

Moravians have become a global church in the last two centuries and have retained their identity as a single *Unitas Fratrum,* "unity of brethren," represented by a single Unity Synod. After World War II the Unity Synod adopted a confessional statement called *The Ground of the Unity,* which has been revised in some ways since that time (most recently in the summer of 1995). In the text that follows, we shall refer to the *Ground of the Unity* at a number of points as reflecting a Moravian consensus.

4.0.5   Evangelical Revival and Great Awakening

In English-speaking and Celtic cultures, the primary expressions of the "religion of the heart" were the Evangelical Revival of the 1700s and the Great Awakening on the North American continent. In Britain, the movement began with the open-air preaching of Howell Harris in Wales in 1735, and it grew further in the preaching ministries of George Whitefield, John Wesley, their followers, and a host of independent preachers. Puritanism, Lutheran Pietism, and Moravianism influenced three of the principal preachers of the Revival: Harris, Whitefield, and Wesley. The Evangelical groups not only employed "itinerant" (wandering) and open-air preaching but organized believers into small home-groups for prayer, scripture study, and for careful discipline, typically by making covenants together and holding one another responsible for their behavior.

The central focus of the Revival and the Awakening was on the "way of salvation," the process by which a person comes to faith in Christ and lives out that faith. The preachers of the Revival stressed the need for heartfelt repentance, especially on the part of those who had no concern for religion, and faith, for those who had sincerely repented and were seeking salvation. The preachers consistently taught that seekers could experience a divinely given assurance of forgiveness when they believed in Christ, so that the central event of coming to faith and receiving this assurance came to be thought of as a conversion experience. The conversion experience is critical and central for the churches described in chapter 4 as "Evangelical."

4.0.6   The Origin of Methodist Churches

The Great Awakening in North America influenced Anglican, Presbyterian, and Congregationalist churches, and it led to the development of prorevival factions in each tradition (an Evangelical faction among North American Anglicans and a "New Light" faction within Presbyterian and Congregationalist churches). The leaders of the Evangelical Revival in Great Britain were almost all Anglicans, and they did not intend to form separate churches. By the end of the 1700s, though, separate churches were forming from the groups who had supported the revival. Some of the supporters of George Whitefield organized themselves as "Tabernacle Methodists," named for Whitefield's famous "Tabernacle," a large preaching house in London. Chapels founded by Selina Shirley Hastings, the Countess of Huntingdon, were formally registered as "Dissenting" (non-Anglican) churches in the 1770s. Welsh Methodists had become effectively separate by the end of the 1700s, but they did not formally organize themselves as the "Welsh Calvinistic Methodist Church" until the 1820s. The title of this denomination should alert us that all these groups were Calvinist in their theology. In fact, the Welsh Calvinistic Methodist Church became the Presbyterian Church of Wales in this century. However, most of the churches that came from the Calvinistic wing of the British Revival eventually dropped the name "Methodist," so that today the title "Methodist" is used almost exclusively of churches that came from the Wesleyan or Arminian wing of the Revival.

The other side of the Revival movement in Britain was an "Arminian" wing, led by John and Charles Wesley. Although the Wesleys had intended their Methodists to be a religious society within the Church of England, their irregular practices (such as open-air preaching and preaching by laypersons) and opposition from Anglicans had led the Wesleyans to be practically independent of Anglicans by the end the 1770s. In 1784 John Wesley authorized the formation of a Methodist church in North America on the grounds that Methodists had limited access to Anglican sacraments there. American Methodists developed a form of church government utilizing bishops, modeled after the Anglican pattern. After John Wesley's death in 1791, the Methodist Conference in Britain took formal steps to reorganize itself as a Dissenting denomination. In Britain and America, Methodists would undergo numerous divisions in the 1800s and some significant reunions in the

1900s, but present-day Methodist churches tend to be either of the American pattern, with bishops and Twenty-five Articles of Religion, or of the British pattern, with "circuit superintendents" and "conference presidents," and using only Wesley's Sermons and *Notes on the New Testament* as doctrinal standards. In the account of Methodist teachings below we shall refer primarily to the Articles of Religion, but at key points we shall also cite the other Wesleyan standards.

4.0.7   The Evangelical Century: African-American Denominations and Restorationist, Holiness, Adventist, and Dispensationalist Movements

By the beginning of the 1800s the "religion of the heart" had deeply influenced European and American Christianity, there were pronounced and strong Evangelical or Pietist parties within Lutheran, Reformed, and Anglican churches, and a host of new Evangelical and Free churches had come into existence. At this point, Methodists and Baptists were by far the largest of these churches, and they left a lasting impact on those areas of global culture where Methodists and Baptists remain the predominant religious groups: for example, in Wales, in the European-American culture of the southeastern and central United States, and in African-American culture at large.

In Britain and North America, Evangelical movements in the early 1800s aligned themselves with movements for democratic society and culture. The British "Primitive Methodists" insisted on the right of public assembly in camp meetings (imported from America), and identified themselves with early trades unions in industrial areas. In North America, Baptists and Methodists flourished as popular religious movements. The trend towards democratic, participatory governance solidified the identification of Evangelicalism with the Free Church principle. Evangelicals in this period involved themselves actively in struggles against slavery and in struggles on behalf of women's rights. All of these democratic tendencies found common expression in a series of revivals on the North American frontier, especially the Appalachians and the Ohio River valley, from the 1790s through the 1830s. These revivals are often referred to as the "Second Great Awakening" in North American religious history, and they themselves provided the background for the rise of some new and distinctly American churches.[194]

A particular expression of the democratic tendencies of this age on

194. Nathan Hatch, *The Democratization of American Religion* (New Haven and London: Yale University Press, 1989).

the North American continent was the development of independent African-American denominations throughout the 1800s. Independent black Baptist congregations had been organized in some southern states as early as the 1770s. From the 1790s, African Americans formed separate Methodist societies (the basis of Methodist congregations) when they were mistreated by white society members. By the earliest decades of the 1800s independent African-American Methodist denominations had been formally organized, including the African Methodist Episcopal (AME) Church, led by Bishop Richard Allen in Philadelphia, and the African Methodist Episcopal Zion (AMEZ) Church, organized in New York. Although most slaves did not belong to separate denominations, slave religion developed its own traditions, an "invisible institution" often concealed from their European-American masters. After the Civil War, more African-American churches became independent. In 1870 black Methodist leaders from the South formed the Colored (now Christian) Methodist Episcopal (CME) Church.

Throughout the decades after the Civil War, black Baptist congregations organized themselves into successively larger conventions, culminating in the National Baptist Convention (1895). This convention was the predecessor of current larger African-American Baptist denominations, including the National Baptist Convention of the U.S.A., the National Baptist Convention of America, the National Missionary Baptist Convention, and the Progressive National Baptist Convention, which was formed in 1961 to uphold more intense support for the civil rights movement. Although a majority of African Americans are Baptists and Methodists (approximately 65 percent are Baptists), many Pentecostal denominations were led by black Americans from the beginning, and black Pentecostal churches have grown consistently through the twentieth century (see 4.0.8).

With respect to doctrine, at least formal doctrine, the African-American Methodist and Baptist denominations follow closely the patterns of other Methodist and Baptist churches. The various National Baptist groups utilize the New Hampshire Confession as their statement of faith, and the AME, AMEZ, and CME denominations utilize the Twenty-five Articles of Religion drawn from the Methodist Episcopal Church. Readers may note, then, that when these doctrinal statements are referred to, they represent the formal teachings of African-American denominations as well as other Baptist and Methodist groups. The AME Church has added additional doctrinal statements on apostolic succession and on "formalism" in worship.

Another movement representative of the trend toward democratization on the part of North American Evangelical and Free churches in the early 1800s was the movement called Restorationism, a movement that grew from the context of independent Presbyterian churches in the 1820s and 1830s. The American Restorationists had a precedent in a secession from the (Presbyterian) Church of Scotland in the 1700s, a secession led by John Glas and Robert Sandeman who had accepted the Free-Church principle of the church as a solely voluntary society. There were numerous schisms from the Church of Scotland over the decades to come, one of them over the issue of whether ministers should be required to "subscribe" formally to the Westminster Confession. Out of this particular group that opposed doctrinal "subscription" were the Scots-Irish preachers Thomas Campbell and his son Alexander Campbell who preached in the Appalachian regions of Virginia, West Virginia, Pennsylvania, and Kentucky.

Although the Campbells considered themselves to be Baptists for a period, by the late 1820s they disclaimed all denominational names, claiming only to be "Christians" or "Disciples of Christ," with their churches called "Churches of Christ" or "Christian Churches." The Campbells opposed speculative theology and doctrine, and they also opposed what they perceived as the excessive emotionalism of the "Second Great Awakening" in North America. They held that baptism and the confession of Christ as Lord were the only requirements of believers, advocated a union of all Christians on the basis of the New Testament alone, and insisted on weekly communion. In 1832 they united their movement with a similar movement led by Barton W. Stone, although Stone's movement had been more revivalistic than the "Campbellites."

The Restorationist "Churches of Christ" flourished in the central United States through the 1800s. By 1906 a marked division had occurred among Restorationists, a division grounded in differing understandings of how the Bible was to be interpreted, but which had several practical points of contention. For example, one division was between those who insisted that musical instruments had no grounding in New Testament practice and those who argued that instrumental music was not forbidden by the New Testament. (It might be important to note that for Restorationists in general, the Old Testament was not considered authoritative as a basis of union or consensus for Christian communities.) Another divisive issue was whether congregations should participate in mission-sending societies. Some who opposed the use of musical instruments and mission-sending societies came to be known as "Churches of Christ." (Sometimes, we may note, the adjective "Noninstrumental" is applied to make it clear that this is the group referred to, but there are also "Instrumental" congregations who claim the title "Churches of Christ.") Most of the group that favored the use of musical instruments in worship and supported mission-sending societies came to be known as "Disciples of Christ." The latter group has in the twentieth century become more and more like other North American Protestant churches, with a liberal/conservative polarization as in other denominations.

Another American movement, one that came into existence at about the same time as Restorationism, was the Holiness movement. But whereas Restorationism had grown from the Reformed tradition, the Holiness movement grew out of Methodist revivalism, also a powerful force in the culture of the Second Great Awakening. Methodists from John Wesley on had stressed the centrality of being "entirely sanctified," that is, loving God with all one's heart, mind, soul, and strength. Methodists had taught believers to expect "perfect love" in this life. The Holiness movement grew from the Methodists' preaching of perfect love, but it differed in some respects: Holiness preachers used the expression "baptism of the Holy Spirit" to describe the moment of Christian perfection, and they tended to expect Christian perfection as a second momentary experience (second after conversion) immediately available to those who had been born again in conversion (see 4.3.6.b).

The Holiness movement was supported by prominent Methodist leaders before the Civil War, but after the war its leadership tended to feel more and more estranged from Methodism. In the 1870s Holiness leaders formed a "National Camp Meeting Association for the Promotion of Holiness," and this brought an organizational structure to their rather loose web of revival movements. By the time Methodist churches passed ugly resolutions condemning the Holiness movement in the 1890s, the formation of Holiness churches was well underway. Many of these took the name "Church of God" (also a popular name for early Pentecostal denominations, as we shall see), but the largest is the Church of the Nazarene, formally organized in 1907. We have used the "Articles of Faith" of the Church of the Nazarene to illustrate Holiness doctrine in the account of Evangelical and Free-church teachings given below.

In addition to the Restorationist and Holiness movements and the churches that grew out of them, the mid-1800s also saw the rise of Evangelical churches that stressed the immediate return of Christ (see 4.2.2.a), although there were two very distinct groups that expressed this concern. Around 1830 in the British Isles an Anglican priest named J. N. Darby separated from the Established church and began teaching that the return of Christ would be soon. Darby also developed the idea that biblical history should be understood in a scheme of discrete periods or "dispensations" in which the terms of human salvation had changed (see 4.1.1.d). He became a popular lecturer, not only in Britain and Ireland but also on the European continent and in North America. The churches that were founded through his direct influence usually have the name "Brethren," and they are often called "Plymouth Brethren" for the city in England where they originated. However, one must be careful at this point because the term "Brethren" is very popular among Evangelical and Free churches. It has been used and is in use to describe Moravians, German Baptist groups, and others. Among the Darbyite Brethren groups, a further distinction grew up between "Exclusive" Brethren, who refused to share communion with other groups on the basis of doctrinal and practical points (sometimes rather fine points), and the "Open" Brethren who (as the title suggests) were more comfortable with doctrinal latitude.

Some of Darby's American followers formed new independent churches, many under the inspiration of C. I. Scofield, an itinerant teacher whose *Scofield Reference Bible* brought Dispensationalist teaching to thousands of followers. American congregations often called themselves "Bible churches" or "Bible-teaching churches." These churches—of both British and North American origin—have spread throughout the world and have undergone a number of divisions in fellowship since the time of their founding. They tend to be Calvinistic in their theology, although (like American Restorationists) they reject "human" creeds in preference for the Bible alone as the sole authority for religious life. I shall refer to these churches in the remainder of chapter 4 as Dispensationalist churches. The narrative of Dispensationalist churches is an intensely complex narrative indeed, involving (among other things) British versions of American Holiness teaching retransplanted to America. But to keep faith with the introduction to this book, we may note here that Garrison Keillor's "Sanctified Brethren," though fictitious, are clearly "Exclusive Brethren" of the Darbyite persuasion.[195]

A different strain of speculation about the second coming of Christ appeared in North America in the 1830s in the teaching of William Miller, who engaged in intense research on biblical prophecies and concluded that Christ's second coming would be very soon. Miller be-

195. Keillor, *Lake,* p. 105.

came convinced that 1844 would be a particularly important year in the divine chronology, perhaps the very year in which Christ would return to earth. Miller's preaching and "Adventist" periodicals, tracts, and publicity attracted thousands of followers, and although 1844 itself came and passed without Christ's visible return, Miller and his followers continued the work of interpreting biblical prophecies anticipating Christ's second advent (see 4.1.1.c).

Churches that developed from the teachings of Miller (and other millennial teachers of his time) are usually referred to as Adventist churches. Many were influenced by the belief that Christians in the last days should restore Old Testament practices, such as the observance of Saturday as the Sabbath (hence, "Seventh-day" Adventists) or Jewish dietary laws. Although early Adventist groups tended to be sectarian (many, for example, were anticreedal, and some were anti-Trinitarian and Arian), there has been a trend for Adventist groups to become more and more like other Evangelical and Free-church denominations. The largest Adventist denomination, the General Conference of Seventh-day Adventists, was influenced by a "Reformationist" movement in the late 1800s, that is, a movement to bring the denomination more in line with historic Reformation churches. As a result of this, the denomination now explicitly affirms Trinitarian theology (see 4.2.1).

4.0.8   The Late 1800s and Early 1900s: Fundamentalism and Pentecostalism

From the time of the emergence of Baptist churches in the early 1600s, we have consistently seen how two distinct strands of Evangelical tradition emerged. One strand was *Arminian Evangelical*, represented by General or Free-Will Baptists, (Wesleyan) Methodists, and the Holiness movement. The other strand was *Reformed Evangelicalism*, represented by Particular or Regular Baptists, George Whitefield, Welsh Calvinistic Methodists (now Presbyterians), the American Restorationist tradition, and the Darbyite Brethren churches. At the end of the 1800s and the beginning of the 1900s these two strands of Evangelical tradition found vigorous expression in Fundamentalism, growing from the Reformed strand of Evangelicalism, and in Pentecostalism, growing from the Wesleyan-Arminian strand of Evangelicalism.

Fundamentalism is a particular expression of Evangelicalism that emerged late in the 1800s. We have seen in chapter 3 how the Reformation churches were influenced by conservative, antimodernist movements in the 1800s. Fundamentalism can be understood as an expression of these same antimodernist tendencies on the part of Evangelical and Free churches, although it also left a strong mark on Reformed churches. Growing from a network of international revival preachers and Bible conferences, the Fundamentalists stressed the need for defining a short list of fundamental, uncompromisable Christian doctrines in the light of Modernism's challenges. Typically, lists of fundamental doctrines would include the following:

1. The "inerrancy" or "infallibility" of the Bible (against scientific claims that appear to have contradicted the Bible's teachings, such as the theory of evolution; see 4.1.1.b);
2. The divinity or deity of Christ (against Modernist tendencies to see Christ as a mere human being; see 4.2.2);
3. The virginal conception of Christ (usually stated as "virgin birth," again against claims that Christ was only human; see also 4.2.2);
4. Substitutionary atonement (against the Modernist tendency to see human salvation as relying on human progress or good works; see 4.3.1); and
5. The literal bodily resurrection of Christ (against Modernist tendencies to interpret the resurrection as a religious "myth"; see also 4.2.2 and 4.2.2.a).

Sometimes the immediate return of Christ was added to this list. In the early twentieth century, a series of pamphlets called *The Fundamentals*, published in the United States, stressed these themes and in 1919 a World Christian Fundamentals Association was organized.

The importance of Fundamentalism for the development of Evangelical and Free churches was not just that some independent Fundamentalist churches were founded. More importantly, Fundamentalism had a deep effect on almost all the Evangelical churches with the possible exceptions of Friends and Methodists, though many Methodist folk were attracted to the Fundamentalists' claims. Most affected were Evangelically oriented churches of the Reformed tradition (especially Presbyterians) and Baptists, but many Holiness and Pentecostal churches also adopted statements of biblical inerrancy or infallibility in the twentieth century even though their own traditions were not closely tied to the origins of Fundamentalism. Perhaps most importantly, Fundamentalism had the effect of sharpening the perception of a chasm between modern life and the ethos of Evangelical churches who adopted its outlook.

Pentecostalism originated at the beginning of the twentieth century and developed at first from Holiness churches and other Evangelical churches that stressed vivid spiritual experiences after conversion. In 1900 and 1901 a preacher in Topeka, Kansas, named Charles F. Parham began teaching his students to expect (1) conversion, followed by (2) "entire sanctification" (cleansing from inward sin), and (3) a "baptism of the Holy Spirit" accompanied by the initial evidence of speaking in unknown tongues (Acts 2:4). The first two points reflect conventional Holiness doctrine (see 4.3.6.b). The third represents a new departure (see 4.3.6.c), and on New Year's Day of 1901, in the first moments of the new century, one of Parham's students claimed this experience. Parham preached throughout the United States, and his teaching on Spirit baptism was taken up by William Seymour, an African-American preacher who began the Azusa Street revival movement in Los Angeles in April of 1906.

The Azusa Street revival was a remarkably interracial phenomenon, and it attracted national and even international press attention. Within months of the revival, the Pentecostal doctrine had spread throughout the United States and also to Chile, Great Britain, and Norway. Hundreds of Pentecostal denominations were formed, many of them taking the name "Church of God" (as Holiness churches had done, so it is important to discern whether a "Church of God" is Holiness or Pentecostal). The original Pentecostal denomination was the Church of God in Christ, which remains the largest predominantly African-American Pentecostal denomination. The Assemblies of God (organized in 1915) are the largest Pentecostal denomination in the world at this time. We have used the Assemblies of God "Statement of Fundamental Truths" in addition to other Pentecostal doctrinal statements to illustrate Pentecostal doctrine in the explication that follows.

The growth of Pentecostalism, especially in developing countries of Africa, South America, and Asia, is one of the most important facts in twentieth-century Christian history. Just as Fundamentalism influenced other churches, so did Pentecostalism, but it took longer for Pentecostalism. Perhaps this was because its first advocates were largely from lower social classes, but by the late 1950s and early 1960s Pentecostalism had attracted considerable support in the middle classes in the United States and elsewhere. The Charismatic movement describes persons within older religious denominations (such as Roman Catholics or Methodists) who teach the Pentecostal doctrine of a baptism of the Holy Spirit, usually associated with the initial evidence of speaking in unknown tongues, though some charismatics allow that a variety of spiritual gifts might be experienced as initial evidence of Spirit baptism.

4.0.9   Evangelical Ferment in the Twentieth Century

Since the middle of the twentieth century the Evangelical and Free churches have undergone important changes. On the one hand, Modernism (and Liberalism) has affected many of these churches, perhaps especially Methodists and Friends, and to a lesser degree Baptists and some of the Restorationist churches. Those most affected by Modernism in the twentieth century have expressed strong social activism, have been consistently involved in the Ecumenical movement, and have tended to adopt modern biblical criticism and Liberal theology, as Reformation and Union churches had done. We might note that one of the most important ecumenical developments in the last twenty years has been the attempt on the part of ecumenical leaders to bring conservative Evangelical and Pentecostal churches into ecumenical dialogue with other churches.

We must also note the growing importance of parachurch organizations in contemporary Evangelicalism. Developing from Camp-meeting associations and Evangelistic associations in the 1800s, there exists an intricate web of Evangelical organizations that cuts across the boundaries of denominations and congregations. With the advent of modern media (radio and television) in this century, these parachurch organizations (for example, the Billy Graham Evangelistic Association and Campus Crusade for Christ) have become extraordinarily powerful, more important for many Evangelical Christians than denominations themselves. Most of them have their own doctrinal summaries or statements, which tend to bear strong resemblances to historic Baptist views of salvation and of the nature of the church.

Fundamentalism remains a very powerful force within many Evangelical and Free churches. In fact, the 1980s witnessed a remarkable revival of Christian Fundamentalism along with other conservative movements throughout the world. At the same time, progressive Evangelical movements have emerged, and although there is no uniformity to them, they tend to stress three points of "revision" in contrast to older forms of Evangelicalism: (1) they stress the need for Christian engagement in modern, critical scholarship (as contrasted with Fundamentalism and the generally anti-intellectual attitude of much American Evangelicalism); (2) they stress the need for Christian involvement in systemic social issues (as contrasted with the individualistic approach to society taken by older forms of Evangelicalism); and (3) they stress the need for a more "catholic" identity, including the use of traditional liturgy, meditative spiritualities, and the practice of an ecumenical outlook (as contrasted with the rather sectarian, and sometimes antiliturgical and antiecumenical outlooks of older forms of Evangelicalism). As we shall see in chapter 5, one of the signs of a new Evangelical outlook in the last two decades has been the significant participation of Evangelicals (including Pentecostals) in the work of the World Council of Churches.

4.1   Evangelical and Free-Church Teachings on Religious Authority

4.1.1.a   *What Evangelical and Free churches teach about the authority of the Bible:* Evangelical and Free-church traditions, with the exception of the Society of Friends, agree in teaching that the Bible is the final authority for faith and practice.

Sources: Dordrecht Confession, 5 (in Leith, p. 297). *Mennonite Confession of Faith (1963),* article 2 (pp. 9–10). *Confession of Faith in a Mennonite Perspective (1995),* article 4. New Hampshire Confession, 1 (in Leith, pp. 334–335). Abstract of Principles, 1 (in Leith, p. 340). Baptist Faith and Message, 1 (in Leith, pp. 345–346). Moravian *Ground of the Unity,* section on "God's Word and Doctrine." Methodist Articles of Religion, 5–6 (in Leith, p. 355). Fundamental Beliefs of Seventh-day Adventists, belief 1. Nazarene Articles of Faith, 4. Assemblies of God Statement of Fundamental Truths, 1 (in Melton, p. 357).

Comparative Cross-References: Eastern Orthodox, 1.1.1–2; Roman Catholic, 2.1.1–4; Reformation and Union, 3.1.1, 3.1.2.a–c; Ecumenical, 5.2.1.

With the important exception of Quakers (see 4.1.2.c), Evangelical and Free churches consistently affirm the Reformation principle that the Bible is the highest and final authority for Christian faith and life. The statements of faith of Baptists, Methodists, Pentecostal, and Holiness groups begin with this principle. Although Restorationist and Dispensationalist churches have no statements of faith as such, the reason they have none is their foundational conviction that the Scriptures are sufficient by themselves. There are some important differences in the way in which various churches express this principle. Some, as we shall see below, assert the "inerrancy" or "infallibility" of scripture (see 4.1.1.b). The Methodist Article of Religion on scripture (following the Anglican Article) is somewhat more guarded, asserting simply that the Scriptures contain everything necessary for salvation.

Within this broad agreement on the centrality and primacy of the Bible, we may further note some important differences in the way in which the Bible is applied in the life of churches. For some, the Scriptures are used simply to rule out that which is unacceptable to a Christian community, but if a practice is not ruled out by scripture, it may be found acceptable by other criteria (such as the long use of the church). This approach allows more of later Christian traditions to be incorporated in the life of the church, and it gives Methodists and Moravians a gift to link Evangelical and Free churches with their roots in older Christian traditions.

Other churches tend to insist on a positive precedent or example in scripture, and they argue that whatever is not specifically mentioned in scripture should not be required of a Christian congregation. The most pronounced example of this trend can be seen in American Restorationist churches, where there have been lengthy debates about what practices have been specifically legitimated by New Testament example. Should musical instruments be used in church? No, some answered, and not because they are evil in themselves, but because the New Testament does not give explicit examples of the use of in-strumental music. How do you name a local congregation? Churches of Christ traditionally insist that the only New Testament example for naming a local church is to name it for its geographical location, like, "the church at Antioch." Following this precedent, then, Churches of Christ are almost always named for their geographical location: "West End Church of Christ," "Highway 79 Church of Christ," and so forth. Some Restorationist congregations reject even the idea of Sunday schools or church roll-books because these are not specifically men-tioned in the New Testament. But even when Evangelical and Free churches do not go to this extreme, there is a strong tendency, espe-cially within Baptist and Dispensationalist churches, to look for ex-plicit biblical precedents.

4.1.1.b   *What Fundamentalists teach about the authority of the Bible:* Fundamentalist churches agree in teaching, further, that the Scrip-tures are "inerrant" or "infallible" in their original manuscripts, due to their divine inspiration.

Sources: Baptist Faith and Message, 1 (in Leith, pp. 345–346). Fundamental Beliefs of Seventh-day Adventists, belief 1. Nazarene Articles of Faith, 4. Assemblies of God Statement of Fundamental Truths, 1 (in Melton, p. 357).

Comparative Cross-References: Eastern Orthodox, 1.1.1–2; Roman Catholic, 2.1.1–4; Reformation and Union, 3.1.1, 3.1.2.a–c.

The Westminster Confession of 1647 had referred to the Bible as "infallible," and as we have seen above (3.1.2.b), it was characteristic of both Catholic and Protestant teachers in the Reformation age to af-firm the "infallibility" of the Bible, among its other perfections. In the context of the controversies of the Reformation age, biblical infallibil-ity was principally understood as an affirmation that the Scriptures do not fail in teaching what is necessary for human salvation, or "saving knowledge," to use the words of the "Abstract of Principles" of Southern Baptist Theological Seminary. Methodist founder John Wesley sometimes spoke of scripture as unfailing in this sense, that is, in reference to human salvation.[196] Fundamentalism stressed the infallibility or inerrancy of the Christian Scriptures in sharp contention with the scientific challenges of the 1800s. Fundamentalism insisted that the Bible is verbally or literally (in its every word or its every letter) inspired by God and is unfailing or infallible in every respect: historical and scientific, as well as religious and moral. The Fundamentalist approach to scripture must be understood in the context of Fundamentalism's sharp reaction against Modernism; Fundamentalists wanted to defend the Scriptures as a definitive, unfailing answer to the challenges of evolutionism, rationalism, secularism, materialism, and the like.

The Southern Baptist report on "Baptist Faith and Message," adopted in 1925, reflects this Fundamentalist outlook. "The present occasion for a reaffirmation of Christian fundamentals," the report notes, "is the prevalence of naturalism in the modern teaching and preaching of religion." In its first article, the report reiterates the assertion of the New Hampshire Confession, that the Bible "was written by men divinely inspired . . . that it has God for its author, salvation for its end, and truth without any mixture of error, for its matter. . . ."[197] We may note, by contrast, that the "Abstract of Principles" of Southern Baptist Theological Seminary does not utilize the language of infallibility or inerrancy, as the New Hampshire Confession had done; the "Abstract" simply asserts that the Scriptures were "given by inspiration of God, and are the only sufficient, certain, and authoritative rule of all saving knowledge, faith and obedience."[198] In recent decades the doctrine of biblical infallibility has again arisen as a major issue dividing Evangelicals, and dividing Southern Baptists in particular. Although some Baptist confessions maintain an "inerrantist" view of scripture, the Baptist confessions are not unanimous in this, and we should recall that the Baptist confessions themselves have never been considered binding on particular congregations or on the liberty of private conscience in interpreting the Scriptures (see 4.1.3.a).

196. John Wesley, preface to *Explanatory Notes upon the New Testament*, 10–12 (London: Epworth Press, 1976), pp. 8–10.
197. "Report of the Committee on Baptist Faith and Message" (in Leith, pp. 344, 345–346).
198. Abstract of Principles, no. 1 (in Leith, p. 340). Note here that the reference to the Bible's certainty is specifically said in reference to "saving knowledge, faith, and obedience" and is not applied to scientific or historical claims. In this respect the "Abstract of Principles" reflects its background in the Westminster Confession and the Reformed tradition.

4.1.1.c *What Adventist churches teach about the interpretation of the Bible:* Adventist churches are characterized by their focused concentration on biblical prophecy, especially as it anticipates the imminent second advent of Christ.

Sources: Fundamental Beliefs of Seventh-day Adventists, beliefs 23–27.

Comparative Cross-References: Eastern Orthodox, 1.1.2–3; Roman Catholic, 2.1.2–5; Reformation and Union, 3.1.2.a–d.

Adventist churches agree with other Evangelical churches in teaching the primacy of scripture (4.1.1.a–b). Their interpretation of scripture, moreover, is especially guided by the belief that Christ will return soon and that the church must prepare for Christ's coming by careful understanding of the biblical prophecies concerning the end of time and by preaching repentance and faith in anticipation of Christ's return. Originally associated with the belief that Christ would return in 1844, the Adventist movement took up William Miller's enterprise of scrutinizing biblical prophecy (see 4.0.7). For some early Adventists, the disappointment that 1844 did not bring the anticipated return of Christ led to more elaborate speculation on the date of Christ's return. For others, the events of this period came to be interpreted as heavenly events. The largest Adventist denomination, the Seventh-day Adventists, states as a point of doctrine that 1844 marked the entrance of Christ into the most holy place of the heavenly temple, based on the prophecies about the 2,300-day period in Daniel 8:14. From this cardinal point, Seventh-day Adventists maintain, the Scriptures can be understood as showing that Christ will return soon. Although most Adventists are clear that Christians cannot know the precise time when Christ will return, they believe that Christians should focus on the time of Christ's coming as being "very near."

The Adventist enterprise of interpreting biblical prophecy has important implications for the Christian community. The church, in anticipation of Christ's return, must function as a special community, a "remnant" that is to call the world to repentance and faith in the light of the impending return of the Lord. Many Adventists take the view that in the remnant community some religious observances of the Old Testament are to be restored to the Christian church, including observance of the seventh day as the Sabbath, and observance of some of the laws of *kishrut*, the Jewish dietary laws. On this point, we should note, Adventist reading of scripture differs widely from those of Restorationists and others who focus solely on the New Testament: for Adventists, the Old Testament stands in continuity with the New Testament and bears particular importance for Christians both as interpreting the coming of Christ and as showing the life of the remnant community.

4.1.1.d   What Dispensationalist churches teach about the interpretation of the Bible: Dispensationalist churches, in addition to accepting the Fundamentalist doctrine of the infallibility of the Bible, agree in teaching that the Bible should be understood according to a scheme of discrete "dispensations" of biblical history in which the particular conditions of human salvation have changed.

Sources: Introduction to *The New Scofield Reference Bible.*

Comparative Cross-References: Eastern Orthodox, 1.1.2–3; Roman Catholic, 2.1.2–5; Reformation and Union, 3.1.2.a–d.

Dispensationalist churches share the Fundamentalist insistence on the inerrancy or infallibility of the Bible (see 4.1.1.b), but they are distinguished by their teaching that the Bible should be interpreted within a scheme of periods or "dispensations" of biblical history, within which the particular conditions of human salvation have changed. Dispensationalist teachers are usually clear that human salvation, in whatever period, is the result of divine grace and human faith (see 4.3.1), but they maintain that the particular conditions by which salvation has been offered by God have changed throughout the biblical narrative. For Adam and Eve, to take the first instance, the sole condition of salvation was not to eat of the fruit of the tree of the knowledge of good and evil, though even this condition was offered by God's grace, and Adam and Eve's obedience would have been the sign of their faith or trust in God. Once they were banished from Eden, however, God set different conditions for salvation. Dispensational schemes vary immensely, but Dispensationalists often list seven particular dispensations (here following the pattern of the *New Scofield Reference Bible*), including

1. the dispensation of "innocence" in Eden (Gen. 1:28 and following), then
2. the dispensation of "conscience or moral responsibility" associated with the state of human beings after the fall of Adam and Eve (Gen. 3:7 and following)
3. the dispensation of "human government" associated with God's covenant with Noah (Genesis 8),
4. the dispensation of "promise" associated with God's promise to Abraham (Genesis 12 and following),
5. the dispensation of the Law, associated with the giving of the Law to Moses (Ex. 19:1 and following),

6. the dispensation of the church, beginning with Pentecost (Acts 2 and following), and

7. the dispensation of the kingdom of God, associated with Christ's second coming (Rev. 20:4).[199]

We should note at this point that although Dispensationalism characterizes some particular denominations, such as Darbyite Brethren churches and "Bible-teaching" churches in the United States, these ideas have had immense popularity within broader Evangelical circles. The *Scofield Reference Bible* has been the best-selling book for the Oxford University Press for decades, and it is a source of Dispensationalist teaching. Dispensationalist ideas have penetrated deeply into many Baptist, Pentecostal, and even conservative Presbyterian churches in this century.

4.1.2.a *What Evangelical and Free churches teach about the role of religious experience in the interpretation of the Bible:* Many Evangelical churches teach that religious experience confirms the truths of the Bible and gives inward knowledge of our relationship to God.

Sources: Mennonite Confession of Faith (1963), article 2 (p. 10). *Confession of Faith in a Mennonite Perspective (1995)*, article 4. Moravian *Ground of the Unity*, section on "Personal Faith." John Wesley, sermon on "The Scripture Way of Salvation" 2:1 (in Leith, p. 364).

Comparative Cross-References: Eastern Orthodox, 1.1.2–3; Roman Catholic, 2.1.2–5; Reformation and Union, 3.1.2.a–d.

Personal religious experience has been a central part of the Evangelical revivals and awakenings from the 1500s through the present time. Early Anabaptist leaders claimed divine revelation as their grounds for opposing national churches. Some Evangelical leaders developed sophisticated accounts of the role of religious experience. Although they did not see religious experience as overturning the centrality of scripture (but see 4.1.2.c on the Society of Friends), they nevertheless maintained that through our human experience of God the truths of the Bible are confirmed for us, and we can know our own relationship to God through these experiences. Perhaps we should recall, at this point, that although the Reformed tradition had long taught that the "inward witness of the Holy Spirit" confirms the truths of scripture, the Evangelical movements grew up at the same time as

199. This scheme of dispensations is laid out in a lengthy footnote on Genesis 1:28 in *The New Scofield Reference Bible* (New York: Oxford University Press, 1969), pp. 3–4.

the Enlightenment was challenging traditional and biblical knowledge. One of the leading Enlightenment options was to argue that our best and surest knowledge is knowledge that comes by experience. Given its classic exposition in the works of Francis Bacon (in the first decade of the seventeenth century) and John Locke (in the 1690s) this "empirical" philosophy dominated British thought in the 1700s and beyond. The views of Evangelical leaders on the central importance of religious experience can be seen as a religious parallel to Enlightenment empiricism.

As a matter of fact, New England revivalist Jonathan Edwards had carefully studied the works of John Locke, and he utilized Locke's philosophical vocabulary in his *Treatise concerning the Religious Affections* to show how religious "affections" or experiences can give an accurate knowledge of God when they confirm biblical truths and when they lead believers closer to God.[200] John Wesley had read both Locke and Edwards, published his own edited version of Edwards's *Treatise*, and consistently defined "faith" as involving an experience of the spiritual. Faith, Wesley claimed, quoting Hebrews 11:1, is "the assurance of things hoped for, the conviction of things not seen." Wesley took "things not seen" to be spiritual as opposed to physical or material realities, and he consistently used the analogy of sense experience to explain "faith" in this sense: just as the bodily senses give us knowledge of the material world, so "faith" or religious experience gives us knowledge of the spiritual world. "Faith" in this broad sense is not necessarily or specifically Christian, since Christian faith always has Christ as its object. It does not necessarily denote strange or weird experiences: faith in this sense is the "spiritual sensation" shared by every human being.

If Edwards and Wesley gave sophisticated expositions of religious experience, we should note further the importance of religious experience in the Evangelical movement as a whole. A good case could be made that this emphasis appears most clearly in the Wesleyan or Arminian expressions of Evangelicalism—among traditional Wesleyan Methodists, Holiness churches, and Pentecostals. This emphasis can lead to a popular Evangelical individualism, the notion that an individual reads the Bible in the light of her or his own experience of God, and little else really counts (such as the experience of the church or her own church community).

The practice of reading the Bible in the light of personal religious experience is not just an intellectual tradition among Evangelical

200. Jonathan Edwards, *Religious Affections*, ed. John E. Smith (New Haven: Yale University Press, 1959).

Christians, it lies at the heart of Evangelical spirituality, as expressed in the following lines from a gospel hymn composed by Mary Ann Lathbury in 1877:

> Break Thou the bread of life, Dear Lord, to me,
>   As Thou didst break the loaves Beside the sea.
> Beyond the sacred page I seek Thee, Lord;
>   My spirit pants for thee, O living Word![201]

4.1.2.b *What some contemporary Evangelical and Free churches teach about the interpretation of the Bible in the light of tradition, reason, and experience:* Many contemporary Christians of Evangelical and Free traditions affirm their belief in the use of scripture, Christian tradition, reason, and experience as religious authorities, recognizing the priority of scripture over all other authorities.

Sources: United Methodist Church statement of "Our Theological Task" (*Book of Discipline of the United Methodist Church* [Nashville: United Methodist Publishing House, 1992], par. 68, pp. 76–82). Moravian *Ground of the Unity,* sections on "God's Word and Doctrine" and "Creeds and Confessions."

Comparative Cross-References: Eastern Orthodox, 1.1.2–3; Roman Catholic, 2.1.2–5; Reformation and Union, 3.1.2.a–d.

In relation to the point last made, about the problems of individualistic readings of the Scriptures, we may note that some contemporary Christians of Evangelical and Free traditions have been influenced by the Ecumenical movement, with its stress on the positive appreciation of Christian tradition, and by Liberal emphases on the use of reason and experience in interpreting religious faith. The United Methodist Church has formally expressed its belief in a quadrilateral of religious authority, in which scripture, tradition, reason, and experience are utilized together, recognizing the priority of scripture over all other authorities. Although the "Wesleyan quadrilateral" was not formulated by John Wesley himself, he set an example of the careful use of early Christian and Reformation traditions, reason, and reflection on religious experience in the interpretation of the Bible. Since 1972 the United Methodist Church (the largest North American Methodist body) has affirmed the use of this pattern of religious authority, although in 1988 it revised its statement to make clearer the priority or "primacy" of scripture within the four elements of the quadrilateral. This formulation has been found helpful by some

201. Hymn by Mary Ann Lathbury in *Assembly Songs: For Use in Evangelistic Services, Sabbath Schools, Young Peoples Societies, Devotional Meetings, and the Home,* ed. J. Ernest Thacker, George A. Fisher, and R. E. McGill (Richmond, Va.: Presbyterian Committee of Publication, 1910), no. 212.

Evangelicals outside of the United Methodist Church as a way of approaching contemporary issues over biblical authority.[202]

The Moravian Church has recently revised its *Ground of the Unity* to indicate how Moravians interpret scripture. Their statement insists that God alone is the fount of all religious authority, and that "the Word of the Cross" is the "center" of scripture. Also according to this statement, Moravians look to the ecumenical traditions of the church as well as their own tradition in interpreting scripture.[203] Though it is more conscious of the limitations of human reason and human language, the Moravian *Ground of the Unity*, like the "Wesleyan Quadrilateral," points the way to a critical reception of scripture in an Evangelical context.

4.1.2.c *What the Society of Friends teaches concerning the role of the Spirit in the interpretation of the Bible:* The Society of Friends is distinguished by its belief that the inward witness of the Holy Spirit holds authority even over the Scriptures.

Sources: Barclay's *Apology*, propositions 1–3 (in Leith, pp. 324–326).

Comparative Cross-References: Eastern Orthodox, 1.1.1–3; Roman Catholic, 2.1.1–5; Reformation and Union, 3.1.1, 3.1.2.a–d.

We have noted at several points above that Quakers would be an exception to the broad Evangelical and Free-Church consensus regarding the primacy of the Scriptures. This should not be taken as meaning that Quakers reject the Bible, but the theory laid out by the early Quaker apologist Robert Barclay and given broad consent in Quaker history is that, because the Bible itself is grounded in the religious experience of its (human) authors, religious experience has a priority over the Bible. Our direct experience of God is the "fountain" or ground of religious knowledge. Thus, in Barclay's own words,

> because [the Scriptures] are only a declaration of the fountain, and not the fountain itself, therefore they are not to be esteemed the principal ground of all truth and knowledge, nor yet the adequate primary rule of faith and manners.[204]

202. On the issue of Wesley's authorship of the quadrilateral, cf. Ted A. Campbell, "The 'Wesleyan Quadrilateral': The Story of a Modern Methodist Myth" (*Methodist History* 29:2 [January 1991]: 87–95; and in Thomas A. Langford, ed., *Doctrine and Theology in The United Methodist Church* [Nashville: Abingdon Press/ Kingswood Books, 1991], pp. 154–161). On the use of the "Wesleyan Quadrilateral" in broader Evangelical circles, cf. Donald A. D. Thorsen, *The Wesleyan Quadrilateral: Scripture, Tradition, Reason and Experience as a Model of Evangelical Theology* (Grand Rapids: Zondervan Publishing House, 1990).
203. Moravian *Ground of the Unity*, section on "God's Word and Doctrine" as revised in 1995.
204. Barclay's *Apology*, proposition 3 (in Leith, pp. 325–326).

This reliance on the "inner light" of the Spirit is one of the chief distinguishing marks of the Quakers. It is probably grounds enough to disqualify Quakers as "Evangelical," although there are some Quakers influenced by American revivalism who describe themselves as "Evangelical Friends." It would be fair to note further that many Quakers after the time of Barclay embraced the Liberal Protestant use of reason and experience as central to their interpretation of religious faith, and some Quakers today have pressed this to the point that they are inclined toward Unitarianism.

4.1.3.a *What Evangelical and Free churches teach about the use of creeds:* Evangelical and Free-church traditions generally agree in teaching that creeds are useful as unifying statements of consensus and as summaries of scriptural truths.

Sources: Mennonite Confession of Faith (1963), preamble (pp. 7–8). *Confession of Faith in a Mennonite Perspective (1995),* introduction. Baptist Faith and Message, preface (in Leith, pp. 344–345). Moravian *Ground of the Unity,* section on "Creeds and Confessions."

Comparative Cross-References: Eastern Orthodox, 1.1.2–3; Roman Catholic, 2.1.5; Reformation and Union, 3.1.2.a–c.

The established churches of the Reformation adopted confessions of faith to which "subscription" (formal agreement) was required for participation in church and even civil leadership. Evangelical and Free churches were born out of a reaction against the "dogmatism" or "creedalism" of Reformation churches and have almost unanimously rejected this confessional principle, so that confessions of faith function in a different way for them. This is especially pronounced in the case of congregational churches, since their congregations are not at all bound to a denomination's confessions. Although some Free churches have gone so far as to reject the use of confessions altogether (see the next subsection), most Evangelical and Free traditions have summaries or confessional statements, but these possess a different kind of authority than in churches defined by confessional allegiance.

Methodists have traditionally asked candidates for ordained ministry if they have studied the doctrines of their church, if they believe these doctrines are in harmony with the Scriptures, and if they will preach and maintain these doctrines.[205] Persons joining local congregations, however, have not been required to profess allegiance to Methodist doctrinal statements. The Methodist Articles of Religion and the "Wesleyan Standards," John Wesley's *Standard Sermons* and

205. *Book of Discipline,* 1992, par. 425, questions 8–10 (p. 226).

Explanatory Notes on the New Testament, can be taken as indicating a historic Wesleyan-Methodist understanding of consensus in the faith, but they are not really binding on individual Methodists.

Similarly, the doctrinal statements of other Evangelical and Free churches are often explained in such a way that they reflect a broad consensus, but they do not require subscription. In the words of the Southern Baptist report on "Baptist Faith and Message,"

> Baptists approve and circulate confessions of faith with the following understanding, namely:
>
> (1) That they constitute a consensus of opinion of some Baptist body . . . They are not intended to add anything to the simple conditions of salvation revealed in the New Testament . . .
> (2) That we do not regard them as complete statements of our faith . . .
> (3) That any group of Baptists, large or small, have the inherent right to draw up for themselves and publish to the world a confession of their faith . . .
> (4) Confessions are only guides in interpretation, having no authority over the conscience.
> (5) That they are statements of religious convictions, drawn from the Scriptures, and are not to be used to hamper freedom of thought or investigation in other realms of life.[206]

The status of confessional documents is a very live issue today in the Southern Baptist Convention. Fundamentalists in the 1980s attempted to require subscription to the "Baptist Faith and Message" statement by all teachers in its theological seminaries, missionaries, and denominational employees. Those who refuse to subscribe often believe all the articles of the statement, but they feel that it contradicts the spirit of the statement (especially the part quoted above) to require subscription to it.

4.1.3.b *What American Restorationist churches teach about the use of creeds:* American Restorationist churches are distinguished by their belief that creeds are destructive of Christian unity and that the New Testament should be the sole criterion of Christian unity.

Comparative Cross-References: Eastern Orthodox, 1.1.2–3; Roman Catholic, 2.1.5; Reformation and Union, 3.1.2.a–c.

Creeds are particularly suspected by some Evangelical and Free churches. Many Dispensationalist churches have historically refused to

206. "Report of the Committee on Baptist Faith and Message," preface (in Leith, p. 345).

use creeds on the grounds that the Bible alone should serve as the basis for a Christian church. But the most radical expression of this anticreedal sentiment comes from the American Restorationist churches. One of its founders, Thomas Campbell, claimed that "WHERE THE SCRIPTURES SPEAK, WE SPEAK AND WHERE THE SCRIPTURES ARE SILENT, WE ARE SILENT."[207] His son Alexander Campbell, an ardent advocate of "Christian union," claimed that the first thing needed for Christian unity was to destroy all "human" creeds, because human creeds had destroyed Christian unity in the first place and stood as an obstacle to evangelization.[208] We might note at this point the particular stress laid on the New Testament by the Restorationist churches: the Old Testament is not considered by them to be valid as providing examples for Christian faith or morals.

4.1.4.a *What Evangelical and Free churches teach about the authority of civil governments: Anabaptist and Quaker views.* Anabaptist churches have historically opposed any compromises between Christianity and civil government, including Christian service in the military, governmental coercion to force religious conformity, and the swearing of oaths before magistrates. Friends (Quakers) opposed military service and the use of titles or forms of address that imply superiority of rank.

Sources: Schleitheim Confession, 4, 6–7 (in Leith, pp. 285–287, 287–291). Dordrecht Confession, 13–15 (in Leith, pp. 303–305). *Mennonite Confession of Faith (1963)*, articles 16 and 18–19 (pp. 21–22, 23–24). *Confession of Faith in a Mennonite Perspective (1995)*, articles 20, 22–23. Barclay's *Apology*, propositions 14–15 (in Leith, pp. 332–333).

Both Anabaptists and Quakers, in their own ways, rejected the notion of Christian cooperation with military power. Early Swiss Anabaptists, and almost all Anabaptists from the 1540s on, adopted the pacifist stance that Christians should not participate in the military. This point of view was linked to their conviction that Constantine's (supposed) conversion marked the point at which the earlier purity of the Christian community had been corrupted by compromise with civil government. Consistent with this view, Anabaptists opposed not only military service but also participation in political offices, the

---

207. Thomas Campbell, an often-quoted statement dated from 1809, cited in Robert Richardson, *Memoirs of Alexander Campbell*, 2 vols. (Philadelphia: J. B. Lippincott, 1868–1879; reprint, Indianapolis: Religious Book Service, n.d.), 1:236.
208. Alexander Campbell, preface to *The Christian System: In Reference to the Union of Christians and a Restoration of Primitive Christianity as Plead in the Current Reformation* (Cincinnati: H. S. Bosworth, 4th ed., 1866; reprint, New York: The Arno Press and the New York Times, 1969), p. 9.

swearing of oaths to civil magistrates, and any hint of governmental coercion to force religious conformity. This historic tradition is carried on today by Mennonite and Hutterite communities, who have worked consistently for the rights of conscientious objectors to military service.

Quakers also opposed military service, but they did not take the stance against participation in government that characterized the Anabaptists. Although some early followers of Fox fought in the English Civil War against the Crown (see 4.0.3), the view prevailed among the Friends that participation in the military was incompatible with the perfection of Christ. The Quaker opposition to the "carnal sword" should be seen as reflecting their opposition to unjust structures of social and economic power. Consistent with this ethic, Quakers rejected the use of titles or forms of address that implied superiority of rank. The Friends' use of "thee" and "thou," though archaic in contemporary English, reflected their preference for the personal and familiar form of address rather than the formal ("you" was actually the more formal second-person pronoun).

4.1.4.b *What Evangelical and Free churches teach about the authority of civil governments: Views of other Evangelical and Free Churches.* Other Evangelical and Free-church traditions agree in teaching that Christians may participate in civil governments and obey civil laws so far as these do not conflict with religious obedience, but they have generally opposed establishments of religion.

Sources: New Hampshire Confession, 16 (in Leith, p. 339). Abstract of Principles, 18 (in Leith, p. 343). Baptist Faith and Message, 18–21 (in Leith, pp. 349–351). Methodist Articles of Religion 23 and 25 (in Leith, p. 360).

Although most Evangelical and Free churches do not reject participation in military or in civil government in the ways Anabaptists (or Quakers) do, one of the characteristics of "Free" churches is their rejection of establishments of religion. Methodists in principle have nothing against establishments of religion, since John Wesley consistently supported the Church of England. But Baptist and Methodist confessions have statements about civil government that in general allow Christians to obey civil governments so long as obedience to government does not conflict with religious conscience and beliefs. Although the Methodist Articles do not deal directly with the issue of state and church (they do allow for Christians to swear oaths before a civil magistrate), Baptist statements call for a clear institutional separation of the two.

4.2   Evangelical and Free-Church Teachings
on God and Christ

4.2.1.a *What Evangelical and Free churches in general teach about the nature of God as the Trinity:* Evangelical and Free-church traditions generally agree in teaching that God is three Persons in one substance, although some churches prefer to state this utilizing only biblical terms.

Sources: Dordrecht Confession, 1 (in Leith, pp. 292–293). *Mennonite Confession of Faith (1963),* article 1 (pp. 8–9). *Confession of Faith in a Mennonite Perspective (1995),* article 1. New Hampshire Confession, 2 (in Leith, p. 335). Abstract of Principles, 2–3 (in Leith, p. 340). Baptist Faith and Message, 2 (in Leith, p. 346). Moravian *Ground of the Unity,* Part 1, "The Belief of the Church." Methodist Articles of Religion, 1 (in Leith, p. 354). Fundamental Beliefs of Seventh-day Adventists, beliefs 2–5. Nazarene Articles of Faith, 1. Assemblies of God Statement of Fundamental Truths, 2 (in Melton, pp. 357–358).

Comparative Cross-References: Eastern Orthodox, 1.2.1; Roman Catholic, 2.2.1; Reformation and Union, 3.2.1; Ecumenical, 5.2.2.1.

The doctrine of God, and specifically of the Trinity, has seldom been a central issue among Evangelical and Free churches. The Methodist Article of Religion is the most traditional, specifically utilizing language of God as "Holy Trinity," one "substance" in three "Persons," following the ancient creeds. The Methodist Article follows the first Anglican Article exactly, except that it omits the Anglican Article's assertion that God is "without passions." Early Methodists were passionate people, and they may have found the ancient notion that God is without passions a very alien idea.

Other Evangelical and Free-church creeds affirm the essence of the traditional doctrine of the Trinity (but see the next subsection), utilizing scriptural language rather than the terms drawn from Hellenistic culture that were found in the ancient creeds (terms such as "Persons" and "substance"). The Anabaptist Dordrecht Confession (1632) affirms one God as Father, Son, and Holy Spirit, but utilizes scriptural language rather than the language of the ancient creeds. Baptist confessions speak of one God "revealed under the personal and relative distinctions of the Father, the Son and the Holy Spirit," or one God "as Father, Son and Holy Spirit each with distinct personal attributes, but without division of nature, essence, or being." The Assemblies of God "Statement of Fundamental Truths" utilizes Trinitarian language cautiously, but it has several paragraphs justifying the use of nonscriptural terminology. This is probably said in response to "Oneness" Pentecostals, to whom we now turn.

4.2.1.b   What "Oneness" Pentecostal churches teach in contrast to the doctrine of the Trinity: "Oneness" Pentecostal churches are distinguished by their explicit rejection of the doctrine of the Trinity and by their teaching that the Father, Son, and Holy Spirit are one without distinction.

Source: United Pentecostal Church Articles of Faith "The One True God," "The Son of God," and "The Name" (*Manual: United Pentecostal Church International, Inc.* [Hazelwood, Mo.: Pentecostal Publishing House, 1991], pp. 20–21).

Comparative Cross-References: Eastern Orthodox, 1.2.1; Roman Catholic, 2.2.1; Reformation and Union, 3.2.1.

A number of Pentecostal churches are described as "Oneness" or "Jesus-name only" or sometimes "Apostolic" churches. These have in common the use of the baptismal formula "in the name of Jesus Christ" (Acts 2:38) and a distinct understanding of the nature of God. According to Oneness Pentecostals, Father, Son, and Holy Spirit are three expressions or phases of the same one God. There is no essential difference between them: the Father became the Son, who then became the Spirit at Pentecost. Not only do Oneness Pentecostals reject the term "Trinity," they also reject the essence of the doctrine, namely, the belief that each of the three Persons is equally and eternally God. Readers may recognize this as a form of "Modalism" (see 1.0.1 and table 2), which originally appeared around A.D. 200. In fact, some Oneness Pentecostals point to ancient Christian Modalism as the true heir of apostolic Christianity. Nevertheless, we should be clear that Oneness Pentecostals do affirm the divinity of Christ and worship Christ as God.

4.2.2   What Evangelical and Free churches teach about the two natures of Christ: Evangelical and Free-church traditions generally agree in teaching that Christ combines divine and human natures, although churches influenced by Fundamentalism stress the divine nature of Christ as evidenced by his virginal conception and bodily resurrection.

Sources: Dordrecht Confession, 3–4 (in Leith, pp. 294–296). *Mennonite Confession of Faith (1963),* articles 1 and 5 (pp. 8–9, 12). *Confession of Faith in a Mennonite Perspective (1995),* article 2. New Hampshire Confession, 4 (in Leith, pp. 335–336). Abstract of Principles, 7 (in Leith, p. 341). Baptist Faith and Message, 4, 16–17 (in Leith, pp. 346, 349). Moravian *Ground of the Unity,* Part 1, "The Belief of the Church." Methodist Articles of Religion, 2–3 (in Leith, p. 354). Fundamental Beliefs of Seventh-day Adventists, beliefs 4 and 9. Nazarene Articles of Faith, 2 and 6. Assemblies of God Statement of Fundamental Truths, 3 and 14 (in Melton, pp. 358, 359–360).

Comparative Cross-References: Eastern Orthodox, 1.2.2; Roman Catholic, 2.2.3; Reformation and Union, 3.2.2; Ecumenical, 5.2.2.2.

Older doctrinal statements of Methodists and Baptists include statements about Christ that utilize the language approved by the Council of Chalcedon to describe the human and divine "natures" in the one Person of Christ. Later doctrinal statements tend to affirm the human and divine identities of Christ, but they do not use the language of "natures" or "substance." This is consistent with attitudes toward Trinitarian language noted above. Doctrinal statements written after 1900, moreover, show the clear influence of Fundamentalism in stressing the divine nature of Christ (against Modernist stress on Christ's humanity), especially as evidenced by Christ's virginal conception, bodily resurrection from the dead, and imminent return. Thus the Southern Baptist "Report on Baptist Faith and Message" repeats the older language of the "New Hampshire Confession," but it goes on to define two new Articles on Christ's bodily resurrection (16) and Christ's bodily return (17). The Nazarene Articles of Faith state the doctrine of Christ in fairly conciliar terms but go on to assert Christ's second coming. The Assemblies of God "Statement of Fundamental Truths" is the most exaggerated, mentioning only (Article 3) Christ's divine nature and evidencing this by scriptural miracles. A further Article (14) asserts the second coming and millennial reign of Christ.

While all Evangelical churches affirm the centrality of Christ's work in bringing about human salvation, not all affirm a particular theory of the atonement. Older creeds, including those of Anabaptists, Baptists, and Methodists, stress the fullness of Christ's incarnation, including his pure life and obedience to God, his death, and his resurrection, as accomplishing the work of human redemption. In the twentieth century, especially among Evangelicals influenced by Fundamentalism, there has been consistent tendency to maintain the substitutionary theory that stresses (1) that all humans are bound to death because of their sin, and (2) that Christ's death on the cross took the place of, or acted as a substitute for, the death that we deserve because of sin. The Nazarene Articles of Faith (Article 6) explicitly affirms substitutionary atonement. Although the substitutionary aspect of Christ's crucifixion is certainly not denied by the older doctrinal statements, some maintain that it does not account for the fullness of Christ's work as the older statements do.

For Evangelical Christians, the worship of Christ as one's personal Savior lies at the center of personal and corporate devotion. Charles Wesley states this faith in classical theological terms in the Christmas hymn "Hark! the Herald Angels Sing" (1734):

> Christ, by highest heaven adored;
> Christ, the everlasting Lord,
> Late in time behold him come,
> Offspring of a virgin's womb.
> Veiled in flesh the Godhead see!
> Hail th' incarnate Deity!
> Pleased as man with men to dwell,
> Jesus, our Immanuel.[209]

But this same faith may be expressed in more personal terms as well. Christ is "the rock of our salvation," as these words by Edward Mote, written in 1834, state:

> My hope is built on nothing less
> Than Jesus' blood and righteousness;
> I dare not trust the sweetest frame,
> But wholly lean on Jesus' name.

> On Christ, the solid rock, I stand;
> All other ground is sinking sand,
> All other ground is sinking sand.[210]

4.2.2.a   *What some Evangelical and Free churches teach about the second coming of Christ:* Some Evangelical and Free-church traditions teach that Christ will return soon. They differ significantly over the issue of whether Christ's coming will precede or follow the millennium spoken of in biblical prophecy.

Sources: Baptist Faith and Message, 17 (in Leith, p. 349). Fundamental Beliefs of Seventh-day Adventists, beliefs 23–26. Nazarene Articles of Faith, 15. Assemblies of God Statement of Fundamental Truths, 14 (in Melton, pp. 359–360).

The belief that the second coming of Christ would come soon has provided the source of much speculation on the part of Evangelical Christians, and it has a long history in medieval and Reformation-age apocalyptic beliefs. Some churches, such as the Southern Baptist Convention and the Church of the Nazarene, simply express their faith that Christ will return in a bodily, historical event. More elaborate theories about the second coming of Christ are often tied to belief about the thousand-year period or millennium described in Revelation 20. Speculation that attempts to locate the millennium and the second

209. Hymn by Charles Wesley, in *Hymns and Psalms* (London: Methodist Publishing House, 1983), no. 106.
210. Hymn by Edward R. Mote, in *Assembly Songs,* ed. Thacker, Fisher, and Magill, no. 215.

coming of Christ as historical events can be described as Millennialism.[211] But within Millennialist circles there have been two main bodies of opinion concerning the prophecies about the millennium described in the Revelation. One group maintained that Christ's second
coming will occur *after* a thousand-year period in which the saints will
rule on earth with Christ. This position is historically described as
postmillennialism, and it often implies concrete Christian social action in the world, which is to be prepared for Christ's return. Postmillennialism prevailed in North American Evangelical circles
through the middle of the 1800s. The other group maintains that
Christ's second coming will occur *before* a thousand-year period in
which Satan will be set loose on earth. This position, which has pre-
dominated in many Evangelical circles since the middle of the 1800s,
is traditionally called premillennialism, and it often has as a concomitant a rather pessimistic view of history according to which the church
should withdraw from the world in order to make itself pure for the
coming of the Lord. The premillennialist view is taken by most Dispensationalist churches.[212] The Seventh-day Adventists assert a premillennialist view of Christ's second coming as part of their Fundamental Beliefs, although they believe that concrete engagement with
the world is in itself a faithful preparation for the Lord's coming.

4.2.3 *What Evangelical and Free churches teach about the present
activity of the Holy Spirit:* Anabaptist, Moravian, Wesleyan, Adventist,
Holiness, and Pentecostal churches agree in teaching that the Holy
Spirit remains actively present in the life of the church.

Sources: Mennonite Confession of Faith (1963), article 2 (section on "The Church and
Healing"). Moravian *Ground of the Unity,* Part 1, "Personal Belief." Methodist Articles
of Religion, 4 (in Leith, p. 355). Fundamental Beliefs of Seventh-day Adventists, beliefs
5 and 16. Nazarene Articles of Faith, 3. Assemblies of God Statement of Fundamental
Truths, 12 (in Melton, p. 359).

In the seventeenth and eighteenth centuries there developed a serious difference over whether miraculous gifts remained in the church after the age of the apostles. One view inherited from the Protestant Reformation saw the biblical age and its miracles as standing in a different
historical period than the postbiblical age. Many Protestants perceived
a clean break between "the age of the apostles" when the Holy Spirit
had worked miracles in the church, and later ages when the church had

211. Another significant option on this point is *amillennialism,* which takes the millennium of Revelation 20 to be a spiritual, not historical, event.
212. Premillennialists are further divided on the issue of whether the church will
be "raptured" to heaven to reign there with Christ during the millennium or the
church will have to undergo the millennium on earth.

been corrupted and miraculous gifts were no longer exercised. Churches influenced by the Reformed tradition took this view of apostolic history. Early Anabaptists taught that the church's early purity was lost when Constantine brought Christianity into compromise with the Roman Empire, but the Anabaptists also believed that the Holy Spirit has been presently active in the true church (restored since the time of the Reformation), for example, in miraculous healings.

Early Moravians insisted on the continuing activity of the Holy Spirit through the church—Orthodox, Catholic, and Protestant. John Wesley and Evangelicals of Wesleyan-Arminian tradition perceived a degree of continuity in history, since they believed that the Holy Spirit was continually active in the life of the church. Wesley himself shared the view of many Protestants that there was a decline of Christian morals and faith after the time of Constantine (early in the fourth century A.D.), but he believed nevertheless that true faith could be found even in the 300s and 400s, especially in the monastic writers of Eastern Christianity. Consistent with this belief, Wesleyan-Arminian churches stress that the Spirit is still active in the church today. The Methodist Article of Religion on the Holy Spirit cited above does not assert the present role of the Holy Spirit in the church, electing to speak in ancient conciliar terms of the unity of the Spirit with God (and asserting the double procession of the Spirit, consistent with Western tradition at this point). The Nazarene Article reflects more of the Wesleyan-Arminian stress on the present activity of the Spirit, stating that the Spirit is "efficiently active" in the church. This belief in the present activity of the Holy Spirit is expressed in the words of Charles Wesley (1740):

> Come, Holy Ghost, our hearts inspire,
> Let us thine influence prove;
> Source of the old prophetic fire,
> Fountain of life and love.[213]

Or in the words of contemporary Christian musician Lanny Wolfe (1977):

> Surely the presence of the Lord is in this place;
> I can feel his mighty power and his grace . . .[214]

On the one hand, this perspective on the Holy Spirit underlies claims of present-day miracles on the part of Holiness and Pentecostal

213. Hymn by Charles Wesley, in *The United Methodist Hymnal*, no. 603.
214. Hymn by Lanny Wolfe, in *The United Methodist Hymnal*, no. 328.

Christians. On the other hand, this perspective can be important in ecumenical dialogue, since it echoes a consistent theme of Orthodox, Catholic, and Anglican thought, namely, the view that God continues to be active in the church. An ecumenical dialogue between the World Methodist Council and the Roman Catholic Church (1981) has found substantial agreement on this issue.[215] Among Evangelical and Free churches, Moravians and Methodists may be the most receptive to the affirmation of postbiblical traditions, precisely because of their stress on the continuing activity of the Spirit in the church. Again, this may give their traditions an ecumenical gift of being able to act as a "bridge" between Evangelical and Free-church traditions and more ancient Christian traditions, just as Anglicanism is able to act as a bridge between Protestants generally and Orthodox and Catholic traditions.

4.2.4 *What Evangelical and Free churches teach about Mary, the mother of Jesus:* Evangelical and Free-church traditions generally agree in rejecting notions of Mary's immaculate conception, perpetual virginity, and bodily assumption into heaven.

Comparative Cross-References: Eastern Orthodox, 1.2.3; Roman Catholic, 2.2.4; Reformation and Union, 3.2.3.

Although Methodist founder John Wesley affirmed the doctrine of the perpetual virginity of Mary (here reflecting an Anglican inheritance from the 1600s),[216] Evangelical and Free churches have almost unanimously rejected the doctrines of Mary's immaculate conception, perpetual virginity, and bodily assumption into heaven.

4.3 Evangelical and Free-Church Teachings on Human Nature and Salvation

4.3.1 *What Evangelical and Free churches teach about human nature and the fall of humankind:* Evangelical and Free-church traditions agree in teaching that the first human beings fell from their original righteousness and that subsequent human beings lack any natural ability to obey God and be saved.

---

215. "Report of the Joint Commission between the Roman Catholic Church and the World Methodist Council" (Lake Junaluska, N.C.: World Methodist Council, 1981), pp. 3–14.
216. John Wesley, "A Letter to a Roman Catholic," par. 7, in *The Works of the Reverend John Wesley, A.M.,* ed. Thomas Jackson, 14 vols. (London: Wesleyan Conference Office, 1873), 10:81.

Sources: Dordrecht Confession, 2 (in Leith, p. 294). *Mennonite Confession of Faith (1963),* article 4 (pp. 11–12). *Confession of Faith in a Mennonite Perspective (1995),* articles 6–7. New Hampshire Confession, 3 (in Leith, p. 335). Abstract of Principles, 6 (in Leith, p. 340). Baptist Faith and Message, 3 (in Leith, p. 346). Methodist Articles of Religion, 7, 8a (in Leith, p. 356). Fundamental Beliefs of Seventh-day Adventists, beliefs 6–8. Nazarene Articles of Faith, 5, 7a. Assemblies of God Statement of Fundamental Truths, 4 (in Melton, pp. 358–359).

Comparative Cross-References: Eastern Orthodox, 1.3.1–2; Roman Catholic, 2.3.1; Reformation and Union, 3.3.1; Ecumenical, 5.2.3.

Consistent with Reformation churches, Evangelical churches teach that human beings, in their "natural" state (that is, by themselves, apart from God's grace), have no power to do what God requires, and so all stand in need of God's grace. This is true not only of Calvinistic Evangelical churches but also of Wesleyan-Arminian churches. The Methodist Articles of Religion, for example (following the Anglican Articles at this point), state that all human beings have inherited the punishment and the guilt of our first human parents (Article 7), and that

> The condition of man after the fall of Adam is such that he cannot turn and prepare himself, by his own natural strength and works, to faith and calling upon God; wherefore we have no power to do good works, pleasant and acceptable to God, without the grace of God by Christ [coming before] us, that we may have a good will, and working within us, when we have that good will.[217]

Almost all Evangelical churches stress the lack of any inborn human goodness, and the implication of this is that our salvation must rely on God's grace. If we have free will, according to these doctrinal statements, we have it only as a gift of grace, not as a natural ability.

The sense of our unworthiness and our reliance on God's grace is a frequent theme of Evangelical spirituality and hymnody. Calvinist Evangelical Augustus Toplady gave this sentiment a classic expression in his hymn "Rock of Ages" (1776):

> Nothing in my hand I bring,
>   Simply to the cross I cling;
> Naked, come to thee for dress;
>   Helpless, look to thee for grace;
> Foul, I to the fountain fly;
>   Wash me, Savior, or I die.[218]

---

217. Methodist Articles of Religion, 8 (in Leith, p. 356). I have elected to render the archaic "preventing" with "coming before" in this article.
218. Hymn by Augustus Toplady, in *The United Methodist Hymnal,* no. 361.

Despite the agreement of traditional Evangelical doctrinal statements that human beings have no natural free will, it must be noted that through the 1800s this was a point often missed, especially by Methodists and other Arminian Evangelicals. In the 1800s, influenced by democratic optimism and popular ideas of individualism and voluntarism, Methodists and others began to speak of human beings as having a "free will" as if it were the natural possession of every human being (as if human beings had "something in [their] hand to bring"). Although this contradicts their own doctrinal tradition, the idea of "free will" as an inborn or natural gift was so popular that it affected Evangelicalism very broadly, even to the point of influencing Baptists and others. It is interesting to note, in light of this, that the Assemblies of God "Statement of Fundamental Truths" does not deal at all with the question of human ability to obey God after the fall, and this may reflect popular Evangelical ideas of natural free will.

4.3.2.a *What Calvinistic Evangelical churches teach about the scope of the atonement:* Calvinistic Evangelical churches agree in teaching that Christ died only for the elect, whom he predestined to eternal salvation.

Sources: New Hampshire Confession, 6, 9 (in Leith, pp. 336, 337). Abstract of Principles, 5 (in Leith, p. 340). Baptist Faith and Message, 6, 9 (in Leith, pp. 347–348).

Comparative Cross-References: Eastern Orthodox, 1.3.1–3; Roman Catholic, 2.3.1–3; Reformation and Union, 3.3.3.a–b.

We have seen that on some issues the massively confusing universe of Evangelical and Free churches can be divided into two historic camps: one group that has been more influenced by the Reformed and Calvinist traditions of the Reformation, and another that has been more consistent with Arminian and later Wesleyan teachings. "Particular" or "Regular" Baptists, Dispensationalist churches, and many independent Evangelical churches teach an Augustinian and Calvinist doctrine of predestination, that is, the teaching that human salvation is entirely the result of God's prior choice or predestination of some particular women and men to eternal salvation. The language of "predestination" and "election" is explicitly used in the New Testament (for example, Rom. 8:30), and this doctrine is understood, in accord with the older churches of the Reformation, as upholding God's initiative in salvation. It is understood as ruling out the arrogance of human reliance on our own abilities, and in this respect it is seen as a "very comfortable doctrine," placing the burden of our salvation on God rather than on us (see 3.3.3.a).

All of the Baptist confessions considered here were developed in churches that were historically "Regular" (that is, Calvinistic), and they all have articles on election. The "New Hampshire Confession" and the Southern Baptist statement of "Baptist Faith and Message" (patterned carefully after the wording of the "New Hampshire Confession"), however, affirm that "election" is compatible with human free will and that Christ's grace is available to all. Only the "Abstract of Principles" of Southern Baptist Theological Seminary offers a clear statement of election in a Calvinist sense. The "Abstract" (article 5) asserts that

> Election is God's eternal choice of some persons unto everlasting life—not because of foreseen merit, but of his mere mercy in Christ, in consequence of which choice they are called, justified, and glorified.

It might be argued that this statement allows for the belief that God's election is based on God's foreknowledge of a free human choice, but it does rule out foreseen "merit." In its most obvious sense, the statement seems to reflect the Regular Baptist teaching of predestination (and the Westminster Confession, on which the "Abstract of Principles" is based).

4.3.2.b *What Arminian Evangelical churches teach about the scope of the atonement:* Mennonite, Moravian, and Arminian Evangelical churches agree in teaching that Christ died for all human beings, and that God gives grace to all that allows them freedom to accept or reject Christ.

Sources: Dordrecht Confession, 4 (in Leith, pp. 295–296). *Mennonite Confession of Faith (1963)*, article 6 (p. 13). *Confession of Faith in a Mennonite Perspective (1995)*, article 8. Moravian *Ground of the Unity*, section on "The Belief of the Church." New Hampshire Confession, 6, 9 (in Leith, pp. 336, 337). Baptist Faith and Message, 6, 9 (in Leith, pp. 347–348). John Wesley, sermon on "The Scripture Way of Salvation" 1:2 (in Leith, pp. 361–362). Nazarene Articles of Faith, 7.

Comparative Cross-References: Eastern Orthodox, 1.3.1–3; Roman Catholic, 2.3.1–3; Reformation and Union, 3.3.3.a–b.

The other large "camp" of Evangelical churches would be those that hold to an "Arminian" understanding of the work of grace. According to this view, Christ's death was for all human beings (not just for a limited number of the elect), and by a special grace, God gives every person a "free will" to choose (or reject) faith in Christ. The Methodist Articles of Religion omit the Anglican Article on predestination, and John Wesley's sermons, including the sermon on the "Scripture Way of Salvation" consistently reflect this view. Similarly, a Charles Wesley hymn of 1747 expresses the universal call of the gospel:

> Come, sinners, to the gospel feast,
> Let every soul be Jesu's guest;
> Ye need not one be left behind,
> For God hath bidden all mankind.[219]

Churches that have followed the Wesleyan pattern, including Holiness churches and Pentecostal churches, will usually affirm this teaching, although (as mentioned in the last subsection) they will sometimes fall into the pattern of claiming that our ability to believe in Christ is a natural gift. The Moravian *Ground of the Unity* also asserts the universal applicability of Christ's work.

Anabaptist and Baptist confessions differ somewhat from the Wesleyan-Arminian pattern in that they consistently utilize the language of God's "election" (choice). However, unlike the "Abstract of Principles" (see the previous subsection), the "New Hampshire Confession" and the Southern Baptist statement of "Baptist Faith and Message" make the points that (1) "the blessings of salvation are made free to all by the Gospel" (this seems to assert the universal scope of the atonement) and (2) that "election" is compatible with "the free agency of man." "Election" is defined in these two documents as meaning "the gracious purpose of God, according to which he graciously regenerates, sanctifies, and saves sinners." These statements, then, seem to allow for the "General" Baptist teaching that Christ died for all of humankind. The 1963 *Mennonite Confession of Faith* states explicitly that election is according to the foreknowledge, but not predetermination, of God.[220]

4.3.3 What Evangelical and Free churches teach about the repentance of sinners: Traditionally, Evangelical Protestant churches agreed in teaching that a crisis of "awakening" or "repentance" generally preceded conversion.

Sources: New Hampshire Confession, 8a (in Leith, pp. 336–337). Abstract of Principles, 9 (in Leith, p. 341). Baptist Faith and Message, 8a (in Leith, p. 347). Moravian *Ground of the Unity*, Part 1, "The Belief of the Church" and "Personal Belief." John Wesley, sermon on "The Scripture Way of Salvation" 1:1–2 (in Leith, pp. 361–362). Fundamental Beliefs of Seventh-day Adventists, belief 10. Nazarene Articles of Faith, 8.

Comparative Cross-References: Eastern Orthodox, 1.3.3; Roman Catholic, 2.3.4; Reformation and Union, 3.3.4.

The previous subsections in this chapter have addressed issues about the human situation and the grounds of human salvation in the

---

219. Hymn of Charles Wesley, in *The Methodist Hymn-Book* (London: The Methodist Publishing House, 1933), no. 323.
220. *Mennonite Confession of Faith (1963)*, article 6 (p. 13).

gracious work of God. The next subsections all deal with the manner in which salvation becomes effective for human beings, a subject of intense interest on the part of Evangelical Christians. One of the topics in formal theological systems in the 1500s and 1600s was described as the *ordo salutis*, the "order" or "way of salvation." This quest to understand the out-working of the religious life became a very large concern of Evangelical Christians.

Two general patterns emerged for describing the way of salvation in the 1600s and 1700s. A typically Calvinist pattern followed Romans 8:30 and saw the stages of salvation as election, "calling" (or "vocation"), justification (forgiveness of sin), sanctification (growth in holiness), and "glorification" (the Christian's final triumphant entry into Christ's kingdom). For Calvinists, this entire process was understood as being grounded in God's sovereign work of election, but it was not a simple or easy path; rather, it was understood as a dangerous road on which a traveler is beset by difficulties and on which the traveler needs constantly the aid of scripture, other Christians, and the means of grace provided by the church. John Bunyan's *Pilgrim's Progress* is a classic, literary exposition of the Puritan understanding of the "way of salvation," and it has been treasured by Evangelical Christians (of all persuasions) for three hundred years.

Another pattern, not harshly different but different in nuance, appeared in the 1700s in the work of John Wesley. According to this pattern, the way of salvation was understood as embracing three major stages, each marked by grace: "prevenient grace," in which the heart is prepared by grace and is led to repentance; "justifying grace" in which a person believes, her sin is forgiven, and she is given an assurance of forgiveness; and "sanctifying grace" in which a believer progressively grows in holiness toward the goal of "entire sanctification," complete love for God.[221]

The present subsection has to do with the first stage in this way of salvation, at least from the human perspective (since divine grace precedes all human action), and this is repentance. Among traditional Evangelicals, repentance was a critically important process, and many understood it to be a kind of crisis event in the life of a human being by which her eyes were suddenly opened to the peril of her soul. Early Methodists spoke of a distinct and terrifying experience of "awakening," when they perceived for the first time the terrors of hell lying before them and the danger of their sinful path in life. This experience

---

221. John Wesley, sermon on "The Scripture Way of Salvation" 1:1–9 (in Leith, pp. 361–364).

was also stressed by Calvinistic Evangelicals, however, who understood sincere, heartfelt repentance to be part of God's "vocation" or "calling" of an individual, one of the signs that grace was indeed active in the life of an individual. Charles Wesley's "Wrestling Jacob" (1742) offers a poetic description of the human soul's wrestling with God (using the image of Jacob wrestling the angel in Gen. 32:24–32) before its deliverance in the gift of faith:

> Yield to me now, for I am weak,
> But confident in self-despair!
> Speak to my heart, in blessing speak,
> Be conquered by my instant prayer.
> Speak, or thou never hence shalt move,
> And tell me if thy name is Love . . .[222]

In traditional Evangelical camp meetings and revivals, the importance of repentance was symbolized by the "mourners' bench," a long bench typically placed between the front seats and the altar. A sinner approached the altar by way of the mourners' bench. In Evangelical circles through the 1800s, it was understood that the period of repentance might last days, weeks, or months (maybe even years), and it was not felt that the sinner should be pressured to the point of faith and conversion, because repentance was God's own way of leading the person to salvation.

One of the most important changes in Evangelical life in the twentieth century has been the consistent loss of the centrality of the experience of repentance. Perhaps this is a point at which Evangelicals have been influenced by the Liberal tendency to downplay sinfulness and to emphasize the positive aspects of human ability, but twentieth-century Evangelicals have tended to press unconverted persons to an immediate experience of conversion, in which there is little or no room for the extended period of repentance that characterized earlier Evangelicalism. Some Evangelicals, concerned with the contemporary renewal of interest in Christian spirituality, have lamented the loss of the place of repentance in the way of salvation and have worked to restore a balanced understanding of repentance as a significant part of Evangelical life.

4.3.4.a *What Evangelical and Free churches teach about justification by faith alone and assurance:* Evangelical Protestant churches agree in teaching that believers are justified by faith in an experience in

222. Hymn by Charles Wesley, in *The United Methodist Hymnal*, no. 386.

which they trust in Christ, and as a result of which they are assured of the forgiveness of sin and born again in Christ.

Sources: Dordrecht Confession, 6 (in Leith, pp. 297–298). *Mennonite Confession of Faith (1963),* article 6 (p. 13). *Confession of Faith in a Mennonite Perspective (1995),* article 8. "New Hampshire Confession," 5, 7–8 (in Leith, pp. 336–337). Abstract of Principles, 8, 10–11 (in Leith, p. 341). Baptist Faith and Message, 5, 7–8 (in Leith, pp. 346–347). Moravian *Ground of the Unity,* Part 1, "The Belief of the Church." Methodist Articles of Religion, 9 (in Leith, p. 356). Minutes of Wesleyan Conferences (in Leith, pp. 373–376). John Wesley, sermon on "The Scripture Way of Salvation" 1:3 (in Leith, p. 362). Fundamental Beliefs of Seventh-day Adventists, belief 10. Nazarene Articles of Faith, 9. Assemblies of God Statement of Fundamental Truths, 5a (in Melton, p. 359).

Comparative Cross-References: Eastern Orthodox, 1.3.3; Roman Catholic, 2.3.4; Reformation and Union, 3.3.4.

As we have seen in the previous chapter, the doctrine of "justification by faith alone" was a hallmark of the Protestant Reformation, and all the Reformation churches express this doctrine in their confessions, catechisms, and Articles of Religion (see 3.3.4). Evangelical churches follow this precedent, often repeating verbatim the wording of Reformation statements on justification by faith. There are, however, a couple of points at which the Evangelical understanding of justification by faith differs significantly from that of the Reformation churches.

The first point of difference is that Evangelicals have typically understood "faith" not only as trust in Christ but as a personal choice to relinquish trust in all other things and place one's trust in Christ alone. Anabaptist confessions stress the importance of faith as a voluntary, personal decision. The classic literary illustration of conversion is the moment when the seeker in Bunyan's *Pilgrim's Progress* comes to a hill where there is a cross, and at this point the huge burden on his back (his sin) falls away. This is his moment of justification. Although Evangelical conversions occurred more freely or spontaneously in the 1700s, by the 1820s on the North American frontier they had fallen into a regular pattern. This pattern was that at the end of an evangelistic sermon, the preacher or an appointed "exhorter" would make a specific plea for sinners to come forward to the front of the revival assembly and indicate publicly their intention to believe in Christ. As the congregation sang an invitational hymn, individuals would lay down their hymnbooks and go forward, where elders of the assembly would pray over them until they experienced faith in Christ. This remains a standard pattern in Evangelical churches and evangelistic missions (such as Billy Graham Crusades) to this day.

The second way in which the Evangelical understanding of justification differed from that of the Reformation churches was that Evangelicals normally expected a divinely given "assurance" of forgiveness to accompany the experience. John Wesley taught his followers to expect this supernatural sense of pardon, and although he later admitted that there were exceptional cases in which women or men had simply believed in Christ without experiencing assurance, he continued to believe that "assurance" normally accompanied justification. If we recall that Evangelicals in the 1700s and 1800s had often passed through a lengthy period of repentance, a period in which they had become intensely aware of their own condemnation by God, it is perhaps easier to understand how central this sense of assurance was for them. Fanny Crosby's hymn of 1873 expresses the joy that accompanies the Evangelical experience of assurance:

> Blessed assurance, Jesus is mine!
> O what a foretaste of glory divine!
> Heir of salvation, purchase of God,
> Born of his Spirit, washed in his blood.[223]

Note that for Evangelical Christians, "justification" (forgiveness of sins) is thought of as happening at the same moment as "regeneration," which denotes the "new birth" in Christ. It is for this reason that a conversion experience will often be described as an experience of being "born again." Justification, we might say, is the end of the old sinful self, regeneration is the beginning of the new self in Christ, and at the same moment the one ends, the other begins. Another typical term for this experience is "being saved," although this term is favored by Baptists and others who believe that justification guarantees one's final salvation (see 4.3.6.a).

This teaching that justification and regeneration occur in a religious experience is perhaps the clearest single teaching that separates Evangelical churches from Anglicans, Lutherans, Catholics, and Orthodox. For each of these latter groups (a very large majority of Christians, especially considered together), regeneration or new birth in Christ occurs at baptism. This raised an acute problem for Lutheran Pietists and for Anglican Evangelicals. Although many Anglican Evangelicals would deny "baptismal regeneration" (the claim that we are born again when we are baptized), Lutheran Pietists and John Wesley made it clear that they believed that baptism does bring about new birth and forgiveness for infants. Here they appealed to the Catholic principle that infants do not *lack* faith, so that baptism is effective for them. However, Wesley and the Lutheran Pietists went on to teach

---

223. Hymn of Fanny Crosby, in *The United Methodist Hymnal*, no. 369.

that most persons "fall away" from the grace received in baptism, and so they stand in need of being renewed or restored to the grace they had once had—not indeed by being baptized again (an idea rejected by almost all Christians), but by experiencing afresh the grace given in repentance and forgiveness.

Again, as at so many other points in our discussions in this chapter, John Wesley himself appears on the very cusp of Evangelicalism, appearing very close to the sentiments of his own Anglican communion. For most other Evangelicals, there is a clear separation between baptism (most often understood as symbolizing or representing new birth in Christ) and the experience of conversion, justification, and new birth.

4.3.4.b *What many Restorationist churches teach concerning justification:* Many Restorationist churches have historically insisted that the belief that Jesus Christ is Lord, accompanied by baptism, is the only condition of justification.

Comparative Cross-References: Eastern Orthodox, 1.3.3; Roman Catholic, 2.3.4; Reformation and Union, 3.3.4.

We have noted in the historical sketch above that Restorationist churches developed out of the merger of two American frontier movements: the movement of Thomas and Alexander Campbell and the movement of Barton W. Stone. Although the followers of Stone were revivalistic and expected conversion experiences like other Evangelicals, the "Campbellites" did not insist on conversion experiences. In fact, their reading of the New Testament suggested that only two things were necessary for salvation: a simple belief or trust that Jesus Christ is Lord, and baptism. The Campbellite view has prevailed in some Restorationist churches, both the "Disciples of Christ" and the "Churches of Christ" varieties. It may well be argued that this view of justification has more in common with classical Protestant views of justification by faith alone than with the views of other Evangelical and Free churches. In fact, some Churches of Christ folk are convinced that baptism itself effects justification and the new birth, and in this respect they have come around to the historic position of Catholicism and Orthodoxy (though practicing believer's baptism only), on the basis of New Testament scripture alone. Other Restorationist churches, however, are conversionist in the same way as other Evangelical churches.

4.3.5 *What Evangelical and Free churches teach about sanctification as growth in holiness:* Evangelical and Free-church traditions agree in

teaching that a process of growth in holiness, "sanctification," follows from the new birth.

Sources: Mennonite Confession of Faith (1963), article 7 (pp. 13–14). *Confession of Faith in a Mennonite Perspective (1995)*, articles 17–18. New Hampshire Confession, 10 (in Leith, p. 337). Abstract of Principles, 12 (in Leith, p. 342). Baptist Faith and Message, 10 (in Leith, p. 348). John Wesley, sermon on "The Scripture Way of Salvation," 1:4–8 (in Leith, pp. 362–364). Fundamental Beliefs of Seventh-day Adventists, beliefs 10, 18–22. Assemblies of God Statement of Fundamental Truths, 9 (in Melton, p. 359).

Comparative Cross-References: Eastern Orthodox, 1.3.6; Roman Catholic, 2.3.5; Reformation and Union, 3.3.5.

In both Reformed and Wesleyan understandings of the "way of salvation," growth in holiness follows after the new birth in Christ. Birth, after all, is supposed to be the beginning of life. This process of growth in holiness is traditionally called "sanctification" (from *sanctus*, "holy"), although a variety of terms may be used to describe it. North American Methodists in this century have preferred to speak of Christian "discipleship"; Baptists often speak of the "lordship" of Christ, because Christians accept Christ as "Savior" (from sin, in justification) and "Lord" (ruler of our lives, in the process of sanctification). Again, an Evangelical of the Calvinist tradition expresses the "double" work of God in justification (being saved from the guilt of sin) and sanctification (being saved from the continuing power of sin) in these terms:

> Rock of Ages, cleft for me,
>   Let me hide myself in Thee;
> Let the water and the blood,
>   From thy riven side which flowed,
> Be of sin the double cure,
>   Cleanse me from its guilt and power.[224]

On this teaching of a process of sanctification there is very broad agreement in Evangelical and Free churches. The Baptist confessions cited above are very careful to point out that it is a "process" or a "progressive work," almost certainly in contention with Wesleyan and Holiness claims about a moment of "entire sanctification" (see 4.3.6.b). But John Wesley and Methodists after him did not hesitate to speak of "the gradual work of sanctification" as the long process leading up to entire sanctification, its completion.[225]

224. Hymn by Augustus Toplady, in *The Hymnal* (Philadelphia: Presbyterian Board of Publication and Sabbath-School Work, 1930), no. 464. Methodists have customarily utilized the revision of this hymn by T. S. Cotterill (1815), which places an even greater stress on sanctification, changing the last line to "Save from wrath and make me pure" (cf. *The United Methodist Hymnal*, no. 361).
225. John Wesley, sermon on "The Scripture Way of Salvation" 1:8 (in Leith, p. 363).

4.3.6.a *What Baptist churches teach about eternal security:* Baptist churches agree in teaching that because of God's providential care, a believer can never fall entirely from God's grace, so a believer has the comfort of "eternal security."

Sources: New Hampshire Confession, 11 (in Leith, p. 337). Abstract of Principles, 13 (in Leith, p. 342). Baptist Faith and Message, 11 (in Leith, p. 348).
Comparative Cross-References: Reformation and Union, 3.3.6.

What, if anything, follows after or culminates the process of sanctification in the way of salvation? At this point, Evangelical churches are seriously divided, and many are distinguished by their beliefs about what "acts of grace" follow after conversion and the process of sanctification. For Baptists and Evangelical churches influenced by the Reformed tradition (such as Darbyite Brethren), no particular "acts" or "moments of grace" follow except for the continuing providential guidance of God. Believers may falter, they may face trials and tribulations, but God who justified them in the first place is able to keep them, to bring them back in the end by grace. Even the "New Hampshire Confession" and the Southern Baptist statement of "Baptist Faith and Message," which do not clearly affirm the doctrine of predestination, hold strongly to the belief in the perseverance of saints, or (as Baptists often express it) in the eternal security of believers. Once justified, a believer can trust that he or she will finally be saved. This belief is so firmly held by Baptists and Reformed Evangelicals that they customarily speak of a conversion experience as "being saved," because once this experience has occurred, final salvation is guaranteed due to the never-failing power of God.

4.3.6.b *What Wesleyan churches teach about entire sanctification:* Wesleyan (Methodist and Holiness) churches agree in teaching that sanctification is culminated in a moment of "entire sanctification," when a believer comes to perfect love for God.

Sources: Methodist Articles of Religion, 12 (in Leith, p. 357). Minutes of Methodist Conferences (in Leith, p. 377–385). John Wesley, sermon on "The Scripture Way of Salvation," 1:9 (in Leith, p. 364). Nazarene Articles of Faith, 10.
Comparative Cross-References: Eastern Orthodox, 1.3.4.

All the churches of the Wesleyan-Arminian pattern, including Methodist, Holiness, and most Pentecostal churches, reject the notion of eternal security, and maintain that the grace of justification is *amissible,* that is, that it can be lost. One is justified so long as one believes or trusts in Christ. Beyond this, the Wesleyan and Pentecostal churches teach that particular "acts" or moments of grace are to follow in the process of sanctification, after conversion.

Methodist and Holiness churches traditionally teach that the goal toward which human life is directed is to love God "with all your heart, and with all your soul, and with all your mind, and with all your strength" (Mark 12:30). They have traditionally described this goal as entire sanctification or Christian perfection. Most distinctively, they have maintained that it is possible, even in this life, to come to this complete love for God. John Wesley was clear that although believers might not notice the moment when this occurs, it nevertheless occurs "in the twinkling of an eye" or "instantaneously."[226] Methodist and Holiness churches ground their teaching of this doctrine in (1) their belief that God *intends* every person to love God completely (here again the "Great Commandment" is cited), and (2) their belief that God is *able* to accomplish what God intends. Charles Wesley's hymn "Love Divine, All Loves Excelling" (1747) describes entire sanctification:

> Breathe, O breathe thy loving Spirit
> Into every troubled breast!
> Let us all in thee inherit;
> Let us find that second rest.
> Take away our bent to sinning;
> Alpha and Omega be;
> End of faith as its beginning,
> Set our hearts at liberty.[227]

Holiness churches are distinguished by their teaching of this doctrine, and many Holiness churches separated from Methodist churches when their leaders felt that Methodists had abandoned this most distinctive of Wesleyan teachings. But although Methodist and Holiness churches do hold this doctrine in common, Holiness churches typically differ in three particular points from the Wesleyan perspective stated above. In the first place, Holiness churches not only speak of this goal as "entire sanctification" or "Christian perfection" but also may speak of it as "baptism in the Holy Spirit" and see the experience of the apostles in Acts 2 as an experience of entire sanctification. Second, Holiness churches tend to expect this experience earlier than in the Wesleyan pattern. Wesley thought that the examples of persons who were entirely sanctified were few, he mistrusted many claims to the experience, and when pressed to

226. John Wesley, sermon on "The Scripture Way of Salvation" 3:18 (in Leith, p. 372). We might note on this point that although Wesley was consistently clear about the instantaneous nature of entire sanctification, a mythology grew up among "mainline" Methodists in contention with Holiness church leaders that Wesley had taught only progressive sanctification.
227. Hymn by Charles Wesley, in *The United Methodist Hymnal*, no. 384.

state *when* the experience might occur, he stated that it should be expected *in articulo mortis*, that is, in the moment of a believer's death. Holiness churches, by contrast, tend to expect entire sanctification to occur fairly soon after conversion, and they think of it as an experience very much like conversion. A third difference lies in the practice of ministerial discipline. Many Holiness churches require pastors to profess that they have experienced entire sanctification. Methodist churches, by contrast, require pastors to pledge that they "expect to be made perfect in love in this life" ("expect" here has the sense "look forward to") but do not require that they have already experienced this.

4.3.6.c   *What "Three-blessing" Pentecostals teach about acts of grace subsequent to conversion:* "Three-blessing" Pentecostal churches agree in teaching that conversion is followed by an experience of entire sanctification, then by the experience of the baptism in the Holy Spirit, accompanied by the initial evidence of speaking in unknown tongues.

Sources: Pentecostal Holiness Articles of Faith, 10–11 (in Melton, pp. 352–353). United Holy Church of America Articles of Faith, 8–9 (in Melton, p. 409). Church of God, Cleveland, Tenn., Declaration of Faith, 6–9 (in Melton, pp. 334–335).

The oldest Pentecostal traditions, those that go back to the teachings of Charles F. Parham and William Seymour, hold that the Christian life is punctuated by three distinct blessings: (1) conversion, followed by (2) entire sanctification, which is then followed by (3) a distinct experience of baptism with the Holy Spirit, which is accompanied by the initial evidence of speaking in tongues. In explaining this pattern of three "blessings," it is often said that "the Holy Spirit cannot fill an unclean vessel," so the experience of cleansing in entire sanctification is necessary prior to the experience of baptism with the Holy Spirit. The International Pentecostal Holiness Church, the Church of God of Cleveland, Tennessee, the United Holy Church of America, and many other denominations follow this pattern.

We should note at this point that what distinguishes Pentecostal churches, in general, from Holiness churches are the Pentecostal beliefs that (1) baptism in the Holy Spirit is an "in-filling" of the Spirit, distinct from entire sanctification (as we shall see below, some Pentecostal churches deny entire sanctification altogether), and that (2) the initial evidence of this experience is the divinely given gift of speaking in unknown tongues. The gift of speaking in unknown tongues is perhaps the single most characteristic mark of the Pentecostal churches and of the Charismatic movement, which has sought to bring the experience of Holy Spirit baptism to expression within older denominational traditions.

How does the baptism of the Holy Spirit take place? In traditional Pentecostal churches, it is understood to be a vivid religious experience, very much as conversion is understood in the Evangelical churches more broadly. At the end of a Pentecostal service, not only are "sinners" (unbelievers) called forward to find faith in Christ, but believers are called forward for a number of reasons: to pray with the elders of the congregation, to profess a special message or ministry, and possibly to seek the baptism of the Holy Spirit. At the conclusion of the service, believers seeking the baptism of the Spirit will be guided to a "Tarrying Meeting" where leaders of the congregation will pray that they receive the baptism. This name comes from the saying in Acts 1:4, where Jesus urges the disciples to "tarry" (KJV) in Jerusalem until they received the Spirit. In this intensive prayer meeting, the congregational leaders will often pray in tongues themselves. Eventually the seeker feels moved by the Spirit and joins in the glossolalia (this is simply a technical term for speaking in tongues).

But just what is meant by "speaking in unknown tongues" or glossolalia? Pentecostal teachers distinguish at least four different phenomena. First, speaking in unknown tongues is regarded as initial evidence of the baptism of the Holy Spirit. Here the "tongues" are understood to be a divinely given language that "assures" the believer that the baptism of the Spirit has occurred. In this respect, the gift of tongues functions as "assurance" does in Evangelical conversion experiences. Second, Pentecostal leaders sometimes claim that "unknown tongues" are actual human languages, given miraculously in order to spread the gospel. This is considered to be an unusual gift. Third, Pentecostal leaders often distinguish speaking in tongues as a way of edifying the congregation, that is, a way of bringing a message from God to the congregation. In this sense, they say, speaking in tongues requires interpretation (1 Cor. 14:27), and in some Pentecostal meetings individuals will speak in tongues and then others will rise to interpret their sayings. Finally, Pentecostal leaders often speak of "praying in tongues," understanding this to be an expression of the private devotion of an individual, and so not requiring interpretation. Sometimes we do not know the words by which we should pray, and in such a case the "Spirit intercedes with sighs too deep for words" (Rom. 8:26).

4.3.6.d What "Two-blessing" Pentecostal churches teach about the baptism of the Holy Spirit: "Two-blessing" Pentecostal churches agree in teaching that conversion is followed by an experience of baptism in the Holy Spirit, accompanied by the initial evidence of speaking in unknown tongues.

Sources: Assemblies of God Statement of Fundamental Truths, 7–8 (in Melton, p. 359).

The Assemblies of God are now the largest Pentecostal denomination in North America, and they represent the "two-blessing" pattern of Pentecostalism that has become normative in many churches. This pattern essentially drops the moment or experience of entire sanctification, leaving (1) conversion followed by (2) baptism of the Holy Spirit, accompanied by the initial evidence of speaking in unknown tongues. In all other respects, the experience of Spirit baptism is like that of the "three-blessing" Pentecostal churches.

The two-blessing pattern also characterizes the Charismatic movement, the movement that has sought to bring the baptism of the Holy Spirit to Christians in more traditional denominations. Among Charismatics, speaking with tongues is the norm, but some progressive Charismatics will say that when a believer is baptized in the Holy Spirit, she or he receives one of the gifts of the Spirit, which might or might not be the gift of tongues.

4.3.7   What Evangelical churches teach about life beyond death:
Evangelical churches generally agree in teaching that those who believe in Christ will share eternal fellowship with Christ and one another beyond death and that those who reject Christ will suffer eternal punishment.

Sources: Mennonite Confession of Faith (1963), article 20 (pp. 24–25). *Confession of Faith in a Mennonite Perspective (1995),* article 24. New Hampshire Confession, 18 (in Leith, p. 339). Abstract of Principles, 19–20 (in Leith, p. 343). Baptist Faith and Message, 16–17 (in Leith, p. 349). Methodist Articles of Religion, 14 (in Leith, p. 357). John Wesley, sermon on "The Scripture Way of Salvation" 1:1 (in Leith, p. 361). Fundamental Beliefs of Seventh-day Adventists, belief 25. Nazarene Articles of Faith, 16. Assemblies of God Statement of Fundamental Truths, 15 (in Melton, p. 360).

Comparative Cross-References: Eastern Orthodox, 1.3.7; Roman Catholic, 2.3.7; Reformation and Union, 3.3.7.

Evangelical Christians have a reputation for preaching "hellfire and damnation," and Evangelical doctrine reflects at the very least the view that beyond death and the final judgment, believers will share fellowship with Christ and with one another through eternity, and those who reject faith in Christ will be cut off from Christ and will suffer eternal punishment. In formal doctrine, however, there is very little speculation on what "heaven" (a cipher for eternal fellowship with Christ) or "hell" (the corresponding term for eternal punishment) will be like. Traditional Evangelical preaching for repentance (see 4.3.3) often relied more on an elaborate folk culture about heaven and hell than on formal church doctrine.

Some Mennonites and Adventists (including Seventh-day Adventists) teach that between death and the final judgment persons would be unconscious of the passage of time. In the nineteenth century some

Evangelical groups speculated that eternal punishment would mean simply the annihilation of those in rebellion against God, rather than conscious eternal punishment. This view has gained currency in some contemporary Evangelical circles, but it has provoked a reaction in others who insist that "conscious eternal punishment" must be a Christian fundamental.[228] Evangelical doctrine has consistently rejected the notion of purgatory, although some Evangelical leaders (including John Wesley) believed in an "intermediate state" between death and the final judgment where believers would be with Christ, anticipating their eternal happiness, and those who rejected Christ would already be subject to torment. We might note that in the wording of these traditional doctrinal statements, the fate of those who have not heard of Christ is not always dealt with explicitly: to say that those who have "rejected Christ" will be eternally punished allows that some who have not heard of Christ may nevertheless be saved (by Christ's grace, even though it remains unknown to them).

4.4 Evangelical and Free-Church Teachings on Church, Ministry, and Sacraments

The notions of personal religious experience in general (see 4.1.2.a) and of a personal experience of conversion in particular (see 4.3.4.a) are central concepts for most Evangelical churches. These central ideas set up a characteristic polarity among these churches on the issues of church, ministry, and sacraments. The role of personal religious experience has had, historically, a tendency to displace the role of church, ministry, and sacraments as mediators of God's grace. The Salvation Army and the Quakers represent the most radical position in their utter rejection of "outward" sacraments, but other Evangelical and Free churches have in varying degrees questioned the importance of outward signs as channels of grace. In almost every case, then, in considering Evangelical and Free-church attitudes toward doctrines of the church, ministry, and sacraments, we shall have to describe a wide range of views, from most traditional to the most radical rejection of historic traditions.

4.4.1 *What Evangelical and Free churches teach about the nature of the church:* Evangelical and Free-church traditions generally agree in teaching that the church should be understood primarily as the fel-

---

228. The Wesleyan Theological Society, an interdenominational Holiness theological society sponsored by the Christian Holiness Association, has a doctrinal statement calling for belief in "conscious eternal punishment."

lowship of believers. Anabaptist churches stress the centrality of church discipline. Methodist churches add to this definition (1) the centrality of the preaching of the Word and (2) the administration of the sacraments.

Sources: Schleitheim Confession introduction and 4 (in Leith, pp. 282–284, 285–287). Dordrecht Confession, 8 (in Leith, p. 299). *Mennonite Confession of Faith (1963),* article 8 (pp. 14–17). *Confession of Faith in a Mennonite Perspective (1995),* articles 9–10, 14. New Hampshire Confession, 13 (in Leith, p. 338). Abstract of Principles, 14 (in Leith, p. 342). Baptist Faith and Message, 12 (in Leith, p. 348). Moravian *Ground of the Unity,* Part 1, "The Belief of the Church," "The Unitas Fratrum as a Unity," "The Church as a Brotherhood," and "The Church as a Community of Service" and the section in Part 2 on "The Vocation of the Unitas Fratrum and Its Congregations." Methodist Articles of Religion, 13 (in Leith, p. 357). Fundamental Beliefs of Seventh-day Adventists, beliefs 11–13. Nazarene Articles of Faith, 11. Assemblies of God Statement of Fundamental Truths, 10 (in Melton, p. 360).

Comparative Cross-References: Eastern Orthodox, 1.4.1; Roman Catholic, 2.4.1; Reformation and Union, 3.4.1; Ecumenical, 5.2.4.1.

The first part of the statement given above expresses what Evangelical and Free churches hold in common concerning the church: the church is simply the fellowship of believers. A familiar hymn by John Fawcett (1782) expresses this central idea of the church as the fellowship of believers:

> Blest be the tie that binds
> Our hearts in Christian love;
> The fellowship of kindred minds
> Is like to that above.[229]

The Anabaptist tradition of the 1500s influenced this view of the church as the fellowship of believers in its stress on the "believers' church," and all the Anabaptist confessional statements considered here stress the role of the church as a pure and visible community. It is pure because it has separated itself from the world; it is visible because it must make its testimony to the world. Anabaptist communities have historically expressed this sense of the church's purity by maintaining a strictly controlled community in which the "ban," a form of excommunication, is employed as the means by which believers are separated from the world. As we have seen above in the introduction to chapter 4, the notion of an entirely "voluntary" church lies at the heart of the identity of Free churches.

Other Evangelical churches also hold that the church is the fellowship of believers, but add that the church is constituted (or at least marked)

---

229. Hymn by John Fawcett, in *The Revivalist: A Collection of Choice Revival Hymns and Tunes,* ed. Joseph Hillman (Troy, N.Y.: Joseph Hillman, 1868), no. 203.

by the preaching of the Word and the administration of the sacraments. In doing so, their definition would answer very carefully to that of Reformation and Union churches (see 3.4.1). The Moravian *Ground of the Unity* stresses the nature of the church as a fellowship of those whose hearts are united to Jesus, but it also maintains that the vocation of the "Unity of Brethren" is "to proclaim [Christ's] Word to [Moravian] congregations and to the world and to administer the sacraments aright."[230] The Methodist Article of Religion reflects the wording of the Anglican Article (in turn reflecting the Augsburg Confession) in defining the church as the fellowship of believers where the Word is preached and the sacraments are administered. Even in Evangelical churches that do not define the church as being constituted by preaching and the sacraments, preaching is nevertheless central, and Baptism and the Eucharist are normative "ordinances" in the lives of their congregations.

4.4.2.a *What Evangelical and Free churches teach about church polity: Wesleyan connectional patterns.* Wesleyan churches typically maintain a connectional polity (in some cases, a modified form of episcopacy) in which preachers can be deployed according to changing situations.

Comparative Cross-References: Eastern Orthodox, 1.4.2; Roman Catholic, 2.4.3–4; Reformation and Union, 3.4.2.a–d.

Among Evangelical and Free churches, there is a spectrum of views of church government (or "polity") that runs from the most radically congregationalist at one end to the most "connectional" at the other end. Wesleyan churches, including Methodists and some Holiness denominations, represent the more connectional expression of this spectrum. Methodists did not originate as a church or denomination but rather as a religious society within the Church of England in the 1700s. Their oldest organizational structures were (1) a system of classes and societies led by laypersons and (2) a loosely related system of traveling or "itinerant" preachers, which included lay preachers. When the Methodists came to be organized as churches in the 1780s (in North America) and 1790s (in the British Isles) they added various elements of Presbyterian and Anglican church polity to these older "society" and preaching structures. The result was that in Britain and in North America and in other places where Methodist churches came into existence, a hybrid polity developed, with significant differences between British and American patterns of Methodist polity.

230. Moravian *Ground of the Unity*, Part 2, chapter 2, "The Vocation of the *Unitas Fratrum* and its Congregations."

Nevertheless, there are some common characteristics to Methodist polity. Common to both British and American patterns is the Annual Conference. Predating the Methodists' origin as a church, the Annual Conference was originally an occasion for Methodist preachers (lay and clergy) to confer together with John and Charles Wesley. In Britain, there remains but one Annual Conference that continues the conferences begun by the Wesleys in 1744. In the United States, by contrast, there are a number of Annual Conferences, organized into Jurisdictional Conferences and then into a single General Conference. Although the Conferences originally consisted only of preachers (including lay preachers), they have evolved in Britain and in North America to include lay representation. In this respect, the Methodist Annual Conferences function much as presbyteries do for Presbyterians (see 3.4.2.b), and it is in the Annual Conference (like the presbytery) that ministers are ordained.

A second factor that characterizes Methodist polity is traditionally described as itineracy, and it might be better described today as a unique appointive system for clergy. In the Methodist polity, pastors are assigned to congregations or other ministries by the Annual Conference and their superintendents (see the next paragraph). In the past, congregations have contributed very little to the process of appointing pastors. This system has given Methodists an unusual flexibility (for example, in adapting to rapidly changing conditions on the North American frontier), but it also leaves Methodists open to the concern that their traditional polity is hierarchical in comparison to more democratic forms of polity.

A third factor in Methodist polity, closely related to this previous point, is the Methodist superintendency, that is, their use of clergy who have oversight over particular areas. In Britain, Methodists have "district presidents" and "circuit superintendents"; North American Methodists have bishops and "presiding elders" or "district superintendents." Because they utilize bishops, North American Methodists have traditionally utilized the term "episcopal" to describe their polity, although it does differ from the historic Anglican (and Orthodox and Catholic) pattern of episcopal polity (see 3.4.2.a) in that it does not recognize bishops as a third order of ministry. Although Methodist churches do maintain separate orders of deacons and "elders," Methodist bishops are understood as a higher rank of elders, and in this respect the Methodist episcopal polity can be understood as mediating between the presbyterian and the Anglican episcopal forms of church governance.

The Methodist "connectional" polity described here influenced many churches of the Wesleyan family, although the general trend on the part of Holiness churches has been to allow greater and greater congregational voice in selecting their pastors, so that many Holiness denominations are entirely congregational. The Church of the Nazarene combines congregational choice of pastors with a Wesleyan system of superintendents. In some cases, non-Wesleyan churches appropriated Wesleyan patterns of governance, especially the Conference structure. Some "Free Will Baptists" in North America adopted (in the 1790s) Methodist nomenclature for their "Annual" and "General" Conferences.[231] The institution of "Annual Conferences" was also incorporated into The United Church of Canada (see 3.4.2.d).

4.4.2.b *What Evangelical and Free churches teach about church polity: polities that combine congregational autonomy and connectionalism.* Mennonites, Quakers, and Moravian churches have historically maintained forms of church polity by which their congregations are united into regional and national assemblies. Although Quakers reject the institution of ordained ministry, both Mennonites and Moravians have maintained ordained ministers and recognize bishops as overseers of their communities.

Sources: Dordrecht Confession, 9 (in Leith, pp. 299–301). *Mennonite Confession of Faith (1963),* articles 8 and 10 (pp. 16–17, 18–19). *Confession of Faith in a Mennonite Perspective (1995),* article 9. Barclay's *Apology,* 10 (in Leith, pp. 330–331). Moravian *Ground of the Unity,* Part 2, chapter 2, "The Vocation of the Unitas Fratrum and its Congregations."

Comparative Cross-References: Eastern Orthodox, 1.4.2; Roman Catholic, 2.4.3–4; Reformation and Union, 3.4.2.a–d.

In the spectrum from the most connectional to the most congregational forms of polity or church government among Evangelical and Free churches, we may recognize in the middle some traditions whose polities have traditionally combined a high degree of congregational autonomy with forms of regional and national connectedness. It is difficult and perhaps dangerous to generalize about Anabaptists in general and Mennonites in particular. Some Anabaptist groups have always maintained a solely independent, congregational polity, but the larger Mennonite groups provide examples of Free-church polity in a historically Anabaptist tradition that combine congregational autonomy and connectionalism by way of assemblies. Mennonite denominations differ as to the level of assemblies at which critical decisions are to be made: for example, in some Mennonite denominations,

231. Even here, we must note, it is not all Free Will Baptists but those who originated in New York State in the 1790s. The so-called "Original Free Will Baptists" of coastal North Carolina and Virginia do not have the conference structures.

appointments of board members for denominational agencies are made at the "district" (regional) level; in other Mennonite denominations these appointments are made by the "General Conference," a national assembly. Mennonites have traditionally recognized three types of ministers: (1) bishops, who preside over baptism and the Lord's Supper and oversee the church at a regional level, (2) preachers, who regularly preach in the congregation and have oversight of the congregation along with the local assembly, and (3) deacons, who assist the bishop in the celebration of baptism and the Lord's Supper. These officers answer fairly exactly to the three traditional orders of Orthodox, Catholic, and Anglican communions, and (like Methodist polity) some forms of Mennonite polity could be described as "episcopal" in a very broad sense, although Mennonites do not speak of these three offices as discrete "orders" of ministry. We can add here that some historic Baptist churches, especially General Baptists, held forms of church polity closely resembling the presbyterian model of church government.

The Moravian Church (also called the "Unity of Brethren") inherited some of its polity from the pre-Reformation movement of John Huss in Bohemia and the church that developed from it. Moravians today refer to this medieval church as "the Ancient Unity." Reorganized in the 1700s by Nicholas, Count von Zinzendorf, the Moravians acquired new and distinctive institutions. Through this historical process, the Moravians have emerged as a strongly connectional church throughout the world. Moravians have maintained the three traditional ministerial orders of deacons, presbyters, and bishops. From the Middle Ages the Moravians inherited a form of ministry including ordained bishops, maintaining a succession of bishops from the ancient church. In 1749, the British Parliament recognized the Moravians as "an ancient Protestant episcopal church" partly because of their maintenance of this episcopal succession.

The Society of Friends (Quakers) represents the most radical expression of independent religious thought in its rejection of the whole idea of ordained ministry, along with its rejection of (outward) sacraments. But despite their rejection of ordained ministry, the Quakers have historically maintained a system of "meetings" by which their local congregations are connected together: (1) the *monthly meeting*, which may denote a single congregation or a group of small local meetings, is responsible for determining membership in the Society and for conducting business related to the local assembly or assemblies, (2) the *quarterly meeting* is a regional meeting at the level of a county in England but varying in size in other parts of the world, and

(3) the *yearly meeting* is typically at a national level, though in some places divisions among Quakers have led to the formation of rival yearly meetings. Although Quakers around the world maintain communication with one another, each yearly meeting is considered to be autonomous.

4.4.2.c What Evangelical and Free churches teach about ministerial orders and church polity: the congregational pattern. Many Evangelical and Free-church traditions agree in maintaining a single order of ordained ministers and a congregational polity according to which most critical decisions are made by a congregational assembly.

Sources: Schleitheim Confession, 5 (in Leith, p. 287). New Hampshire Confession, 13 (in Leith, p. 338). Abstract of Principles, 14 (in Leith, p. 342). Baptist Faith and Message, 12 (in Leith, p. 348).

Comparative Cross-References: Eastern Orthodox, 1.4.2; Roman Catholic, 2.4.3–4; Reformation and Union, 3.4.2.a–d.

The congregational polity that characterizes so many Evangelical and Free churches may be understood as the most radical expression of Evangelical and Free-Church thought concerning church polity. Regular and Particular Baptist churches, Restorationist churches, most Pentecostal churches, and many other Free or Evangelical denominations affirm the congregational principle that the truest expression of the church is a particular congregation (see 3.4.1.b) and reflect the polity that developed among British Congregationalists in the early 1600s (see 3.4.2.c), although some Anabaptist groups had operated as independent congregations from the 1500s. This is evident in the Schleitheim Confession's discussion of pastors, where it is stated that the congregation's pastor "shall be supported of the church which has chosen him."[232] The Baptist form of congregational polity has direct roots in Congregationalism, and it provides an example of this system.

Evangelical and Free churches with congregational polity convene in local assemblies that make the most critical decisions in that congregation's life, including decisions about who will be admitted as members and who will be called as pastor or in other church staff capacities. In addition to the assembly, there are usually lay officers who are called deacons in Baptist churches. Baptist deacons are elected for life, and the deacons together form a committee that oversees the ongoing life of the congregation along with the pastor. Churches organized on the congregational pattern usually recognize only one rank

232. Schleitheim Confession, 5 (in Leith, p. 287).

of ordained minister, and ordination is performed by the local congregation. In formal Baptist doctrinal statements, ordained clergy are recognized as "elders" or even "bishops," though the terms "pastor" and "minister" are more frequently used in congregational life.

In addition to congregational assemblies and congregational officers, Evangelical and Free churches with congregational polity usually participate in larger church assemblies, associations, conferences, or conventions, although these wider assemblies do not hold authority over local congregations. In the Baptist pattern, congregations send "messengers" or delegates to regional and national meetings (for example, the annual Southern Baptist Convention). The convention recognizes delegates and may pass resolutions expressing the viewpoints of its constituent congregations. Perhaps more importantly, the convention elects directors or trustees who govern and determine the policies for institutions (colleges, schools, hospitals, and the like) that are supported by the churches participating in the convention or assembly. In the Baptist pattern, these trustees are accountable to their respective conventions. However, participation in a convention is not exclusive: local Baptist congregations may send delegates to different conventions, for example, many Baptist congregations in the Mid-Atlantic region of the United States participate in the meetings of both the American Baptist Churches, U.S.A., and the Southern Baptist Convention.

The congregational pattern described above is based on the Baptist pattern, which was derived from English Congregationalism as the original pattern of congregational polity among the churches identified in chapter 4 of this book. Other Free or Evangelical denominations have variations on this basic pattern. Dispensationalist and Adventist churches, Restorationist churches, Pentecostal churches, some Holiness churches, and most nonaligned Evangelical churches have adapted the congregational pattern. Because the congregational pattern is characterized by the sovereignty of the local congregation, particular patterns of congregational governance vary immensely. For example, a noninstrumental Church of Christ congregation may adopt a congregational structure considerably different from another noninstrumental Church of Christ congregation close by.

4.4.3.a *What Evangelical and Free churches teach about sacraments: sacraments as means of grace.* Some Evangelical and Free churches hold that the sacraments convey as well as symbolize divine grace.

Sources: Moravian *Ground of the Unity*, Part 1, "The Belief of the Church." Methodist Articles of Religion, 16 (in Leith, pp. 357–358).

Comparative Cross-References: Eastern Orthodox, 1.4.4; Roman Catholic, 2.4.5; Reformation and Union, 3.4.3; Ecumenical, 5.2.4.1.

Evangelical and Free churches are sometimes thought of as "non-sacramental" churches, and, as is said in opening this section, there are grounds for this suspicion in the consistent tendency of Evangelical and Free churches to value personal religious experience over churchly or sacramental (ecclesial) understandings of the ways by which God's grace comes to human beings. Nevertheless, the point must not be missed that many Evangelical churches understand sacraments to be more than mere "symbols" or "ordinances." The Moravian *Ground of the Unity* affirms that Christ "is present with us in the Word and the Sacrament." The Methodist Article of Religion defining sacraments reflects precisely the Anglican Article: both assert that sacraments are not just signs or "tokens" but that through the sacraments God "doth work invisibly in us, and doth not only quicken, but also strengthen and confirm our faith in him." One may find Methodist folk uncomfortable with this understanding of sacraments, but Methodists engaged in liturgical and ecumenical renewal in this century have consistently pointed to the sacramental emphasis of John and Charles Wesley, an emphasis that is enshrined in formal Methodist liturgy and doctrine.

In addition to Moravians and Methodists, we should note the sacramental inclinations of Calvinistic Evangelicals who have maintained the ecclesial and sacramental emphases of the Reformed tradition. Churches such as the Christian Reformed Church have been described in chapter 3 as part of the Reformed tradition, but in fact share much of the culture of Evangelical churches. In many Evangelical churches of Reformed heritage, sacramental piety is prominent. Moreover, the American Restorationist tradition has always held a high regard for Baptism and the Eucharist, with some of the most conservative members of this tradition not only insisting on weekly Eucharist but also insisting that baptism conveys new birth in Christ.

Throughout the 1970s and 1980s Evangelical Christians were consistently attracted to more sacramental expressions of Christian faith. Many Evangelical students at Wheaton College, for example, began reading the works of Anglo-Catholic author C. S. Lewis. Some found their way to Anglicanism (and some to Catholicism and Eastern Orthodoxy), but others have attempted to recover a sacramental sense within the context of traditionally Evangelical churches. Considering the groups mentioned here, along with other Evangelicals (whatever their particular traditions) with sacramental inclinations, we may say with some confidence that there are Evangelical churches and Evangelical Christian leaders whose understanding of sacraments seems closer to that of Reformation churches (see 3.4.3) than to other Free or Evangelical churches.

4.4.3.b *What Evangelical and Free churches teach about sacraments: sacraments as symbols of religious profession.* Other Evangelical and Free churches maintain that the sacraments or "ordinances" symbolize divine grace and human intention.

Sources: Dordrecht Confession, 8 (in Leith, p. 299). *Mennonite Confession of Faith (1963),* articles 11–12 (pp. 19–20). *Confession of Faith in a Mennonite Perspective (1995),* article 11 and the first point of commentary on this article. New Hampshire Confession, 14 (in Leith, p. 338). Abstract of Principles, 15–16 (in Leith, pp. 342–343). Baptist Faith and Message, 13 (in Leith, p. 348). Fundamental Beliefs of Seventh-day Adventists, belief 15. Nazarene Articles of Faith, 13–14. Assemblies of God Statement of Fundamental Truths, 6 (in Melton, p. 359).

Comparative Cross-References: Eastern Orthodox, 1.4.4; Roman Catholic, 2.4.5; Reformation and Union, 3.4.3.

For many Evangelicals, the very idea of a sacrament as conveying God's grace seems to contradict their fundamental belief in God's *direct* and *immediate* giving of grace to women and men. If God communicates grace to us directly and immediately, then why should we need means or intermediaries? The Anabaptist and Baptist doctrinal statements listed in this subsection have no separate article on sacraments, although all three have articles on baptism and the Lord's Supper. Anabaptists, Baptists and many other Evangelical churches prefer not to use the term "sacrament," because the term itself suggests the idea of a means of grace. Instead, they prefer to speak of Baptism and the Lord's Supper as ordinances, a term that suggests that they are acts that Christ ordained to be followed by Christians. "Ordinance" does not carry the connotation of an act in which grace is given. For them, the ordinances are primarily signs or symbols of God's gracious acts and signs of human intention. For an example of the latter point, baptism is often understood as a "sign of profession," by which an individual makes public her or his acceptance of Christ and of a particular Christian community (see 4.4.4.b).

Although the Anabaptist Dordrecht Confession of 1632 lists only baptism and "supper" in discussing the responsibilities of church "teachers," the Dordrecht Confession and the more recent *Confession of Faith in a Mennonite Perspective (1995)* have separate articles on footwashing and marriage. The Seventh-day Adventists also consider footwashing along with other ordinances. Footwashing can be described along with Baptism and the Lord's Supper as an "ordinance" of Christ, since Christ clearly intended for the practice to be imitated by Christians (John 13:3–17). Moravians also practiced footwashing occasionally, and other churches have experimentally followed their example in this century.

4.4.3.c What Evangelical and Free churches teach about sacraments: rejection of sacraments altogether. The Society of Friends and the Salvation Army are characterized by their rejection of "outward" sacraments.

Sources: Barclay's *Apology,* propositions 11–13 (in Leith, pp. 331–332).

Comparative Cross-References: Eastern Orthodox, 1.4.4; Roman Catholic, 2.4.5; Reformation and Union, 3.4.3; Ecumenical, 5.2.4.1.

The reaction against sacraments on the part of Evangelical and Free churches reaches its ultimate conclusion in the decision of Friends (or Quakers) and members of the Salvation Army to discontinue the "outward" practices of Baptism and the Eucharist. Friends affirm the need for "baptism" and "communion," but not as outward acts: they insist that the only baptism needed is the baptism of the Holy Spirit and the only communion needed is the communion of our souls with God. As Friends understand it, then, they have not so much rejected Baptism and Holy Communion as they have rejected the "outward signs" associated with these as being unnecessary, and even dangerous if individuals rely on them in place of the true, inward experience of Christ.

The Salvation Army at some points speaks very much like the Society of Friends, for example in stating that the baptism of the Holy Spirit is the only true baptism. At other points they argue that the sacraments are not necessary for salvation, that Christ did not intend baptism or the Supper to be repeated continually, and for this reason they do not observe them. In practice, the Salvation Army's military style of organization replaces baptism with infant dedication and then a formal signing of the "Articles of War" by mature believers.

4.4.4.a What Evangelical and Free churches teach about baptism: baptism as a means of grace. Some Evangelical and Free churches maintain that baptism is a sign of grace, possibly a means of new birth, and maintain that infants should be baptized.

Sources: Moravian *Ground of the Unity,* Part 2, chapter 2, "The Vocation of the Unitas Fratrum and its Congregations." Methodist Articles of Religion, 17 (in Leith, p. 358).

Comparative Cross-References: Eastern Orthodox, 1.4.5; Roman Catholic, 2.4.5.1; Reformation and Union, 3.4.3.1; Ecumenical, 5.2.4.2.

With the important exceptions of the Friends and the Salvation Army, all other Evangelical and Free Churches practice baptism (with water) as the means by which persons are incorporated into the church. But although there is broad agreement on this general understanding that baptism incorporates women and men into the church, there is a wide variety of teaching among Evangelical and Free churches on the question of baptism's relationship to salvation. On the one hand is the view that baptism is a means of grace, perhaps specifically an instrument of justification and the new birth in Christ.

Although it is difficult to generalize about a tradition as insistent on congregational autonomy as the noninstrumental Churches of Christ, a significant number of their congregations teach that baptism is the means by which we are born again in Christ. Our new birth and justification come about when we believe and are baptized: "The one who believes and is baptized will be saved" (Mark 16:16a). That is to say, their understanding of baptism's saving work seems surprisingly similar to that of Orthodox, Catholic, Lutheran, and Anglican traditions about baptism (see 1.4.5, 2.4.5.1, and 3.4.3.1), although they are clearly distinct from these in that they practice believer's baptism only, by immersion. In this latter respect, their practice of baptism is much closer to that of Baptist and other churches that practice believer's baptism only (see the next subsection).

Methodist churches have historically found themselves in considerable ambiguity about baptism. While all Methodist churches practice infant baptism and typically allow the options of baptism by sprinkling, pouring, or immersion, Methodists have never come to a clear agreement about baptism's relation to salvation, and this remains a point of division among Methodists up to the present time. Methodist founder John Wesley found himself in the position of many Anglican Evangelicals and Lutheran Pietists, who argued that the baptism of infants *does* bring about the new birth in Christ, but that most persons fall away from this baptismal gift and stand in need of new repentance and faith. This view is incorporated into one of the "Standard Sermons" of John Wesley that Methodists accept as a doctrinal standard.[233] On the other hand, though, the Methodist Article of Religion on baptism repeats the initial wording of the Anglican Article, but then omits the significant phrase that speaks of baptism as bringing about new birth "as by an instrument." Without this phrase the Methodist Article seems most compatible with Reformed understandings of baptism (see 3.4.3.1), according to which the water of baptism is the appointed sign of the grace of new birth but must not

---

233. John Wesley, sermon on "The New Birth" 4:1–2, in *Sermons*, ed. Albert C. Outler, 4 vols. Bicentennial Edition of the Works of John Wesley (Nashville: Abingdon Press, 1984–1987), 2:196–198.

be confused with the new birth itself. Moravians, Methodists, and some Holiness churches baptize infants, or at least allow for the baptism of infants.

4.4.4.b *What Evangelical and Free churches teach about baptism: baptism as a sign of faith.* Other Evangelical and Free churches maintain that baptism is a sign of a believer's profession, and so they maintain that infants should not be baptized.

Sources: Schleitheim Confession, 1 (in Leith, p. 284). Dordrecht Confession, 7 (in Leith, p. 298). *Mennonite Confession of Faith (1963),* article 11 (p. 19). *Confession of Faith in a Mennonite Perspective (1995),* article 11. New Hampshire Confession, 14 (in Leith, p. 338). Abstract of Principles, 15–16 (in Leith, pp. 342–343). Baptist Faith and Message, 13 (in Leith, p. 348). Fundamental Beliefs of Seventh-day Adventists, belief 14. Nazarene Articles of Faith, 13. Assemblies of God Statement of Fundamental Truths, 6 (in Melton, p. 359).

Comparative Cross-References: Eastern Orthodox, 1.4.5; Roman Catholic, 2.4.5.1; Reformation and Union, 3.4.3.1; Ecumenical, 5.2.4.2.

Anabaptist churches, Baptist churches, and many other Evangelical churches teach the symbolic value of baptism as a sign of new birth among those who have believed in Christ. It follows that baptism is only appropriately performed for those who have already come to mature faith in Christ. For this reason, their practice is described as believer's baptism. Since this view is shared not only by Baptist churches but also by other Evangelical churches (such as Restorationists, Pentecostal, Adventist, and Dispensationalist churches), we shall refer to churches who practice believer's baptism only as "believer's baptist" churches (with a lowercase b to indicate that we are not referring to Baptist churches only). Those who maintain believer's baptism insist that the only New Testament precedents for baptism are for baptisms of persons who have already believed in Christ. Baptism, then, does not convey forgiveness or new birth in Christ in their understanding; rather, it is the sign appointed by Christ himself by which a new believer publicly professes her or his faith and is made part of the Christian community.

Although some Anabaptist churches baptize by pouring, other believer's baptist churches perform baptism only by immersion; that is, the person is dipped into water (in some churches three times) "in the name of the Father and the Son and the Holy Spirit." For this purpose, their churches will typically have a large baptistery, a pool for performing baptisms by immersion. Often the baptistery is hidden behind a curtain at the front of the church, or in some cases hidden in the floor where a floor-piece can be removed when baptisms are to be performed. One exception we might note to the Trinitarian formula "in the name of the Father and of the Son and of the Holy Spirit" is that of the Oneness Pentecostal churches, who follow Acts 2:38 and other passages in baptizing "in the name of Jesus Christ" only (see 4.2.1.b).

Believer's baptist churches (and other Evangelical and Free churches as well) usually follow the historic consensus that baptism should not be repeated, since it is the one-time mark of entry into the Christian community, just as a marriage ceremony is a one-time mark of union, even though the promises made in baptism as in marriage may need to be renewed, even in a public ceremony. This is true even of churches that practice believer's baptism, although we must note two important points. In the first place, belief in the irrepeatability of baptism appears to be contradicted in the practice of believer's baptist churches when persons baptized as infants, baptized in other denominations, or baptized by a mode other than immersion are "rebaptized." But in this case, some understanding and sensitivity is needed. Believer's baptist churches do *not* regard themselves to be "rebaptizing"; rather, because they in principle do not accept the validity of infant baptisms and (in some cases) baptisms in other modes than immersion or in another denomination, they understand themselves simply as baptizing a person for the first time. Therefore, on the principle that a valid baptism should not be repeated there is broad agreement.

A second case that really is an exception involves those believer's baptist congregations that understand baptism to be a sign of entry into a local congregation, not into the whole Christian church. This view is generally held by "Primitive Baptists" and by some other Baptist groups in the United States. In their understanding, the congregational principle (see 3.4.1.b) is so emphasized that there is no formal fellowship or communion with congregations outside of their own. Consistent with this view, these congregations often rebaptize a person joining their fellowship from another congregation, and consistent with this view, the Lord's Supper is usually restricted to baptized members of their congregation (see 4.4.5.b).

Belief that a valid baptism should not be repeated can set up a crisis of conscience for believer's baptists. What if a person has a conversion experience, is baptized on profession of faith, and then subsequently comes to think that in fact the former conversion was not true, that is, that she had really not believed in Christ at that time? In the logic of believer's baptist churches, this may well lead to the conviction that the former baptism was invalid, because it was not a sign of true Christian faith. Baptism may be repeated in this case, again on the grounds that it is not in fact a "rebaptism" but rather the first true baptism for the believing individual. Informally, this idea has deeply influenced many

Evangelical churches (even Methodist churches and others who practice infant baptism), where baptism can become in practice a repeatable, public sign of sincere repentance and desire for renewal. This practice is problematic in ecumenical discussions with churches who have historically insisted on the irrepeatability of baptism, and many Evangelicals (especially those engaged in ecumenical dialogue) have called on their own traditions to reconsider the practice, especially in light of the fact that their own traditions have historically affirmed in their own ways that baptism should not be repeated.

4.4.5.a *What Evangelical and Free churches teach about the Eucharist: Eucharist as conveying Christ's presence.* Some Evangelical and Free churches maintain that the Eucharist conveys Christ's presence to those who receive it with faith.

Sources: Moravian *Ground of the Unity,* Part 2, chapter 2, "The Vocation of the Unitas Fratrum and its Congregations." Methodist Articles of Religion, 18–20 (in Leith, pp. 358–359).

Comparative Cross-References: Eastern Orthodox, 1.4.6; Roman Catholic, 2.4.5.3; Reformation and Union, 3.4.3.2.a–c; Ecumenical, 5.2.4.3.

Almost all of the Evangelical and Free churches observe "the Lord's Supper" or "Holy Communion" as an act instituted by Christ representing the continuing fellowship of believers. Again we must note the exceptions of Friends and the Salvation Army. Terminology may vary from one church tradition to another: "Eucharist" is used here only to relate what is said to other traditions. Most Evangelical churches prefer to speak of "the Lord's Supper" or "Holy Communion" or perhaps simply "communion." But within Evangelical and Free churches there is a wide range of belief and teaching about Christ's presence in the Supper.

Many Evangelical and Free churches understand the Lord's Supper to be a means of grace, not only a sign or symbol of fellowship. The Supper is a *sacrament,* not just an *ordinance.* Within the scope of Evangelicals with this sacramental concern, some persons interpret the presence of Christ in the Supper as being conditional upon faith and conveying not the "bodily" presence of Christ but the virtue or effect of Christ's presence. The Moravian *Ground of the Unity* affirms that in the Lord's Supper, Moravian congregations

> have the assurance of being united to their Lord, enjoy the fruits of His sufferings and death for the forgiveness of sins, unite with each other anew as members of His body, and rejoice in the hope of His return in glory.[234]

234. Moravian *Ground of the Unity,* Part 2, chapter 2, "The Vocation of the *Unitas Fratrum* and its Congregations."

The "Virtualist" or "Receptionist" view of the Eucharist (see 3.4.3.2.b) seems to be the most natural reading of the Methodist Articles of Religion on the Lord's Supper, taken directly from the Anglican Articles. Charles Wesley's hymns, much beloved by Evangelicals, speak boldly of the reality of Christ's presence in the sacrament:

> Come and partake the gospel feast,
> Be saved from sin, in Jesus rest;
> O taste the goodness of our God,
> And eat his flesh and drink his blood.[235]

On the other hand, the Charles Wesley hymns also speak of the power or "virtue" that is given by Christ in the sacrament:

> Let the wisest mortals show how we the grace receive;
> Feeble elements bestow a power not theirs to give.
> Who explains the wondrous way,
>   how through these the virtue came?
> These the virtue did convey, yet still remain the same.[236]

This seems to reflect very precisely the "Virtualist" understanding of the Eucharist, consistent with the Anglican Articles, so Charles Wesley's references to Christ's presence may be understood as references not to a "bodily" or "corporeal" presence of Christ in the Eucharist but to the practical effect or power of Christ's presence.

4.4.5.b *What Evangelical and Free churches teach about the Eucharist: Eucharist as a sign of Christian communion.* Other Evangelical and Free churches maintain that the Eucharist is a sign of Christ's death and of Christian fellowship or communion.

Sources: Schleitheim Confession, 2–3 (in Leith, pp. 284–285). Dordrecht Confession (in Leith, p. 302). *Mennonite Confession of Faith (1963)*, article 12 (pp. 19–20). *Confession of Faith in a Mennonite Perspective (1995)*, article 12. "New Hampshire Confession," 14 (in Leith, p. 338). Abstract of Principles, 15–16 (in Leith, pp. 342–343). Baptist Faith and Message, 13 (in Leith, p. 348). Fundamental Beliefs of Seventh-day Adventists, belief 15. Nazarene Articles of Faith, 13.

Comparative Cross-References: Eastern Orthodox, 1.4.6; Roman Catholic, 2.4.5.3; Reformation and Union, 3.4.3.2.a–c; Ecumenical, 5.2.4.3.

Many Evangelical churches would prefer to call the Supper an "ordinance" rather than a "sacrament," with the implication that it is not a holy act in itself, not an act that conveys grace itself, but rather a sign of fellowship "ordained" or commanded by Christ (see 4.4.3.b). The Anabaptist and Baptist confessional statements are very clear on this

235. Hymn of Charles Wesley, in *The United Methodist Hymnal*, no. 616.
236. Hymn of Charles Wesley, in *The United Methodist Hymnal*, no. 627.

point: the Lord's Supper was intended by Christ himself "to com-
memorate his death, to confirm the faith and other graces of Christians, and to be a bond, pledge, and renewal of their communion with
Him, and of their church fellowship."[237] This position is quite similar
to the Zwinglian understanding of the Eucharist as a commemoration
of Christ, a view held by many in Reformed churches (see 3.4.3.2.c).

But although these Evangelical churches may think of the Lord's
Supper as being solely a reminder of Christ's death and a visible symbol of Christian fellowship, we should not conclude that it is unimportant for them. True, in some Evangelical churches the Supper is
celebrated only infrequently, and sometimes as a chore that is carried
out with little enthusiasm. But in most churches it is a very meaning-
ful sign of fellowship. American Restorationist churches (Disciples of
Christ and Churches of Christ) have historically insisted that the Supper should be celebrated every Sunday in accord with what they believe to be the churches' practice in the age of the New Testament.
Other Evangelical churches celebrate the Supper less frequently, some
quarterly and others only once or twice a year. Even in these cases less
frequent celebration may be tied to a conviction that the Supper is so
important to the community that it should not be taken lightly.

We may note here as a related point that among some Evangelical
churches the Lord's Supper is "open," that is, members of other denominations are welcome to partake of communion. Moravians, the
various Wesleyan churches, and some Adventist and Restorationist
churches have historically practiced "open" communion. Other Evangelical churches practice "closed" communion, that is, communion is
restricted to members of one's denomination. In certain circles (Primitive Baptists, for example) the restriction has closed communion to all
but members of one's congregation. Among historic Anabaptist communities the "ban" is practiced, that is, persons who have offended the
community are "banned" from fellowship. In the strictest communities, such as the Amish, this may mean that even family members are
forbidden from speaking to an individual under the ban. Evangelical
churches have practiced greater or lesser degrees of moral and doctrinal discipline through their histories by restricting participation in the
Supper to those who are out of fellowship for some reason.

---

237. "Abstract of Principles" of Southern Baptist Theological Seminary, 16 (in
Leith, p. 342).

5

The Ecumenical Core and the Peripheries of Historic Christian Teachings

5.0 Introduction

I recently received a fax from Southeast Asia. "I was just reacting against the Zwinglianism here in Singapore," my correspondent scribbled at the bottom of the page. Although Zwinglianism is a serious matter in Singapore—among both Methodists and Presbyterians—I have the feeling that something has gone seriously wrong in that doctrinal disputes that historically divided European and North American Christianity since the Reformation have now been implanted throughout the world as a result of missionary outreach. As a matter of fact, it was their perception of the *visible dividedness* of the churches that inspired missionary leaders to call together the Edinburgh Missionary Conference of 1910, an event that many understand as the beginning of the twentieth-century Ecumenical movement.

Doctrinal division, our being divided over what we agree publicly to teach, remains a significant factor in the visible dividedness of the churches today, and it has been a concern of the Ecumenical movement through its history. Given the new ecumenical context described in the Introduction (see 0.2), it seems appropriate that after surveying the teachings of Christian traditions in chapters 1 to 4 of this book, we should turn in conclusion to consider how the Ecumenical movement has dealt with issues of Christian doctrine that continue to separate Christians today. This concluding chapter, then, will consider the means by which the Ecumenical movement of the twentieth century has worked to clarify points of divergence and to find greater consensus among Christian traditions (see 5.1). It will then attempt to summarize the most critical points of doctrinal divergence and convergence among historic Christian traditions (see 5.2). Based on this summary, we shall then attempt to make some claims about a distinctive core of Christian teachings (see 5.3) and to discuss the problem of the "peripheries" or boundaries of historic Christian doctrine (see 5.4).

5.1   Doctrinal Understanding and the Ecumenical Movement

The Ecumenical movement in the twentieth century has helped both to clarify doctrinal issues that divide Christian communions and to work toward a new consensus in corporately held Christian teachings. We should stress that both points are important: much of what is said in chapters 1 to 4 of this book is quite different from what would have been said at the beginning of the twentieth century. The difference is to be accounted for by the fact that the Ecumenical movement has brought Christians into closer conversation with one another, so that even if the Ecumenical movement were to fail in its quest for doctrinal *consensus*, its contribution to inter-Christian *understanding* would remain a very substantial contribution. Two different forms of ecumenical dialogue concerning doctrinal division will be considered here: the Faith and Order Movement, which has sponsored multilateral dialogues between churches, and the various international bilateral dialogues that have flourished especially since late in the 1960s.

5.1.1   Faith and Order

The task of understanding doctrinal differences and trying to reach consensus was one of the first tasks of the twentieth-century Ecumenical movement. Although the Edinburgh Missionary Conference (1910) was concerned primarily with the practical outworking of the missionary mandate to win the world for Christ in the new century, a motion was adopted at that conference to establish a new conference to address issues of "Faith and Order" dividing the churches. It is the Faith and Order movement, which grew from this motion at Edinburgh and was first organized in an international conference in Lausanne, Switzerland, in 1927, that addresses most directly the doctrinal differences that have divided the churches. The intention of the original Faith and Order Conference was "to draw churches out of isolation into conference," and it was open to all churches that "accept our Lord Jesus Christ as God and Savior."[238] The name of the Faith and Order movement emphasizes its concern with doctrine ("Faith") and polity ("Order").

238. These quotations are given in the introduction to *The Second World Conference on Faith and Order Held at Edinburgh, August 3–18, 1937,* ed. Leonard Hodgson (New York: MacMillan Co., 1938), p. 3.

After its initial meeting in Edinburgh (1927), the Faith and Order movement held a second international conference in 1937. When the World Council of Churches was organized in Amsterdam in 1948, the Faith and Order organization became a standing Commission of the new Council, and it has continued its work within the context of the World Council. Although in its origins the World Council was overwhelmingly Protestant, the Church of Greece (and the ecumenical patriarch of Constantinople) had participated since the beginning, and other Eastern Orthodox churches became full participants in the council in 1961. Moreover, although the Roman Catholic Church does not participate as a full member of the World Council of Churches, it has participated fully in the work of the Faith and Order Commission since 1968. Moreover, many Evangelical and Free churches who are not formally part of the World Council have participated in Faith and Order. For example, Pentecostal churches (such as the Assemblies of God) and Restorationist churches (such as noninstrumental Churches of Christ) have sent delegates or at least observers to Faith and Order meetings. Faith and Order, then, is by far the most international and comprehensive organization working for ecumenical understanding and consensus in Christian doctrine.

In its earlier years, Faith and Order utilized the method of comparative symbolics (see 0.2), that is, the method of carefully comparing doctrinal statements of particular churches and noting points of divergence and convergence, especially on the issue of ecclesiology, the doctrine of the church. A shift in methodology came at Faith and Order's third international conference, which met in Lund, Sweden, in 1952. Participants in the Lund conference realized that the method of comparative symbolics illumined historic differences between traditions, but it did not afford a way to find contemporary consensus or agreement. Rather than simply comparing traditional doctrines, then, the Lund conference advocated a new strategy in which participants engaged in dialogue from their own church perspectives but looked for new ways to unity, especially by using the common inheritance of New Testament scripture.[239] It has become a commonplace since the time of Lund to say that the Ecumenical movement does not intend simply to restore the historically broken unity of Christian traditions,

239. Cf. John E. Skoglund and J. Robert Nelson, *Fifty Years of Faith and Order: An Interpretation of the Faith and Order Movement* (New York: jointly published by the Interseminary Movement, the Department of Faith and Order of the National Council of Churches of Christ in the U.S.A., and the Commission on Faith and Order of the World Council of Churches, 1963), pp. 68–73. The movement for a renewed "biblical theology," prominent in the 1940s through the 1960s, was influential on the movement in this period.

but seeks rather to build a new unity in our time. At this point, however, we must issue a word of caution. To my knowledge (and I have talked to participants in the Lund conference), this was not intended to mean that the hard work of understanding historic doctrine could be avoided; rather, it was understood as meaning that the comparative study of doctrine by itself could not bring about the contemporary unity of the churches that Faith and Order has so consistently sought. We need to say this because, of course, this work itself utilizes a comparative methodology, and we should be aware of the fact that this method, by itself, cannot bring about new ecumenical consensus. Nevertheless, careful understanding of traditional doctrine remains one of the prerequisites of Christian unity today.

The success of the method proposed at Lund can be seen in the work that Faith and Order accomplished in the years following. The fourth world conference of Faith and Order (Montreal, 1963) adopted a report on "Scripture, Tradition, and Traditions." This report addressed very directly the questions about religious authority, especially the authorities of scripture and Christian tradition, which had stood as primary doctrinal division between Catholics and Orthodox, on the one hand, and most Protestants on the other (see 5.2.1 below). Although Faith and Order did not hold another world conference until 1993, its work was carried on through the assemblies of the World Council and through regular meetings of the Faith and Order Commission.

Through the decade of the 1970s, a central concern of Faith and Order was the church-dividing issues related to the sacraments of Baptism and the Eucharist and to the understanding of ministry and ordination. This work led in 1982 to the publication of *Baptism, Eucharist and Ministry* (*BEM*), a text setting out agreed points of consensus and also points of disagreement on each of these issues. In the decade following the publication of *Baptism, Eucharist and Ministry*, Faith and Order collected an extensive series of official responses to the document on the part of denominations throughout the world (see 5.2.4 below). The work on *BEM* not only presupposed the process developed at Lund but built also on the foundation of the Montreal report on "Scripture, Tradition and Traditions."

For many years now Faith and Order has been at work investigating the doctrines of the Trinity, of Christ, and of the Holy Spirit under the title "Confessing the Apostolic Faith Today." Based on a preliminary report adopted in Lima, Peru, in 1982, the discussions of "Apostolic Faith Today" have been the subject of intense doctrinal investigations since that time. Although these investigations have not yet resulted in a general document such as *BEM*, extensive work has been done, especially on the churches' reception of the Nicene Creed. The most recent world conference of Faith and Order (Santiago de Compostela, Spain, 1993) took note of work in progress on the issues of "Apostolic Faith," and urged churches to consider how common affirmation of the Nicene Creed can promote visible Christian unity today.[240]

5.1.2 International Bilateral Conversations

The ecumenical conversations carried on by Faith and Order under the auspices of the World Council of Churches have been multilateral conversations, that is, conversations in which a large number of church bodies have participated. Another approach is to focus on the issues between two church bodies, or perhaps between two families of churches, each represented by a single sponsoring institution. This approach is described as that of bilateral conversations, and it has been the approach favored by Roman Catholics. Although bilateral conversations have been conducted at national and even local levels, there have been significant international bilateral conversations, especially since the decade of the 1970s, when the bilateral approach encouraged by Roman Catholics seems to have caught on with church communions throughout the world. In the case of Reformation and Evangelical churches, these international bilateral conversations have been undertaken by international organizations representing their traditions, namely, the Lambeth Conference of Bishops and Anglican Consultative Council for Anglicans, the World Alliance of Reformed Churches, the Lutheran World Federation, the Baptist World Alliance, and the World Methodist Council, although in some cases they have been undertaken by specific denominations (the Disciples of Christ) or by an ad hoc group of representatives of an Evangelical tradition (the group of Pentecostals who undertook the Pentecostal-Roman Catholic conversations). The most important international bilateral dialogues to date are listed in table 9.

5.2 Summary of Doctrinal Convergences and Contrasts

What then do Christian churches agree to teach, and on what issues do they remain visibly divided in their attempts to teach the faith? Given the doctrinal summaries in chapters 1 to 4 of this book, and in the light of ecumenical discussions of Christian teachings, we are now

240. "On the Way to Fuller Koinonia: The Message of the World Conference," in Best and Gassman, par. 6, p. 226.

Table 9. Some International Bilateral (and Trilateral)
Ecumenical Conversations[241]

Bilateral Conversation	Reports
Anglican–Old Catholic	1931
Anglican–Lutheran	1972
Anglican–Orthodox	1976, 1978, 1980
Anglican–Roman Catholic	1981, 1994
Baptist–Reformed	1977
Disciples–Roman Catholic	1981
Lutheran–Methodist	1984, 1987
Lutheran–Orthodox	1975
Lutheran–Reformed	1973
Lutheran–Roman Catholic	1972, 1978, 1980 (2), 1981, 1994
Lutheran–Roman Catholic-Reformed	1976
Methodist–Roman Catholic	1971, 1976, 1981, 1986, 1991
Old-Catholic–Orthodox	1975, 1977, 1979, 1981
Pentecostal–Roman Catholic	1976
Reformed–Roman Catholic	1977

in a position to consider more precisely the areas on which doctrinal convergence may be claimed as well as areas where doctrinal divergences appear. Although the account that follows will not be able to examine doctrinal convergences and contrasts at the level of denominational divisions, it will attempt to outline convergences and contrasts between the large families of Christian traditions we have identified in this book.

At some points in the summaries that follow, we are able to rely on earlier work by Faith and Order (such as *BEM*) or reports of bilateral dialogues. In other cases we can state a point of convergence simply as the greatest common denominator of the views considered in chapters 1 to 4. In these cases, though, we cannot truly speak of an ecumenical "consensus," since our descriptive deductions do not represent formal agreement between church bodies.

5.2.1   Convergences and Contrasts on Issues of Religious Authority

Issues about religious authority lie underneath most other issues of Christian faith. For example, Christian teachings about Mary the

241. As given in *Growth in Agreement: Reports and Agreed Statements of Ecumenical Conversations on a World Level*, eds. Harding Meyer and Lukas Vischer (New York: Paulist Press, and Geneva: World Council of Churches, 1984). I have omitted the Faith and Order study of "Baptism, Eucharist and Ministry" as being a multilateral document, which I have discussed above, and I have added dates for some more recent reports of international dialogues of which I am aware.

mother of Jesus will differ very significantly if these teachings are formulated (1) on the basis of the unity of scripture and later traditions, or (2) on the basis of scripture alone, or (3) on the basis of scripture and possibly later traditions read in the light of broader human experience and critical reflection. It is particularly crucial to be clear about issues of religious authority in ecumenical discussion, for without attention to the underlying issues of what authority validates Christian teaching, Christians can simply talk past each other, never seriously engaging what others consider to be valid foundations for faith.

A critical point of convergence among the Christian traditions on the issue of religious authority is the reliance of all the traditions on the Bible, an accepted canon or list of scripture about which the only formal discrepancy between the churches is the issue of the Apocrypha or Deuterocanonical books of the Old Testament that are received as scripture by Orthodox and Catholics. All the Christian traditions agree, at a bare minimum, that no teaching may contradict the meaning of Christian scripture. This is true for Orthodox, who hold that the Scriptures express the infallible holy tradition of the church (see 1.1.1–2), and equally true for Catholics, who maintain that the Scriptures, interpreted by church tradition, are the authoritative source of the church's teachings and practice (see 2.1.1–2). It is obviously true for Protestants, for whom the Bible alone is the final source of Christian teachings (see 3.1.1, 4.1.1.a–b).

We could be a bit more specific and say that in almost all the traditions Christian scripture holds the highest place of authority in the church, although this statement would have to be qualified by two observations: (1) that the Society of Friends would differ formally on this point in their assertion that the experience of God is itself the fount of all religious authority (see 4.1.2.c), and (2) that although the assertion is true for Orthodox and Catholics, the "highest place of authority" in their traditional doctrinal statements is held not by scripture alone but rather by the unbroken unity of Christian scripture and Christian tradition. The papal encyclical *Ut Unum Sint* (May 1995) offers what is perhaps the most important Catholic clarification of this issue to date, asserting that sacred scripture is "the highest authority in matters of faith," with sacred tradition as "indispensable to the interpretation of the word of God."[242]

This last point leads us to the central issue of doctrinal contrast on the issue of religious authority, specifically, the issue of the relationship between Christian scripture and Christian tradition. At the broadest level, there lies a deep division between Catholic and Orthodox

242. Papal encyclical of Pope John Paul II, *Ut Unum Sint*, par. 79 (*Origins* 25:4, p. 66).

traditions, on the one hand, which perceive an unbroken unity between scripture and tradition, and those Protestant traditions, on the other hand, which stress that scripture alone is the final source of religious authority and which tend to see tradition as a corrupting influence in the experience of the church. This division is deep, but we must recall at the same time that many Protestant churches (especially Anglican and Lutheran churches) value early Christian tradition very highly in the next place after scripture.

One of the most significant documents of the Faith and Order movement attempted to address directly the issue of the relationship between Christian tradition and Christian scripture. Adopted at the Faith and Order plenary meeting in Montreal in 1963, the report on "Scripture, Tradition, and Traditions" attempts to formulate a new ecumenical consensus on this issue. The report distinguishes "Tradition" (with a capital T) as "the Gospel itself, transmitted from generation to generation in and by the Church" from "tradition," meaning the traditioning process, and "traditions," particular expressions of the faith, both confessional and cultural. With this positive understanding of "Tradition," the report is able to assert the unity of scripture and tradition in a way in which Protestants had not in the past, though recognizing the Protestant principle that the Scriptures are the primary criterion by which true "Tradition" (meaning the Christian message itself) is to be distinguished from corrupt traditions.[243]

It is difficult to assess the extent to which an ecumenical statement such as this has been received in the churches. The Montreal statement has clearly influenced some contemporary doctrinal statements in Protestant churches, for instance, the United Methodist (USA) definition of the "Wesleyan Quadrilateral" of scripture, tradition, reason, and experience.[244] Moreover, bilateral dialogues have often utilized the concept of "Tradition" and the distinction of scripture, "Tradition" and traditions,[245] and more recent multilateral ecumenical dia-

243. Plenary report of the fourth World Faith and Order Conference on "Scripture, Tradition, and Traditions," in *Documentary History of Faith and Order, 1963–1993*, ed. Günther Gassman (Faith and Order paper no. 159; Geneva: World Council of Churches, 1993).
244. First expressed in the *Book of Discipline* of the United Methodist Church in 1972 (Nashville: United Methodist Publishing House), paragraph no. 70, pp. 76–77. It should come as no surprise that Professor Albert C. Outler of Southern Methodist University who chaired the committee that prepared this statement was also part of the leadership for the 1963 Montreal Faith and Order Conference.
245. For example, the Anglican-Orthodox Moscow statement of 1976, 3:9–12 (in Meyer and Vischer, pp. 42–43), Anglican-Roman Catholic discussions of "Authority in the Church" of 1976, 1:2 (in Meyer and Vischer, p. 90), and Lutheran-Roman Catholic discussions concluded in 1972, part 1 (in Meyer and Vischer, pp. 172–176).

logues have utilized the principles developed at Montreal, most notably in the discussion of *Baptism, Eucharist and Ministry*. Perhaps most importantly, the Montreal statement on "Scripture, Tradition and Traditions" serves as a positive precedent and example of a way in which careful ecumenical discussion can lead to clarification of Christian understandings of biblical and traditional authority and can point toward a definition of consensus on this issue. Discussions of the relationship between scripture and tradition are complicated further by contemporary discussions of the role of cultural diversity in the understanding of both scripture and tradition (this is expressed in the "Message" of the Santiago world conference of Faith and Order).

If the tension between scripture and tradition is the primary area of formal division separating Catholics and Orthodox from Protestants in their corporate understandings of religious authority, a number of other areas of division remain. One further issue has to do with the authority of bishops, and in particular, the authority of the bishops of Rome. Orthodox and Catholics (and Anglicans) have been united in their belief that the office of bishop is necessary for the existence of the church (see 1.1.3, 1.4.2, 2.1.2, 2.4.3, 3.4.2.a, and also 5.2.4 below). Although Orthodox are willing to grant the primacy of honor to the bishops of Rome, they have historically refused to grant supremacy of jurisdiction to the bishops of Rome (see 2.1.3). Protestants have historically rejected both the primacy and the jurisdiction of the papacy. The Roman Catholic definition of papal infallibility (see 2.1.4) remains a critical divisive issue in this area. There have been suggestions that the office of the papacy could be reenvisioned as an ecumenical office linking all Christians (limiting papal jurisdiction or supremacy), and the encyclical *Ut Unum Sint* of John Paul II (30 May 1995) hints at the possibility that Catholics now may be willing to discuss the limits of papal jurisdiction in the church.

Another divisive issue with respect to religious authority involves the conservative Evangelical (Fundamentalist) understanding of biblical inerrancy or (possibly) infallibility (see 4.1.1.b). Although Orthodox and Catholic traditions ascribe infallibility to God and believe that this infallibility is expressed in the tradition of the church (specifically in the papacy, for Catholics; see 1.1.1, 2.1.1, and 2.1.4), they have not taught that the canon of scripture holds unique authority over tradition as Protestants historically have. The Fundamentalist understanding of scripture, moreover, goes beyond that of historic Reformation churches, which did ascribe "infallibility" to the Scriptures in asserting the clarity and unity of the Bible (see 3.1.2.b) but did not hold the Scriptures over against modern scientific and historical claims in the way that Fundamentalists have.

A fourth and very different area of divergence today on issues of religious authority lies in the question of whether human reason and reflection on human experience can serve to interpret or perhaps critique traditional doctrines grounded in scripture and tradition. Reformation and Union churches in particular (see 3.1.2.d), but other Christian communions in varying degrees, have been influenced by the European Enlightenment's severe questioning of traditional knowledge (including knowledge grounded in scripture) and its preference for ways of knowing grounded in unaided human intellect and reflection on common experience (see also 4.1.2.b). Although this issue has not been addressed as formally in ecumenical discussions as the issue of the relationship between scripture and tradition, it nevertheless underlies many ecumenical conversations.

For example, in the issue of the ordination of women to preside at the Eucharist, the question of the relative weight attached to scripture and tradition, and to reason and experience, is a critical underlying issue. A case can be made for the ordination of women grounded in scripture and tradition, but this argument must be made on the grounds that women's voices and roles in scripture and tradition have been silenced or muted by the preponderance of later Christian tradition against them. Those who advocate the ordination of women to preside at the Eucharist also argue that contemporary experience and reflection, especially the experience of expanding leadership roles for women based on modern democratic notions of participatory leadership, provide a foundation for the interpretation of Christian scripture and tradition on this issue. The issue of the ordination of women has been one of the most divisive in ecumenical discussions in the last twenty years, and these divisions must be seen as grounded in deep divisions over the issue of how reason and experience can serve as religious authorities in the interpretation and reception of Christian scripture and tradition. At this point we must ask whether this difference over the role of experience and reason in religious teachings is not in reality more divisive than the issue of the relationship between scripture and tradition.

5.2.2   Convergences and Contrasts on Issues of God and Christ

5.2.2.1   Convergences and Contrasts
on the Triune Nature of God

Teachings about God and Christ lie at the heart of traditional Christian belief, and we shall argue below that the worship of Jesus Christ as God is the constitutive fact of historic Christian faith (see 5.3). At this point we may note two broad areas of consensus in Christian teaching. The first is the broad affirmation of the doctrine of the Trinity, that is, the teaching that God is eternally Father, Son, and Holy Spirit, each of these being equally and eternally God. Eastern Orthodox churches, the Roman Catholic Church, historic Reformation and Union churches, and almost all Evangelical and Free churches have agreed in affirming this doctrine (see 1.2.1, 2.2.1, 3.2.1, and 4.2.1.a), most often in the terms of the Nicene Creed. We have noted as exceptions that many Evangelical churches affirm the essence of the Trinitarian teaching although preferring to state this doctrine in biblical terms (see 4.2.1.a). We have also considered the fact that "Oneness" Pentecostal churches reject the doctrine of the Trinity in favor of a modalistic understanding of Father, Son, and Holy Spirit (see 4.2.1.b). We have seen, further, that some Liberal Protestants have questioned the traditional understanding of the Trinity, often in the direction of Modalism (see 3.2.1).

5.2.2.2   Convergences and Contrasts on the Human and Divine Natures of Christ

A second point of broad doctrinal convergence in teachings about God and Christ lies in the very widespread affirmation of the human and divine identities of Christ, most often stated in the terms utilized by the Council of Chalcedon (451), that is, the affirmation of the one "Person" of Christ known in two distinct "natures," divine and human. The Chalcedonian language about Christ is affirmed explicitly by Orthodox (see 1.2.2), Roman Catholic (see 2.2.3), Reformation and Union churches (see 3.2.2), and by most Evangelical churches (see 4.2.2). Again, some Evangelical churches prefer not to utilize the terminology of "natures" and "Person" that characterized the Chalcedonian statement, although they do affirm the integrity of divine and human in Christ and acknowledge the unity of these in the biblical figure of Jesus Christ. Moreover, we have noted the tendency on the part of conservative Evangelicals to stress the divinity of Christ, though this does not necessarily imply a denial of Christ's humanity (see 4.2.2).

Work in progress on the Faith and Order study of "Confessing the Apostolic Faith Today" shows a consistent tendency since 1982 to utilize the Nicene Creed as a basis for contemporary Christian unity in teaching about God and Christ. This tendency stands in contrast to an earlier attempt in Faith and Order to develop a modern interpretation of the faith in contemporary language, as Liberal Protestant churches had done through the early decades of the twentieth century.[246] From 1982 the Faith and Order discussions have not pursued the attempt to frame a new statement of faith and have preferred instead to ask all churches how they can recognize the apostolic faith as expressed in the Nicene Creed.[247] Bilateral discussions such as those between Anglicans and Lutherans have also reflected the movement to affirm common teachings about God and Christ as expressed in the Nicene Creed.[248] This tendency reflects a very serious attempt on the part of Faith and Order to respond to the concern that it had been dominated by Liberal Protestantism, for the affirmation of apostolic faith as expressed in the Nicene Creed ran counter to the tendency of Liberal Protestantism to frame a new "creedal" statement, and it embraced the approach favored by Orthodox, Roman Catholics, and traditionalists within Protestant churches to reaffirm the faith in the terms utilized by an ancient consensus.

A more particular issue that has been much discussed in ecumenical circles in recent decades concerns the *filioque* clause of the Nicene Creed, that is, the statement in the creed as it is traditionally said in Western churches that the Holy Spirit "proceeds from the Father *and the Son.*" On this issue there has been a growing consensus that the *filioque* clause should *not* be utilized in the creed, primarily because it was not in the form of the creed agreed to at Constantinople in 381. Anglican-Orthodox bilateral dialogues affirmed as early as 1976 that the *filioque* clause should not be utilized in the creed, and some Anglican and Reformed churches have proceeded tentatively to liturgical revisions that will delete or at least make optional the *filioque* clause.[249] In 1979 a report of Faith and Order stated explicitly, after many years of multilateral discussions,

> That the original form of the third Article of the Creed, without the *filioque*, should everywhere be recognized and restored, so that the whole Christian people may be able, in this formula, to confess their common faith in the Holy Spirit . . . [250]

246. Examples of the attempt to frame a contemporary "account of Hope" or "A Common Statement of our Faith" can be seen in Faith and Order documents on 1978 (in Gassman, *Documentary History of Faith and Order, 1963–1993*, pp. 161–170).
247. Faith and Order report "Towards the Common Expression of the Apostolic Faith Today" (in Gassman, *Documentary History of Faith and Order, 1963–1993*, pp. 191–200, and cf. Gassman's comments on this, p. 31).
248. Anglican-Lutheran statement of 1972 (in Meyer and Vischer, p. 17).
249. Anglican-Orthodox statement of 1976 (in Meyer and Vischer, p. 44). The Reformed Church in America has also voted to make the *filioque* optional.
250. Faith and Order Report "The Filioque Clause in Ecumenical Perspective" (in Gassman, *Documentary History of Faith and Order, 1963–1993*, pp. 178–190, quotation is on p. 189).

Although Roman Catholics have maintained the propriety of the *filioque* clause, recent Catholic statements, including the 1992 *Catechism of the Catholic Church*, have expressed clear appreciation for the Eastern understanding of the creed (that is, without the *filioque* clause),[251] and many Catholics and Orthodox now believe that *filioque* no longer stands as an obstacle to their communion with one another.

Another area of historical division where there seems to be considerable healing lies in the Chalcedonian definition of one Person of Christ in two natures, the issue that has historically separated Oriental Orthodox churches from Eastern Orthodox churches. In recent decades a series of meetings between Oriental Orthodox and Eastern Orthodox leaders has been held, some under the auspices of Faith and Order, in which very significant understanding has been reached, so much so that a theological basis for reunion between Oriental and Eastern Orthodox churches appears to be in place, although the practical implementation of these reunions remains to be negotiated.[252]

But granted these widespread and growing grounds for unity, what areas of divergence continue to divide churches in their teachings about God and Christ? Differences over these issues may be ranged in the following order, from most to least serious. In the first place and most seriously would be those groups who originated from historic Christian communities but who have clearly rejected not only the language of the Nicene Creed but the Trinitarian belief itself, and with this have rejected the worship of Christ as God. Here I have reference to Unitarians especially, many of whom explicitly acknowledge that they should not be thought of as distinctly Christian (see 5.4). In the second place would be those who have rejected the doctrine of the Trinity but maintain in some degree the divinity of Christ and perhaps the worship of Christ. Such groups as Jehovah's Witnesses would fall into this category, since they acknowledge that in a certain degree Jesus can be considered "divine," but not in the same sense as God the Father. In this respect, their beliefs resemble those of the ancient Arians, against whose teachings the Nicene Creed was directed in the first place (see 5.4). In the third place would be those who have rejected the doctrine of the Trinity as such but maintain explicitly the worship of Christ as God. In this category we would place the Oneness Pentecostal churches (see 4.2.1.b), whose affirmation of the

251. *Catechism of the Catholic Church*, 246–248 (in American translation, pp. 65–66).
252. Some of the discussions between Eastern Orthodox and Oriental Orthodox are given in *Does Chalcedon Divide or Unite? Towards Convergence in Orthodox Christology*, ed. Paulos Gregorios, William H. Lazareth, and Nikos A. Nissiotis (Geneva: World Council of Churches, 1981).

deity of Christ and whose worship of Christ is unequivocally clear. In the fourth place and least seriously would be those who have rejected the Hellenistic language associated with the doctrine of the Trinity (language of "substance" and "Persons") but who maintain nevertheless the *essence* of the Trinitarian teaching, rejecting Modalism and Arianism, but preferring to speak in biblical terms about the unity of Father, Son, and Holy Spirit in one God. Here would be a variety of Evangelical and Free churches; most notably the Restorationist churches but to some degree other churches as well whose doctrinal statements show a preference for biblical terminology (see 4.2.1.a). We have elected in chapter 4 of this book to consider these churches as affirming the historic doctrine of the Trinity, although the difference in language is significant.

A further area of contrast has to do with the role of Mary in the understanding of the churches. Orthodox, Roman Catholics, and some Protestants affirm Mary as *Theotokos*, "God-bearer" or "Mother of God," and understand this teaching as being linked inexorably to the Chalcedonian assertion of the unity of divine and human in the Person of Christ. Orthodox and Roman Catholic churches teach the doctrines of Mary's perpetual virginity and (in different ways) her assumption into heaven. Catholics teach the doctrine of the immaculate conception of Mary. Moreover, Mary is "venerated" in Orthodox and Catholic churches, and prayers are offered through her. In many Protestant churches, by contrast, the doctrine of Mary as *Theotokos* and related Marian doctrines have not been affirmed and do not represent part of their historic consensus in faith. Ecumenical discussion has clarified some of the issues related to the mother of Jesus (for example, the critical distinction between "veneration" and "worship"), but the remaining differences are significant, both with respect to formal teachings and devotional practice.

5.2.3 Convergences and Contrasts on Issues of Human Nature and Salvation

Protestant churches—including Reformation churches, Union churches, Evangelical and Free churches—have consistently claimed that the primary issue distinguishing themselves from Catholics and Orthodox is the historic Protestant insistence that human salvation comes about solely by God's grace and on the basis of faith alone in Christ's all-sufficient work. A century of ecumenical dialogue and historical study inspired by ecumenical contact has offered a serious corrective to this conventional view. Ecumenical discussions and historical writing in this century have pointed out that early Protestants, on the one hand, reflected more of medieval Catholic theology and spirituality than Protestants in the past had believed: they point, for example, to Luther's continuing belief in and practice of penance, and the many ways in which late medieval spirituality influenced John Calvin. On the other hand, ecumenical discussions and historical works have also shown the extent to which Catholics and Orthodox have both stressed, in their own ways, the priority of divine grace in the out-working of human salvation.

Although the issues of human nature and salvation have not been one of the central issues addressed by the Faith and Order movement, contemporary historical and ecumenical studies, along with some bilateral dialogues (especially the Lutheran–Roman Catholic dialogues) offer the possibility of stating what Christians hold in common on these points. Most notable is the strong consensus between Orthodox, Catholics, and Protestants that because of the fallen condition of humankind, human salvation depends on God's grace. This is stated in distinctive ways in different traditions. Orthodox speak of the human loss of the "likeness" of God that consists of the righteousness and holiness with which human beings are intended to be endowed by God (see 1.3.1–3). The traditional Catholic and Reformation understanding of original sin holds that in their "natural" state, that is, apart from God's grace, human beings lack the freedom to turn to God on their own strength and to be saved (see 2.3.1–2 and 3.3.1–2). Evangelical churches may not define a doctrine of original sin in the classic Augustinian pattern, but at the heart of Evangelical faith is the conviction that human salvation must come about by God's own initiative, not by human works or merit (see 4.3.1).

It might also be possible to express a convergence in the churches' understanding of the roles of faith and good works in salvation, although at this point we would have to state the points of convergence very carefully. It seems appropriate to state that historic Christian traditions agree in teaching (1) that human salvation normally comes about by explicit faith in Christ, (2) that salvation cannot come about when human beings explicitly reject faith in Christ, and (3) that good works follow as the fruit of faith in Christ. The first two claims reflect the historic teachings described in chapters 1 to 4 of this book (specifically at 1.3.3, 2.3.4, 3.3.4, and 4.3.4.a–b). If the reader wonders why we have to state that salvation "normally" comes about by explicit faith in Christ, it is because two exceptions could be noted to this normative pattern. In the first place, many historic Christian traditions teach that infants and other persons incapable of explicit faith may nevertheless be saved by the grace given in the sacraments, so long as they do not explicitly reject faith in Christ. In the second place, some historic traditions maintain that persons outside of the Christian faith may be saved by trusting in the grace of God in Christ, even if they are unaware of the explicit name and nature of Christ. In both cases, the exception to the normative belief in salvation by explicit faith in Christ is made in the case of persons for whom explicit faith is not possible. In all cases, with the exception of Universalists, historic Christian communities maintain that explicit rejection of faith in Christ means cutting oneself off from salvation. Although they may differ on the issue of the particular role played by good works in human salvation, all of the historic traditions considered in this book maintain that good works ought to flow from faith (see 1.3.6, 2.3.4, 3.3.5, and 4.3.5). The Lutheran–Roman Catholic bilateral dialogues, where one might expect the sharpest difference on this issue, have proven extraordinarily helpful in illuminating the degree of consensus on this point.[253]

Beyond these very broad areas of agreement or consensus, considerable divergences continue to divide the churches in their teachings about human nature and salvation. We may observe the following four areas of significant disagreement. First, and perhaps most prominent, is the historic divergence over the Augustinian understanding of human nature and salvation, which has been so influential in Western churches, both Catholic and Protestant. This paradigm involves both (1) the understanding that all human beings inherit the guilt of sin as well as its consequences and (2) a predestinarian understanding of the sovereignty of God's work in salvation, with the concomitant belief that Christ's work was for a limited number of the elect (see 2.3.3, 3.3.3.a–b, and 4.3.2.a). In contrast to the Augustinian paradigm, Eastern Orthodox churches have traditionally insisted that human beings inherited only the consequences of sin but not its guilt (see 1.3.2–3), and many Catholics and Protestants have rejected the Augustinian paradigm in favor of the belief that Christ's work has made salvation available to all human beings (see 2.3.3, 3.3.3.b, and 4.3.2.b). Those traditions that maintain the Augustinian paradigm see it as being inexorably linked to their belief in God's initiative in salvation. We should perhaps note, though, that the divergence on this issue cuts across the boundaries of Catholic and Protestant traditions.

A second area of divergence has to do with the question of the re-

---

253. Lutheran–Roman Catholic agreed statement on "Justification by Faith," especially pars. 108 (on "Merit") and 161 (concluding declaration) in *Justification by Faith: Lutherans and Catholics in Dialogue VII*, ed. H. George Anderson, T. Austin Murphy, and Joseph A. Burgess (Minneapolis: Augsburg Publishing House, 1985), pp. 54 and 73–74.

lationship between faith and good works. Although the statement given above expresses some areas of convergence among historic Christian traditions, Protestants have traditionally asserted that our salvation is itself grounded in grace only, not on human works or merit. That is to say, even though good works flow from faith in Christ, they are not themselves a grounds of our salvation (see 3.3.4–5, 4.3.4.a–b, and 4.3.5). Catholics and Orthodox and in their own way Wesleyans have historically insisted that salvation will not come about apart from good works, and Catholics have historically spoken of good works "meriting" salvation, although they are clear that this "merit" is itself grounded in God's initiative (see 1.3.3, 2.3.5, and 4.3.5).

A third area of divergence lies in the strong tendency of Evangelical churches to deemphasize the role of the church and sacraments in human salvation in their stress on an affective conversion experience. Orthodox, Catholics, and Reformation churches are clear and consistent in their claim that the normal means by which human beings receive grace are the church (as being itself a kind of mystery or sacrament) and its "mysteries" or sacraments (see 1.3.5, 2.3.6; also see 3.4.3). Although some Evangelical churches (such as Moravians and Methodists) have historically maintained the centrality of the sacraments in human salvation (see 4.4.3.a), others have formally disavowed the close relationship between church, sacraments, and salvation (see 4.4.3.b) and in two cases Free-church traditions have rejected "outward" sacraments altogether (see 4.4.3.c). A specific case in point here, perhaps the point of sharpest difference, is the historic teaching of Orthodox, Catholics, and Reformation churches that baptism brings about the new birth in Christ for those who do not reject faith in Christ (see 1.4.5, 2.4.5.1, 3.4.3.1; also see 4.4.4.a), contrasted with the belief of many Evangelical churches that only explicit faith brings about justification and that baptism is only a sign or symbol of this faith (see 4.4.4.b).

A fourth area of divergence lies in the inter-Evangelical question of what experiences or acts of grace are normative for the religious life beyond conversion. In what we might call the Baptist paradigm of Evangelicalism, conversion itself guarantees one's final salvation (see 4.3.6.a). Wesleyan and Holiness churches teach that the goal of the religious life is "entire sanctification," thought of in Holiness churches as a distinct religious experience (see 4.3.6.b), and Pentecostal churches have been distinguished historically by their teaching of a baptism of the Holy Spirit accompanied by the gift of speaking in unknown tongues (see 4.3.6.c–d).

5.2.4   Convergences and Contrasts on Issues
of Church, Ministry, and Sacraments

Throughout the history of ecumenical dialogue in the last hundred years, Christian teachings about the church, its ministry, and its sacraments have been understood as critically divisive doctrinal and practical issues. Many Christians believe that the future unity of the churches hinges on the resolution of these doctrinal and practical issues. Much early ecumenical discussion was given to differing understandings of the nature of the church, and in fact the vision of a new expression of Christian fellowship, or *koinonia*, was the central contribution of the most recent Faith and Order world conference in Santiago de Compostela, Spain, in 1993. Perhaps most importantly, lengthy discussions in the Faith and Order movement have resulted in a single, short document entitled *Baptism, Eucharist and Ministry* (1982) that addresses the crucial divisive issues of the two sacraments of Baptism and the Eucharist and the understanding of the church's ministry. Thus, although issues about church, ministry, and sacraments might be the most divisive of all the categories considered here, we have more ecumenical thought and reflection to rely on as we consider these issues.

5.2.4.1   *Convergences and Contrasts*
on the Nature of the Church

There are significant differences in the ways in which Orthodox, Catholic, and various Protestant traditions define the church. Catholics and Orthodox stress the nature of the church as a divine institution that bears the "character" or impression of Christ in this world (see 1.4.1 and 2.4.1). Reformation and Union churches stress the nature of the church as the coming-together of those who believe in which the Word is preached and the sacraments are administered (see 3.4.1). Evangelical churches have historically stressed the nature of the church simply as a fellowship of believers (see 4.4.1.a–b).

The common denominator in these various definitions would be the agreement of historic Christian traditions in teaching that the church includes those who believe in Christ, but this bare claim would not suffice as a definition for either Catholics or Orthodox, who insist on the divine origin and divine nature of the church, nor would it suffice for Reformation churches or Methodist churches, who would insist on the proclamation of the Word and the celebration of the sacraments as necessary elements in the life of the church. But these historic understandings of the church are not mutually exclusive: Orthodox and Catholics agree that because the church bears the impress of

Christ, it involves proclamation and sacraments, and for their part Protestants would agree at the very minimum that the church *ought* to express the character of Christ, even though Protestants are keenly aware of the church's historic failures to do so. To attempt to find grounds for unity among these varied historic understandings of the church is a very risky matter; an effort that has been tried in the past without fruitful results.[254] But in keeping with the general plan of this section, we might consider the following tentative formulation of common teaching on the nature of the church, based on what has been demonstrated in chapters 1 to 4 above: namely, that historic Christian traditions hold that the church is constituted by the faithful of all ages amongst whom Christ is preached and the sacraments are administered, and in whose faithful proclamation and sacraments the character of Christ is made visibly present to the world. This formulation does not deny that at various times and places all of the historic Christian traditions have failed to proclaim Christ "faithfully," and so it acknowledges that the divine character of the church is often hidden in this world.

If this expresses a degree of unity concerning the nature of the church, however, we must hasten to note some of the most significant points of disunity concerning the Christian community. One point of divergence might be described as the issue of the catholicity, or universality, of the church. Catholics and Orthodox have historically insisted that one of the necessary signs or "notes" of the church is its catholicity, that is, that the church embraces the fullness of Christian faith and includes the body of Christian believers throughout the whole world, not just those of a particular nation or locality. The churches of the Reformation acknowledged the catholicity of the church but maintained that because of the corrupt condition of medieval Catholicism, it was necessary to establish national churches to reform the church in their times and places. Still others maintained that although the church might be spiritually united throughout the world, the only necessary visible unity for the church was at the congregational level (see 3.4.1.b and 4.4.1). Protestants have often failed to recognize the seriousness with which Orthodox and Catholics viewed the disintegration of the churches at the time of the Reformation, not only as schismatic but also as destroying the "catholic" or universal nature of the church.

254. Here I refer to Faith and Order discussions prior to the Lund conference of 1952 in which attempts to reach a consensus on the nature of the church by the method of "comparative ecclesiologies" were seen to have failed. This was what pressed the participants at Lund to seek a new model for finding contemporary consensus in doctrinal matters.

A second area of divergence concerning the doctrine of the church might be termed the issue of the apostolicity of the church, that is, the question of the extent to which the church must be defined by adherence to apostolic teaching, and conversely the extent to which churches can tolerate or allow for a range of teachings on particular issues. Catholic and Orthodox tradition have maintained that it is necessary for the church to discipline and perhaps excommunicate those who publicly teach false or misleading doctrine. Many Protestant churches of the Reformation age are defined doctrinally (for example, by adherence to the Augsburg Confession), so that church membership is defined along doctrinal lines. Among many conservative Evangelical churches and among Anabaptist churches the tendency to division over doctrinal issues, and to define the church by its upholding true doctrine, is a strong impulse indeed. A different strain of conservative Evangelical thinking about the nature of the church, however, deemphasizes doctrine, insisting that believers should express "In essentials, unity; in non-essentials, liberty; and in all things charity."[255] The question of the latitude a church communion can allow in doctrinal matters obviously affects that church's ability to enter into ecumenical dialogue and partnership with other church communities.

A third area of divergence concerns the question of whether a particular form of polity (church governance) or ministry is necessary for the existence or at least for the fullest realization of the church. Orthodox, Roman Catholic, and Anglican traditions have historically insisted that bishops (and perhaps an unbroken succession of bishops from the apostles) are necessary to the church's very existence (see 1.4.2, 2.4.3, and 3.4.2.a). Some Protestant churches insist that only a congregational form of polity expresses the authenticity of the church (see 3.4.2.c and 4.4.2.c). The Faith and Order study of *Baptism, Eucharist and Ministry* recognizes the faithfulness of varied forms of ministry and polity, but suggests that for the future unity of the church, all churches should consider how they might express or embrace the ancient threefold pattern of deacons, presbyters (or "priests" or "elders"), and bishops.[256]

Before we move to other issues, however, we should pause to note that the Faith and Order movement has been concerned not so much with the definition of the church in general but with the question of what *form* an ecumenical unity of Christians might take. Through the

---

255. A quotation traditionally ascribed to the seventeenth-century Moravian Bishop Johann Amos Comenius, but broadly used by Methodists and others.
256. *Baptism, Eucharist and Ministry*, section on "Ministry," 3:A (pp. 24–25).

1970s, when more and more denominational mergers along national or regional lines were coming into existence, Faith and Order advocated an understanding of the ecumenical church as "a conciliar fellowship of local churches." The vision of Faith and Order at that time was of a "conciliar" unity of churches, in which the World Council of Churches or perhaps a successor body would serve as a council (so "conciliar") to link churches together.[257] In more recent ecumenical discussions this vision has given way to a vision of communion, or *koinonia,* in three areas: in faith (especially by the mutual recognition of the Nicene Creed), in life (especially in mutual recognition of one another as Christians, specifically by recognizing the validity of one another's baptisms), and in mission (in common witness and service to the world). This offers a more realistic goal for the Ecumenical movement, while not ruling out the possibilities for organic union between churches.[258]

The question of the nature of the church has already raised the issue of ministry, and here the principal issues concern the differences in church polity, especially the necessity of bishops and of bishops in unbroken succession to the apostles as being necessary for the being or at least the well-being of the church. We must mention another formidably divisive issue at this point, and that is the issue of the ordination of women to preside at the Eucharist. Orthodox, Roman Catholic, and many conservative Protestant churches have historically rejected the ordination of women, on the grounds that the one who presides at the Eucharist must represent Christ, who was male (this is the argument most consistently given by Catholics) or on the grounds that scriptural injunctions against women speaking in Christian assemblies would forbid them from preaching or from presiding at the Eucharist (this is the argument most consistently given on the part of conservative Protestant churches). Protestant churches influenced by Liberalism, as well as very traditional Holiness and

257. The ecumenical vision of the church as a "conciliar fellowship of local churches" was first clearly expressed in a 1973 Faith and Order report entitled "The Unity of the Church—Next Steps" (in Gassmann, ed., *Documentary History of Faith and Order, 1963–1993*), pp. 35–49 and especially pp. 37–38. It was expressed in further Faith and Order documents in 1974 (Gassmann, pp. 50–60), 1975 (Gassmann, pp. 61–68), 1976 (Gassmann, pp. 69–75), and 1978 (Gassmann, pp. 76–80). The vision of a "conciliar fellowship of local churches" was also affirmed in the plenary statement on the Nairobi Assembly of the World Council of Churches (Gassmann, p. 3).
258. The vision of "koinonia in faith, life, and mission" was expressed in the statement on the unity of the church adopted by the plenary of the Canberra Assembly of the World Council of Churches in 1991 (in Gassmann, pp. 3–5), and was the overarching theme of the 1993 plenary meeting of Faith and Order in Santiago de Compostela, Spain; cf. Best and Gassmann, *On the Way to Fuller Koinonia,* passim.

Pentecostal churches, have ordained women for the last century, both on the grounds of liberal participatory notions of authority and on the grounds that women's roles in scripture (and the early centuries of the church) have not been fully recognized. In recent decades this issue has been extraordinarily divisive, in fact it has become the focal point for a variety of divisive issues, such as the issue of the meaning of Christian ministry, and the issue of authority in the church (see 5.2.1 above). Orthodox and many Catholics believe that the ordination of women by Anglicans, for example, threatens earlier ecumenical liaisons between their communions. Many Eastern Orthodox leaders felt in the 1980s and 1990s that their concerns over the ordination of women and underlying questions about the nature of the Ecumenical movement and authority in the church were so vehemently rejected in ecumenical circles that they should perhaps no longer participate.[259]

Related to broader issues of the understanding of the church and its ministry are the issues raised by the most central and most distinctive of Christian practices, namely Baptism and the Eucharist. There is a broad ground of common teaching among the historic doctrinal statements of the churches that Baptism and Eucharist, as outward acts instituted by Christ, hold a special and distinctive place within the life of the church. This is true even in the case of Eastern Orthodox Churches and the Roman Catholic church, who acknowledge seven "mysteries" or sacraments, but nevertheless recognize the Eucharist and baptism as being the "two great sacraments of the Gospel." As we have seen, only the Society of Friends and the Salvation Army diverge from this pattern in their rejection of outward sacraments (see 4.4.3.c). In the cases of Baptism and the Eucharist, it is possible to state a ground of unity (however weak) as well as issues on which there has been historical divergence.

5.2.4.2 Convergences
and Contrasts on Baptism

In the case of baptism, we may state that historic Christian traditions agree in teaching that baptism is the act appointed by Christ by which persons are incorporated into the fellowship of the church. This

259. Orthodox Churches in the U.S.A. withdrew temporarily from the National Council of Churches of Christ in the early 1990s over this and other issues on which they felt that the voice of Liberal Protestantism was so stifling that their concerns could not be fairly heard. See also the "Reflections of Orthodox Participants" in the 1991 Canberra Assembly of the World Council of Churches in Kinnamon, ed., *Signs of the Spirit*, p. 281.

statement, although true, would not at all be a sufficient statement about baptism for most Christian traditions. It does express what Christian traditions teach in common about baptism, again noting the critical exceptions of Friends and the Salvation Army.[260] It is not a trivial point of consensus, and the recent ecumenical vision of "koinonia in faith, life and witness" calls the churches to community in common life by recognizing the validity of one another's baptisms.

Beyond this singular point of consensus concerning baptism, we may note critical points of divergence that continue to divide the churches. Perhaps the most critical issue is the relationship between baptism and salvation, and specifically the issue of whether in baptism God conveys the new birth in Christ. Orthodox, Catholics, and most Reformation churches have historically maintained that baptism is the act in which a woman or man is born again in Christ and is forgiven of past sins (see 1.4.5, 2.4.5.1, and 3.4.1; also see 4.4.4.a). Reformed confessions and Methodist doctrinal statements allow that although this may be generally asserted, the moment of new birth may be separate from the moment when water is applied. Distinctive of many Evangelical churches is the belief that only by affective and explicit faith (conversion) is a person born again in Christ (see 4.3.4.a and 4.4.4.b). Although this divergence does not allow easy resolution, the growing consensus that baptism upon personal profession of faith is the normative pattern (see the next paragraph) recognizes at least that faith is a prerequisite for keeping the grace given in baptism, a point on which Orthodox, Catholics, and Protestants are historically agreed.

This raises a second issue concerning baptism, whether the church should practice infant baptism or whether baptism with conscious and explicit confession of faith is the normative (or only allowable) practice. Orthodox, Catholics, and most Protestants practice infant baptism, but it is distinctive of Anabaptists, Baptists, Restorationists, and many other Evangelical churches to practice believers' baptism only (see 4.4.4.b). There has been in ecumenical circles a growing tendency to recognize that baptism with confession of faith should be regarded as the normative pattern, with infant baptism being considered an exception to this pattern. This is affirmed at least in a descriptive statement about early Christian practice by the 1982 Faith and Order report on *Baptism, Eucharist and Ministry*, which states that "baptism upon personal profession of faith is the most clearly attested pattern in the New Testament documents."[261] The underlying pre-

---

260. *Baptism, Eucharist and Ministry*, section on "Baptism," 2:D, p. 3.
261. *Baptism, Eucharist and Ministry*, section on "Baptism," 4:A, p. 4.

supposition of the Roman-Catholic Rite of Christian Initiation for Adults (RCIA) is that adult baptism should be the normative pattern in the church.

A third historically divisive issue, perhaps of less importance today, is the mode of baptism, that is, whether baptism should be performed by immersion only or by sprinkling or pouring. Orthodox churches, most Baptists and Restorationists, and many other Evangelical and Free-church traditions have insisted on immersion as the normative mode of baptism, whereas Catholics and many Protestants have allowed for sprinkling or pouring. On this point there is again a growing consensus that immersion is historically the preferred mode of baptism, and that if sprinkling or pouring are practiced they should be seen as exceptions to the norm.[262]

5.2.4.3   Convergences and Contrasts on the Eucharist

With the Eucharist, as with Baptism, it is possible to state a weak area of agreement in the common teaching that the Eucharist is the act appointed by Christ in which Christ's saving work is constantly brought to the memory of the church and by which the church's fellowship or communion in Christ is uniquely celebrated. But again, although the assertion is true, it would be seen as quite inadequate for most Christian traditions, in which the commemoration of Christ and the sense of communion together are not the only or even most significant aspects of the Eucharist, in their understanding. Nevertheless we should call attention to these points of consensus, for all the traditions (except Friends and the Salvation Army) do believe that the commemoration of Christ's work is *one* of the elements of the eucharistic celebration and there is broad agreement that the Eucharist represents the fellowship or communion of Christians.[263]

Beyond these areas of consensus lies the divisive question of whether Christ is *present* in the eucharistic celebration, and *how* Christ is present in the celebration. The historic options laid out in this book are as follows: (1) The assertion that in the eucharistic we encounter the very body of Christ who was born of Mary. This claim is maintained in their own ways by Orthodox (see 1.4.6), Roman Catholics (see 2.4.5.3), Lutherans, and many Anglicans (see 3.4.3.2.a). The historic Catholic doctrine of transubstantiation may be understood as a very particular way of understanding the bodily presence of Christ.

---

262. *Baptism, Eucharist and Ministry,* section on "Baptism," 5:17, p. 6.
263. *Baptism, Eucharist and Ministry,* section on "Eucharist," 2:A, p. 11.

(2) The belief that Christ's power is present in the Eucharist to those who receive it with faith (see 3.4.2.b and 4.4.5.a). This belief is associated with many in the Reformed tradition, with many Anglicans, and with historic Methodist doctrine, and it can be described as "Virtualism" or "Receptionism." (3) The view that the commemoration of Christ in the Eucharist is the principal meaning of the event, with no unique or distinctive presence of Christ (see 3.4.2.c and 4.4.5.b), which is a view associated with Zwingli and some subsequent Protestants, including many Evangelical and Free churches.

Ecumenical discussions of the Eucharist, including the influential Faith and Order study of *Baptism, Eucharist and Ministry*, take account of these divisions over the existence and manner of Christ's presence in the Eucharist, but these discussions call the churches to recognize ways in which each of these aspects of the Eucharist can be recognized by all. Moreover, the ecumenical discussions call the churches to consider other depths of meaning and devotion in the Eucharist that have often been overlooked in the disputes over the manner of Christ's presence. For example, *Baptism, Eucharist and Ministry* deals only briefly with the issue of Christ's presence in the Eucharist but it calls the churches to consider other central meanings of the Supper: Eucharist as "thanksgiving to the Father," Eucharist as "invocation of the Spirit," Eucharist as "communion of the faithful," and Eucharist as the "meal of the kingdom."[264] The hope offered by these discussions is that Christians may discover together new depths of meaning in the Eucharist in the light of which traditional divisions may appear less important.

5.3 The Core of Historic Christian Doctrine

As this book demonstrates from beginning to end, the historic differences between Christian communions over the content of the Christian faith are abundant and cannot be minimized. But from all that has been said above, we may now ask if it is possible to identify any teaching or teachings held so broadly by Christians that they may be said to constitute a distinctive core of historic Christian faith. A contemporary theologian has written,

> There is no one "core" or "basic" or "essential" material theme or doctrine, nor any one pattern of them, that *is* the Christian thing. The generally accepted conclusion of historical studies is that there never has been. There is not even a past, perhaps orig-

264. *Baptism, Eucharist and Ministry*, section on "Baptism," 2:A–E, pp. 10–15.

inating, "essential" or "core" construal of the Christian thing
from which Christians have departed in different ways to which
they might return.[265]

Although this book has not been concerned with what this theologian
calls a "material theme" that characterizes Christian faith, it does point
to some important areas of agreement or consensus between the historic teachings considered in chapters 1 to 4. This quotation raises the
question of whether there is any core of meanings shared across
the boundaries of Christian traditions or Christian cultures. Of course,
if one were to argue that there is no constitutive belief or practice held
by Christians *without exception*, then we should grant this claim, although it would be a very trivial claim. Here we must concern ourselves
with a more radical and more important claim, namely, that because of
the vast differences between Christian cultures and traditions there neither is nor has been historically a distinctive and constitutive belief or
practice that marks the Christian community throughout the world and
throughout the historical experience of the Christian communities.

It is my contention, grounded in the study of historic teachings presented in this book, that the Christian faith is historically constituted
by the teaching that Jesus Christ is God. This is, I believe, the distinctive, constitutive assertion of the historic Christian community, although many words of caution must be issued along with it. Most important: the obverse (that "God is Jesus Christ") cannot be simply true
in a framework of Trinitarian thought. We may restate this same conviction as expressing a constitutive practice of the historic Christian
community, namely, that the Christian faith is historically constituted
by the worship of Jesus Christ as God. Moreover, the importance of
the term "historically" must not be minimized in these two claims, for
the evidence presented throughout this book is essentially historical
evidence. Nevertheless, I am convinced that these two closely related
claims accurately describe the faith agreed to by Orthodox, Roman
Catholic, and Protestant churches of varied traditions, that is to say,
the vast congregation of Christian communions present today and the
overwhelming congregation of Christian communions in the historic
experience of Christian faith. The term "historically" implies that
these two assertions purport to be more than mere tautologies (fortu-
itous definitions of terms); rather, they purport to be grounded in the
historic doctrinal agreements of Christian churches examined in chapters 1 to 4 above.

265. David H. Kelsey, *To Understand God Truly: What's Theological about a Theological School* (Louisville, Ky.: Westminster/John Knox Press, 1992), p. 33.

It might be objected that even if these two claims about the constitutive center of historic Christian faith are true, they are nevertheless trivial because they fail in themselves to resolve the many issues that continue to divide the churches. While I will grant that these claims by themselves will not resolve many of the church-dividing issues considered through this book, I shall argue nevertheless that these assertions about the center of Christian unity are significant points of unity, because they are the points that most distinctly define Christianity itself as a religious tradition.

Let us digress from Christianity for a moment to find a larger context in which the importance of these claims can be understood. A helpful way to think about "religion" is to understand it as being concerned with ultimate values, that is to say, what we value above all else, what we treasure, in short, what we worship. Understood in this way, religion is the characteristic of every human being, for to be human is to value or evaluate, and for every human being there is something that is valued above all else, something that is valued ultimately. In the words of Luther's commentary on the First Commandment, "That to which your heart clings and entrusts itself is, I say, really your God."[266] In this sense, religion does not have necessarily to do with a God or gods or spirits, it has to do with whatever it is that humans value above all else, whatever their ultimate vision is for human reality. It is part of every human culture to transmit values, and within these to transmit a vision of what is to be valued ultimately. Another way of saying this is to say that it is characteristic of all human cultures to transmit religious values from one generation to the next.[267] There is a rigorous logic to ultimates: ultimates (by definition) allow of no rivals. That is why religious values, when genuinely held, are

266. Luther's *Large Catechism*, commentary on the First Commandment (in Tappert, p. 365).
267. This understanding of religion is grounded in the work of Frederick Ferré, *Basic Modern Philosophy of Religion* (New York: Charles Scribner's Sons, 1967), pp. 30–83 and of Frederick Streng, *Understanding Religious Life*, 3rd ed., The Religious Life of Man Series (Belmont, Calif.: Wadsworth Publishing Co., 1985), pp. 1–9. Both of these Fredericks were at one time colleagues at Southern Methodist University, and I studied with Frederick Streng there. Ferré defines religion as "one's way of valuing most comprehensively and intensively" (p. 69), and I take his extensive definitions of "most comprehensively" and "most intensively" to denote what I have called "ultimate" valuing. Streng's definition utilizes the term "ultimate" explicitly: he defines religion as "a means to ultimate transformation" (p. 2), where "transformation" denotes an individual's or society's aspirations for how the world should become. I take Streng's process of "transformation," then, as being close to what Ferré denoted by "valuing." Both definitions are functional in that they refuse to define religion as having a particular content, and both are concerned with ultimate valuing or transformation.

held so tenaciously: religious values can be defined as the values for which one would struggle and for which one would perhaps die.

The understanding of religion as concerned with ultimate values is helpful, I believe, because in many cases it enables us to get beneath the surface of a religious tradition to find what is truly distinctive. The claim that "Christianity is historically constituted by the worship of Jesus Christ as God" is a significant claim not only because it tells us what distinguishes Christianity from other religious traditions but more importantly because it tells us what lies at the very center or heart of historic Christian faith; it tells us what Christians have taught is to be valued above all else, namely, God as revealed or known in Jesus Christ. It is a significant fact that the World Council of Churches defines itself as "a fellowship of Churches which accept our Lord Jesus Christ as God and Saviour."[268] Given this center, one can understand the centrality of such practices as baptism (incorporation into Christ) and the Eucharist (communion with Christ), and one can comprehend more readily why the Christian year is traditionally punctuated by the events of Christ's incarnation, especially Christmas and Easter.

Understanding the worship of Christ as God as lying at the center of Christian faith also allows us to understand more readily some of the internal conflicts over Christian teaching that we have seen in this book. Why define a doctrine of the Trinity? The answer, I believe, is that in the church's unfolding understanding of God's revelation in Christ, the Arian belief that Christ was a lesser divine being challenged the logic of ultimacy; it challenged the constitutive practice of the worship of Christ as God. Why engage in a debate over the natures and Person of Christ? Again, the question was an ultimate one for ancient Christians; it was a question of how the eternal God could become a human being in the person of Christ, and the logic of ultimacy forced the church to think about both the integrity of divine and human in Christ and the unity of divine and human in Christ. Each of the seven Ecumenical Councils of the ancient church were concerned in one way or another with the understanding of Christ, including the last council that dealt with the issue of whether and how the divine and human Christ could be depicted graphically.

Historic Christian teachings about Christ, then, involve what I have called the rigorous "logic of ultimates" in the discussion of religion

268. The "Basis" of the constitution of the World Council of Churches, given in *Documents of the Christian Church*, ed. Henry Bettenson, 2nd ed. (London, Oxford, and New York: Oxford University Press, 1963), p. 333.

above. Ultimates do not allow rivals, but the process of discerning what is truly ultimate may be extended over decades or centuries. The New Testament itself includes narratives suggesting that the recognition of Jesus' identity came only with difficulty and often with surprise: Peter's recognition that "you are the Messiah" (or Christ) in Mark (8:29b) and its parallels in Matthew and Luke seems to come as a surprise to him and the other disciples who had been with Jesus, and Jesus tells them not to reveal this secret. Paul was suddenly and unexpectedly confronted with the heavenly figure of "Jesus, whom you are persecuting" (Acts 9:5b) on the road to Damascus. Part of the claim of Christian tradition is that the naming of Jesus as God was only implicit in the earliest decades and did not become fully explicit until the worship of Christ was challenged within the Christian community. Whether Jesus was indeed a *human being* was a point of debate in the second century A.D., when almost all parties seem to have agreed that Christ was a divine figure. But Arianism proved a formidable test of the church's faith and worship in the fourth century, for Arianism seemed to allow for the veneration of Christ while not offering Christ the full worship paid to God the Father. It was only after the Arian challenge arose that the church was forced in the logic of ultimacy to determine, in the words of the Nicene Creed, that Jesus Christ is "God from God, light from light, true God from true God, of the same substance as the Father, begotten, not created."

One further issue may be considered here, and that is the concern that although Orthodox, Catholic, and Protestant traditions appear to agree in this central teaching that Jesus Christ is God, the seriously divergent cultural contexts in which this affirmation is made implies that in reality they are not affirming the same thing. This objection could be grounded in postmodern understandings of human knowledge, which stress the importance of context in cultural-linguistic systems to the point of questioning whether it is really possible at all to communicate significantly between cultural systems. On this point I would suggest two matters for consideration. The first is that the affirmation in one cultural context of a statement developed and affirmed in other cultural contexts means, at the very least, that those affirming it have the *intention* of affirming what it said in its former context. That is to say, the fact that Lutherans in the 1500s included the Nicene Creed in the *Book of Concord* signifies their intention to affirm what ancient Christians, Orthodox, and Catholics had affirmed in that creed. The second thing that should be considered on this matter is that this very practice of affirming central teachings across the boundaries of cultural systems is in itself an argument for the possibility of mutual understanding, or "commensurability" between cultural-linguistic systems. It is not difficult to see that despite the enormous cultural variations within Islam, for instance, there is nevertheless a core of Islamic religious belief that is shared (and understood as being shared) between Muslims of quite varied cultural traditions. A similar case, I believe, should be made for Christian belief, namely, that although Christianity has been expressed in widely divergent cultural contexts, there is nevertheless a significant core of meanings shared across cultural systems.

5.4 The Peripheries of Historic Christian Doctrine

A critical test of any definition is to ask not only what it purports to include but also what it *excludes* or rules out. The belief that Jesus Christ is God, and the related practice of the worship of Jesus Christ as God, distinguishes Christianity from Judaism, Islam, and most other religious traditions. This is not necessarily a definition of who goes to heaven and who goes to hell; it simply describes the difference between historic Christian doctrine and the teachings of other religious traditions, and at the same time points to the heart or core of Christian faith.

A more difficult question has to do with communities often identified as Christian but who have not historically subscribed to the belief that Jesus Christ is God and have not practiced the worship of Christ as God as other traditions examined in this book have done. We may examine these communities as lying at the "peripheries" or borderlands of historic Christian doctrine. If the definition adopted here "marginalizes" or "peripheralizes" these communities, it might be fair to note that "historic Christianity" is not a designation prized by everyone everywhere, not a club (so to speak) to which everyone wants to belong. The communities described in this section are Unitarians, Jehovah's Witnesses, and Latter-day Saints (Mormons). Others could be included here. These communities have not attempted to identify themselves with "historic Christianity," although there may be movements within their communities that would seek such an identification. For example, there is a vigorous reform movement within the Church of Jesus Christ of Latter-day Saints that would like to see their community identified more closely with historic or traditional Christian faith. We should note, moreover, that although these groups have distanced themselves from historic Christianity, each has its own way of accounting for why it represents the truest form of Christian belief.

Unitarianism emerged in the late 1700s, growing from roots in the "Socinians" of the 1500s and British Deism (see 3.0.5), with independent congregations organized from former Anglicans, Presbyterians,

Congregationalists, and General Baptists. Sometimes whole congregations shifted allegiance to Unitarianism (see Interlude 5 A). "Unitarian" stands in contention with "Trinitarian," and it has been distinctive of Unitarianism to insist on the unity or oneness of God to the exclusion of the belief that Father, Son, and Holy Spirit are equally and eternally God. Unitarians have historically considered themselves to be "Christian" in so far as they follow the teachings of Jesus, but they do not regard Jesus as God. The Unitarian Universalist Association, the largest American Unitarian body, acknowledges its grounding in Judeo-Christian tradition, but it does not claim to be explicitly Christian. Unitarians insisted early on that the worship of Jesus Christ as God was not intended by Jesus himself and was an error on the part of the early Christian churches. Unitarians are not excluded from believing historic Christian teachings, because the principal stress of their tradition has come to be on its very broad toleration and inclusiveness rather than its particular views about the doctrine of the Trinity. Since the Unitarian Universalist Association embraces the former Universalist church (which did not deny Trinitarian doctrine) the possibility remains that one can in fact believe Trinitarian doctrine (personally) while being part of a Unitarian Universalist congregation.

Jehovah's Witnesses (the Watch Tower Bible and Tract Society) also stand at the peripheries of historic Christian teaching, but for clearly different reasons than Unitarians. The Witnesses grew from roots in the North American Adventist movements of the 1800s (see 4.0.7) and did not grow into a widespread religious movement until this century (see Interlude 5 B). Although they have no formal creedal documents, Jehovah's Witness literature consistently rejects the doctrine of the Trinity, maintaining that Jesus Christ is the firstborn of God's creation, and the Holy Spirit is God's hidden force or power in the world. It is often pointed out that this teaching bears considerable similarity to ancient Christian Arianism, which also maintained that Christ is a creation or "creature" of God (see 1.0.2 and table 2). Jehovah's Witnesses, however, do not claim any connection to ancient Christian groups except to maintain that theirs is the true following of New Testament Christianity.

The Church of Jesus Christ of Latter-day Saints (Mormons)[269] also grew out of the context of North American Evangelicalism in the 1800s (see Interlude 5 C), but they present a more difficult case to

269. Note that the name of the Utah-based church is the "Church of Jesus Christ of Latter-day Saints" (with a lowercase d in "day") and the Missouri-based church is the "Reorganized Church of Jesus Christ of Latter Day Saints." The Missouri-based church tends to reject the title "Mormon," since it is so closely associated with the Utah-based Latter-day Saints church.

assess, because many of their scriptures and doctrinal statements, such as Joseph Smith's own "Articles of Faith," present what appear to be traditional Christian statements about Christ. For example, the first Article of Faith states that Mormons "believe in God, the Eternal Father, and in his Son, Jesus Christ, and in the Holy Ghost," and the third Article states that human beings are saved "through the Atonement of Christ."[270] Christ's divinity is affirmed clearly in the *Book of Mormon*, which Mormons take as scripture.

The most critical problem presented by Mormon doctrines about God and Christ is that their beliefs about God and Christ are part of a much larger, more elaborate religious system in which, from the perspective of historic Christian faith, the ultimacy of God and Christ is seriously attenuated. On the one hand, Jehovah is believed to be but one of a number of Gods, and is identified with both Adam and Jesus in Mormon thought. On the other hand, Mormons teach that human beings may themselves aspire to become "Gods" in the same sense as Jehovah, and rule over universes of their own. Although traditional Mormon piety holds that this elevates humankind rather than debases God, in both claims the ultimacy of God and Christ is lessened in ways that cannot be reconciled with historic Christian teachings.

We have focused here on Mormon understandings of God and Christ to make sense of our placement of them at the "periphery" of historic Christian teachings, but a number of other matters indicate the distance Mormons have placed between themselves and historic churches. The use of scriptures such as the *Book of Mormon* alongside the Bible, the restoration of the Old Testament priesthood and Temple practices, and the belief that baptisms on behalf of the dead can effect salvation and inclusion into the church for those who have died are beliefs and practices that place Mormons at odds with historic Christian churches.

Many Latter-day Saints, however, have come to deemphasize these most distinctive or divisive aspects of their faith. Within the Utah-based Church of Jesus Christ of Latter-day Saints (LDS), there is a vigorous reform movement that stresses more what Mormons teach in common with other churches. The Reorganized Church of Jesus Christ of Latter Day Saints (RLDS; see Interlude 5 C) does not explicitly mention the *Book of Mormon* or distinctively Mormon teachings

---

270. "The Articles of Faith of the Church of Jesus Christ of Latter-day Saints," nos. 1 and 3, in *The Pearl of Greatest Price: A Selection from the Revelations, Translations, and Narrations of Joseph Smith* (Salt Lake City: Church of Jesus Christ of Latter-day Saints, 1971), p. 60.

about God in its doctrinal statement, which formally appears similar to those of many Evangelical churches. Moreover, the RLDS Church does not subscribe to the distinctive LDS beliefs that attenuate the ultimacy of God and Christ (namely, the beliefs that Jehovah was at one time a human being, is now but one of the Gods, and that humans can aspire to deity in the same way that Jehovah did) and has historically rejected polygamy, baptisms on behalf of the dead, and temple rites. The RLDS Church has voted in recent years to share communion with other Christian churches.

In each of these cases—Unitarianism, Jehovah's Witnesses, and Mormons—there is some degree of ambiguity over that which we have identified here as the center of historic Christian teaching, namely, the belief that Jesus Christ is God. Unitarians originated in the rejection of this teaching, but their latitude allows for this belief among individual members. Jehovah's Witnesses relegate Jesus to semidivine status as the firstborn of creation, but still hold Christ to be divine (in a sense) and above all the rest of creation. Mormons affirm the deity of Christ, but lessen the finality of Christ by extending deity to other gods besides Jehovah and by extending the potential to become gods to human beings; nevertheless reformist Mormons downplay these teachings and stress its similarities to historic churches. Other ambiguous cases could be considered, for example, the role of Jesus as one among many spiritual teachers in contemporary "New Age" religious movements. We should recall in concluding this section that "historic" Christian teaching has very specific content here, that is to say, it refers to the teachings considered in chapters 1 to 4 of this work. While distancing themselves from that which we have called "historic" Christian teaching, each of these traditions makes its own claims to represent "true" Christian teaching.

Interlude 5 A
Unitarian Churches

Unitarian churches originated in the 1700s in England, but had precedents in two earlier movements. *Socinianism* was a movement in the age of the Reformation (the 1500s) that questioned traditional Trinitarian doctrine. *Deism* was a movement dating from the 1690s in the British Isles that also rejected Trinitarian teachings, influenced by the Enlightenment's search for knowledge based on reason and experience (see 3.0.5). A number of British Christians were attracted to Socinian or Deist teachings in the early 1700s. In 1773 Thomas Lindsey seceded from the Church of England and formed the first Unitarian congregation. More congregations were formed in Britain and North America in the decades following and in some cases Congregationalist, Presbyterian, and General Baptist congregations voted to accept Unitarian teachings. More traditional Unitarian congregations retain the liturgies of their parent denominations (such as the *Book of Common Prayer*), revised to exclude Trinitarian formulas and references to Christ as God. Unitarians have historically identified themselves with movements for religious toleration and human rights. In the United States, the American Unitarian Association united with the Universalist Church of America in 1961 to form the Unitarian Universalist Association.

Interlude 5 B
Jehovah's Witnesses

Jehovah's Witnesses grew out of the North American Adventist movements of the 1800s, with their expectation of the immediate return of Christ and their emphasis on the interpretation of biblical prophecies in the light of contemporary history (see 4.0.7). These movements spawned schools led by independent Bible teachers who gathered students together to teach their own systems of interpretation. One of these was Charles Taze Russell (1852–1916), who determined that Christ's coming would be a spiritual event, and who taught that Christ was the firstborn of the creation, rather than an incarnation of the supreme God (see the text above). Russell's followers, sometimes referred to early on as "Russellites," incorporated themselves as an independent organization in 1884, which is now called the Watch Tower Bible and Tract Society. Missionary efforts led to the expansion of the movement into Europe and Australia early in this century, and vigorous expansion has continued in North America. Witnesses were severely persecuted by Nazis during the Third Reich because of their refusal to serve in the military or to pledge allegiance to any human government. In 1961 Witnesses produced their own translation of the Bible, the *New World Translation of the Holy Scriptures*. By the beginning of the 1990s it was estimated that there were at least four million Jehovah's Witnesses throughout the world.

Interlude 5 C
Latter-day Saints (Mormons)

The early decades of the 1800s saw the proliferation on the North American continent of a number of perfectionist and communitarian movements. Almost all of these passed out of existence within a few decades, but one that succeeded on a vast scale is the Church of Jesus Christ of Latter-day Saints (LDS), also referred to as Mormons. The Church was organized in 1830 by Joseph Smith (1805–1844), who claimed that the existence of *The Book of Mormon* was revealed to him by an angel, and that it had been deposited by descendants of ancient Israelites who had lived on the North American continent before the coming of European peoples. Based on his discovery and translation of this book, Smith restored the Old Testament priesthood and priestly rites in 1829, the year before the organization of the LDS church. Mormons were severely persecuted early in their history because of their exclusive claims to have revived true Christian faith. They moved to the Midwest of the United States, but Smith himself was murdered in 1844. After Smith's death, the Mormons were led by Brigham Young (1801–1877) to the site where they founded Salt Lake City, Utah. At this place they built a temple in which ancient Israelite observances could be restored by the Mormon faithful. The denomination continues to have its greatest strength in Utah, but it has become a global church with at least eight million members worldwide by 1990.

A number of splinter groups emerged from the Mormons in the 1800s. The largest of these still in existence is the Reorganized Church of Jesus Christ of Latter Day Saints (RLDS), based in Independence, Missouri. The RLDS established a hereditary line of prophet/presidents from the son of Joseph Smith. They rejected polygamy, the "Adam God" belief held by the LDS church, baptisms on behalf of the dead, and the temple rites, and they have consistently taken a more conciliatory attitude toward other Christian churches. This is reflected in their most recent Statement of Faith, which does not refer explicitly to the *Book of Mormon* or distinctive LDS views of God (see above), and in their recent decision to open communion with other churches.

Conclusion

"Doctrines are not God," C. S. Lewis wrote, "they are only a kind of map. But that map is based on the experience of hundreds of people who really were in touch with God."[271] We should say at the conclusion of this work that although doctrines reflect the consensus of Christian communities, Christian doctrine does not hold Christian doctrine to be the final or ultimate reality. In the end, creeds and doctrines taught in creeds convey to Christians the wisdom of those who have gone before, pointing those who follow them in the direction of Christ. Historic Christian doctrine also maintains that merely knowing historic Christian doctrine cannot be confused with the actual confession and worship of Christ. The devil himself, an old Anglican homily points out, recognized the bare truth that Jesus was "the Holy One of God." He might pass the doctrinal test: but Christian faith itself is more than a matter of knowing doctrines. It is a matter of ultimate valuing; it is a matter of worship.

At the conclusion of this work, I feel that I must restate that this book has been concerned with the historic teachings of Christian traditions. It does not purport to tell what "Lutherans" believe: it purports to tell only what historic Lutheran doctrinal statements have agreed to teach. The book has dealt only obliquely with the Christian Scriptures, as they lay a groundwork for the later development of Christian doctrine. It has not attempted to describe the moral and social teachings of Christian traditions, and these (for example, the issue of abortion) are often as divisive as historic theological issues. The

271. C. S. Lewis, *Mere Christianity* (New York: Macmillan Co., 1960), p. 136.

range of churches dealt with in the book is very broad, but not fully inclusive. Many groups of Evangelical and Free churches will be found missing, and the book does not represent well the teachings of newer non-Catholic churches in various parts of the world amongst whom traditional doctrinal divisions are often (and happily) not as prominent as they have been in Europe and North America. The book has not dealt at length with nondoctrinal matters dividing Christian communities, such as the varieties of ethnic and cultural Christian traditions.

Moreover, the reader must be aware of how limited this book is, even in dealing with its particular subject. Hundreds of books have been written on nearly every topic covered here, and in far greater detail than this work can pretend to offer. Though they do not always make for easy reading, the doctrinal statements of the churches themselves can be found in such a collection as John Leith's *Creeds of the Churches*. Other works such as Jaroslav Pelikan's multivolume study of *The Christian Tradition* offer an understanding of Christian doctrine from a chronological and developmental point of view. Beyond these lie the immense bodies of religious reflection that should be called theology proper, that is, critical reflection on the doctrines historically taught in Christian communities.

I conclude (as a Methodist should) with an exhortation and a benediction. The exhortation is to work hard at the business of understanding Christians of other traditions than your own. It is hard work, but you may find, I think, that other traditions can be means of grace, leading you to understand greater depths of wisdom and spirituality and also helping you to understand your own tradition in comparison with them. The benediction is to pronounce as blessed anyone who has read this far: God has certainly given you a gift of perseverance. To the gifts you have also received, I add my sincerest blessings.

Appendix 1

List of Denominations

The following list is far from exhaustive, but it includes a number of specific denominations, indicating the chapter of this book where their traditions will be found and the tradition, possibly subtradition, or tradition family in which they will be discussed.

Denomination	Chapter	Tradition
Advent Christian Church	4	Adventist
Assyrian Church of the East	1 (Interlude 1 A)	Nestorian
African Methodist Episcopal Church	4	Wesleyan/Methodist
African Methodist Episcopal Zion Church	4	Wesleyan/Methodist
Albanian Orthodox Archdiocese in America	1	Eastern Orthodox
Albanian Orthodox Diocese of America	1	Eastern Orthodox
Allegheny Wesleyan Methodist Connection	4	Wesleyan/Methodist
Amana Church Society	4	Anabaptist (Mennonite)
American Baptist Association	4	Baptist
American Baptist Churches in the U.S.A.	4	Baptist
American Carpatho-Russian Orthodox Greek Catholic Church	1	Eastern Orthodox
Anglican Church of Australia	3	Anglican
Anglican Church of Canada	3	Anglican
Anglican Church in Japan	3	Anglican
Antiochian Orthodox Christian Archdiocese of North America	1	Eastern Orthodox
Apostolic Catholic Assyrian Church of the East	1 (Interlude 1 A)	Nestorian
Apostolic Lutheran Church of America	3	Lutheran
Armenian Apostolic Church of America	1 (Interlude 1 B)	Oriental Orthodox
Armenian Church of America, Diocese of the	1 (Interlude 1 B)	Oriental Orthodox
Assemblies of God	4	Pentecostal (Two-Blessing)
Assemblies of God International Fellowship (Independent)	4	Pentecostal
Associate Reformed Presbyterian Church (General Synod)	3	Reformed (Presbyterian)
Bangladesh Baptist Sangha	4	Baptist
Baptist Bible Fellowship International	4	Baptist
Baptist Convention of Nicaragua	4	Baptist
Baptist General Conference	4	Baptist
Baptist Missionary Association of America	4	Baptist
Baptist Union of Denmark	4	Baptist

Denomination	Chapter	Tradition
Baptist Union of Great Britain and Ireland	4	Baptist
Baptist Union of Hungary	4	Baptist
Baptist Union of New Zealand	4	Baptist
Beachy Amish Mennonite Churches	4	Anabaptist (Mennonite)
Bengal-Orissa-Bihar Baptist Convention	4	Baptist
Brethren Church (Ashland, Ohio)	4	Anabaptist and Baptist
Bulgarian Eastern Orthodox Church	1	Eastern Orthodox
Burma Baptist Convention	4	Baptist
Canadian Yearly Meeting of the Religious Society of Friends	4	Friends
Catholic Diocese of the Old-Catholics in Germany	2 (Interlude 2 A)	Old Catholic
Christian and Missionary Alliance	4	Holiness
Christian Brethren (also known as Plymouth Brethren)	4	Dispensationalist
Christian Church (Disciples of Christ)	4	Restorationist
Christian Churches	4	Restorationist
Christian Methodist Episcopal Church	4	Wesleyan/Methodist
Christian Reformed Church in North America	3	Reformed
Church in Wales	3	Anglican
Church in the Province of the West Indies	3	Anglican
Church of the Brethren	4	Anabaptist and Baptist
Churches of Christ	4	Restorationist
Churches of Christ in Australia	4	Restorationist
Church of Christ in Zaire (Baptist Community of Western Zaire)	4	Baptist
Church of Christ in Zaire (Community of Disciples of Christ)	4	Restorationist
Church of Christ in Zaire (Mennonite Community)	4	Anabaptist (Mennonite)
Church of Christ in Zaire (Presbyterian Community)	3	Reformed (Presbyterian)
Church of England	3	Anglican
Church of God (Anderson, Ind.)	4	Holiness
Church of God (Cleveland, Tenn.)	4	Pentecostal (Three-Blessing)
Church of God General Conference		
Church of God in Christ	4	Pentecostal (Three-Blessing)
Church of God in Christ, International	4	Pentecostal
Church of God in Christ (Mennonite)	4	Anabaptist (Mennonite)
Church of God of Prophecy	4	Pentecostal (Three-Blessing)
Church of Ireland	3	Anglican
Church of Jesus Christ of Latter-day Saints	5 (Interlude 5 C)	Mormon
Church of Scotland	3	Reformed (Presbyterian)
Church of the Lutheran Brethren of America	3	Lutheran
Church of the Lutheran Confession	3	Lutheran
Church of the Nazarene	4	Holiness
Church of North India	3	United

Denomination	Chapter	Tradition
Church of Norway	3	Lutheran
Church of the Province of Burma	3	Anglican
Church of the Province of Burundi, Rwanda, and Zaire	3	Anglican
Church of the Province of Central Africa	3	Anglican
Church of the Province of Kenya	3	Anglican
Church of the Province of New Zealand	3	Anglican
Church of the Province of Nigeria	3	Anglican
Church of the Province of Southern Africa	3	Anglican
Church of the Province of Tanzania	3	Anglican
Church of the Province of the Indian Ocean	3	Anglican
Congregational Christian Churches, National Association	3	Reformed (Congregationalist)
Congregational Christian Church in American Samoa	3	Reformed (Congregationalist)
Congregational Christian Church in Samoa	3	Reformed (Congregationalist)
Congregational Holiness Church	4	Holiness
Congregational Union of Scotland	3	Reformed (Congregationalist)
Conservative Baptist Association of America	4	Baptist
Conservative Congregational Christian Conference	3	Reformed (Congregationalist)
Conservative Lutheran Association	3	Lutheran
Coptic Orthodox Church	1 (Interlude 1 B)	Oriental Orthodox
Cumberland Presbyterian Church	3	Reformed (Presbyterian)
Cumberland Presbyterian Church in America	3	Reformed (Presbyterian)
Duck River (and Kindred) Associations of Baptists	4	Baptist
Ecumenical Patriarchate of Constantinople	1	Eastern Orthodox
Elim Fellowship	4	Pentecostal
Episcopal Church (USA)	3	Anglican
Episcopal Church in Jerusalem and the Middle East	3	Anglican
Episcopal Church of Brazil	3	Anglican
Estonian Evangelical Lutheran Church	3	Lutheran
Estonian Evangelical Lutheran Church (Russia)	3	Lutheran
Estonian Evangelical Lutheran Church (Sweden)	3	Lutheran
Ethiopian Orthodox Church	1 (Interlude 1 B)	Oriental Orthodox
European Continental Province of the Moravian Church	4	Moravian
Evangelical Baptist Union of Italy	4	Baptist
Evangelical Church in Baden	3	Lutheran
Evangelical Church in Berlin-Brandenburg	3	Lutheran
Evangelical Church in Germany	3	Lutheran
Evangelical Church in Hessen and Nassau	3	Lutheran
Evangelical Church in Rhineland	3	Lutheran
Evangelical Church of Germany	3	Lutheran
Evangelical Church of Greifswald	3	Lutheran

Denomination	Chapter	Tradition
Evangelical Church of Kurhessen-Waldeck	3	Lutheran
Evangelical Church of Lutheran Confession in Brazil	3	Lutheran
Evangelical Church of the Augsburg Confession in the People's Republic of Poland	3	Lutheran
Evangelical Church of the Augsburg Confession in the Socialist Republic of Romania	3	Lutheran
Evangelical Church of the Augsburg Confession of Alsace and Lorraine	3	Lutheran
Evangelical Church of the Church Province of Saxony	3	Lutheran
Evangelical Church of the Goerlitz Church Territory	3	Lutheran
Evangelical Church of the Palatinate	3	Lutheran
Evangelical Church of Westphalia	3	Lutheran
Evangelical Friends International- North America Region	4	Friends
Evangelical Lutheran Church in America	3	Lutheran
Evangelical Lutheran Church in Bavaria	3	Lutheran
Evangelical Lutheran Church in Brunswick	3	Lutheran
Evangelical Lutheran Church in Canada	3	Lutheran
Evangelical Lutheran Church in Chile	3	Lutheran
Evangelical Lutheran Church in Oldenburg	3	Lutheran
Evangelical Lutheran Church in Southern Africa	3	Lutheran
Evangelical Lutheran Church in Tanzania	3	Lutheran
Evangelical Lutheran Church in The Kingdom of the Netherlands	3	Lutheran
Evangelical Lutheran Church in Thuringia	3	Lutheran
Evangelical Lutheran Church of Denmark	3	Lutheran
Evangelical Lutheran Church of Finland	3	Lutheran
Evangelical Lutheran Church of France	3	Lutheran
Evangelical Lutheran Church of Hanover	3	Lutheran
Evangelical Lutheran Church of Iceland	3	Lutheran
Evangelical Lutheran Church of Latvia	3	Lutheran
Evangelical Lutheran Church of Latvia in Exile	3	Lutheran
Evangelical Lutheran Church of Mecklenburg	3	Lutheran
Evangelical Lutheran Church of Saxony	3	Lutheran
Evangelical Lutheran Church of Schaumburg-Lippe	3	Lutheran
Evangelical Lutheran Church of Württemberg	3	Lutheran
Evangelical Lutheran Synod	3	Lutheran
Evangelical Mennonite Church	4	Anabaptist (Mennonite)
Evangelical Methodist Church	4	Wesleyan/Methodist
Evangelical Methodist Church in Bolivia	4	Wesleyan/Methodist
Evangelical Methodist Church in the Philippines	4	Wesleyan/Methodist
Evangelical Methodist Church in Uruguay	4	Wesleyan/Methodist
Evangelical Methodist Church of Argentina	4	Wesleyan/Methodist
Evangelical Methodist Church of Costa Rica	4	Wesleyan/Methodist

Denomination	Chapter	Tradition
Evangelical Methodist Church of Italy	4	Wesleyan/Methodist
Evangelical Presbyterian Church	3	Reformed (Presbyterian)
Evangelical Presbyterian Church, Ghana	3	Reformed (Presbyterian)
Evangelical Presbyterian Church in South Africa	3	Reformed (Presbyterian)
Evangelical Presbyterian Church of Portugal	3	Reformed (Presbyterian)
Evangelical Reformed Church in North-West Germany	3	Union
Evangelical Synodal Presbyterial Church of the Augsburg Confession in the Socialist Republic of Romania	3	Lutheran
Fire Baptized Holiness Church (Wesleyan)	4	Wesleyan/Methodist and Holiness
Free Lutheran Congregations, The Association of	3	Lutheran
Free Methodist Church of North America	4	Wesleyan/Methodist
Free Wesleyan Church of Tonga	4	Wesleyan/Methodist
Free Will Baptists, National Association of	4	Baptist
Friends General Conference	4	Friends
Friends United Meeting	4	Friends
Full Gospel Assemblies International	4	Pentecostal
Full Gospel Fellowship of Churches and Ministers International	4	Pentecostal
Fundamental Methodist Church, Inc.	4	Wesleyan/Methodist
General Association of Regular Baptist Churches	4	Baptist
General Baptists (General Association of)	4	Baptist
General Conference of the Evangelical Baptist Church, Inc.	4	Baptist
General Mennonite Society (Netherlands)	4	Anabaptist (Mennonite)
General Six-Principle Baptists	4	Baptist
Georgian Orthodox-Apostolic Church	1	Eastern Orthodox
Greek Orthodox Archdiocese of North and South America	1	Eastern Orthodox
Greek Orthodox Patriarchate of Alexandria and All Africa	1	Eastern Orthodox
Greek Orthodox Patriarchate of Antioch and all the East	1	Eastern Orthodox
Greek Orthodox Patriarchate of Jerusalem	1	Eastern Orthodox
Holiness Church of God, Inc.	4	Holiness
Hutterian Brethren	4	Anabaptist
International Pentecostal Holiness Church	4	Pentecostal (Three-Blessing)
Jehovah's Witnesses	5 (Interlude 5 B)	Jehovah's Witnesses
Joint Board of the Moravian Church in Tanzania	4	Moravian
Korean Methodist Church	4	Wesleyan/Methodist
Korean Presbyterian Church in America, General Assembly of the	3	Reformed (Presbyterian)
Latin American Reformed Church (Brazil)	3	Reformed
Liberty Baptist Fellowship	4	Baptist
Lutheran Church—Missouri Synod	3	Lutheran

Denomination	Chapter	Tradition
Lutheran Churches, The American Association of	3	Lutheran
Lutheran Church in Hungary	3	Lutheran
Lutheran Church in Liberia	3	Lutheran
Malagasy Lutheran Church	3	Lutheran
Malankara Orthodox Syrian Church	1	Eastern Orthodox
Mar Thoma Syrian Church of Malabar	1 (Interlude 1 C)	Mar Thoma
Mennonite Brethren Churches, The Conference of	4	Anabaptist (Mennonite)
Mennonite Church	4	Anabaptist (Mennonite)
Mennonite Church, The General Conference	4	Anabaptist (Mennonite)
Methodist Church (United Kingdom)	4	Wesleyan/Methodist
Methodist Church, Ghana	4	Wesleyan/Methodist
Methodist Church in Brazil	4	Wesleyan/Methodist
Methodist Church in Cuba	4	Wesleyan/Methodist
Methodist Church in Fiji	4	Wesleyan/Methodist
Methodist Church in India	4	Wesleyan/Methodist
Methodist Church in Ireland	4	Wesleyan/Methodist
Methodist Church in Kenya	4	Wesleyan/Methodist
Methodist Church in Malaysia	4	Wesleyan/Methodist
Methodist Church in Samoa	4	Wesleyan/Methodist
Methodist Church in Singapore	4	Wesleyan/Methodist
Methodist Church in Sri Lanka	4	Wesleyan/Methodist
Methodist Church in the Caribbean and the Americas	4	Wesleyan/Methodist
Methodist Church in Zimbabwe	4	Wesleyan/Methodist
Methodist Church Nigeria	4	Wesleyan/Methodist
Methodist Church of Chile	4	Wesleyan/Methodist
Methodist Church of Mexico	4	Wesleyan/Methodist
Methodist Church of New Zealand	4	Wesleyan/Methodist
Methodist Church of Peru	4	Wesleyan/Methodist
Methodist Church of Southern Africa	4	Wesleyan/Methodist
Methodist Church Sierra Leone	4	Wesleyan/Methodist
Moravian Church in America (Unitas Fratrum)	4	Moravian
Moravian Church, Eastern West Indies Province	4	Moravian
Moravian Church in Great Britain and Ireland	4	Moravian
Moravian Church in Jamaica	4	Moravian
Moravian Church in South Africa	4	Moravian
Moravian Church in Surinam	4	Moravian
National Missionary Baptist Convention of America	4	Baptist
National Baptist Convention of America	4	Baptist
National Baptist Convention, U.S.A., Inc.	4	Baptist
National Primitive Baptist Convention, Inc.	4	Baptist
Netherlands Reformed Church	3	Reformed
Netherlands Reformed Congregations	3	Reformed
Nigerian Baptist Convention	4	Baptist

Denomination	Chapter	Tradition
North American Baptist Conference	4	Baptist
North American Old Roman Catholic Church	2 (Interlude 2 A)	Old Catholic
North Elbian Evangelical Lutheran Church	3	Lutheran
Old Catholic Church in Austria	2 (Interlude 2 A)	Old Catholic
Old Catholic Church of Switzerland	2 (Interlude 2 A)	Old Catholic
Old Catholic Church of the Netherlands	2 (Interlude 2 A)	Old Catholic
Old Catholic Mariavite Church in Poland	2 (Interlude 2 A)	Old Catholic
Old German Baptist Brethren	4	Baptist
Old Order Amish Church	4	Anabaptist (Mennonite)
Old Order (Wisler) Mennonite Church	4	Anabaptist (Mennonite)
Orthodox Church in America	1	Eastern Orthodox
Orthodox Church of Czechoslovakia	1	Eastern Orthodox
Orthodox Church of Finland	1	Eastern Orthodox
Orthodox Presbyterian Church	3	Reformed (Presbyterian)
Pentecostal Assemblies of the World, Inc.	4	Pentecostal
Pentecostal Church of Chile	4	Pentecostal
Pentecostal Church of God	4	Pentecostal
Pentecostal Fire-Baptized Holiness Church	4	Pentecostal
Pentecostal Free Will Baptist Church, Inc.	4	Pentecostal
Pentecostal Mission Church (Chile)	4	Pentecostal
Plymouth Brethren	*see* "Christian Brethren"	
Polish Catholic Church in Poland	2 (Interlude 2 A)	Polish Catholic
Polish National Catholic Church of America	2 (Interlude 2 A)	Polish Catholic
Polish National Catholic Church (USA)	2 (Interlude 2 A)	Polish Catholic
Polish Orthodox Church	1	Eastern Orthodox
Presbyterian Church in America	3	Reformed (Presbyterian)
Presbyterian Church in Cameroon	3	Reformed (Presbyterian)
Presbyterian Church in Canada	3	Reformed (Presbyterian)
Presbyterian Church in Taiwan	3	Reformed (Presbyterian)
Presbyterian Church in Trinidad and Grenada	3	Reformed (Presbyterian)
Presbyterian Church in the Republic of Korea	3	Reformed (Presbyterian)
Presbyterian Church in the Sudan	3	Reformed (Presbyterian)
Presbyterian Church in the United States of America	3	Reformed (Presbyterian)
Presbyterian Church of Africa	3	Reformed (Presbyterian)
Presbyterian Church of Cameroon	3	Reformed (Presbyterian)
Presbyterian Church of East Africa	3	Reformed (Presbyterian)
Presbyterian Church of Ghana	3	Reformed (Presbyterian)
Presbyterian Church of Korea (Tong-Hap)	3	Reformed (Presbyterian)
Presbyterian Church of Mozambique	3	Reformed (Presbyterian)
Presbyterian Church of New Zealand	3	Reformed (Presbyterian)
Presbyterian Church of Nigeria	3	Reformed (Presbyterian)
Presbyterian Church of Rwanda	3	Reformed (Presbyterian)
Presbyterian Church of Southern Africa	3	Reformed (Presbyterian)

Denomination	Chapter	Tradition
Presbyterian Church of Vanuatu	3	Reformed (Presbyterian)
Presbyterian Church of Wales	3	Reformed (Presbyterian)
Presbyterian Church (U.S.A.)	3	Reformed (Presbyterian)
Presbyterian-Reformed Church in Cuba	3	Reformed (Presbyterian)
Primitive Baptists	4	Baptist
Primitive Methodist Church in the U.S.A.	4	Wesleyan/Methodist
Progressive National Baptist Convention, Inc.	4	Baptist
Protestant Conference (Lutheran), Inc.	3	Lutheran
Protestant Methodist Church in the People's Republic of Benin	4	Wesleyan/Methodist
Protestant Reformed Churches in America	3	Reformed
Province of the Episcopal Church of the Sudan	3	Anglican
Reformed Christian Church in Slovakia	3	Reformed
Reformed Church in America	3	Reformed
Reformed Church in Hungary	3	Reformed
Reformed Church in Yugoslavia	3	Reformed
Reformed Church in the United States	3	Reformed
Reformed Church of Alsace and Lorraine	3	Reformed
Reformed Church of Equatorial Guinea	3	Reformed
Reformed Church of France	3	Reformed
Reformed Church of Romania	3	Reformed
Reformed Churches in the Netherlands	3	Reformed
Reformed Episcopal Church	3	Anglican and Reformed
Reformed Methodist Union Episcopal Church	4	Wesleyan/Methodist
Reformed Presbyterian Church in Southern Africa	3	Reformed (Presbyterian)
Reformed Presbyterian Church of North America	3	Reformed (Presbyterian)
Religious Society of Friends (Conservative)	4	Friends
Religious Society of Friends: Friends General Conference (USA)	4	Friends
Religious Society of Friends: Friends United Meeting (USA)	4	Friends
Religious Society of Friends (Unaffiliated Meetings)	4	Friends
Remonstrant Brotherhood (Netherlands)	3	Reformed
Roman Catholic Church	2	Roman Catholic
Romanian Orthodox Church	1	Eastern Orthodox
Romanian Orthodox Church in America	1	Eastern Orthodox
Romanian Orthodox Episcopate of America	1	Eastern Orthodox
Russian Old Ritualists	1 (Interlude 1 D)	Old Ritualists
Russian Orthodox Church	1	Eastern Orthodox
Russian Orthodox Church in the U.S.A., Patriarchal Parishes of the	1	Eastern Orthodox
Russian Orthodox Church Outside of Russia	1	Eastern Orthodox
Salvation Army	4	Holiness
Samavesam of Telugu Baptist Churches	4	Baptist
Scottish Episcopal Church	3	Anglican
Separate Baptists in Christ	4	Baptist
Serbian Orthodox Church	1	Eastern Orthodox

Denomination	Chapter	Tradition
Serbian Orthodox Church in the U.S.A. and Canada	1	Eastern Orthodox
Seventh-day Adventist Church	4	Adventist
Seventh Day Baptist General Conference, USA and Canada	4	Baptist
Silesian Evangelical Church of the Augsburg Confession	3	Lutheran
Slovak Evangelical Church of the Augsburg Confession in the CSSR	3	Lutheran
Slovak Evangelical Church of the Augsburg Confession in Yugoslavia	3	Lutheran
Southern Baptist Convention	4	Baptist
Southern Methodist Church	4	Wesleyan/Methodist
Sovereign Grace Baptists	4	Baptist
Syrian Orthodox Church of Antioch (Archdiocese of the United States and Canada)	1	Eastern Orthodox
Union of Baptist Churches of Cameroon	4	Baptist
Union of Evangelical Christian Baptists of USSR	4	Baptist
United Church of Canada	3	United
United Church of Christ (USA)	3	United
United Church of Christ in Japan	3	United
United Evangelical Lutheran Church (Argentina)	3	Lutheran
United German Mennonite Congregations	4	Anabaptist (Mennonite)
United Holy Church of America, Inc.	4	Pentecostal (Three-Blessing)
United Methodist Church	4	Wesleyan/Methodist
United Pentecostal Church International	4	Pentecostal
United Presbyterian Church of Brazil	3	Reformed (Presbyterian)
United Presbyterian Church of Pakistan	3	Reformed (Presbyterian)
United Reformed Church in the United Kingdom	3	Reformed
Uniting Church in Australia	3	United
Unity of the Brethren	4	Moravian
Waldensian Church	4	Reformed
Wesleyan Church	4	Wesleyan/Methodist
Wesleyan Holiness Association of Churches	4	Wesleyan/Methodist and Holiness
Wisconsin Evangelical Lutheran Synod	3	Lutheran

Appendix 2

Sequences for Anglican and Protestant Tradition Families

Growth in Holiness	4.3.5
Life beyond Death	4.3.7
The Church	4.4.1
Synodal Polity	4.4.2.b
Sacraments as Signs of Faith	4.4.3.b
Believer's Baptism	4.4.4.b
The Lord's Supper as a Sign of Faith and Fellowship	4.4.5.b

Anglican Sequence

Anglican Origins	3.0.4
The Authority of Scripture	3.1.1
Anglican Interpretation of Scripture	3.1.2.c
Effects of Protestant Liberalism	3.1.2.d
Belief in the Trinity	3.2.1
Divine and Human Natures of Christ	3.2.2
Mary the Mother of Jesus	3.2.3
Original Sin	3.3.1
Loss of Human Free Will in the Fall	3.3.2
Predestination and Its Alternatives	3.3.3.b
Justification by Faith	3.3.4
Good Works following Justification	3.3.5
Life beyond Death	3.3.7
The Church	3.4.1
Episcopal Polity	3.4.2.a
Sacraments	3.4.3
Baptism	3.4.3.1
Eucharist: Corporeal Presence/Virtualism and Receptionism	3.4.3.2.a *or* 3.4.3.2.b

Baptist Sequence

Baptist Origins	4.0.3
African-American Baptist Denominations	4.0.7
Priority of Scripture	4.1.1.a
Fundamentalist Interpretation of Scripture	4.1.1.b (Some)
Use of Creeds	4.1.3.a
Civil Government	4.1.4.b
Belief in the Trinity	4.2.1.a
Divine and Human in Christ	4.2.2
Mary the Mother of Jesus	4.2.4
The Human Need for Grace	4.3.1
Predestination (Particular or Regular Baptists)/Universal	4.3.2.a *or*
Availability of Grace (General or Free-Will Baptists)	4.3.2.b

Congregational Sequence

Dispensationalist Sequence

Belief in the Trinity	4.2.1.a
Divine and Human in Christ	4.2.2
The Second Coming of Christ	4.2.2.a
Mary the Mother of Jesus	4.2.4
The Human Need for Grace	4.3.1
Predestination	4.3.2.a
Justification by Faith	4.3.4.a
Growth in Holiness	4.3.5
Eternal Security of Believers	4.3.6.a
Life beyond Death	4.3.7
The Church	4.4.1
Congregational Polity	4.4.2.c
Sacraments as Signs of Faith	4.4.3.b
Believer's Baptism	4.4.4.b
The Lord's Supper as a Sign of Faith and Fellowship	4.4.5.b

Friends (Quaker) Sequence

Quaker Origins	4.0.3
Religious Experience in the Interpretation of the Bible	4.1.2.a
Unique Authority of Religious Experience for Quakers	4.1.2.c
Pacifism and Objection to Titles of Superiority	4.1.4.a
Belief in the Trinity	4.2.1.a
Divine and Human in Christ	4.2.2
Mary the Mother of Jesus	4.2.4
The Human Need for Grace	4.3.1
Universal Availability of Grace	4.3.2.b
Repentance	4.3.3
Faith and Assurance	4.3.4.a
Growth in Holiness	4.3.5
Life beyond Death	4.3.7
The Church	4.4.1
Synodal Polity	4.4.2.b
Rejection of Outward Sacraments	4.4.3.c

Holiness Sequence

Origins of Holiness Denominations	4.0.7
Priority of Scripture	4.1.1.a
Fundamentalist Interpretation of Scripture	4.1.1.b [Frequently]
Religious Experience in the Interpretation of the Bible	4.1.2.a
Use of Creeds	4.1.3.a
Civil Government	4.1.4.b

Lutheran Sequence

Methodist/Wesleyan Sequence

Priority of Scripture	4.1.1.a
Religious Experience in the Interpretation of the Bible	4.1.2.a
Use of Tradition, Reason, and Experience in Interpretation of the Bible	4.1.2.b
Use of Creeds	4.1.3.a
Civil Government	4.1.4.b
Belief in the Trinity	4.2.1.a
Divine and Human in Christ	4.2.2
The Present Activity of the Holy Spirit	4.2.3
Mary the Mother of Jesus	4.2.4
The Human Need for Grace	4.3.1
Universal Availability of Grace	4.3.2.b
Repentance	4.3.3
Faith and Assurance	4.3.4.a
Growth in Holiness	4.3.5
Entire Sanctification or Christian Perfection	4.3.6.b
Life beyond Death	4.3.7
The Church	4.4.1
Methodist Connectional Polity	4.4.2.a
Sacraments as Means of Grace	4.4.3.a
Baptism	4.4.4.a
The Lord's Supper as a Means of Grace	4.4.5.a

Moravian Sequence

Origins of Moravianism	4.0.4
Priority of Scripture	4.1.1.a
Religious Experience in the Interpretation of the Bible	4.1.2.a
Use of Tradition in Interpretation of the Bible	4.1.2.b
Use of Creeds	4.1.3.a
Civil Government	4.1.4.b
Belief in the Trinity	4.2.1.a
Divine and Human in Christ	4.2.2
The Present Activity of the Holy Spirit	4.2.3
Mary the Mother of Jesus	4.2.4
The Human Need for Grace	4.3.1
Universal Availability of Grace	4.3.2.b
Repentance	4.3.3
Faith and Assurance	4.3.4.a
Growth in Holiness	4.3.5
Life beyond Death	4.3.7
The Church	4.4.1
Connectional Polity	4.4.2.b

Restorationist Sequence

Appendix 3

A Doctrinal Comparative Schema

The following table is organized by topics and allows users to follow topics across the boundaries of the traditions considered in this book. The numbers in parentheses indicate that the topic is discussed in the chapter referred to, but as a subpoint in the chapter and not as the main point.

Topic	Eastern Orthodox	Roman Catholic	Reformation and Union	Evangelical and Free	Ecumenical Consensus
Teachings about Religious Authority					
Tradition as Embracing Scripture	1.1.1				
Tradition and Scripture Complementing Each Other	1.1.2	2.1.1			
The Bible as Primary Authority			3.1.1 3.1.2.a 3.1.2.b 3.1.2.c	4.1.1.a	5.2.1
Biblical Infallibility			(3.1.2.b)	4.1.1.b	
Authority of Ecumenical Councils	1.1.2	2.1.5	(3.1.2.c)	(4.1.2.b)	
Authority of Later Traditions	1.1.3	(2.1.5)	3.1.2.a 3.1.2.b 3.1.2.c	(4.1.2.b)	
The Use of Creeds	(1.1.3)	(2.1.5)	(3.1.2.a–c)	4.1.3.a 4.1.3.b	
Role of Bishops in Interpreting Scripture	(1.1.3)	2.1.2			
The Teaching Office of the Bishop of Rome		2.1.3			
Papal Infallibility		2.1.4			
The Inward Witness of the Spirit Confirming Scriptural Truth			3.1.2.b	4.1.2.a 4.1.2.c	
The Authority of Civil Governments				4.1.4.a 4.1.4.b	
Reason and Experience as Authority			3.1.2.d	4.1.2.b	

(table continues.)

312

(table continued.)

Topic	Eastern Orthodox	Roman Catholic	Reformation and Union	Evangelical and Free	Ecumenical Consensus
Teachings about God and Christ					
God as Holy Trinity	1.2.1	2.2.1	3.2.1	4.2.1.a	5.2.2.1
Oneness Pentecostal Assertion of God's Unity				4.2.1.b	
The Double Procession of the Holy Spirit		2.2.2	(3.2.1)	(4.2.1.a)	
Christ as One Person in Two Natures	1.2.2	2.2.3	3.2.2	4.2.2	5.2.2.2
The Second Coming of Christ				4.2.2.a	
The Present Activity of the Holy Spirit				4.2.3	
Teachings about Mary the Mother of Jesus	1.2.3	2.2.4	3.2.3	4.2.4	
Teachings about Human Nature and Salvation					
Human Nature	1.3.1	2.3.1	3.3.1	4.3.1	5.2.3
The Fall of Humankind, Original Sin	1.3.2	2.3.1	3.3.1	4.3.1	
Reason and Freedom after the Fall	1.3.3	2.3.2	3.3.2	(4.3.1)	
The Goal of Human Life as Divinization	1.3.4				
The Human Need for Grace	(1.3.3)	2.3.3	(3.3.2)	(4.3.1)	5.2.3
Predestination		(2.3.3)	3.3.3.a 3.3.3.b	4.3.2.a 4.3.2.b	
Repentance		(2.3.4)	(3.3.4)	4.3.3	
Justification		2.3.4	3.3.4	4.3.4.a 4.3.4.b	
The Role of Sacraments in Christian Life	1.3.5	2.3.6			
Growth in the Christian Life, Sanctification	1.3.6	2.3.4	3.3.5	4.3.5	
Entire Sanctification	(1.3.4)			4.3.6.b (4.3.6.c)	
Holy Spirit Baptism (Pentecostal)				4.3.6.c 4.3.6.d	

(table continues.)

(table continued.)

Topic	Eastern Orthodox	Roman Catholic	Reformation and Union	Evangelical and Free	Ecumenical Consensus
The Role of Merit in Human Salvation		2.3.5			
Perseverance of the Saints			3.3.6	4.3.6.a	
States of Persons after Death	1.3.7	2.3.7	3.3.7	4.3.7	

Teachings about Church, Ministry, and Sacraments

Topic	Eastern Orthodox	Roman Catholic	Reformation and Union	Evangelical and Free	Ecumenical Consensus
The Nature of the Church	1.4.1	2.4.1	3.4.1	4.4.1	5.2.4.1
Necessity of Discipline			3.4.1.a		
The Congregational Principle			3.4.1.b		
The Necessity of the Church for Salvation	(1.4.1)	2.4.2			
The Hierarchical Nature of the Church, and Episcopal Polity	1.4.2	2.4.3	3.4.2.a	(4.4.2.a)	
Presbyterian Polity			3.4.2.b	4.4.2.a 4.4.2.b	
Congregational Polity			3.4.2.c	4.4.2.c	
Other Forms of Polity			3.4.2.d		
Orders of Ministry	(1.4.2)	2.4.4	(3.4.2.a) (3.4.2.b) (3.4.2.c) (3.4.2.d)	(4.4.2.a) (4.4.2.b) (4.4.2.c)	
Use of Religious Images or Icons	1.4.3				
Definition of Sacraments or "Mysteries"	1.4.4	2.4.5	3.4.3	4.4.3.a 4.4.3.b 4.4.3.c	5.2.4.1
Baptism	1.4.5	2.4.5.1	3.4.3.1	4.4.4.a 4.4.4.b	5.2.4.2
Confirmation (Chrismation)	(1.4.4)	2.4.5.2	(3.4.3)		
The Eucharist or Lord's Supper	1.4.6	2.4.5.3	3.4.3.2.a 3.4.3.2.b 3.4.3.2.c	4.4.5.a 4.4.5.b	5.2.4.3
Penance and Reconciliation	(1.4.4)	2.4.5.4	(3.4.3)		
Anointing of the Sick	(1.4.4)	2.4.5.5	(3.4.3)		
Marriage	(1.4.4)	2.4.5.6	(3.4.3)		
Holy Orders	(1.4.4)	2.4.5.7	(3.4.3)		

Glossary

Absolution. The formal proclamation of "acquittal" or release from the guilt of particular sins (Latin *absolutio*, "acquittal").

Adventist. Stressing the imminent second coming of Christ (Latin *adventus*, "coming").

Amissible. Capable of being lost. Those who teach that the grace of justification is amissible differ with those who teach the eternal security of believers.

Anabaptist. Literally "rebaptizers," the term refers to a variety of groups that emerged during the 1500s and practiced believer's baptism, held to the Free Church principle of a completely voluntary church, and (for most groups after the 1540s) advocated pacifism. Members of these churches accept the term "Anabaptist" only grudgingly, since in their belief they do not recognize the validity of infant baptisms and so do not understand themselves as actually "rebaptizing."

Anathema. A "curse" or condemnation.

Anglican. Specifically, this term refers to the Church of England but more broadly describes the churches historically derived from or in communion with the Church of England.

Anglo-Catholic. Anglicans inclined to more Catholic liturgy and doctrine.

Anointing, Anointing of the Sick. (1) Anointing itself simply denotes the application of oil, customary in ancient cultures as a sign of purification (oil was used for cleansing) or as a sign that a person had been set apart for a particular task (such as the anointing of a priest, prophet or ruler). (2) The anointing of the sick refers to the mystery or sacrament or simply the church practice of anointing those who are seriously ill, accompanied by prayers for their healing. Chrismation (q.v.) is also an anointing.

Antidoron. Greek "after-gift"; the blessed but unconsecrated bread that in Orthodox eucharistic practice is shared after the Eucharist proper, a relic of the ancient love feast.

Apocrypha. The books included in Orthodox and Catholic Bibles that existed in the Greek text (*Septuagint*) and Latin text (*Vulgate*) of the Bible but not in the Hebrew and which were consequently not included in Protestant Bibles. Also referred to as *Deuterocanonical Books*.

Apostolic. (1) The general meaning of the term is faithfulness to the teaching and practice of the apostles. (2) A more specific usage is as a title claimed by Oneness Pentecostal churches (q.v.).

Arianism. The belief that Christ was a creation of the Father and had an origin in time; the view condemned by the First Council of Nicaea (325) and the First Council of Constantinople (381).

315

Assumption of the Blessed Virgin Mary. Literally, "taking up"; the assumption of the Blessed Virgin Mary is the teaching that Mary was taken up or "assumed" into heaven at the end of her earthly life.

Baptist. Churches derived originally from English Separatism in the early 1600s that practice believer's baptism only.

Baptistery. A place for baptisms, especially baptisms performed by immersion.

Believer's Baptism. Baptism performed only upon profession of Christian faith, as contrasted with infant baptism.

Cardinal. One of the "college" or council of Roman Catholic clergy (now all cardinals are bishops) who are called together to elect a Pope.

Catechesis, Catechism. Teaching or instruction for those who are candidates for Christian baptism or confirmation.

Catholic. (1) The most general sense of the term is "universal" (Greek *kath' holos*, "through the whole"), that is, reflecting Christianity through the whole world and also reflecting the wholeness of Christian teaching. (2) Specifically, when capitalized, the term can be used as a shorthand substitute for "Roman Catholic."

Chalcedon. The Council of Chalcedon (451) is reckoned as the Fourth Ecumenical Council. This council defined the doctrine of one Person in two natures of Christ.

Chrismation. Literally "anointing," the term refers to the anointing following baptism in which the gift of the Holy Spirit is prayed for; when it became customary to postpone it until after catechesis in the Western church, chrismation became confirmation (q.v.). Chrismation is regarded as one of the seven mysteries acknowledged by Orthodox churches.

Conciliarism. The movement in the Western church in the late Middle Ages that sought the reform of the church (and the papacy) through church councils.

Confessional orthodoxy. Movements to define Reformed and Lutheran faith by careful explication of doctrinal statements, especially prominent in the 1600s and then again in the early 1800s.

Confirmation. The laying on of hands and prayer for the gift of the Holy Spirit on those who have been baptized and catechized; in the Western church confirmation takes the place of chrismation. It is regarded as a sacrament by Roman Catholics and is practiced by many Protestant churches, including Lutheran, Presbyterian, Congregational, and Anglican churches.

Congregational, Congregationalist. (1) In the broadest sense (with a lowercase c), congregationalism denotes the form of church polity characterized by the independence of local congregations. (2) In a more particular sense, the term denotes a family of Reformed churches distinguished by this polity.

Consistory. The term is used to describe a variety of church assemblies or courts. In presbyterian polity, "consistory" or "consistory court" now denotes the local church session (q.v.), although early on it could denote the church judicatory for a whole city (like the consistory of Geneva over which Calvin presided).

Constantinople. The capital of the Eastern Roman (Byzantine) Empire, present-day Istanbul. The city was the venue for three of the seven Ecumenical Councils, the First Council of Constantinople (A.D. 381), the Second Council of Constantinople (A.D. 553), and the Third Council of Constantinople (A.D. 680).

Consubstantiation. The belief that Christ's true body and blood are present with (Latin *con*) the substance (Latin *substantia*) of bread and wine in the Eucharist.

Corporeal Presence. The specific form of eucharistic teaching maintained in Lutheran tradition that holds that Christ's true body (Latin *corpus, corporis*) is present in the *Eucharist.*

Deacon. From Greek *diakonein,* "to serve." (1) In Orthodox, Catholic, Anglican, and some Protestant churches the office of deacon is a transitional office for persons preparing to become priests. (2) The term may also denote in these same traditions a person holding a permanent office of servant ministry in the church. (3) In Presbyterian, Baptist, and some other Protestant churches, the deacon is a lay official of the local congregation, usually elected for life.

Deuterocanonical Books. Another term for the Apocrypha (q.v.).

Dispensations. The term used in some Conservative Evangelical churches to refer to discrete periods of biblical history in which specific terms for salvation have changed. This is the teaching that characterizes Dispensationalist churches.

Divinity. The nature or character of God (Latin *divus,* "divine").

Donatism. The belief prevalent in northern Africa in the fourth century A.D. that sacraments are invalid if performed by an unworthy minister (especially one who had lapsed during the times of persecution).

Dormition of the Blessed Virgin Mary. The celebration in Eastern Christian churches of the "sleeping" (Latin, *dormitio*) of Mary, that is, her death. This celebration is paralleled in the Western Church by the celebration of the Assumption.

Double Predestination. The specific form of the doctrine of predestination favored in historic Reformed teaching that maintains that God has chosen some to eternal salvation and others to eternal damnation; as contrasted with the doctrine of single predestination (q.v.).

Double Procession. The doctrine maintained in historic Western churches (Roman Catholic and Protestant) that the Holy Spirit proceeds from the Father and the Son, implied in the *filioque* clause (q.v.) of the Nicene Creed.

Ecumenical Council. A council recognized as representing the consensus of the church through the whole world (from Greek *oikoumene*, "the inhabited world"). For a list of councils regarded as ecumenical in both Eastern and Western churches, see table 1.

Ecumenical Movement. The movement between Christian churches in the twentieth century that seeks their visible unity.

Elder. The term is a direct translation of the Greek *presbuteros*, which may also be rendered "presbyter" or "priest." (1) In episcopal Methodist churches, the term elder denotes an ordained minister authorized to preside at the Eucharist, thus the equivalent of priest. (2) In Presbyterian churches ordained clergy are often recognized as "teaching elders," and there is a separate order of "ruling elders," lay members of the congregational session. (3) In many Evangelical and Free churches "elder" designates a lay office.

Election. God's act of choosing (Latin *electio*) some human beings for salvation; a corollary of the doctrine of predestination is that some human beings have been elected to salvation.

Episcopal. (1) The most basic meaning of the term is simply that which pertains to bishops (Greek *episkopos;* Latin *episcopus*). (2) In a more specific sense, a form of church polity in which bishops play a central role.

Established; Establishment. An established church is a church supported by a particular political state, and so establishment refers to state support for a church.

Eternal Security of Believers. The belief implied in the doctrine of predestination and also maintained by Baptists and others that those who have been given the grace of justification will persevere and will not finally fall away from their faith.

Eucharist. From Greek *eucharistein*, "to give thanks"; the sharing of bread and wine following Christ's command, regarded as a mystery in Orthodox churches, as a sacrament by Roman Catholics and many Protestants, or as an ordinance by some Evangelical churches. Other terms for *Eucharist* may be the Lord's Supper or Holy Communion, and Roman Catholics typically use the term "mass" to describe the celebration of the Eucharist.

Evangelical. The term is used in two discrete senses in this book: (1) "Evangelical" can denote Protestant as opposed to Roman Catholic and specifically Lutheran as opposed to Reformed. In this sense the term functions as an equivalent to the German *evangelisch* and Spanish *evan-*

gelico. (2) "Evangelical" can also denote those pietistic Protestant groups that stress the necessity of an affective experience of conversion along with a belief in the centrality of scripture. In this sense the term functions as the equivalent of the German *evangelikal* or the Spanish *evangelico conservador* ("conservative Evangelical").

Ex Cathedrā. Latin, "from the [bishop's] throne." This has particular reference to the condition under which the pope speaks in virtue of his office as supreme teacher in the church, and this is one of the conditions for an exercise of papal infallibility.

Extreme Unction. The now-outdated term that was utilized until 1973 for the sacrament of the anointing of the sick in Roman Catholicism. Under this title, the sacrament was performed only once for an individual when the individual was believed to be near death.

Filioque. Latin "and the Son." The clause added to the Nicene Creed in Western (Roman Catholic and Protestant) churches that states that the Holy Spirit proceeds from the Father "and the Son" and so asserts the doctrine of double procession (q.v.).

Free Church. A "free church" is, most technically, a church not established by a political state. More broadly the term represents those communities that stress the voluntary nature of the church; that is, that the church is a fellowship of believers who have consciously chosen to identify with that community, as opposed to membership by virtue of the fact that one is part of a Christian state or family.

Free Will. (1) The term "free will" most generally refers to the ability of human beings to choose to accept or reject Christ; however, the use of this term itself does not clarify the underlying issue of whether free will is a natural human capability or itself the gift of grace. (2) In North American Baptist circles, Free Will (capitalized) denotes specific Baptist groups who believe that Christ died for all human beings, the term denoting the same as British General Baptists and standing in contrast to Particular or Regular Baptists (qq.v.).

Fundamentalist. Conservative Evangelicals (see the second definition of Evangelical above) who define Christian faith by a list of specific necessary or fundamental doctrines, one of which is almost always a belief in the inerrancy or infallibility of scripture.

General Baptist. In British Baptist circles, General Baptist denotes specific Baptist groups who believe that Christ died for all human beings and who maintained a synodal polity, the term denoting the same as Free Will Baptists in North America and standing in contrast to Particular or Regular Baptists (qq.v.).

Glossolalia. The practice of speaking or praying in unknown tongues (from Greek *glossa*, "tongue" or "language," and *lalein*, "to speak"), a practice that characterizes Pentecostal churches.

Gnosticism. The term "Gnosticism" is used to describe a number of early Christian groups, which were not necessarily related to one another. Some characteristics associated with Gnosticism are (1) a stress on secret or esoteric knowledge (Greek, *gnosis*) as the way of salvation (as contrasted with faith), (2) belief that the creator of the material world was a demiurge or secondary god (not the god associated with Jesus Christ), (3) rejection of the Hebrew Scriptures, and (4) a christology that denied the human suffering and death of Christ.

Immaculate Conception. The belief affirmed by Roman Catholics that Mary was conceived by her parents without the taint or stain of original sin associated with human conception and birth.

Immersion. Baptism by "dipping" or "dunking," practiced by Eastern Orthodox Christians, allowed as an option by some, and insisted upon as the primitive mode of baptism by most Baptists and many other Evangelical and Free churches.

Incarnate, Incarnation. Incarnate means "in the flesh"; the incarnation is God's act of becoming human in Christ for the sake of human salvation.

Inerrant, Inerrancy. That which does not err, or the characteristic of that which does not err. The term is a linguistic equivalent of infallibility (q.v.), although inerrancy is the term preferred by Fundamentalists to describe their belief that the Bible does not err in any matter.

Infallible, Infallibility. That which does not fail, or the characteristic of that which does not fail. The term is a linguistic equivalent of inerrancy (q.v.), but is (1) the term preferred by Orthodox and Catholics in speaking of the church's infallible teaching authority (for Roman Catholics, papal infallibility is a specific exercise of the church's infallible teaching authority), and (2) the term preferred by some Evangelicals who speak of the Bible's infallibility in teaching the way of salvation but may not affirm that the Bible is inerrant in other respects (e.g., with respect to its historical or scientific claims, or perhaps its culture-specific claims).

Infant Baptism. Baptism of infants or young children incapable of mature faith, a practice formally disavowed by churches that practice believer's baptism (q.v.).

Infralapsarianism. A particular version of the doctrine of predestination that maintains that God's act of election occurred after (Latin, *infra*) or with regard to the human fall (Latin, *lapsus*) into sin.

Instrumental Cause. The cause that designates the means or instrument by which something happens; in many forms of historic Christian thought, baptism is said to be the instrumental cause of justification.

Intermediate State. Term denoting a state between death and the final judgment where believers anticipate their joy in Christ and those who rejected Christ experience torment or punishment.

Interpenetrations. The belief that all the members of the Holy Trinity operate together in all actions toward the world; the term translates the Greek *perichoresis,* which is frequently used to describe this teaching.

Jesus-Only. Or Jesus' Name Only; a designation for Oneness Pentecostal churches (q.v.).

Justification. The act by which God regards human beings as righteous (Latin, *iustus*) or forgiven.

Koinonia. Greek, "fellowship" or "communion."

Liberalism. A tendency within Protestant circles from the early 1800s that stressed the critical reception of traditional religious beliefs by the use of reason and experience, and an optimistic view of the human condition.

Logos. Greek, "Word," a designation (in John 1:1–14) for Christ's eternal nature.

Mass. A term used by Roman Catholics for the celebration of the Eucharist.

Methodist. Churches founded as a result of the Evangelical Revival of the 1700s in Great Britain. Although some Calvinistic churches have utilized the title "Methodist" (for example, the Welsh Calvinistic Methodist Church), the term is used in contemporary English almost exclusively of churches founded as a result of the evangelistic work of John and Charles Wesley.

Modalism. The belief that the members of the Trinity name only modes or activities of the one God, thus minimizing any distinction between them; also referred to as Sabellianism and Patripassianism.

Modernism. The term may be used (1) in a broad sense to denote belief in modern scientific and cultural developments (as in "Catholic Modernism"), and (2) in a somewhat more specific sense to denote cultural movements since the late 1800s that stress the need for a global culture overcoming the particularities of traditional cultures (the sense in which "Postmodern" reacts against Modernism).

Modes of Origination. The three modes by which the members of the Trinity are distinguished in their relations to one another; specifically, the Father is unbegotten, the Son is begotten, and the Spirit proceeds.

Monasticism, Monk. The rejection of secular life in favor of life devoted entirely to God, either as a solitary individual (an anchorite or hermit) or as a member of a religious community. Traditionally, monks take vows of poverty, chastity, and obedience.

Monenergism. The belief that the human and divine natures of Christ share but one (Greek, *monos*) common "energy" (Greek, *energeia*) or outward operation.

Monophysitism. The belief that in Christ there is but one (Greek, *monos*) nature (Greek, *physis*). The Monophysite belief has been carried on in churches today identified as Oriental Orthodox.

Monothelitism. The belief that the human and divine natures of Christ share but one (Greek, *monos*) common will (Greek, *thelema*).

Mortal Sin. A sin that leads to spiritual death (Latin, *mors, mortis*), as distinguished from a venial sin (q.v.).

Mystery. In Eastern Orthodox teaching, a mystery denotes a privileged moment of communion with the divine that is accompanied by an outward form; the equivalent of a sacrament in Western Christian teaching.

Nature. The term is used in two rather discrete senses. (1) In historic teaching about Christ, nature is the term that designates the integrity or distinctness of human and divine in Christ (so that two natures are affirmed in Christ, one human and one divine). (2) In historic Western teaching about human nature and salvation, nature denotes the status of human beings from birth (Latin, *natus*) or apart from the influence of grace.

Neo-Orthodoxy. Twentieth-century Protestant theological movement that stressed the critical reception of scripture and tradition in the light of contemporary historical crises, the omnipotence of God, and the fallenness of humankind.

Nestorianism. Belief condemned at the Council of Ephesus (A.D. 431) that insisted on the complete integrity of divine and human in Christ to the point of affirming two Persons in Christ, and which denied the title *Theotokos* ("God-bearer") to the Blessed Virgin Mary. The Nestorian tradition continues today in the Assyrian Church of the East.

Nicaea, Nicene. The setting for two of the seven Ecumenical Councils acknowledged by East and West, the First Council of Nicaea (A.D. 325) and the Second Council of Nicaea (A.D. 787). Nicene is the adjective formed from this place name.

Nicene Creed. In this book, the expression Nicene Creed actually denotes the creed first stated by the First Council of Nicaea in 325 but subsequently revised at the First Council of Constantinople in 381.

Novatianism. A Roman movement of the mid-third century A.D., similar to the later Donatist movement, which refused to recognize clergy who had compromised with non-Christian religious practices. Novatianists set up a rival episcopal succession in Rome.

Omnipotent, Omnipotence. Having all power (Latin *omnis*, "all," and *potens*, "powerful"); the characteristic of God, who is all powerful.

Oneness Pentecostal. Pentecostal churches characterized by their rejection of the traditional doctrine of the Trinity in favor of the belief that the Father, Son, and Holy Spirit are three temporal modes of the one God (a close parallel to ancient modalism), and characterized by their practice of baptizing "in the name of Jesus" only. Sometimes referred to as Jesus-Only or Apostolic churches.

Operations. The divine operations or "energies" are those actions of God that affect the world apart from God, as contrasted with the internal relationships between members of the Trinity.

Ordinance. The term ordinance is preferred as a term for baptism and the Eucharist in many Evangelical churches, to stress that they are carried on because Christ ordained them. The term is used in contrast to sacrament, which implies that divine grace is actually given in these events.

Ordo Salutis. Latin, "order of salvation." Evangelical churches (in the second sense defined here) described a number of patterns of the *ordo salutis*, usually involving repentance, justification, and the pursuit of holiness.

Oriental Orthodox. Churches that historically rejected the Chalcedonian Definition of Faith because of their objection to its doctrine of two natures in Christ. Armenian, Syrian, Ethiopian, Malankara (Indian) and Coptic churches are the five major ethnic (but not theological) divisions of Oriental Orthodox churches.

Original Sin. The belief that all human beings are infected with the inheritance of sin from their first parents; in Western thought original sin is specifically associated with the belief that both the guilt and the consequences of sin are inherited by every human being (with the possible exceptions of Mary and Jesus).

Orthodox. The term denotes the holding to right (Greek, *orthos*) belief or worship (Greek, *doxa*). Though claimed (with a lowercase o) by almost all Christian groups, the term with an uppercase O denotes Oriental Orthodox churches and the Eastern Orthodox churches described in chapter 1 of this book.

Pacifism. The belief held historically by Anabaptist churches and by Quakers that Christians should not engage in warfare (from Latin *pax, pacis,* "peace").

Papacy, Papal. The office of pope (papacy), or pertaining to the office of pope (papal).

Particular Baptist. In British Baptist circles, Particular Baptist denotes specific Baptist groups who believe that Christ died for the particular number of the elect and who maintained a congregational polity, the term denoting the same as Regular Baptists in North America and standing in contrast to General or Free-Will Baptists (qq.v.).

Patriarch. The bishop of one of the ancient (patriarchal) sees of Christianity, such as Jerusalem, Alexandria, Antioch, or Rome.

Patripassianism. Belief that the Father (Latin, *pater*) suffered (Latin, *passus*) in the Son; a variation of Modalism (q.v.).

Pelagianism. The belief ascribed by Augustine to the British monk Pelagius that maintains that human beings in their natural state (without the aid of divine grace) can obey God's law and be saved.

Penance. The term denotes (1) the mystery or sacrament by which a penitent individual is reconciled to the church by confession and the priest's proclamation of absolution. In a secondary sense, (2) the term may denote a particular act required by a priest, the penitent's promise to fulfill this act being a condition of the priest's proclamation of absolution.

Pentecostal. Although in its broadest sense the term denotes the season of Pentecost, when the Holy Spirit was given according to Acts 2, it specifically denotes churches that teach a baptism of the Holy Spirit accompanied by the initial evidence of speaking in unknown tongues.

Perichoresis. Greek, "interpenetration." The term is often used to refer to the doctrine of interpenetrations (q.v.).

Perpetual Virginity. The belief that Mary's virginity was preserved through the conception and birth of Jesus and forever thereafter.

Person. In historic Trinitarian theology, the term used to describe the distinctness of the three members of the Trinity, as contrasted with substance, which describes the unity of the godhead. In christology, the same term Person is used to represent the unity of Christ (the second Person of the Trinity) as contrasted with the natures of Christ, describing the distinctness of divine and human in Christ.

Polity. A form of government or governance (from Greek *polis*, "city-state").

Pontiff. An alternative designation for the pope (q.v.), derived from Latin *pontifex* (originally "bridge builder," but later used to designate the highest religious official in ancient Rome).

Pope. The term traditionally used to describe the bishop (also patriarch) of Rome (from Greek *pappas*, "father").

Postmillennial. Referring to the belief that Christ will return after (Latin, *post-*) a thousand-year period (millennium).

Postmodernism. The term denotes, in this work, cultural outlooks prevalent since the 1970s that stress the particularities of cultural traditions, in contrast to Modernism's attempt to transcend cultural particularities.

Predestination. Belief that human salvation is the result of a sovereign choice made by God alone without consideration of human merit.

Premillennial. Referring to the belief that Christ will return before (Latin, *pre-*) a thousand-year period (millennium).

Presbyter. Transliteration of the Greek *presbuteros*, "elder," which can also be translated "priest." The term generally denotes a minister ordained to celebrate the Eucharist, thus denoting the same rank as priest in Orthodox, Catholic, and some Protestant churches.

Presbyterian. (1) In its broadest sense (lowercase p) the term designates a form of church polity in which significant governing functions, including the ordination of ministers, is vested in a presbytery. (2) In its more specific sense (uppercase P), the term denotes those Reformed churches characterized by presbyterian polity.

Presbytery. Originally denoting the assembly of presbyters or elders (or priests) in an area or city, the term designates in presbyterian polity the regional governing assembly, an assembly of ministers and elders from the congregational sessions in a region. The same sort of assembly may also be designated a *classis* in some Reformed churches.

Prevenient Grace. Grace "coming before" (Latin, *preveniens*) human belief in Christ.

Priest. In Orthodox, Catholic, Anglican and some other churches, priest designates the minister who is designated to preside at the Eucharist. Derived from the Greek *presbuteros*, the terms "presbyter" and "elder" may designate the same office.

Purgatory. The intermediate state between death and the final judgment where believers are purged of remaining venial sins, according to Roman Catholic teaching.

Quadrilateral. (1) The Chicago-Lambeth Quadrilateral of 1886 and 1888 was an agreement that Anglican pursuit of visible unity with other churches rested on four principles, namely, (a) the canon of Holy Scripture, (b) the Nicene and Apostles' creeds, (c) Baptism and the Eucharist, and (d) the "historic episcopate." (2) The so-called Wesleyan Quadrilateral formulated in the *Discipline* of the United Methodist Church since 1972 recognizes (a) scripture, (b) tradition, (c) experience and (d) reason as four criteria that should guide Methodist reflection in contemporary theological issues.

Real Presence. The term, historically used to describe Anglican views of Christ's presence in the Eucharist, is problematic since (1) it originally seems to have denoted corporeal presence of Christ in the Eucharist (in this sense "real presence" was disavowed by the so-called Black Rubric of the 1552 Anglican Prayer Book); nevertheless, (2) later Anglicans (from the 1600s) affirmed the term but with a weaker meaning, essentially the same as Virtualism (q.v.). In a still further development (3) the term was utilized by Anglo-Catholics from the 1800s to denote a stronger form of belief in Christ's presence in the Eucharist, more like corporeal presence than Virtualism.

Receptionism. Belief that Christ's presence in the Eucharist is contingent on the faith of the recipient; usually conjoined with the belief in Virtualism (q.v.).

Reformed. Churches derived from the reforming efforts of Zwingli, Calvin, and their successors are designated as Reformed in contrast to Lutheran or "Evangelical" churches (in the first sense of the latter term defined here). The two large divisions of Reformed churches are Presbyterian and Congregational churches.

Regular Baptist. In North American Baptist circles, Regular Baptist denotes specific Baptist groups who believe that Christ died for the particular number of the elect and who maintained a congregational polity, the term denoting the same as Particular Baptists in Britain and standing in contrast to General or Free-Will Baptists (qq.v.).

Religious. In Roman Catholic parlance, the noun *religious* (the same form is used for singular and plural) denotes a person or persons in religious orders.

Restorationist. The American Restorationist movement grew from the efforts of Thomas and Alexander Campbell, Barton W. Stone, and others on the North American frontier in the 1820s and thereafter seeking the restoration of New Testament Christianity. The tradition is represented today by the Christian Church, Disciples of Christ, and by various groups identified as Churches of Christ.

Sabellianism. Another term for Modalism (q.v.), named for the teacher Sabellius.

Sacrament. The classic definition of sacrament, in the catechism of the *Book of Common Prayer*, is "an outward and visible means of an inward and spiritual grace given to us; ordained by Christ himself. . . ."[272] Eastern churches prefer the term mystery, and many Evangelical churches prefer the term ordinance (qq.v.).

Salvation. Deliverance or healing from the sinful condition of humankind and from the consequences of sin (both the Latin term *salvatio* and the Greek term *soteria* denote "healing").

Sanctification. Growth in holiness (Latin *sanctus*, "holy"). In some Holiness churches and three-blessing Pentecostal churches, the term sanctification by itself has come to be a shorthand term for entire sanctification or Christian perfection, that is, the moment when a believer comes to love God completely.

See. The jurisdiction of a bishop (from Latin *sedes*, "seat"); the jurisdiction of the pope is referred to as the "Holy See."

Semipelagianism. The belief condemned by Augustine and by subsequent Western synods, that human salvation relies on the cooperation of human nature and divine grace.

Septuagint. The Greek translation of the Hebrew Scriptures, regarded as an inspired translation in Eastern Christian churches (from the Greek *septuaginta*, "seventy," referring to the seventy translators believed to have produced it).

Session. Literally a "sitting" (Latin, *sessio*). (1) In reference to church councils, the term may be used to refer to different periods in which a council met, e.g., the four sessions of Vatican II. (2) In Presbyterian polity, session denotes the governing assembly of the local congregation, consisting of the elders and pastor(s) of that congregation, also referred to as a consistory or consistory court (q.v.).

272. Anglican Catechism (in Schaff, 3:521).

Single Predestination. The specific form of the doctrine of predestination favored in historic Lutheran teaching that maintains that God has chosen some persons to eternal salvation out of the whole mass of human beings who would otherwise be condemned to eternal damnation by the choice of their first parent (in other words, the choice to damn some human beings is not attributed directly to God); as contrasted with the doctrine of double predestination (q.v.).

Substance. The "stuff" of which something consists. (1) In Trinitarian theology substance is the term used to denote that which all the members of the godhead have in common, so the Son is said to be "of the same substance" as the Father in the Nicene Creed. (2) In eucharistic theologies, substance is used to denote the reality of Christ, as in the doctrine of transubstantiation, in which it is maintained that the substance of bread and wine in the Eucharist is transformed into the substance of Christ's body and blood.

Substitutionary Atonement. The belief that Christ's death served as a substitution for the death that all human beings owe as a result of their implication in original sin.

Supralapsarianism. A particular version of the doctrine of predestination that maintains that God's act of election occurred before (Latin, *supra*) or without regard to the human fall (Latin, *lapsus*) into sin.

Synergy. "Cooperation" (Greek, *sunergeia*) between human nature and divine grace, especially associated with Semipelagianism.

Synodal. A form of polity characterized by various levels of church assemblies or synods; functionally an equivalent to presbyterian (q.v.), except that assemblies may not be termed presbyteries.

Teleosis. Greek "perfection."

Theotokos. Greek "God-bearer," a term applied to Mary, later rendered "Mother of God."

Total Depravity. The belief that original sin has corrupted human beings in all of their capacities, including the exercise of will and the ability to do any good.

Transubstantiation. A way of accounting for the presence of Christ in the Eucharist in Roman Catholic teaching, which maintains that the substance of bread and wine is transformed into the substance of Christ's body and blood.

Tridentine. Referring to the Council of Trent (Latin, *Tridentinum*).

Trinity, Trinitarian. Historic belief in the Trinity involves both the assertion of the oneness or unity of God (as opposed to polytheism and Arianism) and at the same time the belief in the eternal distinctness or integrity of each of the three members of the Godhead (as opposed to Modalism).

TULIP. An acrostic identifying the five points of historic Reformed belief about human salvation as taught at the Synod of Dort, namely, T—total depravity, U—unconditional election, L—limited atonement, I—irresistible grace, and P—perseverance of the saints.

Venerate, Veneration. As clarified at the Second Council of Nicaea (A.D. 787), veneration is the degree of respect paid to saints and religious images, as contrasted with true worship which is to be paid to God alone. (The Greek term translated veneration is *proskunesis,* which means "bowing the knee.")

Venial Sin. In historic Roman Catholic teaching, a lesser sin, one not leading the believer to spiritual death, as contrasted with mortal sin (q.v.).

Via Media. Latin "middle of the road"; the expression often used to describe the position of historic Anglicanism in the "middle of the road" between Roman Catholicism and Reformed faith.

Virtualism. The specific form of eucharistic teaching favored in many Protestant churches that maintains that although Christ's body remains in heaven after the Ascension, the Eucharist conveys the "virtue" or power of Christ's presence just as if Christ were bodily present (from Latin, *virtus,* "power").

Vulgate. The Latin translation of the Bible, prepared by Jerome in the fourth century A.D. and revised numerous times since then, which is the official version of scripture utilized by Roman Catholics.

Worship. The degree of reverence or adoration that is due to God alone. The Second Council of Nicaea (A.D. 787) distinguished this degree of worship from veneration (q.v.), the lesser degree of respect that may be paid to saints and religious images.

Index of Names and Subjects

Names of denominations are included only where particular mention is made of them in the text; in all other cases readers should consult Appendix 1 for names of denominations. Confessional documents are referenced so frequently in the text and "sources" paragraphs that the index refers to them only at the point at which they are originally described. Page numbers followed by *t* represent tables.

Disciples of Christ, 261. *See also* Restorationist Churches
discipline in the church, 164–65
Dispensationalist Churches, xx, xxi, 187*t*, 188, 199–200, 209–10, 306–7
dispensations of biblical history, 209–10, 317
Divine Liturgy. *See* Eucharist
divinization. *See theosis*
divorce, 111
doctrine, 2–5, 133–34, 138, 171, 188–89, 192, 276, 293
Dodd, C. H., 12 n.18
dogmatics, 5 n.7
Dominic and Dominicans, 71, 73, 93, 158
Donatism, 67, 317
Dordrecht Confession, 190
Dormition of Mary, 47, 317
Dort (or Dordrecht), Council of (A.D. 1619), 154–55
Dositheus, Confession of, 31, 33
double predestination, 155, 317
double procession of the Holy Spirit, 27, 29–30, 69, 85–86, 146, 223, 268–69, 318. *See also* single procession of the Holy Spirit

Eastern Orthodox Churches, xx, xxi, 19–61, 75, 259
Eastern-Rite Catholics, 30, 73
Ecumenical Councils, 22–26, 23*t*, 37, 82–83, 284, 318
Ecumenical movement, 5–11, 31–32, 55, 66, 75–76, 130–31, 258–62, 276–77, 318
Edinburgh Missionary Conference, 257–58
Edward VI, King, 125
Edwards, Jonathan, 211
elder, 170, 243, 247, 276, 318. *See also* presbyter; priest, priesthood
election. *See* predestination
Elizabeth I, Queen, 125
energies (Divine). *See* operations
Engelder, Theodore Edward William, 4 n.7
England, Christianity in. *See* British Isles
English Revolution, 126
Enlightenment, 127, 144, 266, 290
entire sanctification, 235–37, 273. *See also* perfection; sanctification
Ephesus, Council of (A.D. 431), 25, 43
episcopacy. *See* bishop
episcopal polity, 167–69, 318. *See also* bishop
Erasmus, Desiderius, 122
establishments of religion, 115–17, 126, 132–33, 216–17, 318

eternal security of believers. *See* perseverance of the saints
Eucharist, 27, 60–61, 96, 106–8, 179–83, 254–56, 280–81, 318
Evangelical, 115–17, 127–28, 185–87, 187 n.192, 318–19
Evangelical Orthodox Church, 32
Evangelical Revival, 127, 194–95
ex cathedrā, 80–81, 319
experience, religious, 210–14
extreme unction. *See* anointing of the sick

faith, 45, 94–95, 158–59, 211, 271–73
Faith and Order, 258–61, 268
fall of humankind, 49–50, 90–94, 151–53, 225
Farel, William, 123
Fawcett, John, 241
fencing of communion, 165, 256
Ferré, Frederick, 283, n.267
filioque. See double procession of the Holy Spirit
First Communion, 105–6
Florence, Council of (A.D. 1439), 29, 102–3
footwashing, 249–50
forgiveness of sins, 59, 94–95, 96, 104, 108–9, 158–59, 230–33
Formula of Concord, 121, 122*t*
Fox, George, 192–93
France, Christianity in, 124, 170
Francis of Assisi and Franciscans, 71, 73
Free Churches, 115–17, 186–87, 319
free will, 48, 49–50, 94, 152–53, 224–26, 227–28, 319
Free Will Baptist Churches, 192, 228, 244, 319
Friends (Quakers), 187, 187*t*, 192–93, 217–18, 245–46, 250, 278, 307
Fundamentalism, 8–9, 201–2, 206–7, 220, 265, 319

General Assembly, 170
General Baptist Churches, 191–92, 228, 245, 319
General Synod, 168
Geneva, 123–24
German states, Christianity in, 120–22, 124, 128–29, 172, 190, 193–94
glossolalia, 203, 238, 273, 319
Gnosticism, 21, 320
God, 23–24, 27, 38–45, 83–87, 145–49, 218–24, 266–70, 281–89. *See also* Christ; Holy Spirit; Trinity
good works, 53, 95, 160–61, 271–73

Sacrifice of the Mass, 106–8
salvation, 47–54, 90–97, 150–62, 224–40, 270–73, 326
Salvation Army, 250, 278
sanctification, 50–52, 95–96, 160–61, 233–34, 326
Sanctified Brethren, 1, 200
Santiago Conference (Faith and Order), 261, 274
Scandinavia, Christianity in, 122
Schleiermacher, Friedrich, 128, 144, 147
Schleitheim Confession, 190
Schmalkaldic Articles, 121, 122t
Scofield, C. I., 200
Scofield Reference Bible, 200, 209–10
Scotland, Christianity in. *See* British Isles
"Scripture, Tradition, and Traditions," 260, 265
second coming of Christ, 221–22
Semipelagianism, 90, 326
Septuagint, 36, 326
Serbia, Christianity in, 28–29, 30
Session, in Presbyterian polity, 170, 326
Seymour, William, 203
sign of the cross, 45, 61, 104
Silesia, Christianity in, 122
Simons, Menno, 190
sin, 48–49, 90–92, 151–52
single predestination, 155, 327. *See also* predestination
single procession of the Holy Spirit, 40, 268–69. *See also* double procession of the Holy Spirit
Slavic Christianity, 29–30
Smith, Joseph, 288, 291
Socinianism, 290
Southern Baptist Convention, 215
Stone, Barton W., 198, 233
Stookey, Laurence Hull, 180 n.183
Streng, Frederick, 283 n.267
substance (Divine), 40, 83–85, 327
substitutionary atonement, 220, 327
superintendent, superintendency, 172–73, 243
Supralapsarianism, 155, 327
Switzerland, Christianity in, 122–23, 124
symbolic theology. *See* dogmatics
symbolics, 4–5 nn.6–7. *See also* comparative symbolics
synergy, 53, 90, 327
synod, synodal polity, 170, 244–45, 327

tarrying meeting, 238
Teresa of Avila, 72
Tertullian, 21, 67
theology, 2, 75

theosis, 50–53
Theotokos, 45–46, 87–88, 149, 270, 327. *See also* Mary the Mother of Jesus
Thirty-nine Articles of Religion, 125–26, 132t
Thirty Years' War, 126
Thomas à Kempis, 71
Thorsen, Donald A. D., 213 n.202
Three-Blessing Pentecostal teaching, 237–38
toleration, religious, 126, 287
tongues, speaking in unknown. *See* glossolalia
Toplady, Augustus, 225, 234
total depravity, 152, 154, 327
Tractarianism. *See* Oxford movement
tradition, Holy Tradition, 33–38, 76–78, 137–38, 141–43, 144, 212–13, 263–65
transubstantiation, 60, 106–8, 180–81, 280, 327. *See also* Eucharist
Trent, Council of (A.D. 1545–1563), 72–73, 98–99
Trinity, 23–24, 27, 39–42, 83–86, 145–47, 218–19, 266–70, 327
TULIP, 154, 161, 328
Two-Blessing Pentecostal teaching, 238–39

Ukrainia, Christianity in, 29, 30
Union of Soviet Socialist Republics, Christianity in, 31, 32
Union, United, Uniting Churches, xx, xxi, 116, 117t, 128–29, 131, 158, 170, 173
Unitarians, Unitarianism, 286–87, 290
United Church
  of Canada, 116, 173, 244
  of North India, 116, 173
  of South India, 116, 173
Uniting Church of Australia, 116
U.S.A., Christianity in, 190, 194–204

Vatican
  First Council (A.D. 1869–1870), 73–74, 100
  Second Council (A.D. 1962–1965), 74–76, 98–99, 100, 102
veneration, 26, 46, 57–58, 88, 270, 328
venial sin, 92, 97, 328
vestry, 168–69
via media, 125–26, 328
virginity of Mary. *See* perpetual virginity
Virtualism, 181–83, 255, 281, 328. *See also* Eucharist; real presence
visible church, 164
Vladimir, 29
Vulgate, 77–78, 328